W9-BSD-647

A DEATH IN ITALY

ALSO BY JOHN FOLLAIN

Jackal
Zoya's Story
City of Secrets
Mussolini's Island
The Last Godfathers
Vendetta

A DEATH IN ITALY

THE DEFINITIVE ACCOUNT OF THE AMANDA KNOX CASE

JOHN FOLLAIN

St. Martin's Press ✷ New York

www.stmartins.com

ISBN 978-1-250-02424-4 (hardcover)
ISBN 978-1-250-01872-4 (e-book)

First published in Great Britain under the title *Death in Perugia*
by Hodder & Stoughton, an Hachette UK company

First U.S. Edition: August 2012

10 9 8 7 6 5 4 3 2

To my parents

Contents

Sources

My research for *Death in Perugia* began on the day the murder of Meredith Kercher was discovered, when *The Sunday Times* sent me to cover the case. It was a trip that was to be repeated many times over the next four years.

I have done my best to give a voice to as many of those involved as possible, with the help of both case files and author interviews, and with the aim of writing an objective, chronological account. The book is based on the 10,000-page files of the prosecutors' investigation, which include photographs and films of the crime scene; autopsy and forensic police reports; transcripts of witness statements; interrogations of suspects; and of Amanda Knox's taped meetings with her family in prison. The files also contain her diaries, which were seized at the time of her arrest and later from her prison cell. I drew on a complete set of the verbatim transcripts of the first, eleven-month trial of Amanda Knox and Raffaele Sollecito, much of which I attended; I also attended the appeal trial that followed.

The book is also based on dozens of in-depth author interviews with prosecutors, police detectives, lawyers for Amanda, Raffaele and Rudy, forensic pathologists and other expert consultants, among others. Arline, Stephanie and Lyle Kercher gave me an interview in Perugia after the verdict of the appeal court. Amanda's parents, Edda Mellas and Curt Knox, and her sister Deanna, granted me a lengthy interview in Seattle – their first with a non-American journalist. I also interviewed her step-father Chris Mellas in Perugia. I met Amanda briefly during one of two visits I made to the Capanne prison outside Perugia where I also spoke to prison officials, guards, the prison chaplain and Amanda's fellow inmates. I was also allowed access to the scene of the crime, inside the cottage where Meredith and Amanda lived.

Meredith's close friend Sophie Purton – the last friend to see her alive – gave me an exclusive six-hour interview at her home, and has patiently answered more questions since. Amy Frost, another close friend also speaking for the first time, answered questions by email. I have also drawn on articles written by John Kercher in several British newspapers including *The Sunday Times*.

The dialogues in the book are as recorded in official transcripts, or as recalled by one or more speakers in witness statements and author interviews.

PERUGIA

N

0   200 metres

1   Amanda and Meredith's cottage, Via della Pergola

2   Piazza Grimana

3   University for Foreigners, Piazza Grimana

4   Raffaele's home, Corso Garibaldi

5   Rudy's home, Via del Canerino

6   Garden where Meredith's mobile phones were found,
    Via Sperandio

7   Sophie Purton's home, Via del Lupo

8   Le Chic Pub, Via Alessi

9   Merlin Pub, Via del Forno

10 Domus Deliri nightclub, Piazza Morlacchi

11 Cathedral, Piazza IV Novembre

12 Piazza IV Novembre

13 Corso Vannucci

14 Lawcourts, Piazza Matteotti

Principal Characters

The Investigators

Giuliano Mignini, prosecutor

Manuela Comodi, prosecutor

Detective Superintendent Monica Napoleoni, head of the Homicide Squad

Chief Detective Inspector Rita Ficarra, Homicide Squad

Deputy Chief of Police Giacinto Profazio, head of the Flying Squad

Chief Superintendent Marco Chiacchiera, deputy head of the Flying Squad

Chief Detective Inspector Michele Battistelli, postal police

Meredith Kercher

Arline and John Kercher, Meredith's parents

Stephanie, Lyle and John Kercher, Meredith's sister and brothers

Giacomo Silenzi, Meredith's boyfriend

Sophie Purton, Robyn Butterworth and Amy Frost, Meredith's friends

Francesco Maresca and Serena Perna, the Kercher family's lawyers

Amanda Knox

Edda Mellas and Curt Knox, Amanda's parents

Chris Mellas, Amanda's stepfather

Carlo Dalla Vedova and Luciano Ghirga, Amanda's lawyers
Diya 'Patrick' Lumumba, bar-owner and Amanda's employer
Father Saulo Scarabattoli, prison chaplain

Raffaele Sollecito

Giulia Bongiorno, Marco Brusco and Luca Maori, Raffaele's
   lawyers

Rudy Guede

Giacomo Benedetti, Rudy's friend

Witnesses

Filomena Romanelli and Laura Mezzetti, Meredith's flatmates
Paola Grande, Filomena's friend
Nara Capezzali, retired neighbour
Hekuran Kokomani, Albanian farmhand
Antonio Curatolo, tramp

Expert witnesses

Luca Lalli, forensic pathologist
Patrizia Stefanoni, biologist, Rome forensic police

A DEATH IN ITALY

Prologue

2 November 2007 – Festa dei Morti (Feast of the Dead)

Ever since the Middle Ages, the people of Perugia have flocked to the yearly *Fiera dei Morti* (Fair of the Dead), a sprawling festival of market stalls loaded with local specialities and arts and crafts. In a traditional tribute to the departed, many of the stalls sell *stinchetti dei morti*, biscuits shaped liked bones, and the *torcolo*, a ring-shaped cake dedicated to St Costantius, one of the city's patron saints, who was decapitated by barbarian invaders.

On a sunny but freezing Friday lunchtime Monica Napoleoni, the dark-haired chief of Perugia's Homicide Squad, had just detained some Romanian pickpockets at the fair when the operations room called her mobile.

'The body of a young woman's been found. Suspicious death,' the duty officer told her. 'Number 7, Via della Pergola.'

A Detective Superintendent, Napoleoni had turned forty-four the previous day and cut an unusual figure in the Italian police force, not only because of the rank she'd achieved in spite of her sex, but also the strikingly feminine way she dressed, as if set on defying any macho colleagues. She liked to wear her silver, shield-shaped police badge as a pendant on a chain around her neck, and occasionally tucked her semi-automatic ordnance pistol into a Louis Vuitton handbag.

She set off immediately in an olive-green Alfa Romeo, her colleague, Inspector Stefano Buratti, beside her. They already knew the part of the city they were headed for. While tourists flocked to the town centre, with its mix of medieval and Renaissance homes and picturesque cobbled streets, this house was just to the northeast of the ancient city walls. It was very close to the University for Foreigners, in a neighbourhood popular with both students and the North African drug dealers who were forever trying to attract their attention.

Number 7, Via della Pergola was a whitewashed cottage with a tiled roof and green wooden shutters, perched on the hillside by a bend in the road winding above a valley. Behind it unfolded a landscape of rolling hills, olive groves, vines and cypress trees typical of the region of Umbria. Napoleoni drove through the open black gate and parked in an unkempt drive of gravel and patchy grass.

Napoleoni noticed a young couple who looked like students standing only a few feet away from the cottage – an attractive blonde girl in a long white skirt and a boy with glasses and a bright yellow scarf – who were hugging and smothering each other with kisses. It was odd.

'How can they do that with a dead girl inside?' she thought to herself. 'Maybe things aren't as bad as that then.'

A police officer came to brief Napoleoni. He had been sent to the cottage after a woman living 400 yards away reported finding two mobile phones lying on the ground in her garden. The phones had been traced to a British student, Meredith Kercher, who lived in the flat on the first floor. The young couple Napoleoni had just seen kissing each other had shown him a broken window, saying there must have been a burglary. Once inside, he found the door to Meredith Kercher's room was locked, and could hear no sound from inside. When the door was kicked down, he said, the body of a young woman had been found lying on the floor in a pool of blood. He couldn't tell who the victim was.

Preparing to go inside, Napoleoni pulled on sterilised gloves and shoe covers – she always had some with her – and went into the tiny hallway, followed by her colleague Buratti and a woman doctor from the emergency services who had just arrived.

Napoleoni went straight across the sitting room and turned left to get to the room with the broken window, which she was told belonged to a trainee lawyer called Filomena Romanelli.

Napoleoni looked around the room, trying as she always did at a crime scene to make a mental photograph of everything she saw. A jumble of clothes and oddments looked as though they had been thrown on the floor; a stone as big as a human head, partially wrapped in a paper bag, lay beside a chair – presumably it'd been used to break in. But several things weren't quite right. Shards of broken glass from the window lay on top of the mess of clothes, not under it – as if someone had first made a mess in the room and then broken the window.

More shards were on the windowsill. But if the stone had been thrown from outside, she thought, the glass should have fallen to the floor. And a stone of that size would have shattered the shutters, which were ajar, before it ever hit the window, but they were undamaged. And why was the stone in a paper bag? Outside, the window was almost a dozen feet above the ground.

'That's strange. It looks as though someone's done all this to make us think it's a burglary,' Napoleoni told Buratti.

They walked down the narrow corridor to Meredith Kercher's room. Napoleoni took just one step inside and stopped abruptly. The walls, a cupboard and the undersheet of the unmade single bed were streaked and splashed with blood. There was more blood on the floor. A beige quilt covered the body, which was lying between the bed and the cupboard; a naked left foot poked out from under it close to the door, and at the opposite end of the quilt, between the small bedside table and the wall, Napoleoni could see a crown of dark hair matted with blood.

A pair of black knickers and a slightly bloodstained white bra lay close to the foot. On the bedside table lay a copy of Ian McEwan's *Enduring Love*, a postcard of Perugia and a sealed envelope addressed to John Kercher.

The doctor from the emergency services bent down and slowly, delicately lifted the quilt. The girl lay on her back, her head in a pool of blood, her face turned towards the left, towards the window and the view beyond it; her brown eyes were open. She was naked save for two thin cotton tops that had been pulled up above her chest. There were splashes of blood on her breasts.

On the front and right side of her neck were what looked like two knife wounds; it was hard to tell because of the blood smearing her neck and face. On the left side of the neck was a bigger, gaping wound the shape and size of half an orange. Napoleoni had seen awful things in her time – a sixteen-year-old boy who'd committed suicide with a rifle, and babies playing with needles their parents had just used to inject themselves with heroin – but tears came to her eyes at the sight of what had been done to this young woman.

'*Mamma mia*, she's been butchered,' she exclaimed softly. Her first impression was that it had been a sexual attack. But why was the body covered with a quilt? Since when did thieves – if it was a thief who had done this – undress a body and then cover it up again?

The eyes of the young woman were to haunt her for a long time to come. 'It was as if she was looking at me,' Napoleoni said later. 'She looked terrified. She looked as if she had seen and understood everything she'd been through, from beginning to end.'

As delicately as she had lifted it, the doctor lowered the quilt back over the body.

Part 1
Path to Murder

1

Surrounded by hills in the heart of Umbria, a region known as Italy's 'green lung' for its unspoilt landscape, the beauty of Perugia has long attracted both tourists and students from overseas. The narrow, cobbled streets of the hilltop city, which lies roughly half-way between Rome and Florence, trace crooked paths through charming squares with ornate fountains, past austere palaces and frescoed churches. Far above the intricate maze of streets, and mostly invisible to the visitors strolling through them, terraces are draped with jasmine and wisteria.

Perugians are fiercely proud of their city – which since its foundation by Etruscans in the sixth century BC has been besieged, conquered and looted by ancient Romans, barbarians, Byzantines and most recently Austrians – but they are also notorious for being rather parochial. An Italian actor performing there for the first time was upset by the lukewarm applause of his audience and joked that it was because the locals saw nothing but hills day in, day out. 'If only they could see the sea, or a flat horizon, they'd be more receptive to the world around them and have more open minds,' he said.

At the city's University for Foreigners, founded under the dictator Benito Mussolini to spread Italy's language and culture abroad, no fewer than 350 different ethnic groups coexist peacefully, making Perugia the most cosmopolitan city of its size – it has a population of 160,000 – in Italy. But in recent years the city's growing prosperity and its student population have attracted drug dealers who skulk in its dark alleys as they wait for customers. In

2007, twenty-five people died of a drug overdose in the province of Perugia, the highest number of such deaths in any Italian
province.

A student in languages and politics, Meredith Kercher was at
first torn between Milan and Perugia for her year's study abroad.
She worried that Perugia might be too small; so few of her friends
had heard of the place. But in the end she chose Perugia, attracted
by the city's beauty, and she put her name down for the university's Italian language course. She had first fallen in love with Italy
as a child, when her parents John, a London-born freelance journalist, and Arline, who was from Lahore in India, took her there
on family holidays. Meredith grew so fond of Italy she also went
on school exchange trips as a teenager. She loved everything from
the Italian way of life to the country's art treasures and its food,
especially pasta and pizza.

Almost a Christmas baby – she was born on 28 December
1985 in Southwark, London – Meredith was a pretty, cheerful
and studious girl. Brought up in Coulsdon, Surrey, she had two
brothers, Lyle and John, but she was closest of all to her sister
Stephanie, three years her senior.

'Mez [Meredith's nickname] and I were friends as well as
sisters,' Stephanie recalled. They had the same sense of humour
and used to charge around the house singing, dancing and laughing for all they were worth. When they were little, the girls went to
ballet and gym classes together. Later on, Meredith played football and when she was seventeen she took a year's karate lessons,
reaching her third belt.

Meredith's parents divorced when she was eleven. The two
girls stayed with their mother but Meredith talked to her father
on the phone almost every day, going to see him at his home in
London once or twice a week. She won a scholarship to the Old
Palace School, an independent private school for girls in Croydon.
Gifted in languages, she took Latin and French for her A-levels
and went on to study European politics and Italian at Leeds
University, which often sent students for a year abroad as part of

their course through Erasmus, the European student exchange programme. Her heart was set on Italy. Meredith loved reading, and wrote poems and stories. She had no definite career plans – she thought of becoming a teacher, or a journalist like her father, or using her languages at the European Parliament in the French city of Strasbourg.

In the summer of 2007, Meredith won a university grant worth some £2,600 towards her year abroad and worked for three months as a guide on tourist buses in London to raise more money for it. She was excited about the course, which started with a month of intensive Italian, after which she would study both Italian and European politics. However, Meredith's plans were almost ruined when she was mistakenly enrolled on a course which had no year abroad. Meredith didn't give up and helped to resolve the problem. 'She fought so hard to come to Perugia,' Stephanie said later.

Meredith hated leaving her sixty-one-year-old mother Arline. But she left England in high spirits, promising Stephanie that after her year in Italy they would travel around the country together.

'We laughed about making sure she would have lots of Italian friends for us to stay with,' Stephanie remembered.

Late that August, a twenty-one-year-old Meredith arrived in Perugia and went first to a hotel near the majestic Cathedral of St Lawrence, where the most highly worshipped relic is an agate ring which according to legend was slipped on to the Virgin Mary's finger at her wedding. One evening, a couple of days later, Meredith went out for a pizza in a restaurant behind the cathedral with two new friends, Sophie Purton and Amy Frost, who had also just arrived in Perugia as exchange students. Like Meredith, Amy was studying languages at Leeds University, and the two had emailed each other a few weeks earlier and arranged to meet in Perugia.

Sophie, who was studying chemistry and Italian at Bristol University, met Meredith for the first time that evening. Sophie usually found meeting new people difficult and was a year and a half younger than Meredith, but she immediately felt comfortable with her. She found Meredith fun, bubbly and quick witted; it was as if she'd known her for years.

Over their pizzas, the three students talked about their families. Meredith's parents, like Sophie's, were divorced, but Sophie's had separated when she was only six years old. Meredith talked about her sick mother, and how close she was to her sister Stephanie. When Sophie fondly praised her teenage brother Joe and pulled out a picture of him, Meredith and Amy burst out laughing. 'You're just like a proud mum!' Meredith joked.

Soon after her arrival, Meredith saw a note on a university student noticeboard about a room for rent in a nearby cottage. She called the mobile phone number and went to see the cottage as quickly as she could.

Filomena Romanelli, a lively, fast-talking blonde, and Laura Mezzetti, a keen guitar player, both in their late twenties, were old friends and worked as trainee lawyers. They made Meredith feel very welcome in their home. Although it was only a two-minute walk from the university and the old Etruscan Arch, along a steep street leading to the city centre, the cottage felt as if it was in the middle of the countryside. An old farmhouse, it used to belong to a man known simply as 'the market gardener' in the neighbour-hood because he grew fruit and vegetables on its sloping land. The current owner, an elderly banker who lived in Rome, had fully renovated it a decade earlier and divided it into two flats.

Olive, fig, pear, cherry, chestnut and magnolia trees grew in the sloping, unfenced garden, which fell steeply away from the cottage down the hillside, stretching a fair distance down into the valley. Filomena had once walked around it trying to find out how big it was but had given up because the slope was too steep.

Filomena and Laura showed Meredith round, careful to explain that the front door didn't close properly unless it was locked shut. Both their rooms were off the sitting room, which had a small kitchen in one corner. Four male students lived in the semi-basement flat. The two bedrooms they wanted to let were just down the corridor, and Meredith was enchanted when she saw the view from the square window in the end room. She loved art history, and the gentle, serene landscape framed by the window was straight out of a Renaissance painting. It plunged down the wooded hillside below her, stretching over hills of varying shades of brown and green, with rows of cypress trees on their crests, as far as the Apennine Mountains on the horizon to the east.

Meredith followed the two friends out through a glass door on the other side of the corridor. She found herself on a big terrace from where she had a 360-degree view of the old churches, houses and walls that marked the edge of Perugia's historic centre, only a stone's throw away to the south, and of the countryside.

The rent was £270 a month, with a deposit of two months' rent. Meredith worried about having to pay so much upfront before even moving in, and mentioned it to her friend Sophie.

But Meredith was in a hurry to leave the hotel which was eating into her funds. She decided to take the end room partly because the cottage was so close to the university but above all because the view enchanted her. She told Filomena and Laura that she would like to stay there until the university year ended in June. The two women were both delighted with Meredith; she was good-looking, clearly well-brought-up and reliable. Besides, they looked forward to practising their English with her just as Meredith wanted to practise her Italian.

A week after first arriving in Perugia, Meredith checked out of her hotel and moved into the cottage. On some mornings she would wake to see the bottom of the valley shrouded in banks of mist that the sun soon dispelled.

A couple of weeks after she moved in, Meredith's new flatmates told her, another student would be coming to live in the room next door to hers – an American girl called Amanda.

2

The blue-eyed Amanda Knox was only five when someone invented the nickname that was to become famous, or infamous, worldwide many years later. In her hometown of Seattle – a rainy, hard-working city on America's north-west coast, best known as the birthplace of Bill Gates, Boeing and Starbucks – Amanda started playing soccer at a very young age and spent hours kicking a ball around the backyard of her house with her sister Deanna, her junior by a year and a half.

It was on the playing field that she earned the nickname 'Foxy Knoxy'. There was nothing sinister behind the name, according to Amanda's German-born mother Edda Mellas, a maths teacher.

'Amanda was like a fox. She played as a defender and she was so intense, so focused; she was short and she'd crouch down and she'd stop people out of nowhere. I don't know how she did it,' Edda recalled.

In all the sports she took up – gymnastics, swimming, softball or whatever it was – Amanda was always fiercely competitive. 'She just liked the thrill of the competition. She was going to do it and do it well. That's Amanda,' Edda said.

Edda and her husband Curt Knox, a vice-president of the local Macy's department store, broke up when Amanda was a year old and Edda was pregnant with Deanna.

'We divorced when Amanda was fairly young. Her dad was there for games and things but for a long time afterwards it was just the three of us,' Edda recalled.

Curt lived five blocks away and the girls were always walking back and forth between the two homes. 'My parents decided to live very close to each other because they wanted to make me and my sister feel that we were a family, even if we were in two different houses,' Amanda said later. A few years later, Edda fell in love with Chris Mellas, an IT consultant with dual American and Mexican nationality thirteen years her junior, and he became Amanda and Deanna's stepfather.

The family turbulence didn't appear to affect Amanda's schoolwork. She was exceptionally studious and at thirteen won an award 'in recognition of an extraordinary student'. When she had to choose a high school, she told Edda: 'Find me the most academically challenging.' Edda picked the private Seattle Preparatory School, a very traditional, Jesuit-run establishment charging fees of $11,800 a year, which expected its students to give their best in both schoolwork and sport. Edda was told that as a private Catholic school, it made all applicants take an entrance test and from those with the highest scores, took first the Catholics and then 'picked the cream of the non-Catholics'.

The only advice Edda gave Amanda before the test was: 'Do your best, feel happy with what you're doing.' She didn't believe in telling her daughters they must get top marks. Amanda took the test and did so well that the school accepted her even though her family couldn't afford the full fees.

Amanda thrived at Seattle Prep. The school's head, Kent Hickey, later described her as 'a good and thoughtful girl, very talented in drama. A very strong student.' Amanda had a passion for performing, acting in a string of musicals – *Annie*, *Guys and Dolls*, *Fiddler on the Roof*, and *Honk!*, the musical adaptation of Hans Christian Andersen's story 'The Ugly Duckling'. She preferred what she saw as the 'interesting' characters to the lead roles – the rowdy orphan Pepper in *Annie* and Chava, the daughter who runs away to get married in *Fiddler on the Roof*.

For Chris Mellas, Amanda was an easy child to raise. 'Amanda loved her school and her schoolwork; she's a nerd. All of her friends are goofy nerds; one guy is in love with biochemistry and talks only about that,' Chris said. 'Sweet as can be, dumb as a stump, and incredibly intelligent. That's Amanda.'

She led what he called 'a fairly regimental life': 'Same breakfast every day, school, homework, a break to watch *The Simpsons*, more homework, then bed – the same every stinking day. All you had to do was tell her to stop doing homework and go to bed. She always played lots of sport at weekends. I took her rock climbing when she was thirteen, and she even got into the US Youth Soccer Olympic Development Programme, but she dropped it because it was too much of a commitment.'

Although successful in both schoolwork and in sport, Amanda was, according to her sister Deanna, 'book smart, but not street smart. She doesn't always pick up social cues.' This could be embarrassing. Once when Amanda had eaten too much in a restaurant she suddenly got up and stretched her arms out. Everyone stared at her. Another time, when her hairdresser asked what she thought of her new shoes, Amanda replied bluntly: 'They're hideous.'

On yet another occasion, when Deanna was with some friends, Amanda walked up to them, looked Deanna up and down in disgust and asked loudly: 'What the heck are you wearing?' She often approached perfect strangers, greeting them breezily: 'Hi, I'm Amanda. How are you?' Men often thought she was flirting with them, but according to her family she just wanted to get to know people.

Edda said her eldest daughter was not only 'not street smart', she was much too trusting. 'She sees good in every person she meets; she doesn't realise that you have to kind of protect yourself. For me as a mother, it was scary,' Edda said.

Late one night when Amanda was seventeen or eighteen, she called Edda to say she was on her way home, had taken a shortcut through an alley and a man was walking close behind her. 'Keep talking to me, get out on to the main street,' Edda urged her. When

Amanda got home she and Edda rowed about the risk she took and Amanda promised to be more careful in future.

It was when she was in her early teens and starting to learn Latin and the history of Ancient Rome that Amanda first got interested in Italy. At the age of fifteen, she made her first trip to the country with her family, visiting Pisa, Rome, the Amalfi Coast and the ruined city of Pompeii. She became fascinated by Italian culture and way of life. Edda gave her *Under the Tuscan Sun*, the best-selling, idyllic portrait of life in Tuscany by Frances Mayes. Amanda loved the book, and the film *Stealing Beauty* by Bernardo Bertolucci, starring Liv Tyler as an American teenager who has decided to lose her virginity during a stay in a stunning Tuscan villa.

Amanda started telling her parents: 'I wanna get out, I wanna study abroad. Italy is cool.'

After graduating with high marks from Seattle Prep, Amanda chose to study Italian, German and creative writing at the city's University of Washington. She hesitated between becoming a writer, becoming an interpreter or, as she put it later, 'doing a bit of both'. What mattered most to her was to be close to her family; she would go abroad to study, but only for a year, and then come back to live in Seattle. At university, as at school, Amanda 'ran by her own agenda', as her father Curt put it.

Edda explained: 'Amanda didn't need to be popular, she never needed to follow what the other girls were doing; if they all did their hair a certain way, she'd do it different. She liked being unique and doing her own thing; she never wanted to be one of the pack.' Few female students shared her love of soccer and rock climbing, for instance.

Jeff Tripoli, a student friend who edited the campus newspaper, confessed later to having had 'a huge crush on Amanda – but I had no luck' and described her as 'the girl next door – cute and wholesome.'

Amanda stuck out like a sore thumb: 'She was nerdy in a good way: she threw tea parties with her friends – in Seattle that's weird, we're obsessed with coffee – and the tea was always exotic. She was sporty and actually a bit of a tomboy rather than sexy.' Tripoli never saw Amanda dress provocatively. 'At a Halloween party – usually it's an excuse for girls to dress up slutty – but Amanda wore the least revealing clothes of all. I felt like telling her she hadn't got the point of Halloween.'

She never slept around, Tripoli remembered – she had what he called 'two long-term relationships during her two years at the university.' Her Seattle boyfriend DJ (short for David Johnsrud) shaved his hair Mohawk-style, wore a kilt because he was proud of his Scottish blood and shared her passion for tea parties and rock climbing.

Tripoli once joked to Amanda: 'You're cute, but you have a weird taste in men.'

She shot back: 'Tell me about it.'

But Amanda was a late bloomer as far as boyfriends went. Like Tripoli, Deanna thought she was a bit of a tomboy. Keen on photography, Deanna once asked Amanda to dress all in black and wear make-up so that she could take a portrait of her for a photography assignment at high school. The moment Deanna had finished, Amanda exclaimed, 'Get this off of me!' and then ran off as soon as her sister had removed the make-up.

Amanda's first kiss was when she was sixteen or seventeen but she didn't have a regular boyfriend until she was at university and was by all accounts naïve where boys were concerned. She once went to a friend's house and started showing yoga poses to some high-school kids there.

'Amanda was wearing jeans and a T-shirt, and there she was bending and posing and it never occurred to her that the guys were kind of looking at her. She doesn't even realise when guys are flirting with her. I'll say to her: "That guy was totally hitting on you," and she'll say: "What? I didn't see anything!" ' Deanna said.

Later, Chris laughed when asked whether he had taught Amanda about the birds and the bees. 'It wasn't me, I didn't have to. Edda did it, I'm sure.' When a chatty Amanda wanted to talk to him about intimate details of her relationship with a boyfriend, Chris cut her off: 'Don't tell me, I don't tell you when I do something.'

'You're telling me you don't have sex just with Mom?' Amanda asked.

'I'm not having this conversation,' Chris said.

In an autobiographical account of her childhood – which has a detached, dreamy tone, partly because she wrote it in the third person – Amanda makes only passing references to the first two boyfriends she had as a student and wrote at much longer length about DJ, whom she met in the university's climbing gym *'where . . . people were adventurers, and it was with these people that Amanda felt most at home.'* DJ was in love with her for two years but said nothing, afraid of rejection, and the two were just close friends.

They finally got together when Amanda asked DJ, as he walked her home after a party: 'Whatcha thinking about?'

He replied: 'I'm thinking about you.'

Amanda saw nothing unusual about herself, or so she wrote: *'Once upon a time there was a very normal girl. She practised yoga, played the guitar and loved to sing . . . Some of this girl's friends were musicians . . . It amazed her to see people who could use tools to create a sensation so beautiful, and so heartfelt.'*

She had kept a diary since she was a little girl; her dream was to become a writer. 'For me, writing really is a way of expressing myself, it's a way of being creative, of producing something and that for me means emotions,' she said later.

Amanda had 'an incredibly active imagination', according to her stepfather Chris. 'Little things would spark huge novels in her head. She loved to lie out in the backyard and look at clouds going over. She'd say a cloud looked like a bunny or a dog, and then she'd turn it into a short story. Or she'd see an expression in her dog's face and write about that. Her dreams and nightmares were always so incredibly vivid they bothered her,' Chris said later.

When her creative writing teacher asked the class to write a dark short story about events ten minutes before the discovery of a body,

Amanda's had a deceptively cosy title: 'Baby Brother'. The main character, called Edgar, asks his younger brother whether he has drugged and raped a girl they both know. '*A thing you have to know about chicks is that they don't know what they want. You have to show it to them,*' Kyle replies. Soon afterwards, Kyle punches his elder brother in the face. '*Edgar dropped to the floor and tasted the blood in his mouth and swallowed it. He couldn't move his jaw and it felt like someone was jabbing a razor into the left side of his face … Edgar let himself fully rest on the carpet and felt the blood ooze between his teeth and out of his lips onto the floor. He spit into the blossoming smudge beside his head.*'

When Amanda told her stepfather she wanted to go and study in Italy, Chris told her frankly: 'I don't think you're ready for it.' He thought she was too immature to live abroad. 'Amanda was too naïve, too trusting. She was harebrained,' Chris said later. She would think nothing of setting out at 1 a.m. for a two-hour bicycle ride from the campus to Edda and Chris's home.

'I need a challenge,' Amanda said.

'It's your decision, but I want you to know that I'm worried. I hope you'll reconsider,' Chris said. He didn't want to smother his stepdaughter.

But Amanda had made up her mind. She wanted to combine languages and creative writing and found out about a course in Rome that taught both. She loved Italy and wanted somewhere that would feel 'new' to her. But she worried that if she went to a big capital city like Rome, she would spend too much time with fellow Americans. She decided to go 'somewhere much smaller where I could really be with Italians instead of with other Americans' and picked Perugia. She had never been to Perugia and there was still so much to discover in Italy.

As soon as term began at the University of Washington, she started doing odd jobs in her spare time to help pay for her year abroad. She worked for a year in one of the campus cafeterias and in an art gallery, but the job she enjoyed most was helping seven- and eight-year-olds with their homework. Edda, Chris and Curt told her how much they could afford to contribute and Amanda surprised them all by budgeting as precisely as she could, working out how much she was going to need to pay for flights, rent and food, then saving her earnings to make up the difference.

By spring of 2007, with only a few months to go before she was due to leave for Perugia, Amanda was so excited she talked of little else and went regularly to practise her rather basic Italian with a neighbour who used to live in Rome.

When Edda and Curt took her out for dinner one evening and Amanda was talking as usual about her preparations, a worried Curt asked: 'Hey, how are we going to be able to help you if something happens? What happens if you get sick? We're not a short distance away.'

She reminded him that several of Edda's relatives lived in Switzerland, Germany and Austria, near enough for them to help in an emergency, but she would be fine anyway. Nothing bad was going to happen.

In early July, Amanda had her only brush with the law in Seattle. She and the five female students she shared a house with threw a leaving party. The grey-painted wooden house was on a quiet, leafy street north of the university and neighbours called the police when some of the boys who had had too much to drink started throwing stones, empty beer bottles and cans around the front of the house and down an alley at the back. Amanda was inside comforting a drunken friend who had quarrelled with her boyfriend when the police arrived. 'We'll tell these boys to go home,' Amanda promised the officer in charge.

'That's all right, but we're also writing you a ticket,' he replied.

Amanda and her friends had to club together to pay the $269 fine.

Amanda was due to leave for Europe that August, but she and Chris kept clashing over her year abroad. 'You're still immature. Not everyone has good intentions,' Chris told her.

'OK, but everyone has some good in them.'

'Amanda, you're just not ready for it. I'm scared you're going to go over there and something is going to happen to you. What if you're in an accident? You don't speak the language that well. What would you do?'

'You always worry too much. I'll be fine. I'm a big girl, I can take care of myself.'

In her diary, Amanda listed all the things she had to do before setting off for Italy. '*Number 1: sex store,*' she wrote. In the packing list was a reminder to include condoms. She talked to DJ about their relationship; while she would be in Perugia, he would be on a long stay in China. They agreed that each of them would be free to have other relationships while they were overseas.

On her Facebook site, Amana filled in the section 'Interested In' with the single word: '*Men*'. Of her 'Relationship Status', she wrote: '*It's Complicated*'. Her favourite group was The Beatles, her favourite books the Harry Potter series, her favourite films anything by Monty Python. The section 'About Me' indicated she no longer thought of herself as 'just a normal girl': '*A lot of my friends say I'm a hippy, but I am thinking I am just weird. I don't get embarrassed and therefore have very few social inhibitions ... I love new situations and I love to meet new people. The bigger and scarier the roller coaster the better.*'

Just before Amanda left Seattle, she accidentally stepped on a flower, crushing it. She felt so bad about it that she dug a little hole outside her house and buried it there, telling Deanna: 'The spirit of the flower can't be released until it's buried.' Deanna explained that Amanda was incapable of hurting anyone or anything: 'My sister can't kill a spider. When I'd find a spider in my room I'd tell her "Kill it!" but she would get a glass and take it outside.'

The only time Deanna could remember Amanda hurting anyone was when she was seven years old and got into a fight with a boy at school who was picking on Deanna. 'Hey, don't mess with my sister!' Amanda shouted and gave the boy a good punch.

When the sisters rowed, they screamed at each other but never came to blows. Amanda didn't do violence, and she didn't do drugs – or only a little – according to Deanna. In the entire time that Amanda lived in Seattle, she had smoked a joint maybe twice, 'because she likes experimenting, she wants to try everything.'

Edda gave Amanda a lot of advice before she left, including a warning about Italian men. One of the guidebooks said they had a habit of whistling at foreign women and pinching their bottoms. 'Just be careful,' Edda warned.

But Edda had more serious worries than bottom-pinching. 'Try to be wary, to pay attention to what's going on around you. Don't trust everyone you meet. Be more on your guard. It's a foreign country you're going to.'

'OK, Mom, I will. I'll be fine!' Amanda replied breezily.

But Edda was still worried. 'I hoped she would learn a bit of fear before she left. I didn't want her to go through life afraid, but I wanted her to have a little fear as far as self-preservation goes,' Edda said later.

3

A month after celebrating her twentieth birthday, Amanda left Seattle in mid-August with her sister Deanna, stopping on the way in Hamburg in Germany to stay with an uncle and aunt. 'She drove me nuts,' Deanna recalled. Amanda was in such a hurry to get to Perugia she kept asking her: 'Can we go to Italy now?' Deanna just told her: 'Amanda, you've got to wait.'

The sisters also stopped in Austria on their way south, and went to a museum in Graz full of soldiers' uniforms and military exhibits. Deanna photographed Amanda crouching behind a nineteenth-century Gatling gun and pretending to fire it. She burst out laughing when she saw what Deanna was doing. Amanda wrote '*The Nazi*' on the back of the photograph.

'We were just goofing around. Here we are, of German descent, sitting behind this gun. We're proud of our German heritage, we were just goofing off,' Deanna was to explain. She also filmed Amanda in their hotel room.

'Amanda, are you anxious about where you're going?' Deanna asks her sister.

'Yeah, I'm really anxious to find out where I'm going to live.'

From Graz they travelled on to Munich, flew to Milan and then took a train to Florence. On the train, they met Federico, a young Italian who spoke no English but made friends all the same and the three went all the way to Florence together where they spent the night in the same hotel. Federico took the sisters out to dinner and after Deanna had gone off to bed – as Amanda wrote on her MySpace page – '*we smoked up together, my first time in Italy . . .*' In her diary she was more explicit, writing that she had sex with him.

The sisters finally reached Perugia in late August. On their first day there, they walked around for two hours, getting lost repeatedly as they looked for their hotel before, tired and sweaty, they hitched a lift to reach it outside the city centre. The driver, who was in his forties, pestered them to go out with him but the sisters turned him down. He wasn't the first man who tried to flirt with the sisters since their arrival in Italy, and Deanna noticed that her previously tomboyish sister was now very much aware when men showed interest in her. Amanda thought the way Italian men stared at women was 'very abrupt' and as the guidebook had warned, the girls were whistled at twice, which irritated them both.

The next day, Deanna would have liked to go shopping but Amanda wanted to go to the university. As they walked through Perugia, Amanda chatted excitedly about the beauty of the old buildings they passed. When they reached the university, Amanda went inside to ask about her course while Deanna sat outside enjoying the warm sun on her skin, facing the tree-lined Piazza Grimana, which had a basketball court in the middle of it. She noticed a skinny young woman putting up a notice near the entrance of the university; Deanna couldn't speak Italian but when she saw the word '*appartamento*', exclaimed, 'Hey, one minute!' to the woman and then raced inside to fetch Amanda.

Laura Mezzetti told them in English about the room she had to let in the cottage where she lived on Via della Pergola, very near the university. 'Would you like to see it now?' Laura asked. Amanda accepted immediately, and Laura led them to the cottage.

Amanda fell in love with the cottage, the garden and the wonderful view from the moment she walked into the drive. Amanda and Deanna met Filomena, who picked two ripe figs and offered them to the sisters, neither of whom had ever eaten one before.

Deanna was nervous about tasting it. 'I don't know if I should eat this.'

'Go on, eat it.' Amanda had already stuffed hers in her mouth.

Inside the flat, Amanda kept exclaiming: '*Fantastica! Fantastica!*' She didn't mind that the bedroom she was shown was tiny, that the ceiling was low or that the window looked out onto the drive and the road above it. When she stepped out onto the terrace, she was bowled over. 'Oh my gosh!' she cried. She gazed out over the hills, her mouth open in wonder. 'I love it; I've never seen anything like it.' Amanda added: 'It's perfect, it's perfect. I'll take it.'

The four of them sat down on the terrace to talk about the details of the rental contract. Amanda sat on the floor – as Deanna explained, it was one of her eccentricities, she preferred the floor to a chair. Amanda told her new flatmates that she had to leave Perugia the next day as she was going to see some relatives in Germany but she would be back in September and could move in then.

As with Meredith, the beauty of the view had drawn Amanda to the cottage.

Meredith moved into the cottage in early September, and quickly began making the most of her year in Perugia. She left the cottage every morning just before 8 a.m. for the intensive, month-long Italian course at the university. She came back just after 1 p.m., had lunch and then settled down to study in the afternoon. She bought an Italian newspaper every day to help her learn the language, and asked Filomena how to pronounce a new word, writing it down in her notebook. Filomena was impressed by how meticulous she was.

Meredith soon made new friends through her course, especially with a group of half a dozen English women in their early twenties; her closest friends were Sophie, Amy and another fellow student from Leeds University, Robyn Butterworth. They often went out to bars and pizzerias popular with foreign students in Perugia; on Mondays they went to see films in English at a cinema on Corso Vannucci – an elegant pedestrian street lined with *caffè* terraces where Perugians like to take their traditional *passeggiata* (stroll). Meredith always arrived late but her friends were so fond of her they just pulled her leg about it; Sophie didn't mind at all, because she was usually only a little less late than Meredith. Their favourite spot was the Merlin Pub, a rustic-looking bar and pizzeria painted red and orange in an old vault near the cathedral. The first evening that Meredith went there, she met the friendly owner Pasquale Alessi, known to all as 'Pisco'.

A former engineering student, he too had studied in Leeds. 'I hope Perugia isn't as cold and rainy as Leeds,' Meredith said to him after ordering a pizza with Nutella spread – she loved chocolate.

She tried a few words of Italian with him but they chatted mainly in English. She was full of enthusiasm for her new life in Perugia. 'It's an adventure for me, I love it. I'm so happy to have chosen Perugia, it's beautiful – I know I did the right thing!' Meredith said with a big grin, her eyes shining. She told Pisco she loved the fact that Perugia was both a city and 'a little town' – wherever you went, you met people you knew. She was looking forward not only to her year in Perugia but also to travelling across Italy. 'I'm going to be here for a long time!' Meredith said with another smile.

She told her family she loved everything about Italy. Concerned about her mother Arline's health, Meredith always kept her English mobile phone in a pocket of her jeans, and called her every day, sometimes several times a day. Arline constantly tried to reassure her daughter, and would tell her to take care of herself – so much so that Meredith once burst out: 'Why are you telling me to take care? You're the one who should be taking care of yourself!' Meredith used a mobile with an Italian number that Filomena had given her to make calls in Italy because it was cheaper than using her English one.

Meredith often emailed and texted her sister Stephanie. 'Mez was very excited. She talked of her nervousness because it was the first time she'd gone abroad,' Stephanie said later. She loved the cottage because it had 'a big terrace with a spectacular panorama.'

Meredith's Italian was getting better, partly thanks to Filomena and Laura. 'That's what she wanted – to improve her Italian. Mez was a really conscientious, very intelligent person and she wanted to make the most of her year in Italy,' Stephanie said.

Only one thing about Perugia worried Meredith: drugs. One night Meredith, Sophie and Amy walked down a steep, narrow street from the cathedral towards Sophie's home on Via del Lupo. As they reached the front door, they saw two men smoking heroin; the men were openly heating the powder on a piece of aluminium foil.

Meredith told her friends that drugs scared her. She said she had been very shocked to find a used syringe lying in the grass in the garden of the cottage. She discovered that the area around Piazza Grimana in front of the university was home not only to students who gathered there to chat between lectures or play basketball but also to drug pushers who skulked in the doorways of ancient houses flanking narrow, poorly-lit alleyways.

Meredith mentioned Perugia's drugs problem only briefly to Stephanie: she said she had seen drugs in the city, but didn't specify where. Stephanie thought little of it: she knew that Meredith wasn't into drugs and didn't even smoke cigarettes. It's likely that Meredith didn't want to alarm Stephanie by telling her what she'd seen.

One night, a couple of days before Amanda was due in Perugia, Meredith and Sophie came across a big group of American students who had just arrived in the city. They were clearly drinking heavily and so boisterous that the two friends commented on how loud and overpowering they were.

'What's Amanda going to be like?' Sophie asked.

Meredith laughed.

Meredith, like Filomena and Laura, gave Amanda a warm welcome when she arrived at the cottage in late September. Amanda had been supposed to do an internship at the parliament in Berlin – a job she'd obtained through her relatives – but she found the work non-existent and got so bored with spending most of the day reading Harry Potter books in German that she walked out on the job after just two days, to her family's dismay.

As Filomena described it later, Meredith and Amanda got on well at first. The two had much in common – they were about the same age (Meredith was a year and a half older than Amanda), they spoke the same language, both were a long way from home and would only be in Perugia for a year. Meredith had arrived in Perugia before Amanda and had already made friends, so she took Amanda under her wing, showing her around local food shops. 'Come on, you've got to meet people too. Come on, let's go out. I'll introduce you to my friends,' Meredith urged her. After dinner on Amanda's very first day in Perugia, Meredith took her out for a drink at the Merlin Pub with Sophie. Exhausted after her trip, Amanda was quiet but friendly. She made a good impression on Sophie, who thought she seemed very laid-back. As they sipped cocktails, Sophie asked her whether she had a boyfriend.

'I've got an open relationship with my boyfriend DJ; he's in China. We're together but because we're so far apart we can meet other people; we're OK with that,' Amanda explained.

'What if you meet someone and it becomes serious?' Sophie asked.

'I can tell him, he'll be happy for me. And he can tell me if he meets someone; I'm not going to be jealous. I understand that's a possibility,' Amanda said.

'Cool,' Sophie thought to herself; it sounded to her like an open, honest arrangement.

Amanda was so tired she left the pub after an hour or so to get some sleep. When she had gone, Sophie turned to Meredith. 'Are you happy?' Sophie asked.

'Yeah, I'm happy. She's really nice,' Meredith replied.

'It's good, it's going to be OK,' Sophie said.

'Yes, it's going to be OK,' Meredith agreed.

The next evening, Meredith again invited Amanda out for a drink with Sophie, this time at the Tana dell'Orso, a short walk uphill from the University for Foreigners. As they walked into the bar, Amanda said to Sophie: 'Oh, you're really popular with the guys.'

At first, Sophie couldn't work out what Amanda meant; they'd only met once the previous evening. Then, Sophie guessed Amanda was talking about Pisco, the owner of the Merlin Pub who was fond of her and had given them a round of free drinks. Sophie thought Amanda's comment had a hint of jealousy about it.

Amanda started chatting animatedly with the barman, who was American; they talked about Seattle and rock climbing. The three students then sat down and Sophie asked Amanda: 'What was your first day like?'

Amanda said she'd got up at six o'clock, had done some yoga, painted a picture, and played the guitar among many other things. Amanda's answer took Sophie aback; she was surprised by how active Amanda appeared to be. She couldn't put her finger on exactly why, but that evening Sophie felt less friendly towards her.

Sophie cooled even further towards Amanda the following evening – the third in a row that Meredith took Amanda out with her. Meredith's other friends Amy and Robyn joined them. Over dinner in the pizzeria Il Bacio off Corso Vannucci, Amanda sat silently for a while, talking to no one. Then, she suddenly started singing in a loud voice, throwing her head back as she stared up at the ceiling.

That same evening, Amanda launched into something that was more of a monologue than a conversation – she talked 'in your face', Sophie thought, and exclusively about herself. Amanda talked loudly about her passion for exotic teas – 'I could talk about it all day,' she said – and then about her open relationship with her boyfriend DJ. When DJ had told her that he'd met a Chinese girl and would surely meet her again, she'd replied: 'Oh great, what's she like? Describe her.'

'Weird,' Amy thought. 'If my boyfriend had met another girl I wouldn't be pleased.'

Later, Meredith and her friends talked about Amanda's behaviour. A few days earlier, Meredith had said her flatmate was 'sweet and nice'. But now she told them: 'The things she does, they're a bit weird.' Meredith thought it odd that Amanda had brought a suitcaseful of several kinds of teas, complete with a teapot, all the way from Seattle.

And when Amanda first arrived at the cottage, Meredith said, she'd put a beauty case in the bathroom, with a vibrator and some condoms clearly visible. 'How's it possible, you arrive and . . . I can't believe it, she left it on display. It's a transparent beauty case and it's there for all to see!' Meredith said with a laugh.

Soon after Amanda's arrival, Meredith flew off to London for a long weekend to see her family and buy some warmer clothes for the winter.

During her visit to London, Meredith arranged to meet her father John at an Italian restaurant. She kept him waiting for a full hour, but as he said later, 'when I saw her, wreathed in that famous smile, my annoyance instantly evaporated.' She delightedly showed him some boots she had bought. It was the last time John ever saw his daughter.

When Meredith got back from London, Sophie gave her a T-shirt and a certificate marking the end of their Italian course which she'd picked up for her in her absence. It had a prancing griffin – the mythical creature with the head and wings of an eagle and the body of a lion which is Perugia's symbol – and the name of the university stamped on the front.

For Sophie, the T-shirt was just that: a T-shirt. But Meredith was delighted with this souvenir of her first weeks in the city. Sophie understood – she herself felt that her stay in Perugia was turning out to be the happiest time of her life.

A few days later, Meredith went out for a night's dancing with Sophie and Robyn at the Gradisca nightclub not far from Perugia. When they left, a young Moroccan man they'd just met offered them a lift home; they nicknamed him 'Shaky' because of the way he danced but his real name was Hicham Khiri. During the drive,

Hicham told them he had three jobs: he worked mainly as a chef in a pizzeria but he also worked in a nightclub and in a clothes shop.

Meredith and her friends saw Hicham again some time later at the Domus nightclub in Perugia. Meredith asked him to dance but moments later, Robyn heard Meredith shouting that he'd pulled his trousers down and was showing her his pants. The friends just laughed it off.

4

Amanda, who had given her room a personal touch by decorating it with perfumed candles, spent her first days in Perugia just walking around the city. On her first Sunday, as the shops were closed, she stayed home and did eleven pages of language exercises in her diary, which she also used as a notebook. A few days later, copying Laura, she had eight piercings done in one ear, and three in the other. She noted with satisfaction in her diary that the woman who did the piercings must have admired her for having so many done in one go: she had kept repeating 'strong woman, strong woman'. If she had done that in Seattle, Amanda knew, Edda would have seen red and Chris would have called her pigheaded or 'Terminator'.

The speed with which Amanda had copied Laura's piercings surprised Meredith.

'Amanda's a bit obsessed with Laura. She got herself exactly the same piercings Laura had, and they've only just met!' Meredith told her friend Sophie.

Soon after moving into the cottage, Amanda started teaching Laura yoga and asked to borrow her guitar – Amanda had just started learning to play – to practise with Giacomo Silenzi, a quietly spoken, awkward student of international relations who lived in the semi-basement flat. Giacomo was a bass player with a rock and punk band and played Amanda's favourite music – The Beatles – with her. At the end of September, when Giacomo celebrated his birthday at the cottage, his flatmates told Amanda that he fancied her.

Amanda emailed Edda during the first two weeks of her language course that she was having 'the time of her life' – she loved her flatmates and her studies. She also emailed and talked to Chris on Google Talk. 'She said everything was great, amazing, she was really happy to be there,' Chris recalled later. 'It was all right up her alley. She was living life completely, without any strings attached.' She loved the Italian lifestyle: 'everything shuts down in the middle of the day so everyone can have a three-hour lunch break.' In an email to Deanna, Amanda said her third flatmate was a girl called Meredith – she was from England, she was 'beautiful, nice and fun and caring'. As Amanda recalled later, she took pictures of Meredith at her request, posing in front of the view from her bedroom window. The two sunbathed together on the terrace – Meredith reading a thriller, Amanda playing the guitar. And when Amanda made a list of friends and relatives she wanted to buy presents for, Meredith's name was on the list.

The flatmate Amanda looked up to most was Laura, whom she admired for being strong-minded. She saw Filomena as ever-cheerful and funny. Meredith was the most studious of them all, and the most solitary because she often isolated herself from the others to read, although she would sometimes watch stupid Italian TV programmes with them.

As they got to know Amanda better, her flatmates began to find her increasingly bizarre and even irritating. Filomena thought Amanda was weird and too extrovert because she would suddenly jump up to do yoga exercises in the middle of a conversation, or start playing the guitar when the others were talking or watching TV. Filomena also thought Amanda lacked common sense and started to mother her, trying to make her understand that they expected her to do her share of the housework.

Writing about Amanda in an email to her sister, Meredith remembered when she and Stephanie used to dance around the house laughing and singing at the top of their voices. She realised only now, she wrote, how annoying it must have been for other people because Amanda did the same thing.

To her friend Sophie, Meredith complained about the way Amanda seemed to crave constant attention. One evening when the students from the downstairs flat had come upstairs for a drink, Amanda came in and started doing yoga in front of everyone. 'It was like she wasn't getting enough attention. She was showing off,' Meredith told Sophie.

Sophie noticed that Meredith was colder towards Amanda than she had been at first when they spent an evening together at Le Chic, a bar in the centre of Perugia. Amanda insisted on speaking in Italian to a Dutch classmate of Meredith's who spoke perfect English. Talking loudly all the time, Amanda kept saying the word '*verde*' (green) when she didn't mean to say 'green' at all.

Meredith looked annoyed. 'It's embarrassing. Why is she being so loud?' she asked Sophie.

'Yes, why doesn't she just talk English?' Sophie said. It was the first time, Sophie realised, that Meredith had expressed irritation with Amanda when they were together.

Sophie thought Amanda must be showing off. Sophie knew Amanda wanted to get a job at the bar, and she was flirting with the barman, being all touchy-feely.

Amanda came up to the two English girls. 'Oh, I'm really drunk,' she said.

Sophie thought she might be faking.

In early October, Amanda started work as a waitress at Le Chic, run by thirty-eight-year-old Diya 'Patrick' Lumumba. Born in Zaire, Patrick had settled in Italy at the age of twenty-one and was well known to students in Perugia because he helped to organise gigs, often taking the stage with his own band, playing a mix of reggae and contemporary music. He was always ready to help his friends and even strangers; he once ran after a drug addict who had stolen a woman's bag and recovered it for her. Patrick worked hard at making Le Chic a success: he would often close his bar at 2 a.m. or later, and be out the next morning at 9 a.m. outside the university, distributing leaflets to promote it. But despite his efforts, only a few foreign students went to Le Chic, and it was often nearly empty.

For the first ten days, Patrick hired Amanda every night from 10 p.m. to about 2 a.m., for £4.50 an hour. But he wasn't very impressed by her work – he noticed she didn't clean the table after some customers left – but instead of reprimanding her, he asked her to hand his leaflets out in the street, going in for only two nights a week, on Mondays and Thursdays.

When Amanda emailed her to say she'd got the job, Edda worried about her walking home late at night. 'What time are you getting off work?' Edda asked.

'Sometimes late,' Amanda replied.

'How are you getting home?'

'I walk home.'

Edda persisted. 'Is someone walking you home?'

'There are always people out, it's not as if you walk home alone; there are people on the steps of the cathedral late at night,' Amanda told her mother – who didn't know the cathedral wasn't on her way home.

Soon after starting work at Le Chic, Amanda badgered Meredith to go there for a drink. Meredith eventually agreed and Amanda introduced her to Patrick. As they chatted, Patrick found out that Meredith had learnt to make a mojito cocktail with a special kind of vodka, and asked her to make them in his bar. From then on, every time Patrick bumped into Meredith in the street, he would say to her: 'So, when are you coming to my bar to prepare your cocktails?' She told him that she went to the Merlin Pub with her friends, and he complained that English girls always went to the Merlin and never to his bar.

A few days later, Amanda tagged along when Meredith and her friends spent an evening at the Velvet nightclub. Suddenly, Amanda emptied her glass over the head of the disc jockey. She was promptly thrown out, but Meredith sprang to her defence.

'Poor girl, she's on her own. We don't know why she did it but she won't do it again,' Meredith promised the staff. Amanda was allowed back in.

The episode may have been too much for Meredith, because it was around this time, in mid-October, that Filomena noticed that relations between Meredith and Amanda had cooled.

'My impression is that Meredith is a bit sick and tired of Amanda,' Filomena told Laura. As far as she could tell, it was just Amanda's extrovert personality that irritated Meredith. From then on, according to Filomena, Amanda and Meredith saw less and less of each other. Amanda herself told Meredith that she only wanted to socialise with Italians because that way she would learn the language – which ruled out the English friends Meredith had tried to share with her.

Meredith complained increasingly about Amanda to her family and friends. She told her sister Stephanie that her relationship with Amanda was superficial as she had her friends and Amanda had hers and they were now doing different courses at the university. Meredith described her flatmate as 'very exuberant and sometimes tiresome'.

To her English friends, Meredith listed the things that irritated her about Amanda. Amanda was always trying to grab people's attention. She would play the same chord over and over again on the guitar. She insisted on speaking Italian all the time, even to Meredith. She brought men into the house, including an Albanian she met at Le Chic and a man Meredith and her friends nicknamed 'Internet Man' – because Amanda had met him in an Internet café – who was 'a bit strange'.

One afternoon, a flustered Meredith bumped into her friend Sophie in front of the law courts.

'I've just called my Dad, I don't know what to do,' Meredith said. 'Amanda keeps leaving the toilet unflushed. She doesn't flush the toilet, not even when she's got her period. I can't stand it, but it's so awkward having to say something to her. What do you think, should I say something?'

'You've got to be diplomatic about it. You could say: "I'm really sorry to bring this up, but did you know that you left the toilet that way?" ' Sophie suggested.

Meredith nodded. 'You know, one time she left the toilet unflushed and there was a guy around. How could she do that? What if he goes in the toilet? Isn't she embarrassed she did that?'

Sophie had never seen Meredith so worked up about Amanda.

A few days later, Meredith told Sophie she'd talked to Amanda about the toilet. 'Amanda, you know, you can't leave it like that,' Meredith had said.

The way Meredith described it, it had been just a conversation, not a row. Besides, Sophie thought, Meredith wouldn't let something like that get between her and Amanda. She had to live with her.

At first, Meredith had no intention of getting romantically tied up with anyone in Perugia. She confided to Filomena that she didn't want to get involved with any men there, because she had come to Italy to study. But after a few weeks she couldn't stop herself thinking about Giacomo, the student who lived downstairs. His flatmates fuelled her interest; initially they said that he fancied Amanda, but now they told Meredith that he preferred her.

Meredith told Amanda she couldn't make up her mind whether she was interested or not. But she added that he was 'a very sweet boy'. Amanda insisted that Giacomo really liked her (Amanda); he had followed Amanda practically all night during a party that Meredith had missed.

'I like Giacomo too but you can have him,' Amanda said.

The comment stung Meredith. 'I don't need Amanda's permission to be with someone. I don't think he does like her, so why is she saying this to me?' Meredith asked Sophie afterwards. Sophie thought Amanda was jealous; the fact that Giacomo liked Meredith made Amanda feel insecure, and that was why she had made her irritating comment. Once, Meredith told Sophie, Amanda asked her to help her put some make-up on – Amanda rarely wore any – and for some advice on how to do her hair. 'I'm not good at girlie things like that,' Amanda had said.

Insecure or not, Amanda spoke openly about men and her sex life to Meredith – so much so that Meredith felt embarrassed listening to her. Amanda told her she had no problem being seen nude and that in America she had once talked to a friend's boyfriend even though she was stark naked. She also told a shocked Meredith that she had had an erotic dream, written it up and sent it to DJ.

Meredith talked about Amanda's sexuality with her friend Sophie. For Meredith, it was strange the way Amanda would meet a man and be straightaway 'very full on', either spending hours with him, or sleeping with him. For Meredith and Sophie, it wasn't a question of judging Amanda; they simply found her hard to understand. Sophie's impression was that Amanda slept with men simply because she could – there didn't seem to be any romance involved.

At first, Meredith told Sophie, she'd thought Amanda was sexually very self-confident in the way she approached men, but the more Amanda told her about her men the more Meredith became convinced there was more to it than that. It was as if Amanda felt she had to have these relationships.

'Amanda's actually quite vulnerable. I feel a bit sorry for her,' Meredith told Sophie.

Meredith's friends began to see less and less of Amanda, but what they did see made them sympathise with Meredith. Once, when Sophie went to the cottage, Amanda greeted her with a very loud '*Ciao! Come stai?*' (Hi, how are you?), drawing out the last word: '*staaaiiii*'.

Why couldn't Amanda just speak English to her? Sophie thought to herself, not for the first time; Meredith and Sophie were both shy about speaking Italian in front of their English friends, even though Meredith's Italian was pretty good. Amanda suffered from no such shyness, and Sophie thought her insistence on speaking

Italian to her was over the top, that she was clamouring for attention rather than simply practising. With Amanda, everything was
so exaggerated, all the time, Sophie thought.

Meredith still missed her family, and worried about her mother.
Arline had just had two operations, only to be taken ill as soon as
she returned home and rushed back to hospital by the emergency
services.

'Meredith was very upset and wanted to come home but I
didn't want to disrupt her studies and I was better . . . Her brother
and her sister rang her to tell her not to worry,' Arline recalled
later. Meredith was however set on flying home again to celebrate
Arline's sixty-second birthday on 11 November; Arline's children always got together to celebrate the birthday together, and
Meredith's absence and Arline's poor health made her want to be
with them all the more.

Meredith was so concerned about Arline that she walked out of
a cinema halfway through a film she had gone to see with Sophie
to call her father for news. Sophie was impressed by the fact that
even when Meredith was anxious about her mother, she was as
bubbly and smiling as ever with her friends.

In a phone call in mid-October, Meredith talked about her
plans for the trip with Stephanie. The sisters discussed where they
would take Arline for her treat and what presents they were going
to give her. Stephanie told Meredith she had booked time off from
her job to be completely free when Meredith came home.

'I'm glad I said that because she was looking forward to it,'
Stephanie said later.

It was the last time Stephanie spoke to her sister.

5

At about 2 a.m. one night in mid-October, Meredith, Amanda, Giacomo and one of the other students who lived downstairs were heading home past the Shamrock pub opposite the cathedral when they bumped into a twenty-year-old immigrant from the Ivory Coast, Rudy Guede, whom Amanda had met a few days earlier at Le Chic. Tall and with an athletic build, Rudy had lived in Perugia since he was a child. He spoke perfect Italian and had a Perugian accent.

Rudy had often played basketball with the students from the downstairs flat on Piazza Grimana and as they walked down the steep hill leading to the cottage, he asked them if Amanda had a boyfriend; they didn't think so. When they reached the square, the two boys invited Rudy to the cottage. Amanda went to her room while Rudy sat in the kitchen with them talking about her. They all thought she was good-looking.

'I'd like to screw her,' Rudy said.

Moments later, Amanda herself knocked on the door; the men burst out laughing but couldn't tell her what the joke was. One of them rolled a joint and passed it round. Rudy was impressed by how deeply Amanda inhaled when she smoked it. 'She's a great smoker, she often comes here and we smoke joints together,' one of the boys told him.

They were still smoking when Meredith joined them. She took just one pull on the joint; she was no habitual smoker. Rudy said later he found her attractive and they talked until about 4.30 a.m. when Meredith announced: 'I'm off, I'm going to sleep.' Amanda followed her out. That night, a drunken Rudy went to the toilet, leaving the door open, and fell asleep on it. He woke up later, failed to flush the toilet, and then crashed out on the sofa.

Not wanting to be on bad terms with her flatmate, Meredith made an effort to get on with Amanda and the two went together to Perugia's Eurochocolate festival. Every year, for a week, stands selling chocolate mushroomed on the Corso Vannucci and nearby streets, as well as in palace courtyards and in the city's parks.

Meredith and Amanda strolled between stands offering lessons in chocolate tasting, in making chocolate cakes and ice cream. There were elaborate chocolate sculptures, and a beauty salon selling only chocolate-based products. Meredith bought a chocolate-scented bubble bath and a candle and went back to the cottage loaded with presents she intended to give to her family when she flew home in three weeks' time. She put them in a suitcase under her bed. Amanda emailed Edda to say she'd got to taste all this chocolate and eaten far too much of it. Meredith was fun, she wrote, they'd had a great time together.

When a kitten suddenly turned up outside the cottage one day, both Meredith and Amanda befriended it. They fussed over the kitten, stroking it and leaving a bowl of milk out for it; the kitten kept coming back. But some days later it was found lying still outside the cottage; it looked as if it had been hit by a car. The kitten's death greatly saddened Meredith and she told Sophie she was shocked that no one had been willing to move it, and bury it.

On the night of 20 October, a Saturday, Giacomo and the three other students from the downstairs flat took Meredith and Amanda to the Red Zone nightclub outside Perugia, where they danced to throbbing house music until dawn the next morning. With them was Daniel De Luna, a student from Rome who, at Giacomo's birthday party the previous month, had made a pass at Amanda.

He had never met Amanda before but he had gone straight up to her at the party and pointed at her lower lip: 'I like you because you've got herpes.'

'No, it's a cold sore,' Amanda replied.

'No, it's herpes. It means you like sex,' Daniel said.

At the Red Zone nightclub, Amanda and Daniel danced under the fake, gold-lit palm trees until about 5.30 a.m. Back at the cottage, Amanda took him to her room. He left the following afternoon but the two didn't bother to exchange phone numbers.

Meredith and Giacomo were also flirting at the Red Zone that night. They kissed for the first time and spent the rest of the night together. Afterwards, Giacomo confided to a friend that he was 'with' Meredith; he felt happy with her, he said, but it wasn't love or anything big.

Giacomo's lack of commitment weighed on Meredith. One evening, when she was strolling down Corso Vannucci with her friends Sophie and Pisco, the owner of the Merlin Pub, he asked her abruptly: 'Don't you have a boyfriend?'

'To be honest, there's a boy I like very very much, I think I'm almost in love with him but I can't make him out. When we're alone together he's very nice and gentle with me, but if we meet in the street he barely says hello. He behaves as if I was just a friend,' Meredith replied.

'Maybe he doesn't know what he wants himself. Why don't you tell him you want a more steady relationship – tell him you want to be his girlfriend?' Pisco suggested.

Moments later, they came face to face with Giacomo who was heading in the opposite direction with some friends. He didn't stop; he just gave a little wave and shouted '*Ciao!*' to Meredith as he walked past her.

'You see!' Meredith said to Pisco.

'That was him?'

'Yes,' she replied, looking unhappy.

From Amanda's diary:
[Amanda lists the names of seven men she has had sex with, grouping them under the two headings '*US (Seattle, New York)*'

and '*Italy (Florence, Perugia)*'. Three of the men she names are in Italy.]

Interesting, isn't it? I think it means that my sex life doesn't correspond to my emotional romantic life. An obvious statement because the only one I'm in love with (even if to tell the truth he's not the only one I want to have sex with) is incredibly far away.

At a loose end on the afternoon of Sunday, 21 October, Rudy went to the cottage to see if he could watch a Formula One race in Brazil with the students in the semi-basement flat. They let him in, and as they watched Ferrari win the race and the championship, Rudy talked again about Amanda. One of the students bet that sooner or later, he would sleep with her.

Shortly afterwards, Meredith found out that the elderly banker who owned the cottage had died. 'It's really weird!' she laughed when she told her friend Sophie. 'First the cat dies, and now the landlord's dead.'

To Amy, Meredith said: 'It's spooky. Things keep dying.'

Amanda met her fourth conquest since arriving in Italy two months earlier at a concert of music by Mozart, Schubert and other composers at the university on 25 October. A shy, meek-looking computer science student from southern Italy who was due to graduate the following month, the twenty-three-year-old Raffaele Sollecito had moss-green eyes and wore glasses; later, Amanda's friends said he looked like Harry Potter.

Amanda had gone to the concert with Meredith, who left during the interval. After the interval, Raffaele overcame his shyness enough to take Meredith's place next to Amanda and start talking to her. The two '*liked each other immediately*', as he wrote to the author later. She suggested they meet that evening at Le Chic. Raffaele's English was better than Amanda's broken Italian, so they often resorted to English.

That night, Amanda slept at Raffaele's flat. He lived in an old, ochre-coloured house a short walk up a medieval street which wound its way up a hill behind the university. She practically moved in from then on, sleeping in his ground-floor bedsit and going back to the cottage every other day to fetch some clothes and talk to her flatmates. '*From the outset, Amanda and I had an intense, albeit brief, relationship,*' Raffaele wrote.

6

Raffaele entered the world virtually asleep; the obstetrician had to shake him to make him cry and open his lungs. After that brusque birth, he was mollycoddled by his parents like many sons of Italian families. Brought up in the small town of Giovinazzo in the heel of Italy's boot, the son of a wealthy surgeon who was also an urologist and a forensic doctor, Raffaele had what he called an 'idyllic' childhood. His mother gave up her career as an accountant to devote herself to the care of Raffaele and his elder sister. '*I was always the darling of my mother and father, but above all of my mother. My mother's world always revolved around the family and especially around me,*' he wrote to the author. As a result, he had always lived in an environment '*softened*' by his parents' unsparing care and attention.

Raffaele was eight years old when his parents separated. '*My mother only ever loved my father but he didn't settle down until he found his current wife,*' Raffaele wrote. His parents continued to fuss over him – albeit separately – and he grew up, as he described himself, '*very discreet, calm and introverted. My shyness has sometimes made me "scared of talking to people" because I didn't want to be a nuisance or say something stupid.*' But he added: '*I've always tried to force myself to overcome my limitations.*'

It was when he was still a boy that he started collecting knives as a hobby. His parents had a house in the country and he amused himself using a knife to carve inscriptions on the bark of pine trees. From then on, he carried a knife all the time. 'Raffaele wore knives as if they were part of his wardrobe,' a friend said. But he was careful with them. 'He didn't let anyone use his knives because he was scared we'd get hurt,' another friend said.

As a teenager, he was unpopular at school. Children made fun of him because he was mad about the cartoon *Pretty Soldier Sailor Moon*, a Japanese manga series in which teenage girls with magical powers defend Earth against evil forces. He went so far as to dye his hair yellow, cut it in strange shapes and wear earrings like the cartoon characters.

When he came to choose a university, he enrolled at the main university in Perugia, far from his hometown, to avoid his parents' constant fussing. Shortly before leaving, he had his first brush with the law when police found him and two friends in possession of 2.6 grammes of hashish.

Once in Perugia, he found it hard to settle in the private, men-only college his father had chosen, which had originally been founded for the orphan sons of doctors. He said he was too introverted and too homesick. But thanks to a generous allowance from his father, he lived comfortably and drove around in a costly Audi A3, sporting Dolce & Gabbana jeans and Jean Paul Gaultier shirts.

College friends described Raffaele as 'a good man, but shy and reserved, who could become emotional very easily'. When college staff talked to him, they often had the impression that his mind was elsewhere, that he was thinking about something totally different from what they were saying to him. He blushed easily, as for example when they told him off for parking his car in the wrong place outside the college.

Raffaele was given a more serious warning when a friend told the staff that he watched pornographic DVDs full of explicit violence. One administrator discovered to his disgust that one of the films had scenes showing a woman having sex with an animal. He told Raffaele off and started watching him more closely. The staff came to suspect that he smoked cannabis but were never able to prove it. He also liked horror films and the controversial American artist Marilyn Manson. But surprisingly on one website he said that his favourite film was *Hamlet*. He defined himself as 'very honest, peaceful, gentle but sometimes completely crazy'. One crazy moment was recorded by a college friend who took a photograph of him covered in toilet paper and holding a cleaver and a bottle of alcohol.

Raffaele's mother died in 2005, when he was twenty-one and still living in college. The doctor attributed the death to a heart attack, and no autopsy was carried out. The college's administrators were told however that she had apparently committed suicide, upset by her ex-husband's relationship with the woman who became Raffaele's stepmother that September; they also heard that Raffaele's mother had a weak personality and was excessively protective of her son, so much so that she was reluctant even to allow him out of the house. Raffaele later denied that she had committed suicide.

He left the cottage that summer and eventually moved into his bedsit on Corso Garibaldi. In a blog, Raffaele vented his frustration at his years in the college in stark terms: the ex-resident he most admired was Luigi Chiatti, the so-called 'Monster of Foligno' – a waitress's son who was serving a thirty-year sentence after confessing to killing two boys, aged four and thirteen. Raffaele added: '*My impression is that all sorts of down-and-outs went through that college and they all had one thing in common: "depression".*'

The college '*castrated*' people: '*it looks as if a place with 350 males cooped up together and where you can't invite anyone in was meant to keep everyone's instincts in check.*' What he wanted was to find '*bigger thrills which will surprise me*'.

In the week following their meeting, Amanda and Raffaele spent hours on end together. A couple of days after they met, Amanda brought Raffaele to the cottage and he cooked spaghetti with mushrooms for her and Meredith.

Filomena and Laura were struck by how much he clung to Amanda, especially since the two had only just met. They kept hugging and kissing each other. When Amanda got up to wash the dishes, he got up too, followed her and hugged her from behind as she stood at the sink, giving her little kisses. Later, when Amanda went to play the guitar, Raffaele again followed and sat next to her. Later, Laura called them 'lovebirds', but both she and Filomena felt Raffaele was so clingy that they kept their distance; they felt as if they risked being treated like intruders, butting in on something they didn't understand.

Raffaele told his father that he treated and pampered Amanda 'as if she was a little girl', and had washed and dried her hair. He drove her to nearby Assisi for a day out and, keen on boxing and martial arts, fooled around with her trying to teach her kickboxing. Later, Amanda wrote in her diary that one of her favourite things to do with Raffaele was to kiss and look at him in bed, pull funny faces at each other and rub their noses together – '*an Eskimo kiss they call it in the US, although I call it "unca wunca".*'

On the nights she worked at Le Chic, he would meet her there at about 10 p.m., and go back at midnight to walk her to his flat. Amanda had become increasingly dissatisfied with her work at the bar; she complained in an email to her mother that Patrick wanted her to drink wine when she was serving customers, so she could help them choose their wine. Amanda thought it very weird of him to ask her to drink while working. To her flatmates, Amanda complained that Patrick wasn't paying her (an accusation he later denied); she said she was going to quit.

In one heart-to-heart conversation which Amanda described later, Raffaele confided that one night, at a concert with some friends, he had had 'a terrible experience'. He had taken cocaine and marijuana, drunk rum as well and then driven his friends home. He decided 'to change' after that, but he still smoked marijuana often. He also told Amanda that he felt guilty about his mother's death because he had gone away and left her alone before she died. She had told her son she felt lonely, had nothing left to live for and wanted to die. Amanda also opened up to him, telling him that she had been unpopular in high school 'because the people in my school thought I was a lesbian'.

On one call home, Amanda put Raffaele on the phone for her stepfather to talk to. 'I know where you live,' Chris joked and Raffaele laughed. The two chatted for a bit. Raffaele spoke decent English and kept calling Chris 'Mister'; Chris kept telling him not to. 'Raffaele seemed an alright guy. A nice kid, very soft-spoken, a computer nerd – definitely the kind of guy I could see Amanda going out with,' Chris said later.

Amanda's relationship with Raffaele caused her some soul-searching and she looked depressed when she sat down with her three flatmates around the cottage's sitting-room table on the afternoon of 30 October. Amanda told them she felt guilty towards her American boyfriend DJ because she was 'cuckolding him' by sleeping with Raffaele. But Amanda then added: 'But I don't really feel guilty because with Raffaele I'm happy, he treats me well.'

'But at least, you've told Raffaele that you've got a boyfriend in America?' Laura asked.

'Yes, yes, but he doesn't care.'

Filomena and Laura reassured her, saying things like that happened when lovers were far away from each other. Meredith was the only one of the four to say firmly that she had never cheated on anyone, that she would never do it and that fidelity was important in a relationship. The other young women knew that Meredith was going out with Giacomo, and they were sure that she wasn't interested in anyone else and would never flirt with other men.

Later that day, Filomena and Laura reminded Amanda and Meredith that the rent was due the following week, by 5 November. Meredith said she had the money ready: 'If you want, I can give it to you now,' she said. Filomena said it could wait until 4 November, when they would put all the money together before paying the agency. 'Meredith is a real English girl, she's more precise than we are,' Filomena joked.

That last week in October, Meredith and her sister Stephanie texted and emailed each other often to talk about her flight home in early November. They were chatting about Giacomo when Meredith suddenly told her sister: 'By the way, I quarrelled with my American flatmate.' Meredith mentioned it in passing, and Stephanie didn't think of asking what the row had been about.

7

31 October 2007

On the afternoon of Halloween, a Wednesday, Meredith sent a text message to her friend Sophie: could Sophie come round to the cottage? Giacomo had asked her a favour that worried her. He and the three other students in the semi-basement flat had five marijuana plants in a small room, and had asked her to water them because they'd gone to spend the All Saints holiday with their families near the Adriatic Coast.

Meredith was a little nervous; she worried whether it was right to water the plants. She was also concerned because they'd told her not to tell anyone about them, not even her three flatmates. Sophie texted Meredith back saying she was sorry but she was too busy to come over then; they could meet later. Meredith and her English friends planned to have dinner together and then go on to the Merlin Pub for a Halloween party.

Early that evening, after a long chat with her mother, Meredith went out to buy the things she needed for celebrating Halloween. As a child, she'd use bin liners to make herself a costume, and tie pumpkins with candles in them to sticks before setting out with her parents to call on neighbours. That evening in Perugia, she decided to dress up as Count Dracula and found a long black cloak with a stiff high collar, a pair of plastic vampire teeth and the fake blood she wanted. It came in a packet with some false teeth, marked in big letters 'BLOOD AND FANGS'.

Pleased to have got everything she needed, she walked back to the cottage. Filomena was at home and the two chatted about Halloween and how the British celebrate it. Meredith put the cloak on and fixed the false teeth and Filomena lent her some make-up. As Meredith was about to leave, she asked Filomena hesitantly: 'Do I look all right?'

Filomena said yes, and the two said goodbye. Laura had already left to stay with her family and Filomena was about to go and spend the next couple of days at her boyfriend's. The cottage would be empty, save for Meredith and Amanda.

It was the last time Filomena saw Meredith.

Amanda tried hard to meet up with Meredith that evening and sent her a series of text messages. She asked Meredith about her plans. Just after 7 p.m., Meredith replied: *'I'm going to a friend's house for dinner. What are your plans?'* Almost an hour later, just before 8 p.m., Amanda again texted Meredith: *'What are you doing this evening? Want to meet up? Got a costume?'* Less than ten minutes later, Amanda texted Meredith yet again: *'I'm going to Le Chic and after who knows? Maybe we'll meet up? Call me.'* Meredith stuck to her dinner plans but told her friends later that she felt guilty for not meeting up with Amanda.

At Amy and Robyn's flat on Via Bontempi, where ruts on the stone thresholds of smart *palazzi* still mark the passage of medieval carts, Meredith and half a dozen friends, all of them women students, had dinner, drank wine and put the final touches to their costumes before going out. Sophie was dressed up as the Devil, Amy as another vampire. Sophie, Amy and Meredith helped each other make themselves up with the fake blood and plenty of bright red lipstick. They got the blood to trickle down from the sides of Meredith's mouth but it was messy and there was more on Meredith's face than she wanted. She just laughed about it.

At about midnight, Meredith and her friends went dancing at the Merlin Pub, then when it closed at 2 a.m. went on to the Domus nightclub. Meredith was too tired to dance, and sat at a table chatting. At about 3.30 a.m., she suggested they leave. The group headed home, passing by the cathedral on their way. They agreed to meet again at Amy and Robyn's flat that afternoon; they would watch a film and have dinner together. The group accompanied Meredith as far as the top of the stairs on Piazza Grimana, where they said goodbye to her at about 4 a.m.

The dark, narrow streets were filled that night with vampires, witches and ghosts. The atmospheric heart of Perugia had become haunted, just for the one night.

1 November 2007

According to Amanda's own account, she woke up late, at about 10 a.m., in Raffaele's flat. The previous night, she'd made up her face to look like a cat, and had gone alone to Le Chic where she chatted with Patrick over a glass of red wine, and then on to the Merlin and other pubs before meeting up with Raffaele. He took her to his flat where they smoked a joint together before going to bed. After breakfast, Amanda went to the cottage to have a shower and change her clothes.

Just after 12.30 p.m., Filomena returned to the cottage with her boyfriend Marco Zaroli, a twenty-five-year-old engineering student, for a quick half hour to get changed before hurrying out again to a friend's birthday party. Amanda was sitting on her own at the table in the sitting room, wearing a sweatshirt that had belonged to her American boyfriend DJ. Filomena asked Amanda to wrap up the birthday present she'd bought – thinking that, as a woman, she would make a better job of it than Marco. Amanda did as she was asked and because Marco's handwriting was so poor, Filomena also asked her to write a birthday message. Before leaving, Filomena closed the window in her room. She closed one shutter, leaving the other one slightly ajar to let in some light.

Not long after Filomena and Marco had gone, Meredith woke up. Amanda noticed as Meredith had her breakfast that she still had traces of fake blood on her face from the previous night. The two told each other how they'd spent Halloween. They also talked once more about Amanda going out with Raffaele, while also still supposed to be DJ's girlfriend. Raffaele arrived at about 2 p.m. and had lunch with Amanda. She then played the guitar for a while. Meredith left the cottage at about 3 or 4 p.m., saying only '*Ciao!*'

Meredith spoke to both her parents on the phone that afternoon. At 3.15 p.m., she called her father John and asked how he was. John was in a bank and they chatted for only a couple of minutes.

'It's expensive for you to call, I'll call you this evening,' John told his daughter.

'But I'm going out this evening,' Meredith said.

'Well, I'll speak to you tomorrow then,' John said. As he said goodbye, he told her that he loved her.

Meredith had a much longer conversation later with her mother, asking how that day's dialysis had gone. She told her that she had booked a ticket to fly home on 9 November, in time to celebrate her mother's birthday two days later. She told Arline about all the presents she was taking her, but wouldn't say what they were. She also had a suitcase full of chocolates for her sister, she said. Mother and daughter also talked about another trip home which Meredith was planning for mid-December; she wanted to go to a ball she had been invited to. After that, Meredith said, she would try to get all her work done so she could be back once again for Christmas.

She was really tired, she said, because she'd been out for Halloween and had got back very late. She was going to a friend's house to watch a film in the afternoon but would come back early because she had an essay to finish and a lecture at ten o'clock the next morning.

Meredith arrived at Amy and Robyn's flat – a little late as usual – around 4.30 p.m. She wore a pair of very faded and very worn jeans that an ex-boyfriend had bought her in England. She also wore a light blue, striped zip-up Adidas sweatshirt which she took off as she came in because she was too hot, and a sleeveless beige cotton top over a long-sleeved T-shirt, also beige.

Meredith had a huge smile on her face. 'I've found my first grey hair! It's a mother's blessing,' she announced delightedly as she walked in.

She told her friends that her Dad had told her that's what people call the first grey hair – 'a mother's blessing'. She was thrilled because it made her feel close to Arline.

While Amy and Robyn made pizza – with a rich topping of ham, tomato, tuna, aubergines, peppers, Gorgonzola and other kinds of cheeses – Meredith and Sophie used a laptop to look at photographs they'd taken during Halloween and posted on their Facebook pages. They talked about the wonderful time they were having in Perugia, and gossiped about men. Meredith showed Sophie a photograph of an ex-boyfriend of hers. They also chatted about Patrick's repeated requests to Meredith to go to his bar. But Meredith preferred the Merlin and hadn't been back to Le Chic.

The girls put on a DVD of *The Notebook*, a romantic drama by Nick Cassavetes, and started eating some time after 5.30 p.m., picking at cherry-sized mozzarella balls before tackling the pizza. They stopped the film while they put an apple crumble Robyn had made in the oven, finishing the meal at about 8–8.30 p.m.

'I'm tired, I'm going to go now,' Sophie said. She wanted to get home before 9 p.m. in time to watch the MTV Europe Music Awards that night.

'I'll come with you,' Meredith said; she was tired too.

Meredith borrowed an Italian history book from Robyn and the two arranged to meet for a class the next morning at 10 a.m. As they said goodbye, Meredith and Sophie thanked Amy and Robyn for the evening.

'I wish you didn't have to go. I wish we could all live together!' Robyn said.

'Yes, that would be really good!' Meredith exclaimed.

As she walked out the door, Meredith said to Robyn: 'See you tomorrow at ten!' Meredith then pretended to shut the door, before opening it again suddenly and adding with a giggle: 'Not really. Half ten!' – a reference to her constant tardiness.

At about 8.40 p.m., Meredith and Sophie walked out into the night. Meredith carried her beige imitation-leather shoulder bag, in which she'd put the book Robyn had just lent her. It was very cold and windy, and the streets were deserted; the only sounds were those of the wind and of their footsteps as they walked down Via Bontempi.

Sophie asked her friend: 'When is Giacomo back?'

'Tomorrow,' Meredith said.

'How's it going with him?' Sophie asked.

'He's not my type looks-wise, but there's something really nice about him. He's quite shy compared to the other boys but he's always really sweet,' Meredith replied. She said she was in two minds about Giacomo; she liked him very much but she wasn't sure she wanted things to become serious because she would be leaving Italy in a year's time. Plus he lived downstairs from her, and she didn't want anything awkward. They walked under the graceful Arch of Lilies – in Etruscan times one of Perugia's five main gates – and on down the steps that wound down the hillside, stopping briefly on the corner of Via del Lupo, a rundown dead end where Sophie lived and where they had once seen two men smoking heroin.

Sophie suggested they go out the next evening, a Friday.

'Yes, I'll text you,' Meredith said as they hugged each other goodbye. 'See you tomorrow.'

As she walked into her flat, Sophie switched the TV on in her kitchen; five minutes later, at 9 p.m., the MTV Awards ceremony started.

Meredith walked on alone down the dark, steep street, towards the cottage some five minutes away, the cold northern *tramontana* wind sweeping up from the valley towards her.

8

Nara Capezzali, a short, stout widow in her late sixties with a mass of big brown curls, went to bed at 9.30 p.m. For the past twenty years she'd lived in her east-facing, first-floor flat just opposite the cottage. From her window, Capezzali could see Via della Pergola and the cottage roof and part of the terrace. It was some seventy yards away, on the other side of a car park.

Her flat was a noisy one and she was often woken up by people talking in loud voices below her window as they walked back to their cars after an evening out, or by rowdy students joking and laughing together. Sometimes, even – the neighbourhood wasn't what it used to be – she could hear people shouting after pick-pockets, or drug addicts squabbling when they couldn't get a fix. She often saw used needles on the ground outside her window. And as if that wasn't enough, people going up and down the iron staircase to the car park made an awful racket, especially at night, their shoes clanging loudly on the metal steps.

Widowed only that summer, Capezzali felt so lonely at night that her daughter Sabrina, who also lived in the flat, slept with her in what used to be the marital bed; sleeping alone in it reminded Capezzali too much of her loss.

Before going to bed Capezzali took her usual pills – since her husband, a schoolteacher, died she suffered from swollen feet and they helped her bladder – and watched TV in the bedroom for a short while. But the programmes were all boring, so she turned it off and fell asleep.

She slept for two hours or a little more – she wasn't sure

precisely how long but she always got up anyway after a couple of hours because that was when the pills took effect – and walked towards the bathroom. As she passed the large window in the dining room which gave out onto her terrace, she said later: 'I heard a scream . . . such a scream . . . an agonising scream which gave me gooseflesh.' The scream went on for a long time and she heard it very clearly.

It was a woman's scream, and she thought it came from the cottage. Startled and confused, Capezzali went into the bathroom and it was only there that she looked outside. She looked out over the tiny cactus plants she kept on the ledge of the small bathroom window; she could see part of the car park and the iron staircase to her right. There was no one to be seen.

'Two seconds, maybe a minute' after the scream, she walked out of the bathroom and as she closed the door behind her, she heard the sound of someone running on the iron staircase. Almost at the same time, she heard a 'scurrying' sound, as if someone was running along the cottage's drive of stones and dry leaves, towards Piazza Grimana and the university.

Capezzali looked out again, but still couldn't see anyone. Then the night was quiet once more.

She went back to bed. Her daughter Sabrina was sleeping soundly. That didn't surprise Capezzali; Sabrina always slept like a log. 'Even if you were to lift her up and carry her away, I don't think she'd hear anything, she's such a heavy sleeper!' she said later. Besides, the bedroom was at the opposite end of the flat from the dining room, away from the cottage.

Capezzali lay awake for some time, still shocked by what she'd heard. She tried to work out what the scream could have been. Perhaps someone had tried to rape a girl. Or perhaps it had just been another student prank. She got up again to make herself a camomile tea to soothe her nerves then went back to bed. She had become used to sleeping in fits and starts; she usually got up two or three times a night and thought often of her late husband.

But that night, Capezzali kept hearing the scream in her head, over and over again. 'What with the scream and the wind blowing, I had the impression I was in a house of horrors,' she said later.

Antonella Monacchia, a primary schoolteacher, lived in a street parallel to Capezzali's and just a few yards further up the hillside. The bedroom window of her fifth-floor flat gave out on the car park and the cottage. That summer, she'd called the police because a loud party at the cottage was still making a racket at 3 a.m., stopping her sleeping.

On 1 November, Monacchia went to bed at 10 p.m.; she remembered the precise time because she looked at her watch. She fell asleep but was woken up some time later – she guessed it was about 11 p.m. – by the loud voices of a man and a woman speaking in great agitation. They were talking Italian, but she couldn't make out what they were saying. The voices became louder and she then heard a very loud scream, a woman's scream. Alarmed, she opened the window and looked outside but she saw no one. She looked at the cottage and thought the sounds had come from there. But everything was dark and she closed the window again.

Still worried, Monacchia walked down to her elderly parents' bedroom on the floor below. They were sleeping but Monacchia woke them up and told them what she'd heard. They'd heard nothing – but they slept in another part of the flat and their window gave out on an alley. Monacchia went back to bed and fell asleep.

Part 2

Investigation

9

2 November 2007 – Festa dei Morti (Feast of the Dead)

Meredith failed to turn up for the 10 a.m. class but Robyn wasn't worried – Meredith was always late and in any case she'd just arrived to find the class was cancelled because of a holiday. Today was the *Festa dei Morti*, when many Italians traditionally went to put flowers on the tombs of their lost ones. Robyn stayed and waited a bit for her friend.

Robyn tried to call her on her mobile but the phone just rang and rang. She assumed Meredith was sleeping. At a loose end, Robyn went for a walk in the city centre and bought some books. She kept trying Meredith's phone, and sent her several text messages; at first the phone just rang, then there was a message that the person she was calling couldn't be reached.

Robyn needed the history book she'd lent Meredith the previous evening, because she had to prepare for an exam in a few days' time. But Robyn got no reply to her texts and her messages became more and more insistent.

'*Where are you? Can you bring the book back to me? I need it. Are you awake?*'

While Robyn was trying to reach Meredith, Elisabetta Lana, who lives in a large, isolated villa on Via Sperandio some 400 yards from the cottage, was in the offices of the postal police – who specialise in tackling crime involving the Internet and communication technology in general – reporting two bizarre events. The previous evening, she'd received a worrying phone call. 'Careful, don't use the toilet, don't wee in the toilet because there's a bomb inside,' the anonymous caller, a man, had said. Lana thought it might be a trick by a burglar who wanted to get her out of the house so he could break in. Then, that morning, Lana's son had found a Motorola mobile phone in the garden; she handed it to the police.

After she'd finished with the police, Lana left and went to do some shopping. She was still out when her daughter called her from the villa. At about 11.45 a.m.–12 p.m., Lana's daughter had found a second mobile phone, this time a Sony Ericsson, close to where the first one had been discovered. It was hidden in some bushes, and she would never have found it if it hadn't started ringing. It rang again when she brought it into the house. A name appeared on the display screen as it rang: '*Amanda*'.

Lana took the second phone to the police who were able to trace the Motorola phone to Filomena Romanelli and sent two officers to the cottage.

Sophie got up early that morning and didn't bother to get washed or dressed. She was behind in her studies and decided now was the time to catch up, as it was a holiday and she had no classes.

About midday, as she sat in her pyjamas working on her chemistry lecture notes at her laptop, a 'ping' sound from the Windows Live Messenger service she was logged onto told her that Robyn wanted a chat.

'*Meredith didn't turn up, have you heard from her?*' read Robyn's message.

God, I hope she's OK, I hope nothing's happened to Meredith, Sophie thought. But then she told herself nothing could have happened to her and so she just replied that no, she hadn't heard from her.

'*It's OK, I'm going to a shop and then I'll go round to her flat on my way back,*' Robyn typed back.

'I'll let you know if I hear anything,' Sophie replied. Then she got back to her work.

At 12.08 p.m., Filomena and her friend Paola Grande, a feisty character who came from southern Calabria like her, were driving to the Fair of the Dead market festival outside the city when Filomena's mobile rang. Filomena answered and drove on as she listened.

'*Ciao*, there's something strange in the house,' Amanda said.

'*Ciao* Amanda. What happened? What do you mean?' Filomena asked in her slightly husky voice.

'I slept at Raffaele's. This morning I went to the house and I found the front door open, and blood in my bathroom. I took a shower but I'm scared, I don't know what to do.'

Filomena blanched. 'Where's Meredith?' she asked.

'I don't know.'

'Maybe Meredith hurt herself, maybe she cut herself. Amanda, go round the house and make sure everything is all right,' Filomena said. She told Amanda to call the police.

'What's happened?' Paola asked as soon as the call was finished. 'You looked very strange.'

Filomena told her friend what Amanda had said. The girl was 'the most *cretina* [stupid] of them all'. How could she calmly have a shower after finding the door open and blood in the bathroom? It made no sense. She told Paola that Laura had gone away for a long weekend, so Amanda and Meredith were alone in the cottage.

'Perhaps Meredith did cut herself,' Paola suggested. 'She went to the bathroom, and some blood fell on the floor. Maybe she didn't manage to stop the bleeding so she went out and left the door open. Maybe she's at the chemist's. Call her.'

Filomena parked the car and as she and Paola walked towards the stalls of the fair she tried Meredith first on her Italian mobile and then on her English one; she got a ringing tone on both of them, but no answer.

'Maybe she's sleeping,' Filomena said.

Filomena called Amanda once more, but there was no reply. Then she tried Meredith's phone again, and this time she got a recording saying the person called was unavailable.

Filomena kept trying Amanda until she got through. 'Amanda, what happened? Do check on the house, because I'm at the fair and I can't come straightaway. Do look around please, I'm worried there might be something wrong,' Filomena said, speaking in both English and Italian.

'OK, OK, I'll go now and call Raffaele. I'll check the house,' Amanda promised.

Filomena and Paola started to walk round the stalls. Paola tried to reassure her. 'Come on, it's probably nothing serious,' she said.

Still at the fair, an increasingly anxious Filomena called Amanda yet again, at 12.34 p.m.

'Filomena, I've checked the house and the window of your room is broken and everything's a big mess. We've had burglars. And there's some shit in the bathroom,' Amanda said.

'Call the police now!' Filomena burst out.

'I'll call them,' Amanda said.

As Filomena and Paola hurried back to the car – Filomena was so flustered it took her a while to find it – she started listing the things she thought burglars might have stolen: the laptop she had left in its case on the desk, the Versace sunglasses next to it, and the box of gold jewellery and a digital camera in unlocked drawers.

On the way home – Filomena was so agitated she drove at a snail's pace – she called her boyfriend Marco, told him what had happened, and asked him to rush to the cottage to help her and to bring Paola's boyfriend, Luca Altieri, with him. Filomena still couldn't make head or tail of Amanda's explanations; they sounded like 'the ravings of someone dreaming'.

At 12.47 p.m., Amanda called Edda and Chris who were asleep in bed in Seattle – it was nearly 4 a.m. for them. Edda answered the phone.

'Mom, I'm home and I'm OK,' her daughter said, sounding worried but not in a panic.

Edda was instantly alert. 'OK, what's going on?' she asked.

'Well, something strange is going on. I think someone may have been in the house.'

'What's going on?' Now Edda was alarmed. She woke Chris up and put Amanda on the speakerphone.

Amanda told them how she'd found the front door open with blood in the small bathroom and excrement in the bigger one. She'd gone to fetch Raffaele and when they got back to the cottage she saw that the toilet had been flushed. She had managed to get hold of Filomena – but not Meredith.

'I can't get hold of Meredith. Meredith's door is locked. We tried to pound on the door to wake her and she's not answering,' Amanda said.

When Amanda said the toilet had been flushed, Edda thought immediately that someone might have been in the house when Amanda was having her shower. But she didn't say that to her daughter; she didn't want to worry her. 'Hang up and call the police,' Edda told her.

Chris butted in. 'Amanda, get the hell out of that house, something's not right. Call the police,' he said.

'I don't know how,' Amanda said weakly.

'Try 911 or ask Raffaele,' Chris said.

'OK. He's going to do that now,' Amanda said, adding that he was just finishing talking to his sister who was a lieutenant in the *carabinieri*.

At 12.51 p.m., Raffaele called the emergency hotline for the *carabinieri*.

'*Carabinieri*,' said Lance Corporal Daniele Ceppitelli, who was manning the switchboard. The call was recorded automatically.

Raffaele, in a feeble, almost sleepy voice: 'Hello, good morning. Listen, someone has entered the house by smashing the window and has made a big mess, the door's closed, the street is . . . What's the street?' he asked Amanda.

'Via della Pergola,' Amanda said.

'Via della Pergola, number 7, in Perugia,' Raffaele repeated.

'Does anyone live there? The name?'

'Um, Amanda Knox. A group of students live here – one's Amanda Knox.' Raffaele spelt out the surname, asked Amanda her mobile number, and gave it to the officer.

'This is a burglary?'

'No, there hasn't been a burglary, they broke the glass, they made a mess . . .'

Ceppitelli, sounding baffled: 'So look, you're saying someone got in and then broke a window? How do you know anyone got in anyway?'

'You can see they have from the traces they left, there are bloodstains in the bathroom.'

Ceppitelli, sounding more baffled: 'They went in and . . . Why? Did they cut themselves when they broke the window?'

'Um . . .' There followed a sound as if the mobile phone was being handled.

Ceppitelli: 'Hello?'

The line went dead.

Raffaele called again at 12.54 p.m.

Ceppitelli took the call: '*Carabinieri*, Perugia.'

Raffaele, sounding slightly more awake: 'Yes hello, I called two seconds ago.'

'Someone's been in the house and broke the window?'

'Yes.'

'Then they went into the bathroom.'

'I don't know, if you come here perhaps . . .'

'What did they take?'

'They didn't take anything, the problem is one of the doors is closed, there are bloodstains.'

'A door's closed? Which door's closed?'

'The door of one of the flatmates who isn't here. We don't know where she is.'

'And this girl, do you have her mobile number?'

'Yes, yes, we tried to call her but she's not answering.'

'OK, I'll send you a patrol car now and we'll check the situation out.'

'OK.'

The cold *tramontana* wind was still blowing when Chief Detective Inspector Michele Battistelli from the postal police and a colleague arrived at the cottage a little after 12.30 p.m., according to their later testimony. (The prosecution was to insist that they arrived at the cottage *before* Raffaele called the *carabinieri*.) A wiry figure with an army-style crew cut, Battistelli went up to speak to Amanda and Raffaele, who were sitting necking and embracing each other in the sunshine near the front door. Battistelli introduced himself and asked if they lived in the cottage. Was this where Filomena Romanelli lived?

'Ah, but you're not from the *carabinieri* police?' Raffaele asked.

'No, we're from the postal police,' Battistelli replied.

'We're waiting for the *carabinieri*, because when we came back here this morning we found the door open and the window broken,' Raffaele said. He said he thought there must have been a burglary.

To Battistelli, Amanda and Raffaele looked surprised and embarrassed by his arrival; both spoke in a low voice. They took him to Filomena's room where he noticed pieces of broken glass lying on top of a pile of clothes that had apparently been dumped on the floor. There was a laptop by a desk and under the broken window lay an eight-inch-long stone which looked as if it weighed between four and five kilos.

'I don't think this is a robbery, it looks more like a put-up job to me,' Battistelli said.

Amanda and Raffaele said nothing.

Battistelli asked Amanda for Filomena's mobile number but he recognised the number she gave him as identical to that of one of the two mobiles that had been found that morning. He asked Amanda for another number, and she went to her room to fetch it and wrote it down for him. Battistelli tried it, without success.

MEREDITH AND AMANDA'S COTTAGE

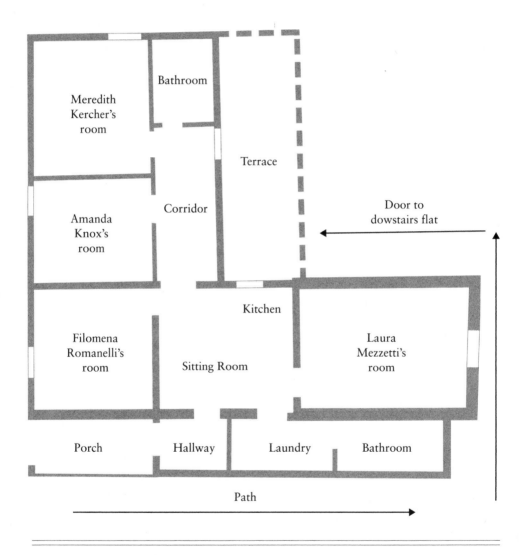

Via della Pergola

10

Filomena and Paola arrived at the cottage a few minutes later, at about 1 p.m. Their boyfriends, Marco and Luca, were already there. Filomena saw Amanda and Raffaele, as well as a man who introduced himself as Battistelli from the postal police, who had come with another officer. Filomena assumed they were there because of the burglary.

Her nerves on edge, Filomena went straight to her room and found it a mess of broken glass with clothes piled up on the floor. The left windowpane was broken and shards of glass lay on the windowsill with more on the floor below it, on a rug near her bed, and near her desk. Under the desk chair, a torn paper bag lay on the floor; she took a closer look and saw there was a large stone inside.

The shock made her whole body begin to shake. Amanda and Raffaele looked on in silence.

'*Signorina*, try to keep calm. It's obvious someone's been here so check if something is missing so you can report it,' Battistelli said.

Filomena made sure first of all that her box of gold jewellery was still in its drawer, then she opened all the other drawers and had a good look round the room.

'Everything's here, my jewellery, my computer,' she told Paola. The Versace sunglasses were still there, and even the digital camera. Filomena breathed a sigh of relief.

Filomena reached for her computer, and realised there were shards of glass on top of it. She looked around again and saw not only that the thief hadn't stolen anything, but also that bits of broken glass from the window were scattered both underneath and on top of the pile of her things on the floor. Her beauty case was open; it was empty.

'He's a strange burglar, but that's fine by me. The only thing he's taken is my make-up!' she told Battistelli.

While Filomena rummaged through her things, Paola went into the narrow corridor – a clothes horse that had been opened out next to the plastic bookcase made it even more cramped than usual – and nearly bumped into Amanda and Raffaele. They shook hands and introduced themselves.

'What about your room?' Paola asked Amanda bluntly.

'Everything's fine in my room,' Amanda replied.

Paola pointed to a door at the end of the corridor, a few feet behind Amanda and Raffaele. She didn't know whose it was.

'Have you looked in there?' Paola asked.

'No, that room's locked,' Amanda said.

'Why on earth is it locked?' Paola asked.

Amanda replied that the girl who lived there locked the door when she went out.

Puzzled, Paola went back to Filomena and asked: 'Filomena, does the other girl who lives here usually lock her door when she goes out?'

'No, absolutely not. What makes you think that? She's only ever locked it once and that was when she went home to London.'

'Well then open that door! Try another key,' Paola said.

Paola went back into the corridor. Amanda and Raffaele were still standing there. They gave her a key: 'See if this one works.'

Paola tried the key but it was no good. She saw someone else had tried to force the door.

'I've already tried to open it but I couldn't manage it,' Raffaele explained.

An agitated Filomena went into the sitting room and said she wanted to call the lawyer she worked for; she was worried the landlady would make her pay for the broken window.

'Let's all keep calm,' Battistelli tried to reassure her again. 'It's not as if we've found a body under the sofa.'

It was only then that he told them that, following an anonymous phone call, two mobile phones had been found in a nearby garden and one of them had been traced to Filomena. He showed her a note with two phone numbers.

At first they meant nothing to Filomena; she didn't know her own number by heart. But she checked on her own mobile and found out they were both Meredith's; she explained that she had given one of her SIM cards to Meredith so that she could make cheaper calls to Italian numbers.

'But where's Meredith?' Filomena asked.

'The door's closed,' Amanda said.

Filomena and Paola looked at each other, a sudden realisation dawning on them. 'We've got to open her door. Knock on it – wake her up. Maybe she's sleeping? But how can she be sleeping with all this racket going on?' Filomena felt her panic rising again.

But Battistelli was still fussing over how Meredith's phones had been found that morning. 'But did you make an anonymous phone call?' he asked.

'No, I didn't do anything, but I'm worrying about this girl,' Filomena answered.

'Why's that?' Battistelli asked.

'Because I know her – forget about the Italian number. She often switches that one off but never her English one . . . Look, this girl always has that phone shoved into her jeans – always. Her mother's ill and they talk to each other five, six or seven times a day. If Meredith hasn't got that phone, she can't possibly be all right. We've got to find her, you *must* open the door,' Filomena said, adding that she hadn't seen Meredith for a day now.

'No, *signorina*, we can't open the door,' Battistelli said – his instructions were not to risk being accused of damaging private property if he could avoid it.

'What?' Filomena was appalled. She tried to make her voice

sound as authoritative as possible. 'You have my permission to break that door down.'

'No, we can't do it. If you want to break it down, you have to do it yourselves,' Battistelli insisted.

Filomena turned to Paola's boyfriend: 'All right then, Luca, break the door down.'

'OK, you're the lady of the house,' Luca said.

Luca and Marco, followed by Filomena and Paola, went up to Meredith's door. Battistelli stood just next to them in the cramped corridor. Raffaele was at the other end of the corridor, near the sitting room, while Amanda was standing close to the front door.

Luca bent down to look through the keyhole but all he could glimpse was part of a bed and a wall. He first tried ramming his shoulder against the door. He tried again, several times. It didn't budge. He then started kicking it, aiming at the door handle, again and again, half a dozen kicks in all.

The door swung open and Luca almost went sprawling into Meredith's room but managed to get his balance back in time. The first thing he saw was a pool of blood in the far corner of the floor to his right. Then he saw there was a beige quilt on the floor and a bare foot poking out from underneath.

'Oh my God, there's a sea of blood!' Luca shouted, raising his hands to his head.

Filomena saw both Luca and Marco blanch, and followed their gaze. 'Meredith! No!' she screamed. She was convinced it could only be Meredith lying there.

Marco shouted: 'Everybody out! *Via, via, via!*'

Filomena, Paola and their boyfriends turned to rush towards the front door out into the fresh air. As he turned away from Meredith's room, Marco saw Amanda standing in the sitting room; she was staring down the corridor with a vaguely surprised, dazed expression that struck him as strange; he himself felt as if he was about to vomit. He said later that from where she stood, she couldn't see inside Meredith's room.

Outside in the garden, Filomena was in shock, terrified; Paola was crying; Marco shook uncontrollably; Luca looked deathly pale.

Amanda and Raffaele were dry-eyed; they moved away from the others and started hugging, caressing and kissing each other – to the bewilderment of the others.

Battistelli emerged from the cottage saying he had to send for the emergency services and call his colleagues. The cottage was now sealed off, he said.

In Seattle, Edda was sitting up in bed wide awake, waiting for more news from her daughter when Amanda called again more than half an hour after her first call. This time, she was much more agitated.

'Oh my God! They're screaming about a foot near the cupboard, the cops are screaming. I'm outside the house, I don't know what's going on. I gotta go,' Amanda said before hanging up.

Shortly afterwards Amanda called a third time, extremely upset. 'It's not a foot, there's a body. They've found a body near the cupboard or in the cupboard, I can't make out which,' Amanda exclaimed.

'Who is it?' Edda asked. She could hear a lot of screaming in the background.

'I don't know, I haven't seen but no one can get hold of Meredith. It's Meredith's room – it's in the cupboard or next to the cupboard,' Amanda repeated.

Edda heard some more shouting. 'I gotta go, the police want to talk to me,' Amanda said and then hung up.

11

Detective Superintendent Monica Napoleoni had first dreamt of joining the police force when she was only seven years old, because her father was a respected, much-liked officer in the Flying Squad and she wanted to follow in his footsteps. Dedicating heart and soul to her work, Napoleoni learnt the nuts and bolts of policing with the patrol section she eventually commanded, spending long hours at night trying to persuade prostitutes to turn against their pimps, get off the streets and start a new life.

She had risen to head the Homicide Squad. Respected for her tenacity and encyclopaedic memory of what suspects or witnesses had said or done in the investigations she worked on, she did long hours of unpaid overtime and often caught only a few hours of sleep at night, sacrificing time with her fifteen-year-old daughter and four-year-old son. 'What matters is the quality of the time I spend with my children, not the quantity,' Napoleoni, who had two failed marriages behind her, would say.

A passion for justice she inherited from her father kept her going through the pressures of the job. 'I keep going for the victims' sake, because I can't stand injustice. My job's about good against evil, and the strong against the weak. My dad taught me to always help the weakest and never the powerful, and never to betray your principles,' she explained. When asked about her rather flamboyant looks – long black hair with a fringe just over her eyebrows, a tanned face, heavy mascara, tight blouses and black leather boots that reached just below the knee – she said cheerfully: 'Maybe I don't look soft on the outside, but you shouldn't judge by appearances.'

Shortly after Napoleoni arrived at the cottage at about 1.30 p.m., her boss Marco Chiacchiera joined her – the deputy head of the Flying Squad was in the cemetery with his mother, laying flowers on a family grave, when the operations room told him there was a 'suspicious death' at Via della Pergola. A patrol car sent by the *carabinieri* also arrived, but they left when they saw the rival, national police force had got there first.

'You go inside to see what you can find out right away,' Chiacchiera told Napoleoni.

After a doctor from the emergency services had lifted and then lowered the quilt back over the body, Napoleoni gazed slowly around Meredith's room. A small blue and silver container marked 'Vaseline pocket-size lip therapy' lay on the desk; it was empty. She walked out of the room and turned left into a small bathroom; she saw a big bloodstain on the tap above the sink, and a footprint that looked like a mix of blood and water on the blue bathmat. She also noticed bloodstains on the light switch – as if someone had switched the light on with a bloody finger.

The key to Meredith's bedroom was missing. What burglar, she wondered, would stop long enough to close and lock the door instead of simply running for it as fast as he could? Was he trying to delay the discovery of the body? That seemed the most obvious explanation. But why did he need to?

Napoleoni walked outside. The young woman had to be identified as soon as possible and her family told before the media could reach them. She asked a colleague to make this a priority.

Napoleoni and Chiacchiera talked alone for a while, trying to make sense of a crime scene they found very confusing. First, there was no sign of the front door having been forced. Second, the green wooden shutters of Filomena's window were ajar and undamaged despite the shattered window. And third, the window was almost a dozen feet from the ground, and the wall below it was quite smooth without any footholds for anyone wanting to climb up and reach the window.

But oddest of all: in the bedroom lay an almost naked young woman, wounded several times in the neck, and covered by a quilt. A burglar wouldn't cover his victim with a quilt. A burglar didn't lock the door and get rid of the key. Nor would he steal two mobile phones only to throw them away in a neighbouring garden.

Napoleoni asked the shocked Filomena a few questions about Meredith and about Amanda's phone calls that morning, then went to speak to Amanda and Raffaele who were still standing some distance away from Filomena and her friends, giving each other little kisses and caressing each other. The couple seemed to her to be completely indifferent to Meredith's death.

'*Buongiorno*,' she greeted them as she opened her wallet and showed them her police badge. 'You must tell me everything you think could help us understand this girl's last moments.'

Napoleoni asked them about the last time they had seen Meredith, and why Amanda had gone into the cottage and taken a shower after finding the front door open and bloodstains in the bathroom.

With Raffaele occasionally acting as an interpreter, Amanda said she had come back to the cottage at about 10 a.m., found the front door open and blood in the bathroom she shared with Meredith, had taken a shower there then gone into the bigger bathroom to dry her hair, where she found the excrement in the toilet.

Amanda's story didn't make much sense to Napoleoni. 'But excuse me, you find the front door's open when you know it's always kept closed but you don't look in the bedrooms. You find blood in the bathroom but you have a shower, then you dry your hair and you find the excrement. Then after all that you go out calmly and you don't call anyone?' she asked Amanda.

'Yes, I thought someone had gone to throw the rubbish out,' Amanda replied. She said she had knocked on the front door of the semi-basement flat, but no one had answered.

As she quizzed Amanda, Napoleoni couldn't help thinking that she was hiding something from her – but she had no idea what. She checked on the rubbish bins and saw they were just outside the gate – so Amanda was bound to have seen anyone carrying rubbish out as she came in. Napoleoni learnt that the four students who lived in the downstairs flat had all gone away for a long weekend with their families, and that Amanda and Meredith had been alone in the cottage.

Later, after sheltering from the cold with Amanda in Luca's car, Raffaele got out to speak to Napoleoni. 'My girlfriend has just remembered that when she went into the big bathroom on her own this morning there was excrement. When we went back to the flat it wasn't there anymore,' Raffaele said. The toilet had been flushed in their absence, he added.

Napoleoni went back into the cottage and to the big bathroom that Filomena and Laura shared, and saw that contrary to what Raffaele had told her, the excrement was still there. She was puzzled and guessed that for some reason or other, Amanda and Raffaele wanted to make sure that she would notice it.

12

Giuliano Mignini, a respected public prosecutor in his late fifties, was packing his cherrywood pipe before taking his dog Argos, a cross between a hunting dog and an Alaskan sled dog, for an early afternoon walk – Mignini was banned from smoking at home by his wife and three teenage daughters – when the detective Chiacchiera called him from the cottage. The prosecutor was on call that week, twenty-four hours a day.

'We've found a girl's body. She was definitely murdered,' Chiacchiera told Mignini, a tall, well-built figure in his late fifties with a bald patch and short, curly grey hair streaked with silver.

'Who is she?' Mignini asked.

'We don't know yet.'

They agreed the officer would pick up Mignini and drive him to the scene. Perugia's prosecutors often caught rides off the Flying Squad; the twelve prosecutors had only one office car between them, a small Fiat. The squad had many more, some of them confiscated from criminals.

Mignini's wife Cristina, whom he'd met in the choir of the cathedral where he used to sing as a bass baritone, guessed instantly from her husband's quiet but forceful tone that there had been a murder; that meant she wouldn't be seeing much of him over the next few days.

'That's the last thing we need,' Cristina said after he put the phone down.

'Well . . .' Mignini shrugged, anxious to get started.

Moments later, his wife wished him good luck as he walked out of their home, a two-century-old house built on top of the ancient Etruscan wall that circles Perugia.

Unlike his British or American counterparts, Mignini dealt with dozens of cases at the same time, from routine expulsions of illegal immigrants to Mafiosi gangsters trying to settle in Umbria and Muslim preachers supporting terrorism. Placid and courteous – even when flustered in court he rarely raised his voice – he was a determined investigator. 'He's tenacious like a bulldog; when he bites he doesn't let go,' one local crime reporter said.

When Mignini was a small boy, his father – a teacher of shorthand – had predicted that he might become a judge. Mignini never found out why his father thought that – the boy was four when a car crashed into his thirty-three-year-old father as he rode his Lambretta motorcycle. An officer from the barracks of the *carabinieri* police, seeing the boy baffled by his mother's tears, took him in his arms and played with him for a long while. The officer's kindness is one of Mignini's most vivid memories and may be one reason why he later wanted to become an officer himself; he chose the air force. But he was rejected because of imperfect vision and became first a lawyer, then a judge, then a prosecutor.

He much preferred the task of discovering the truth behind a crime to playing the judge's role of arbiter. His fascination was rooted in the tales of Sherlock Holmes and the French fictional detective Jules Maigret which he had read as a teenager. Mignini admired Sherlock Holmes as 'a philosopher', making extraordinary deductions from his armchair. He admired Maigret for his honesty and his humanity; he got results because he liked to watch people and work out what made them tick.

Outside the cottage, Mignini looked at Filomena's window, puzzling over it with Chiacchiera and Napoleoni. He agreed with them that it was an unlikely point of entry for a burglar to choose. The window was too high up for anyone to scale the wall; the wall was bare save for a small nail that would have bent under the weight of an intruder. Besides, the wall was in full view of anyone passing the cottage and even the stupidest burglar would have chosen an easier and more discreet way in, such as a ground-floor window. Alternatively, out of sight at the back of the cottage, a burglar could have easily scaled the metal grating outside the front door to the downstairs flat, climbed onto the terrace and used the table or one of the chairs left out on it to break the glass door leading into the corridor opposite Amanda and Meredith's rooms.

Mignini slipped on protective gloves and shoe covers and, accompanied by Chiacchiera, walked slowly inside. The Perugia forensic police, dressed in white overalls, were already there and had begun their search for bloodstains, fingerprints and other traces, placing white cards printed with letters of the alphabet to flag anything they thought important. One officer told him that excrement had been found in the bigger of the two bathrooms, off the sitting room. *Perhaps an outsider,* Mignini thought – surely the four young women living in the flat always flushed the toilet.

He stared around the sitting room and kitchen area; he never took notes at crime scenes, preferring to just look, let his mind wander and absorb what he saw and heard. Through his half-moon glasses, he read some handwritten notices stuck to the fridge – they were bawdy, student-humour jokes. He then glanced at the DVDs on a shelf just above the fridge – Italian comedy classics and *Shall We Dance* with Richard Gere.

He looked into Filomena's room and like Napoleoni before him, he noticed the shards of glass on top of the piles of clothes and the large stone on the floor; it was obvious to him too that it could never have come through the window without shattering the shutters. He thought immediately that the window must have been broken by someone standing inside the room.

'There's a traitor in this house, someone who participated in the crime or helped to cover it up or who did both,' Mignini thought to himself. Perhaps the killer had entered through the front door, and staged a fake burglary to throw suspicion on an outsider, assisted by someone living in the cottage – in either of the two flats – who at the very least, acted as an accomplice to the murder.

Mignini walked down the corridor and stopped in the doorway to Meredith's room. He didn't go in because there was too much blood; besides, he didn't want to risk touching anything. The foot that emerged from under the quilt looked pale, unnaturally so; the blood on the floor was the colour of dark chocolate and had apparently been there for some time. Mignini noticed the knickers, the bra and the pot of Vaseline on the desk and thought the motive for the murder might have been sexual. He stared at a trace of blood on the wall, which looked as if it had been made by the victim as she tried to steady herself.

He puzzled over the quilt covering the body. Why would a thief bother to delay his escape long enough to cover the body of his victim, he wondered. It had to be a mark of pity, which meant some form of relationship between the killer and the victim. Maybe there was a female hand in the murder, he speculated; a woman who knew the victim and felt pity for her naked, mangled body. Mignini thought of a popular French saying: 'Cherchez la femme' – look for the woman.

Mignini asked Luca Lalli, a bearded, heavily built forensic pathologist from the University of Perugia whom the Flying Squad had summoned, to go into the room but to touch the body as little as possible for now; he wanted the forensic police to do their job first. Lalli crouched down and established simply that rigor mortis – the stiffening of the joints and muscles that begins a few hours after death – had settled in the left ankle and toes. Lalli told Mignini that he needed to examine the body and above all to take its temperature to help estimate the time of death – the more time went by, the less data he would be able to gather – but the prosecutor was firm. Mignini insisted that he couldn't risk modifying or contaminating the crime scene and losing any biological traces. He was adamant that both the local forensic police, and the elite forensic unit which was on its way from Rome, should do their work first.

The flat was crowded by now, what with the forensic police milling about and placing their letter cards, so Mignini went outside. A detective kicked the locked door of the semi-basement flat open, and Mignini and Napoleoni went in, the prosecutor worrying there might be another body there. They saw small traces of blood on a quilt, a bed, a pillowcase, a sofa and on the floor. Mignini had no idea what that blood meant; there was no indication that anyone had broken in. Did it mean one or more of the students living there had been involved in the murder in some way?

The prosecutor talked to Filomena, who told him that Amanda's account of that morning made little sense to her. She also told him about Meredith and her sick mother – how Meredith always had her English mobile on her so she could talk to her mother, and about her planned trip to London to see her. Filomena's words moved Mignini; he thought with sadness of what the news of her fate would do to her sick mother.

A detective pointed Meredith's flatmates out to Mignini. 'The girl Amanda's saying a lot of strange things,' the detective said.

'Let's try and make sense of what she says,' Mignini said.

The prosecutor glanced at Amanda – she was pretty, a fresh-faced beauty. Mignini asked her a few questions and fascinated as always by body language, noticed that she occasionally put both hands up to press her temples and then shake her head. It was as if, he thought, she wanted to empty her mind of something.

That afternoon, as journalists who'd heard the news gathered in the road just above the cottage, a TV camera caught one of Amanda and Raffaele's embraces. Amanda, her eyes closed, raised her slightly parted lips to Raffaele's and they kissed three times in quick succession. Then they each gave the other a quick, light rub on the back.

Shortly after 3 p.m., Napoleoni asked Meredith's flatmates and their boyfriends to go to the police station for questioning. She asked Luca to drive Amanda and Raffaele there.

As they skirted the city centre, Raffaele asked Luca bluntly: 'Is she dead?'

'Yes,' Luca said. He was surprised that Raffaele hadn't worked it out for himself. It seemed obvious to him given that the forensic police were there, that no ambulance had come to take anyone away.

'How did the girl die?' Raffaele then asked.

'Well, from what I heard they cut her throat,' Luca said.

'But with a knife?' Raffaele asked again.

Luca, irritated by the question, replied curtly: 'Yes.' Luca thought to himself: 'What did Raffaele think? That Meredith's throat had been cut with a piece of bread?' It had to be a sharp weapon, a knife or a sword or something. He thought that perhaps Raffaele was in shock, and that was why he was asking stupid questions.

Amanda, head bowed, made a brief sound as if she was crying.

They drove the rest of the way in silence.

13

In the Flying Squad's offices on the third floor of Perugia's police station, Napoleoni briefed her colleagues on the little she knew ahead of the rounds of questioning they were about to begin. She argued that the first step should be to find as many friends or acquaintances of Meredith's in Perugia as possible. The search should focus on a male attacker given the apparent sexual nature of the murder – most likely someone whom Meredith had either allowed into the house or someone she knew. The search was definitely not for a burglar, because Napoleoni was convinced the burglary had been staged. Over the next few hours, the number of Perugian police working on the case grew to over fifty, and several more arrived from the Central Operations Service in Rome, which works on high-profile and mafia cases.

As they sat on white plastic chairs in the waiting room outside the Flying Squad's offices, Filomena asked Amanda about that morning. Amanda sometimes hesitated when replying. Filomena noticed how Raffaele jumped in to explain what Amanda wanted to say, effectively acting as her interpreter.

Amanda continued to make little sense to Filomena and she asked Raffaele: 'How's it possible that Amanda gets to the house, finds the door open, there's blood in the bathroom and she has a shower? Surely you would run into the street and call for help first, or you call me first. But how on earth could you have a shower without checking the house?'

'She's irresponsible,' Raffaele replied.

'You'd have to be massively irresponsible,' Filomena retorted.

Later, Filomena saw Amanda pull a big notebook out of her bag and, head bowed, write in it at length. She then showed it to Raffaele, pointing a section out with her pen. They did this several times in silence, Raffaele nodding or shaking his head. Filomena thought it was odd.

Filomena kept asking Amanda why she hadn't called the police immediately – she couldn't help thinking that if Amanda had called an ambulance, Meredith might still be alive.

Amanda was among the first to be questioned by detectives. She told them she had last seen Meredith at about 3 or 4 p.m. the previous day when Meredith had left the cottage; Amanda had no idea where she was going. Amanda was with Raffaele at the time, and they had stayed at the cottage until 5 p.m. when they went to his flat. They spent the whole night there, and at 11 a.m. the next morning she had gone back to the cottage. Earlier, she had told Napoleoni that she had got back home at about 10 a.m.

She then described the morning's events as she had earlier; she'd discovered the broken window only after she'd gone to fetch Raffaele, and had decided to call the *carabinieri* after Raffaele phoned his sister for advice. Amanda said that Raffaele had told her that the body of a girl covered by a sheet had been found in the cupboard, and that the only thing that could be seen was a foot.

In his statement to police, Raffaele confirmed all that Amanda had said. The only variation he made was to point out that he had found the toilet clean, while Amanda had told him it hadn't been flushed.

At her home in Surrey at about 5 p.m., Meredith's mother Arline saw on the TV news that a British girl student had been found murdered in Perugia. She called John, her sixty-four-year-old ex-husband, and he tried to stay calm by focusing on the fact that there were thousands of British students in Perugia. He too tried calling Meredith on her mobile. John tried about a dozen times but all he got was the answering machine telling him to leave a message. He kept trying and at about 5.30 p.m., Meredith's phone started ringing when he called it. John felt relieved, thinking she had switched the phone back on. But there was no answer although he kept trying for another half hour.

As he had worked for many years as a freelance journalist for the *Daily Mirror*, he called its foreign desk at about 6 p.m. But his colleagues had heard little and told him to call again in an hour's time in case they managed to find out more. Meredith's sister Stephanie also tried to contact her, sending several text messages after Arline told her about the news on TV. *'Mez, call us as soon as you wake up. We're worried, an English girl's been killed,'* Stephanie texted her sister.

When John called the *Daily Mirror* again, a colleague had some news for him: the Italian police had found the girl's phone and had contacted people in London. John again felt relieved: surely her family and the British police had been informed by now?

Half an hour later, a woman from the newspaper called him back. She told John they had heard a name. She hesitated, apparently reluctant to tell him more.

Then she said: 'The name going around Italy is Meredith.'

John dropped the phone. At first he couldn't believe it, he was sure someone had made a mistake. But he quickly realised it was probably true. Numb with shock, he couldn't cry.

Meredith's friend Sophie was still working on her chemistry lecture notes, in her pyjamas, when Cornelia, a friend from the university's Erasmus student exchange office, called her at about 5 p.m.

'Hello Sophie, how are you? How was Halloween?' Cornelia asked.

Sophie told her what she'd been up to.

'Do you have a friend called Meredith?' Cornelia asked.

'Yeah, she's my friend. I was with her on Halloween,' Sophie said, thinking that perhaps Cornelia knew Meredith too.

'Does she have a boyfriend?' Cornelia asked.

This is weird, Sophie thought. 'Why, do you know Meredith?'

Cornelia went quiet for a bit. Then she said: 'I'm really sorry but a girl called Meredith has been found murdered.'

Sophie was too stunned to take in what she'd just heard. Cornelia quickly asked: 'What's your friend's surname?'

'Kercher,' Sophie said.

'Oh, I don't think it's her then. Do you mind if I give your number to the police?' Cornelia said.

'No, OK,' Sophie managed to say before they said goodbye to each other.

Sophie didn't know what to think. As soon as Cornelia got off the phone, Sophie tried to ring Meredith. There was no reply.

Sophie then called Robyn. 'Robyn, have you heard from Meredith yet?' Sophie asked.

'No, I haven't,' Robyn said.

'Right, I'm coming round,' Sophie said.

Sophie sounded so upset that Robyn asked: 'Are you OK?'

'I'll tell you when I get there,' Sophie said before hanging up.

Sophie couldn't believe that something like that could have happened to Meredith. But something must be wrong because Robyn hadn't heard from her. A girl called Meredith had been murdered, Cornelia had said. But she'd also said she didn't think it was the Meredith Sophie knew. But then again, why had she called Sophie in the first place, and why did she want to give her number to the police? It didn't make sense.

All Sophie knew was that she wanted to get to Amy and Robyn. She was badly shaken, breathing heavily and making little crying noises. She was in such a hurry she took off her pyjama bottoms and put on a pair of jeans, but then just slipped a cardigan over her pyjama top before rushing out.

Sophie walked fast, nearly running, to Amy and Robyn's flat – retracing the route she'd taken with Meredith, in the opposite direction, only the previous evening.

Worried by the sound of Sophie's voice on the phone, Amy and Robyn were both waiting for her in the street when she hurried up to them.

'What's wrong?' Amy and Robyn asked as soon as they saw her.

'It's really hard to tell you. I don't know how to say it. I don't know whether it's true or not,' Sophie replied, breathing more heavily than before, after her fast walk.

Amy and Robyn both took hold of her and led her through the big front door and up to their flat on the first floor. The two friends held on to her all the way and kept asking her what was the matter as they went up the steps, but Sophie found the strength to tell them only when they reached the landing.

'I really don't understand but this woman called me and said a girl called Meredith has been found murdered,' Sophie finally blurted out.

Amy stared at her, aghast. Robyn cried out. After a moment of silence, they both started saying that couldn't be right, Meredith must be OK.

'It's fine, we'll just go to the house,' Amy said.

Amy and Robyn quickly fetched their coats and they all started down the stairs again. They were still on the stairs when Sophie's mobile phone rang; it was the police. An officer told her he needed to speak to her and would be sending a car to pick her up; it would be waiting outside the university in five minutes' time. Then he hung up; he didn't tell Sophie why he needed to speak to her.

'Something's definitely not right,' Sophie said. She started crying. Perhaps something had happened to Meredith on her way home after they'd said goodbye the previous evening, she thought.

Outside, Amy charged on ahead, not saying anything, while Robyn walked next to Sophie, holding on to her arm.

'What if it's true?' Sophie asked Robyn.

'No, it can't be. It's somebody else, there's another Meredith. It's not her, it's not her,' Robyn insisted.

'What if it is?' Sophie asked.

The three friends got to the university on Piazza Grimana but there was no police car there. As they waited, they found out from a local man that there were several journalists in the *caffè* opposite the university. The journalists were saying the victim was apparently Welsh, and twenty-three years old – Meredith wasn't Welsh, and she wasn't twenty-three, the friends said to each other. Apparently the house where it happened was just round the corner, the man said, pointing down the road which led to Meredith's cottage.

Amy called her father. He told her everything would turn out fine; she should just go to the cottage, and she'd see that Meredith was fine. Amy started walking across the street towards the cottage but Sophie and Robyn shouted after her: 'Amy! Amy, don't go there.'

'I'm just going to see if she's OK,' Amy said.

'No, don't go,' Sophie said. She and Robyn were afraid of what Amy might find.

When the police car arrived, the three all got into the back together. On the way to the police station, they asked the officer driving them what had happened, but all he knew was that an English girl had been killed. He didn't know her name.

It couldn't be Meredith, the three friends kept saying to each other.

At the police station, they were shown into the waiting room, which was empty at the time. Moments later Meredith's flatmate Laura walked in.

'Does that mean it's her?' Sophie asked – seeing Laura at the police station must mean the victim was Meredith, she thought. Her question went unanswered; Laura walked out without saying anything. Sophie, Amy and Robyn waited, crying quietly. Sophie now had few doubts that it was Meredith who'd been killed. And yet she still hoped it wasn't, because no one had told her it was.

Shortly afterwards, Sophie was led into an office of the Flying Squad, where she sat across a desk from two officers who began by asking her questions in Italian about what she'd done the previous evening. Sophie asked them several times what had happened, but they didn't answer her; they just said, 'It's really bad,' and kept on asking her questions.

The questions were mostly about Meredith. When had Sophie last seen Meredith? What had they done together yesterday? What the friends had eaten together seemed to be very important, for some reason Sophie didn't understand. Sophie said they'd had ice cream. 'What ice cream?' one of the officers asked. Struggling to understand what the point of the question was, Sophie said she couldn't remember. They asked her about drugs, but Sophie said she didn't know anything about that – she didn't want to get the students in the semi-basement flat into trouble by mentioning the marijuana plants there.

She asked again what had happened, but still they didn't reply. They pressed on with their questions. Tell us about Meredith's friends, they said. What about her foreign friends? Did Meredith know any black men? Adding to her confusion, one or the other of the officers kept going away to talk to some colleagues before coming back again. One officer gave her some dark chocolate to eat.

Sophie's phone rang and she asked if she could answer it. The officers nodded, and Sophie took the call from her father, Terry.

'Oh, so you're not the British girl who's been murdered in Perugia then!' Terry exclaimed with relief.

The sound of her father's voice made Sophie burst into tears.

When Sophie was led back to the waiting room after an hour or so of questioning, she found it crowded with Meredith's Italian flat-mates and their boyfriends, her English friends and other people she didn't know. They were sitting or standing around looking devastated, several of them in tears.

Sophie heard someone say that Meredith had been found dead in the cottage, and that Amanda had found her. Just then, Amanda walked into the waiting room. 'God, what she's gone through . . .' Sophie thought to herself and quickly went up to her.

'Oh, Amanda, I'm so sorry!' Sophie exclaimed as she instinctively put her arms around her and gave her a bear hug.

Amanda didn't hug Sophie back. Instead she stiffened, holding her arms down by her sides. Amanda said nothing.

Surprised, Sophie let go of her after a couple of seconds and stepped back. There was no trace of emotion on Amanda's face. Raffaele walked up to Amanda and took hold of her hand; the couple just stood there, ignoring Sophie and gazing at each other.

Sophie was puzzling over Amanda's manner when an officer came in and told the two girls to follow him; they must have their fingerprints taken, he said. In her agitated state, Sophie began to worry; she had hugged Meredith the previous evening – would the police find her fingerprints on her friend and think she had something to do with the murder?

The officer led them and Samantha Rodenhurst, another friend of Meredith's, down a corridor. As Raffaele tagged along, Sophie turned to Amanda. 'Amanda, what's going on? Can you tell me exactly what happened?' Sophie asked.

'I know everything. What do you want to know? Are you OK?' Amanda said.

'I can take it. Just tell me what you know because I don't know anything and I'd like to know. Tell me what you know,' Sophie said. She braced herself.

'Her throat was cut, and then she was put in the cupboard,' Amanda said in a flat, matter-of-fact tone – as if what she was describing happened every day, Sophie thought. Amanda was the first to tell Sophie how Meredith had died.

Amanda explained she hadn't seen the body herself. Raffaele and Filomena had told her Meredith's foot was practically dangling out of the cupboard.

Amanda paused when they reached the lift and the officer told Raffaele he couldn't come up with them. The couple kissed each other on the lips before Amanda got into the lift with the others. Amanda then talked in a loud voice to Sophie; she was very animated, gesticulating a lot.

Amanda told Sophie she'd gone home, found the front door open and then seen blood in the bathroom – 'I thought it was menstrual blood.' Then she had a shower. It was only when she went to the other bathroom, and saw 'shit' in the toilet there, that she thought something was wrong.

'I freaked out a bit; I thought hang on, something's not right,' Amanda said.

Despite her shock at what she was hearing, Sophie felt more and more annoyed with Amanda – with the way she was acting and with the way she was talking about it all. 'How can she be so indifferent about it?' Sophie thought to herself. She stopped asking her questions.

When they reached the forensic police offices, Sophie and Samantha sat down on chairs in the corridor. Amanda stood in front of them, still talking.

'The worst thing about all this is that if I'd been home last night it could have happened to me,' Amanda said.

The comment infuriated Sophie. She was so angry with Amanda she wanted to give her a good slap in the face. But instead Sophie just sat there, head bowed, weeping, not looking at Amanda; she didn't want to see her, or hear her, anymore.

Later, as they waited for the fingerprint testing, Amanda fished two pieces of paper out of her pocket, on which she'd already written her phone number. She handed them to Sophie and Samantha.

'Here's my number, if ever you need anything,' Amanda said.

Amanda was the first to have her fingerprints taken and came back complaining that her hands were dirty. She was calmly rubbing them together in an effort to clean them.

Soon afterwards, while Samantha was comforting Sophie, Amanda suddenly raised her eyes to the ceiling and shouted vehemently: 'Those fucking bastards!'

Sophie and Samantha stared at each other, bewildered. They thought Amanda must mean the murderers, because she then started to talk about what could have happened to Meredith. She repeated: 'Why? Why? Why?'

Sophie and Samantha had assumed there was only one murderer. 'Are you all right?' Samantha asked Amanda.

'I'm angry because I've been here a long time. I'm hungry, I can't go and get my clothes, I'm tired,' Amanda explained. Then, after buying something to eat from the vending machine she complained it gave her 'a hell of a stomach ache'.

The fingerprinting finished, they were led away back to the Flying Squad's waiting room. Sophie left the piece of paper Amanda had given her with her phone number on her chair. She felt she never wanted to talk to her again.

Back in the crowded waiting room, Sophie kept her distance from Amanda. She sat quietly with Amy and Robyn, but couldn't help staring at Amanda and Raffaele; Amanda sat with her feet resting on Raffaele's lap. As they talked to Laura and Filomena sitting opposite them, the two caressed and kissed each other; sometimes they'd even laugh.

How could Amanda act like that? Sophie asked herself. *Doesn't she care?*

Laura noticed that Amanda had a long vertical red scratch in the middle of her throat. Laura was certain that Amanda didn't have that scratch on the day Meredith died – the last day Laura had seen Amanda. Questioned by Napoleoni, Laura said, 'I absolutely rule out that it could have been a love bite or an injury other than a scratch.'

Most of Meredith's friends were in tears or looked devastated, but Amanda and Raffaele made smacking noises with their lips when they kissed or sent kisses to each other. Amy saw Amanda sitting with her knees raised close to Raffaele and making faces at him. She stuck her tongue out, curled it up, and crossed her eyes; the two then burst out laughing and kissed each other. *She's either going mad or she's mad already*, Amy thought.

14

Pisco, the owner of the Merlin Pub, was among Meredith's acquaintances summoned by the police. In the waiting room, he went up to Amanda – he knew her by sight as she'd been to his bar.

'You're Meredith's flatmate, aren't you?' Pisco asked.

'Yes, I am.' Amanda told him about how the body was found, saying: 'I went inside the room with the police.'

Soon afterwards Patrick, the owner of the bar Le Chic where Amanda worked, called her.

'Amanda, is it true that your friend, the English girl, is dead?' Patrick asked.

'It's true. I can't talk now because I'm with the police,' Amanda replied.

'Oh, OK, sorry.'

'How do you know?'

Patrick said friends of his had told him, then hung up.

Late that evening, after four hours of questioning, Natalie Hayward, an English friend of Meredith's, was shown into the waiting room where she heard Amanda say, in an aggressive tone, that if she had been in the cottage that night, she too would be dead now.

'Let's hope she didn't suffer,' Natalie said.

'What do you think? They cut her throat, Natalie. She fucking bled to death!' Amanda retorted.

Amanda's words chilled Natalie; she was surprised both by Amanda talking of several killers, and by the coldness of her tone. Natalie thought it was as if Meredith's death didn't concern her.

That evening, Robyn too was shocked by Amanda's manner. Describing in a loud voice how she had found 'shit' in the toilet, Amanda kept on repeating the word: 'shit'. Robyn thought this was strange as Meredith had told her she had argued with Amanda, criticising her for failing to flush the toilet even when she was menstruating. Amanda kept talking too about how she had found Meredith; she seemed proud of it.

Talking in English, again loudly, to someone on her mobile phone, Amanda repeated over and over again 'I found her', 'I was the first to find her' and 'It could have been me in her place'. She repeated that she had seen Meredith's body in the cupboard, with a blanket over her. All the time, Amanda's tone was exuberant, which for Robyn was inappropriate and disrespectful.

Robyn was also shocked to see the way Amanda translated the word '*minaccia*' – threat – for Raffaele when Meredith's friends talked about an English media report of a threat made before the murder. This was in fact the phone call received by Elisabetta Lana who lived near the cottage, telling her not to use the toilet 'because there's a bomb inside' – police quickly established it was a prank. It was in her garden that Meredith's mobile phones had been found.

Robyn saw Amanda repeat the Italian word '*minaccia*' to Raffaele several times, her face up close to his. She would say the word, then kiss him, then repeat it, kiss him again and then they both laughed.

Throughout the long hours at the police station, Amanda tried several times to talk to Meredith's English friends in Italian, just as she always did. *How could she be thinking about improving her Italian at a time like this?* Sophie asked herself. At one point Amy answered Amanda in Italian just to shut her up.

As she waited, Sophie suddenly realised she hadn't told the police about Hicham Khiri, the Moroccan chef whom she'd met with Meredith a couple of times, and who had dropped his trousers while dancing with Meredith. The police had asked Sophie repeatedly about any foreign friends of Meredith's, so she went to talk to an officer.

This time, she was questioned by a senior detective who asked her many questions about Hicham. Sophie felt awful telling the police about him; she'd even kissed him once on the night of Halloween, and now the detective was asking her whether he could have killed Meredith.

I don't know, perhaps, was all she could say.

Like Amanda, Raffaele complained about being kept at the police station. At one point, he went up to an officer to ask: 'We're tired, can we go home?'

The policeman was taken aback by the question – if a friend or an acquaintance of his had died, he was sure he wouldn't dream of asking to leave – but he simply asked Raffaele to be patient.

Like Amanda, Raffaele seemed bizarrely unemotional to Meredith's friends. Speaking to his sister on his mobile, he told her in a cold tone: 'They've slit the throat of my girlfriend's flat-mate' – he stressed the words 'slit the throat' and he too spoke of several killers. But they noticed that Raffaele kept rubbing his hands and, from time to time, he would go red in the face.

When Filomena's boyfriend Marco emerged from his questioning, Raffaele bombarded him with questions about the murder – to Marco, it felt like a second interrogation.

'What do you think happened?' Raffaele asked first. 'Who do you think did it?' he asked next.

'I'm sure it was someone who knew her,' Marco replied.

Napoleoni and her colleagues asked Meredith's flatmates and friends about the students in the semi-basement flat, and which men had been to the cottage. They wanted to know if anyone had taken a fancy to Meredith or flirted with her in Perugia or if anyone had ever bothered her, and they searched for men pictured with her in the photographs taken on Halloween night, which the friends had given them. The detectives quickly learnt that Meredith went out almost exclusively with her English girl-friends, and had met Giacomo several times in the past few days.

Napoleoni went back and forth between the waiting room and the offices where the questioning took place. She saw that most of Meredith's friends were either tearful or in shock, while Amanda was pulling faces at Raffaele, and putting her feet up on his knees.

'These two are crazy,' Napoleoni thought. She considered telling them off but thought better of it; she didn't want to make things worse for Meredith's English friends who looked in such a bad way.

Napoleoni was irritated to learn that of all the people who had been brought in for questioning, Amanda and Raffaele were the only ones to complain they were tired and hungry. Napoleoni herself, like many of her detectives, got no sleep for several days that followed – she would rush home just to have a shower and change her clothes, then rush back to the police station.

'After what I'd seen at the cottage, I couldn't stop thinking about whether we had everything covered, let alone sleep,' Napoleoni said later. From then on, she often talked of the victim as '*la povera Meredith*' – poor Meredith.

From Amanda's diary:
And so I'm at the police station now, after a long day spent telling how I was the first person to arrive home and find my compagna [companion] dead. The strange thing is that all I want to do now is write a song about this. It would be the first song I've ever written, and it would talk about someone who died in a horrible way and for no motive. How morbid is all this?

I'm dying of hunger. And I would so much like to say that I could kill for a pizza, but it's just that it doesn't seem right.

Laura and Filomena are pretty shocked. Raffaele too. I'm angry. At first I was scared, then sad, then confused, then pissed off, and now ... I don't know. I really can't concentrate with my brain. I didn't see her body and I didn't see her blood, so it's almost as if it didn't happen. But it happened, right in the room next to mine.

The Homicide Squad kept Meredith's friends at the police station late into the night. As they talked about the murder, Meredith's English friends heard Amanda say that Meredith had been alone in the cottage for the first time the previous night, and that the killer 'must have watched the house from outside to make sure Meredith was alone'.

Amanda and Amy talked briefly about the days ahead. 'What do you think you're going to do? Are you going to stay in Perugia?' Amy asked Amanda.

Amanda had no intention of leaving. 'This kind of thing happens everywhere, murders happen everywhere,' she said.

Amanda then turned to her flatmates Filomena and Laura. 'What shall we do about the house? Will we find another house to go and live in?'

Amy thought to herself: 'How can she think about another house at a time like this?'

It was gone midnight when the police told Meredith's English friends they could go. An officer drove Sophie, Amy, Robyn and Natalie to Amy and Robyn's flat. The four decided to stick together that night; they were all badly shaken, and very scared. They had no idea who had killed Meredith and, whoever the killer was, he was still at large. They were afraid he could seek them out too.

Amy and Robyn started packing their suitcases as soon as they got into their flat – they'd decided to fly back to London in the morning. Sophie would have liked to go with them, but her parents had already told her they'd booked a flight to come to Perugia and fetch her later that day.

Natalie insisted they all eat something and she quickly prepared some spaghetti bolognese. As the friends ate, they discussed what Amanda had said about the discovery of Meredith's body; they all agreed her behaviour at the police station had been inappropriate, insensitive and annoying. They couldn't understand how she could act like that.

Shortly after the meal, they were alarmed to hear shouting and banging on the front door to their house. The four were so on edge they rang the police and asked them to come over, but the street soon went quiet again; it was only a couple of drunks.

None of the four could face spending the night on their own, so they carried some quilts into Robyn's room, spread them on the floor and tried to get some sleep. Sophie managed to doze off for an hour or so before the realisation that Meredith had been murdered yanked her awake at about 4 a.m. She lay awake for hours, thinking. She wondered if the murder had been a random one, but didn't know what to think.

Amanda and Raffaele spent the whole night at the police station. They took turns resting; Amanda stretched out on several chairs and Raffaele caressed her throat.

At about 4 or 5 a.m., as dawn was about to break, Fabio D'Astolto, an officer who spoke English, saw Amanda pacing nervously up and down a corridor, beating her head with the palms of her hands. She was so agitated that D'Astolto asked himself: 'God, what if she hits her head against the wall and hurts herself?'

D'Astolto called out to Amanda: 'Would you like some water? Would you like a coffee?'

'No, no, no, I don't need anything,' Amanda replied.

D'Astolto saw later that she went back to sit next to Raffaele and they started hugging, laughing and kissing again. At about 6 a.m., Filomena and her boyfriend Marco drove Amanda and Raffaele to Raffaele's home.

That night, Amanda told a relative on the phone: 'No, they're not letting me go home, I can't take that flight.' Amanda's family had suggested to her that she could fly home to Seattle.

Later, Edda confided: 'The biggest mistake of my life was not putting that kid on a plane.'

15

At about 8 p.m. as the Homicide Squad continued to question Meredith's friends at the police station, Patrizia Stefanoni from the Rome forensic police arrived at the cottage. Stefanoni was an attractive, no-nonsense biologist; thirty-eight years old, she had dealt with dozens of Italy's most serious crimes in recent years and her team had a strong international reputation. She worked from gleaming modern offices on the outskirts of the Eternal City, situated between an ancient Roman aqueduct and the old Cinecittà studios – known as Hollywood-on-the-Tiber during the *dolce vita* (sweet life) heyday of Italian cinema in the 1950s and '60s.

At the cottage, Stefanoni's forensic police team began by photographing and filming the flat, the scene illuminated by lights the police had brought with them. A photographer used a digital Spheron SceneCam to take a full, high-resolution 360-degree image from floor to ceiling and from wall to wall. Without touching the quilt or the body, Stefanoni's team and their Perugian colleagues made a detailed survey of Meredith's room, which measured eleven by nine and a half feet.

Black knickers and a white bra – the latter stained with blood, especially on the right strap and on the top outer part of the left cup – lay on the floor a few inches away from Meredith's right foot. The left shoulder strap of the bra was severed and the cloth and metal clasp at the back had been cut off and was missing. A pair of blue Levi's jeans lay partly under the quilt and was smeared with blood around the right back pocket. In a big pool of dried blood by Meredith's head was a blue hot-water bottle and a pair of brown leather boots.

On the bloodstained undersheet of the single bed lay an ivory-coloured towel heavily soaked with blood, a beige fake leather handbag, a big notebook, and a bloodstained Italian history book. On the white desk to the right of the window lay an empty container of Vaseline, an Apple laptop, a notebook and another Italian history book.

Part of the door handle was broken and smeared with blood. To the right of the door, some beauty and hygiene products had fallen over on their wooden shelf. On the opposite side of the room, there were more than twenty bloodstains on the white door of the plywood cupboard. On the inside of the open left door of the cupboard, towards the bottom, was a bloody smear that seemed to have been left by someone's fingers. There was another similar smear on a wall opposite the door of the room, four feet from the floor, and more bloodstains on the lower part of the desk.

From Meredith's bedroom, Stefanoni would later take thirty objects and biological samples including the bra, the jeans, the quilt, three blood-soaked towels, samples from the blood on the floor, on the walls and on the door handle, bloodstained fragments she cut from the undersheet, and two blonde hairs – not Meredith's – from her left hand and from her vagina.

In the small bathroom next door which Meredith and Amanda had shared, the forensic police found several traces of blood: on the basin, on the tap over the basin, and on a box of cotton buds left on the basin. There was more on the blue mat under the basin, as well as on the bidet, the toilet lid, some floor tiles close to the toilet, the light switch and the door frame.

At the other end of the flat, the switch on the washing machine outside the big bathroom which Filomena and Laura shared was in the 'on' position; it had finished running and warm, damp clothes were still inside. Outside the cottage, nine small bloodstains were found on the staircase and on the concrete parapet that ran down to the semi-basement flat.

Stefanoni had the DNAs of her Rome colleagues on file but she took saliva swabs of the Perugia investigators, including Mignini who was smoking his pipe as he waited for her to finish her work. Stefanoni asked no questions about who might have killed Meredith. At crime scenes, she preferred to concentrate simply on the job at hand.

Unknown to Stefanoni, her team had missed a single small object that was to prove a key piece of evidence – the clasp from Meredith's bra. The Perugian forensic officers had placed a letter-card by the clasp, but Stefanoni's team failed to see it when they took the bra. It was only several days later, back at their offices in Rome, that the team realised the clasp was missing.

Luca Lalli, the forensic pathologist, had never waited so long at a crime scene. On first arriving, he had been allowed into Meredith's bedroom only just long enough to establish that rigor mortis was present in her ankles and toes. Since then he had been obliged to wait outside in the garden while the forensic police teams did their job.

Lalli found it hard to be patient: he couldn't stop worrying about the effect the delay would have on his work. It was never possible to give a precise time of death – only pathologists in Hollywood films could do that – but the more time passed, the more data he would lose and the more vague his estimate would be. From time to time, he asked one of the investigators if he could begin working, but each time he was told to wait until the forensic team had finished.

As he waited, Lalli became first irritated and then exasperated at the failure of the police to drive the journalists, photographers and TV crews away from the garden railing that ran along the street just a few yards from the front door. How could the investigators do their job properly when they were constantly being watched, photographed and filmed from such close quarters? Making things worse, the journalists shouted out questions at Lalli and his assistant Giulia Ceccarelli, who was also his girlfriend: 'Was the girl raped? How did she die? When did she die?'

'How on earth are we supposed to know?' Ceccarelli thought angrily to herself – she and Lalli had only spent a short time inside the cottage.

It was only at about 12.30 a.m. on 3 November, more than eleven hours after Meredith's body was found, that the forensic police finally told the prosecutor Mignini that Lalli could examine the body.

In Meredith's bedroom, as Mignini and Stefanoni watched, Lalli took a couple of steps to the edge of the quilt, bent down and, holding it between finger and thumb, lifted it – he noticed it was thick and heavy – to uncover Meredith's face and breasts. He folded the top of the quilt to one side. Meredith lay on her back, her head turned to the left and slightly bent backwards, her left temple resting against a boot. Her eyes were open and her mouth closed. Her hair was soaked in blood, rivulets of blood streaked her face, and patches of blood covered part of her right cheek, the base of her nose and much of her neck. In the front of the neck was a wound less than an inch long, and on the right side of the neck another wound of the same size.

Lalli gently took hold of Meredith's head and turned it to her right, revealing a gaping wound in the left side of her neck some three inches long. From the wound emerged what experts called a 'foam-like mushroom', a grey and red mix of air and blood which showed Meredith had breathed in her own blood. There were similar 'mushrooms' in the nostrils and in the mouth. The left cheek was covered in blood save for three small, roundish areas where the skin was bare. Lalli thought that the weapon that caused the three wounds might be a knife, or a piece of glass, perhaps from the broken window in Filomena's room.

Mignini leant to one side to examine the wounds on Meredith's neck and started, stunned by the size of the most serious wound; it was so deep – deeper than any he had ever seen. Mignini was well-accustomed to dealing with corpses, but this time he was moved by Meredith's beauty and by what had been done to her.

Lalli lifted the quilt completely off Meredith. Her two cotton tops, one light-coloured with short sleeves and the other a long-sleeved beige one, had both been raised above her breasts; blood had splashed onto her chest and the tops were damp to the touch and smeared with blood. A cushion lay under her bottom. Her right arm was outstretched; the hand half-closed and slightly smeared with blood on the back, rested on the edge of the quilt. Her left arm was bent at the elbow. The left hand – stained with blood, especially on the index finger and around the nails – was half-closed and close to her head. Her legs were wide apart. The right leg was folded at the knee at a 100-degree angle and rested on the edge of the quilt. The left leg, which was stretched out, rested on the floor.

Lying on the floor by the body, and previously hidden by the quilt, were two towels, one green and the other ivory-coloured, both completely soaked with blood. There were bloodstains on the white sheet from the bed and on a light blue, zip-up sweatshirt lying by it.

Meredith's hands were smeared with both blood and hairs. Lalli made a note of the position of the body and, with Mignini's approval, placed two transparent plastic covers over her hands to protect them and preserve any substances that might be under her fingernails. He couldn't get a good look at the hands because this would have meant removing the blood on them. He would only do this when he did the autopsy.

Moving Meredith as little as possible, he felt her arms and legs and noted rigor mortis had spread widely. Down the back of the body were the wine-red marks typical of hypostasis, showing the accumulation of fluid or blood in parts of the body due to the lack of circulation after death. The marks paled when he pressed them with his finger, indicating the death had taken place less than forty-eight hours earlier. At 12.50 a.m., Lalli took the body temperature – 22°C – against a room temperature of 13°C. Finally, he took three vaginal swabs and three rectal swabs, which he handed to Stefanoni, and decided to stop there. He didn't want to lose any vital biological traces he might need to study. He would continue his examination of the body at the morgue later that day.

Meredith's body was removed from the cottage at about 1.30 a.m. As it was lifted from the floor in her bedroom, Lalli noticed the missing bra clasp under the cushion that had been placed under her bottom. He pointed it out to the forensic police officers who were also in the room.

He had been careful as ever to do his job as dispassionately as possible. Lecturing his university students, he always insisted that a pathologist should never allow himself to feel anything at the crime scene or during an autopsy; if he did, he would do a bad job. He made the point that in his profession, all corpses were equal; you should care as much about an ugly old woman who had died in her sleep as you would for a baby who had been murdered.

But as he walked out of the flat after an hour in Meredith's room, Lalli turned to his assistant and said in a low voice: 'Poor girl.'

16

Just before 7 a.m., Sophie and Natalie walked Amy and Robyn down Corso Vannucci to the stop for the airport bus. Later that morning, Sophie went back to the police station. She realised she'd been wrong not to tell detectives about the marijuana plants, and this time told them all she knew. They also questioned her again about Hicham, the Moroccan chef.

Sophie had been counting on leaving Perugia to fly back home as soon as her parents arrived, but the police called to tell her they needed her to stay on; they would let her know when she could leave. She couldn't help wishing she'd left that morning with Amy and Robyn.

After going to bed at 3 a.m. to catch only a few hours' sleep, Mignini spent the morning of 3 November at the offices of the Homicide Squad with Napoleoni and the other detectives. Meredith's English friends and others had given accounts of her last days, and of her relationships with her flatmates and various acquaintances in Perugia. But so far Mignini and the police had precious little else to go on.

Mignini – who loved reading history books and saw his job as a bit like that of a historian, working backwards in time to reconstruct the past – couldn't fathom who would commit such a crime, or why. Could it have been pre-meditated? Was the attack sexually motivated? And if so, was there also a motive for the murder?

He ruled out the possibility that it was a '*crime passionnel*', a fit of jealous rage and a sudden impulse to kill. One detective suggested that because Meredith's throat had been slit, the killer might be a Muslim, maybe a North African immigrant.

Mignini persisted in thinking as he had at the outset that an insider must have betrayed Meredith, let their accomplice into the cottage and then helped to stage the fake burglary. He was inclined to rule out Filomena – she said she had been with her boyfriend that night – and Laura, who said she had been away visiting her family. That left Amanda and the students in the semi-basement flat; Mignini asked the Homicide Squad to keep a close watch on them. He ordered phone taps on mobiles belonging to Amanda, to Raffaele, to the students in the downstairs flat and to other people who had known Meredith.

Detectives checked her flatmates' alibis, as well as those of Raffaele and the students in the downstairs flat. Other officers searched the garden of the cottage, using metal detectors in the hope of finding the murder weapon and Meredith's keys to her room and the front door. All they found were big stones similar to the one in Filomena's room.

They trawled the neighbourhood asking if anyone had seen anything suspicious; and collected videos made by all the CCTV cameras belonging to the municipal police. One from a camera placed inside the car park opposite the cottage showed for just one second someone walking on the cottage side of the street, near the gate, at 8.41 p.m. on 1 November. The figure was just a shadowy blur dressed in light-coloured clothes, impossible to identify even as male or female. More officers went from hospital to hospital to see if anyone had been treated for cuts that could be traced to the murder; all they found was a football fan who had hurt himself while cutting some salami for a snack after a match.

At times of stress, Mignini usually liked to walk his dog – he did much of his thinking about cases then – or go to the shooting range where he found firing the two pistols he owned, an Italian Beretta and a Swiss SIG Sauer, deeply relaxing. But now he couldn't afford to do either; he felt the clock ticking and knew that if he didn't get any results in the first week, it would be much, much harder to solve the case as time dragged on. He knew from bitter experience that things easily got bogged down if there was no break early on; investigators would become more and more anxious, and less and less lucid. He dropped all his other cases in order to concentrate exclusively on Meredith's murder.

The pathologist Lalli gave Mignini his first estimate of the time of death – about 11 p.m. on the night of 1 November, or anytime between 10 p.m. and midnight. He based his conclusions on Meredith having had her dinner at 9 p.m. and on her weighing fifty-five kilograms; he also took into account the fact that the quilt covering the body had slowed its cooling. But her English friends had told the Homicide Squad that she had eaten earlier, so the estimate would have to be revised.

It was vital for Mignini to establish whether Meredith had been sexually attacked or not, so at midday Lalli examined the body with a gynaecologist – the day before he was due to carry out the autopsy – in the morgue on the ground floor of the Monteluce general hospital outside Perugia, a former convent. He found no unequivocal signs of sexual violence, which he pointed out didn't rule out the possibility that Meredith had been forced into a sexual relationship because an attacker could have threatened her and obtained what he wanted without leaving signs of sexual violence on her body.

He did however find purple bruise-like marks in the vagina, and concluded that they indicated sex had taken place and that it had been hurried, before lubrication could take place – possibly against Meredith's will. There was also more, minute purple bruising around the anus and some dilatation, which could be compatible with constipation, he commented.

That morning Kate Mansey, a 26-year old journalist who had flown in from London, abandoned the crowd of Italian and British colleagues massed by the cottage. Too many hacks, she thought – she would never get a good story there. Mansey, from the *Sunday Mirror*, decided to look for a friend of Meredith's – ideally a boyfriend or a flatmate. She set off towards Piazza Grimana, asking anyone who looked like a student whether they knew her.

Carrying her laptop in a rucksack on her back, and a thick bunch of newspapers under an arm, she went up to complete strangers and asked, in rather shaky Italian: '*Sono giornalista d'Inghilterra. Conoscere Meredith Kercher?* (I am journalist from England. Know Meredith Kercher?)' She had studied Italian in her first year at Leeds University – where Meredith had been studying.

Several of those she went up to replied in English. One gave Mansey a number for an American called 'Amanda'. She tried the number but without success. By about 1 p.m., she was almost ready to give up. She had talked to a dozen groups of students and had nothing to show for it, she'd done a lot of walking, the laptop and newspapers felt heavier and heavier, and her hands were freezing.

As she walked up Corso Garibaldi – nothing in particular had led her there – she spotted a young man with glasses and a floppy fringe who looked a bit scruffy; his duffel coat hung off his shoulders. Mansey put her question once more.

She had stumbled across Raffaele. 'Yes. I knew her. I found her body,' he replied in broken English.

Mansey quickly overcame her surprise to say: 'Can I talk to you? Would you like a coffee?'

Raffaele again surprised Mansey by agreeing to talk to her. They walked into a bar and Raffaele asked for an espresso. Mansey invited him to sit down but he stayed standing, shifting his weight from foot to foot, while she sat down. He sat down a few minutes later.

Mansey was only three years older than Raffaele, but he seemed like a lost little boy to her. As they talked, in English, he kept pushing his glasses up his nose and fiddling with his mobile phone. He seemed nervous except for his face, which had a calm expression.

Mansey kept asking him if he was ok. 'Are you OK? Are you OK?' she repeated. She worried about him; he had been through a traumatic event but he wasn't showing any emotion – he was quite blank, as she put it later. Perhaps he was in shock, she thought. The only time Raffaele did show emotion was when she checked small details with him – his age, or the spelling of 'Sollecito' and 'Knox' – which irritated him. He blew his cheeks out in frustration.

In a flat, emotionless voice, Raffaele described what Amanda had told him she'd seen when she first walked into the bathroom. 'Spots of blood . . . The bathroom was speckled with blood,' he said. He repeatedly flicked his fingers as if flicking the blood.

Amanda had then brought him to the cottage. 'We went into the bedroom of Filomena and it had been ransacked, like someone had been looking for something.' He continued: 'It seems her killer came through the window because it was smashed and there was glass all over the place. It was so sinister because other parts of the house were just as normal.'

Mansey asked him about the discovery of the body.

'I couldn't believe what I was seeing,' he said. 'It was hard to tell it was Meredith at first but Amanda started crying and screaming. I dragged her away because I didn't want her to see it, it was so horrible.'

Raffaele said he had followed the police into Meredith's room. 'There was blood everywhere and I couldn't take it all in,' he said. 'My girlfriend was her flatmate and she was crying and screaming, "How could anyone do this?"'

'Tell me about what happened that night,' Mansey said.

'Meredith had been out at the Halloween party,' Raffaele said.

Mansey corrected him, saying this had been the night before the murder. 'So what was she doing on that night?' she asked.

'I was out with Amanda at a party and Meredith was at a Halloween party with her friends,' Raffaele said.

Mansey corrected him once again. Raffaele looked irritated. 'Amanda and I had been out to a party and we went back to my place,' he said.

'Who were you with?' Mansey asked.

'One of my friends,' Raffaele replied.

'You're sure it wasn't Halloween night?'

'No, no, it was that Thursday night,' Raffaele insisted – the night of the murder. Mansey thought he was probably confused.

'What was Meredith like?' Mansey asked.

'Meredith was always smiling and happy. She was normal,' he said. Pressed by Mansey, he added: 'She was a really good person, she studied. She was really calm, she was so normal.'

Mansey noticed that Raffaele kept using the word 'normal'. Raffaele and Amanda's actions had been 'normal', it was 'normal' that the police should want to speak to him. Mansey was also struck by the interest Raffaele showed in her newspapers – he seemed desperate to see them. He asked to look at them and then thanked her over and over again before scanning the articles about the murder.

Mansey pointed to a sketch of a man and a woman standing over a body, which was sprawled out on a bed. 'Is this right? Is this how you found her? And who is the girl with you in the picture?' she asked.

'It is right but it's not if you know. It's a cartoon but yes I was there with Amanda.'

Mansey said he could have the papers, and he thanked her. She asked whether he could call Amanda for her.

But Raffaele said he had to go. He had left the police station only half an hour earlier. 'Amanda is still with them, she's with the police. I know they wanted her to show them something, I don't know what. I'm going to her soon.'

Mansey's photographer took a picture of Raffaele out in the street. He was smiling as he posed for the picture.

'You probably shouldn't be smiling,' Mansey told him. 'Can we do a serious one?'

The two shook hands and Mansey wished him the best for the future. Later, she found out that Raffaele lived just a few yards further up the street.

                              ★   ★   ★

That afternoon, Mignini and Napoleoni returned to the cottage and took Amanda with them, hoping she might be useful, even though they were still puzzling over her story. They asked her to accompany them on a visit to the semi-basement flat, where small traces of blood had been found the previous day. But Amanda was of no help there.

Back at the police station, detectives questioned her for the second day running, but learnt little that was new. She talked a little about her relations with the students in the downstairs flat, and denied ever smoking joints. She described her work at Le Chic, mentioning that a man known as 'Shaky' had flirted insistently with her.

In Seattle, Amanda's mother Edda received a phone call from a cousin. 'The police are talking to Amanda an awful lot. Are you sure they don't think she's a suspect?' the cousin asked.

The idea was ridiculous to Edda. 'Oh no, she's been helping them and that's why they've been talking to her,' Edda replied.

But Edda thought it might be best for Amanda to come home for a bit; for one thing, she was now homeless in Perugia and her clothes were all in the cottage, which the police had sealed off. Edda called Amanda and asked her: 'Don't you want to come home?'

'No, I'm helping the police. I want to be here to answer their questions and I want to finish school,' Amanda replied.

Edda didn't want to tell Amanda to come home; she didn't order her daughters about. But she decided she would fly over herself; at the very least, she could take Amanda some clothes.

Sophie spent the day in her flat, thinking constantly of Meredith as she waited for her parents Terry and Sue to arrive from England. She didn't feel up to going out so her friend Pisco, the owner of the Merlin Pub, met them in a square and brought them to the flat. It was the first time Sophie had been with both her parents since they'd divorced when she was six.

She told them how annoying she'd found Amanda's coldness at the police station.

'She knows. She's involved,' Terry said at once.

'Dad, you can't say things like that! Don't be ridiculous,' Sophie said.

At about 7 p.m., Carlo Scotto di Rinaldi, owner of the Babbol clothes shop off Perugia's main square opposite the cathedral, noticed a young couple walking around his store, caressing, kissing and embracing each other in such a way that customers kept looking at them. The young woman chose a thong and a pullover and, as they neared the till to pay for them, the owner overheard the young man tell her in English: 'Later you'll put them on at home and we'll have hot sex . . .'

A few days later, the shop-owner recognised the couple as Amanda and Raffaele. He called the police, thinking that what he'd seen might be of use, and handed over footage from the shop's CCTV.

17

4 November 2007

On the Sunday following the discovery of Meredith's body, Amanda sent a long, detailed email to her parents, sister, relatives and friends. In all, twenty-five people, chiefly in Seattle, received what she called '*my account of how I found my roommate murdered.*' Amanda began with the morning of Meredith's last day:

> *The last time I saw Meredith, English, beautiful, funny, was when I came home from spending the night at a friend's house. It was the day after Halloween, Thursday. I got home and she was still asleep, but after I had taken a shower and was fumbling around the kitchen she emerged from her room with the blood of her costume (vampire) still dripping down her chin. We talked for a while in the kitchen, how the night went, what our plans were for the day. Nothing out of the ordinary.*

Raffaele arrived to have lunch with Amanda.

> *As we were eating together, Meredith came out of the shower and grabbed some laundry or put some laundry in, one or the other and returned in her room after saying hi to Raffaele. After lunch I began to play guitar with Raffaele and Meredith came out of her room and went to the door. She said bye and left for the day. It was the last time I saw her alive.*

Amanda played the guitar a little while longer. Then:

me and Raffaele went to his house to watch movies and after to eat dinner and generally spend the evening and night indoors. We didn't go out. The next morning I woke up around 10.30 and after grabbing my few things I left Raffaele's apartment and walked the five-minute walk back to my house to once again take a shower and grab a change of clothes. I also needed to grab a mop because after dinner Raffaele had spilled a lot of water on the floor of his kitchen and didn't have a mop to clean it up.

She then repeated the story of finding the front door of her house open – she noticed Meredith's bedroom door was closed *'which to me meant she was sleeping'* – taking a shower and finding bloodstains in the bathroom.

At first I thought the blood might have come from my ears which I had pierced extensively not too long ago, but then immediately I knew it wasn't mine because the stains on the mat were too big for just droplets from my ear, and when I touched the blood in the sink it was caked on already. There was also blood smeared on the faucet [tap]. Again, however, I thought it was strange, because my roommates and I are very clean and we wouldn't leave blood in the bathroom, but I assumed that perhaps Meredith was having menstrual issues and hadn't cleaned up yet. Ew, but nothing to worry about.

She went to dry her hair in the other bathroom.

It was after I was putting back the dryer that I noticed the shit that was left in the toilet, something that definitely no one in our house would do. I started feeling a little uncomfortable and so I grabbed the mop from our cupboard and left the house.

She went to Raffaele's home, used the mop with him to clean up the kitchen and then had breakfast. While they ate, she told him about what she had seen and he said she should call one of her flatmates.

After breakfast, Raffaele walked back to the cottage with her, and they found what they later described as evidence of a break-in. Amanda knocked on Meredith's door.

At first I thought she was asleep so I knocked gently, but when she didn't respond I knocked louder and louder until I was really banging on her door and shouting her name. No response. Panicking, I ran out onto our terrace to see if maybe I could see over the ledge into her room from the window, but I couldn't see in. Bad angle ... Raffaele told me he wanted to see if he could break down Meredith's door. He tried, and cracked the door, but we couldn't open it. It was then that we decided to call the cops.

Her priority for now, she wrote, was to retrieve important papers of hers that were still in the cottage and find somewhere to live – '*it kind of sucks that we have to pay the next month's rent,*' she complained. She expected to continue her studies the next day:

I guess I'll go back to class on Monday, although I'm not sure what I'm going to do about people asking me questions, because I really don't want to talk again about what happened ... I still need to figure out who I need to talk to and what I need to do to continue studying in Perugia, because it's what I want to do.

One of the recipients of the email, the owner of a bar in Seattle where Amanda had worked, promptly sent it to the city's police, who sent it on to Perugia's Homicide Squad.

That morning in the morgue of the Monteluce hospital, Lalli and his assistant Ceccarelli began the autopsy, watched for a while by Mignini and four detectives. Autopsies didn't unsettle Mignini as they did several of his colleagues, and he didn't bother to wear a mask. Lalli first made a detailed observation of Meredith's body and took photographs. He then carefully cleaned the body, washing the blood away so that he could take more precise measurements of the wounds and bruises now that he could see them clearly, and made a revised list.

Lalli counted a total of twenty-three wounds on Meredith's body. Seven were compatible with cuts caused by a knife; the rest were lesions caused by a bruising action. The most serious wound, on the left side of her neck, was just over three inches long, just as deep and a maximum of one-and-a-half inches wide. It was caused by a slightly upward thrust from front to back, going from Meredith's left to her right.

Lalli found two slight cuts and several bruises on the palm of her right hand, and another cut on her left index finger. There were more bruises on her nose, inside her nostrils, on her mouth, on and below her jaw, and bite marks on the tip and sides of her tongue. Her left elbow was also bruised, as were the small of her back, her left thigh and the lower part of her right leg.

The autopsy revealed the complete severing of the superior right thyroid artery and the breaking of the hyoid bone at the base of the tongue and above the larynx. Lalli attributed the fractured hyoid bone to either an attempt to strangle Meredith, or to a blow from the blade of a knife. Lalli also discovered what he called 'lakes of blood' inside the lungs – Meredith had breathed in a great deal of her own blood, an indication that it had taken her several minutes to die. The bruises on her nose, inside her nostrils and inside her lips were compatible with an attacker clamping a hand over her mouth and nose, in an apparent attempt to suffocate her.

As he scrutinised the body, Lalli fielded questions on his mobile phone from Marco Chiacchiera, the deputy head of the Flying Squad, calling him from the cottage. Chiacchiera's questions were blunt, as he knew the autopsy would take a long time and he was anxious for any clues as to what to look for. Lalli's replies were cautious, as was to be expected from a pathologist just starting work.

'Was she killed with one knife or more than one knife?' Chiacchiera asked.

'It's possible a small knife was used to inflict the smaller wounds but I don't know whether the same knife could have been used for the biggest wound.'

'Was she sexually assaulted?'

'There are signs of dilatation, both vaginal and anal.'

'Was she attacked from in front or behind?'

'If you want my opinion, someone held the girl from behind with his hands under her jawbone and she was then stabbed by someone standing in front of her.'

Mignini was convinced that the positions of the injuries on the body showed without doubt there had been more than one attacker. He pointed to the wounds on the front, left and right of Meredith's neck and asked Lalli: 'Look here, surely these were caused by two different knives?'

'Well, my guess is that they were caused by the same knife,' Lalli replied, pointing with his index finger to show how he believed each of the three wounds had been inflicted.

The autopsy lasted eight hours, during which Lalli removed portions of the neck, genital area and stomach, which he preserved in formalin. After the autopsy, he concluded that Meredith had died from cardio-respiratory failure due to asphyxiation caused by an attempt to strangle or suffocate her, and to a subsequent haemorrhage from the biggest wound to the neck, 'caused by a pointed and cutting weapon'. The wound hadn't touched her carotid artery, which meant it had taken Meredith several minutes to die.

In the early afternoon, while Lalli was still at work and as Mignini and the Homicide Squad were becoming increasingly worried that their investigation was making little progress and risked becoming stalled, detectives summoned Meredith's flatmates back to the police station in the early afternoon for another round of questioning.

Napoleoni had been questioning Amanda about her friends and about Meredith's friends for half an hour when a colleague walked in to tell her that Raffaele was downstairs – Raffaele was insistent, he said, that he should be allowed in to talk to his girlfriend. Napoleoni thought it odd that Raffaele should stick to Amanda so much – they'd only known each other nine days. 'Maybe he's obsessed,' she thought. Or perhaps what Amanda told the police mattered to him – but if so, why? Napoleoni decided to let him, but only because she wanted to make the couple wait together in an office she had bugged.

At 4.30 p.m., Amanda and Raffaele were shown into the room; the microphone lay hidden in an open cardboard box on top of a cupboard. The microphone however picked up only part of their conversation – they often dropped their voices and noise from a nearby fairground made it difficult to make out what they said.

Amanda talked to Raffaele about a friend she called 'Shaky' who had been 'sweet' in finding her work, then added that he was terrifying and crazy when he had to end a relationship with a girl. He harassed women and had once kept her in a room against her will.

Speaking to someone on her mobile, Amanda complained: 'I was the only one who was with her so they want to squeeze my brain to make me say things . . . They asked me to remember who came to the house, who met her. They asked me about her sex life and I said: "What? I don't know that." . . . I'm feeling sick. They yelled at me. I slept only two hours last night . . . I saw the body [the word is unclear] . . . under the sheet.'

She added: 'It's only the police who are stressing me out . . . If they ask me to stay until Christmas, I'll ask someone for help . . . I have my studies here . . . On Monday I've got my classes . . . I can't be at their disposal all the time.'

After Raffaele left the police station to go and buy some pizzas, Napoleoni escorted Amanda, Filomena and Laura to the cottage. The investigators wanted the flatmates to check on the knives in the kitchen. They met Mignini at the cottage just as night had fallen. They all put on gloves and shoe covers, then went through the knives; they said there was no knife missing.

As Mignini showed the young women the knives, Amanda suddenly started to sob. She broke down in tears, her body trembling. It was the first time either Mignini or Napoleoni had seen Amanda in tears. Napoleoni thought Amanda must be upset at being in the cottage for the first time since the day Meredith's body was found. Amanda was helped to a sofa but she kept crying, so Napoleoni covered her with some jackets to hide her from the TV cameras waiting on the road by the cottage, and took her outside to sit in a car in the drive.

Filomena was asked whether the clothes still in the washing machine were hers; she glanced inside and said they weren't. Later, she and Laura said that most of the clothes were Meredith's, and the rest Amanda's.

Back at the police station, Amanda and Raffaele were again left on their own in the bugged office.

'What are you thinking?' Raffaele asked Amanda.

'That I don't want to be here,' she replied.

Raffaele told her funny stories of things that had happened to him at school, and the two laughed. They laughed again when Raffaele started translating Italian insults for Amanda, such as 'Vaffanculo' – Fuck off – and 'Li mortacci tua' – literally, to your lousy dead ancestors.

The two became serious for a short while as Amanda described her visit to the cottage and how the police had asked her to check the knives. Then they again started joking and laughing together.

18

Once they had finished the autopsy, the pathologist Lalli and his assistant Ceccarelli painstakingly eliminated as far as possible any trace of their work as Meredith's family, who had flown in earlier that day, were due to come to the morgue to see her. They carefully stitched together the edges of the cuts they had made, including to the neck, and then washed the body. They usually dressed the corpse but they had none of Meredith's clothes, so they simply spread a white sheet over her, leaving her face uncovered and closed her eyes.

The stitches and wounds on the neck were still very visible. Lalli and Ceccarelli tied a white handkerchief around Meredith's neck but it only partly covered them. Then Ceccarelli combed Meredith's hair, and arranged some pink roses sent by the mayor in vases on the floor next to her. She was moved by Meredith's beauty, and her youth; it was odd, but her body seemed to have the same smell as the roses.

When Meredith's parents Arline and John and her sister Stephanie arrived at the morgue to formally identify the body, accompanied by Mignini and Moira MacFarlane, the British consul in Florence, Lalli was impressed by how dry-eyed and dignified Meredith's family was. He was used to seeing what he called 'Neapolitan melodramas': relatives weeping, screaming and sometimes even berating the body of their loved one. Sometimes he had to hold screaming relatives back from the corpse.

John himself was surprised to see that many of the people who greeted him at the morgue were close to tears. He decided not to go and see his daughter. 'It would have put a full stop to my memory of her,' he said later. He recalled the last time he'd seen her, when they'd met for coffee on her last trip to London and she'd showed him some boots she'd bought for the winter: 'I want that to be the one memory of my daughter that I hold in my mind for ever.'

Before taking Arline and Stephanie in, Lalli warned them that Meredith was naked under a sheet, explaining that he didn't have any of her clothes. The relatives were then accompanied into the room where Meredith lay.

'Can I go up to her?' Arline asked Mignini.

Mignini nodded, surprised that she had asked.

Arline reached out as if to lift the sheet but Lalli gently advised her not to. The wounds were to the neck, he explained, and it might be better if she didn't see them. Arline nodded.

'Can I kiss her?' Arline asked Mignini.

'Yes, of course, you can,' the prosecutor said. Arline's request moved him so much he made his excuses and went outside.

Arline bent down over Meredith's face and kissed her daughter on the forehead.

Soon after her return to her home in Northampton, Meredith's friend Robyn Butterworth was questioned again, this time by English police, and her statements were quickly sent on to the Homicide Squad in Perugia.

From Robyn, Napoleoni learnt more about the man called 'Shaky' whom Amanda had described to Raffaele as terrifying and crazy in their bugged conversation at the police station. His real name was Hicham Khiri; a Moroccan, he worked as a chef and he was the one who'd once pulled his trousers down and shown Meredith his pants as they danced in a nightclub.

But that lead led nowhere. Napoleoni established that Hicham had nothing to do with the murder, and began to suspect that Amanda had perhaps been trying to throw suspicion on him.

Detectives kept poring through the photographs taken on Halloween night and quizzed Meredith's friend Sophie, who had stayed on in Perugia, about the men in the photographs and about Giacomo and other friends of Meredith's including Pisco, the owner of the Merlin Pub. The detectives tracked down an American student pictured next to Meredith on Halloween dressed as Harry Potter. He said his costume was so popular that lots of women had their picture taken with him. He'd seen Meredith's picture in the newspapers but he didn't remember ever meeting her, or having his picture taken with her. His name was taken off the list of possible suspects.

Napoleoni also eliminated as suspects Meredith's boyfriend Giacomo and the three other students in the semi-basement flat. Their alibis – that they had been away visiting their families on the Adriatic Coast – all checked out. Detectives also established, with the help of their forensic colleagues, that the bloodstains on the staircase outside the cottage and in the semi-basement flat had been left by a black cat the students owned who had injured an ear.

From Giacomo's friends, Napoleoni learnt that he was with them on the train back to Perugia when Filomena called him on the afternoon the body was found to tell him Meredith was dead. Giacomo had blanched, thinking immediately that she had been killed in a car crash, but Filomena told him she had been murdered. He was too shocked to ask any questions. 'I'm coming,' was all he managed to say.

While questioning Giacomo's flatmate Stefano Bonassi together, Mignini and Napoleoni learnt that recent visitors to the cottage included a young man nicknamed 'The Baron', a 'South African' who had a gym-toned body and was strongly attracted to Amanda. Bonassi couldn't remember his name, but he did remember seeing 'The Baron' with his flatmates at their home one night: he was very drunk, went to the toilet and fell asleep there without flushing it. Over the next few days Napoleoni tried to track down 'The Baron'– she remembered that someone had failed to flush the toilet in Meredith's flat around the time she was killed. It was only much later that Napoleoni found out that 'The Baron' was Rudy.

*   *   *

Anxious to resolve a host of practical matters after their home had been sealed off by police, Filomena and Laura arranged to meet Amanda at the flat where Laura was staying. She arrived with Raffaele. They discussed how they could recover their belongings from the cottage, whether they would have to pay the rent for that month, how to go about finding a new home, and how to deal with requests for interviews from the media – they all agreed to reject them.

But Amanda's flatmates were still puzzled by her account of the morning she had returned to the cottage and they asked her one question after another, with Raffaele helping to translate. How could she have had a shower, after finding the front door open and blood in the bathroom? Amanda gave a lengthy reply, which Raffaele summarised in a couple of sentences; he said that she had done it absentmindedly.

Filomena and Laura were surprised to learn that detectives had asked Amanda about Meredith's sex life.

Raffaele claimed to know the reason: in an ice-cold tone, he said it was because Meredith's body had been found completely covered in Vaseline.

That evening, Raffaele drove Amanda to a flat where two of his friends were watching the Juventus–Inter Milan soccer match on TV. They asked Raffaele about the murder but he replied that he didn't want to talk about it; he had been to the police station and he was stressed out.

Amanda hadn't met Raffaele's friends before and didn't speak to them, spending most of the time on her mobile; when she spoke to Raffaele, it was only in English. The two friends both noticed that the couple didn't look upset by Meredith's death; they kissed and caressed each other continuously.

19

Amanda began the week following Meredith's murder by going to her 9 a.m. Italian class on Monday, as she had before the death. But this was to prove little relief, as at the beginning of the lesson the teacher mentioned the murder; Amanda, sitting at her desk, bent forward and rested her head on her arms. The teacher talked to Amanda after the lesson and she complained that police had sealed off the cottage and she couldn't get to her clothes.

She complained again at lunchtime when, outside the university, she bumped into Patrick, the owner of the Le Chic bar where she worked.

'How are you?' Patrick asked.

'We spent a long, long time with the police. It's really very tiring. I'm tired,' she said.

The university had asked Patrick to help them find an English-speaking student willing to talk about life in Perugia, so he asked Amanda if she would do it.

'Me and my flatmates, we've agreed not to talk to anyone,' Amanda said. She gave Patrick a hug and added: 'Patrick, you're a good man, you've helped me a lot; you can call me anytime. I've got to go to my friend's place, I'm tired.' She then walked away.

Ninety miles away in the heart of Florence, a short walk from the old jewellery shops squatting on top of the Ponte Vecchio over the river Arno, Meredith's parents, Arline and John, and her sister Stephanie, walked into the office of Francesco Maresca, a lawyer who had been recommended to them by the deputy consul Jane Ireland.

Ireland had advised Meredith's family to get a lawyer because, under the Italian system, this would enable them to follow the investigation closely – a lawyer could have access to the files of the case, and could seek briefings from the prosecutor – and to play an active role in a trial if there ever was one, questioning witnesses in court.

Maresca, who'd turned forty-seven the previous day, was the son of a *carabiniere* general and had himself served as a *carabiniere* during his military service and before deciding to become a lawyer. A keen sportsman and motocross enthusiast – he had once dreamt of becoming a professional surfer – Maresca was more used to defending alleged murderers than their victims or their families. His clients had included mafia gangsters – he'd been to meals in Sicilian restaurants at which each Mafioso placed a gun on the table by his plate – and a paedophile; the photographs in that police file were so awful that Maresca, married with a young daughter, had only been able to look at them once.

Maresca sat the Kerchers down on the other side of his desk, facing him and his colleague, Serena Perna. Behind Maresca was a massive bookcase with a red and gold sign propped up on top of it which had once hung in a church and read: *Plenary Indulgence*. To the Kerchers' left, framed by heavy red velvet curtains, the windows looked out on the imposing, fifteenth-century Palazzo Strozzi.

Maresca briefly expressed his sympathy; the Kerchers just nodded. The lawyer was struck by how shattered Arline looked and by her gentle manner; it was almost as if she didn't understand where she was or what was happening. Arline seemed to be struggling to find a reason for Meredith's death. John also looked bewildered and was clearly trying to smile, making a couple of wry jokes as if wanting to lighten the atmosphere. Stephanie, who sat between her parents, was the most collected of the three and she often helped them to understand what Maresca said.

'What happened? What did they do to Mez?' Arline asked Maresca.

The question took Maresca by surprise. He'd read stories in the newspapers about the wounds inflicted on Meredith, the possibility that she had been sexually abused, and the speculation that friends of hers might be involved, but he knew little else. He told Arline what he did know, promising he would find out more from the investigators soon.

Over coffee from the office espresso-maker, they asked Maresca what was going to happen in the coming weeks and months: what was the procedure for the investigation, and what if someone was arrested and there was a trial? Maresca gave them a brief explanation of the Italian system – if someone was accused of the murder, a preliminary hearing lasting maybe several weeks would decide whether he should go on trial. If the judge at the hearing decided there should be a trial, the trial itself might last a year or more.

The Kerchers looked surprised; they were used to the British system in which trials were much swifter. The two Englishwomen became tearful as Arline said something to her daughter and Stephanie said quietly: 'But we want to know the truth about what happened. Why would anyone want to hurt her? Did she suffer? Was she raped? How was she killed?' Arline and Stephanie quickly wiped away their tears. The Kerchers found the system baffling, and kept asking for more explanations.

As the meeting drew to an end, Maresca asked if the Kerchers wanted him to start working for them immediately or whether they wanted to think about it. The family appointed him and Perna there and then. After more cups of coffee, the lawyers promised to send them daily updates on the investigation, and the family then left to catch a flight back to London. Moved by their suffering and by their self-control, Perna kissed the three Kerchers on the cheek as they said goodbye.

Having made little progress in four days – they still had no culprit, no murder weapon and no motive – and struggling that afternoon to relaunch the investigation, Mignini and Napoleoni questioned Meredith's friend Sophie in the prosecutor's office. For the past few days, Sophie had been staying with her parents in a hotel outside Perugia. She knew that journalists were looking for her and rarely left the hotel, spending much of her days either reading about the investigation or watching the news on television.

Mignini went over the ground that the detectives had covered a few days earlier. He asked Sophie about Giacomo, Hicham and Meredith's other male friends. Had she and Meredith met a young South African man? he asked. No, Sophie replied. He asked about the Halloween party, showing Sophie photographs of men who'd been there.

Mignini also asked her about the last evening at Amy and Robyn's flat – what Meredith wore, what she ate, when she left the flat with Sophie, and when did Sophie say goodbye to her? Sophie said she'd looked at the time when she walked into her flat and it was 9 p.m.

That evening, Napoleoni and her colleagues decided to question Raffaele once more because his account – like Amanda's – was still confusing. The detectives also wanted to check why phone records showed that his and Amanda's mobiles had become inactive within minutes of each other on the night of the murder, and had remained inactive all night – Amanda's from 8.35 p.m. to midday the next day, and Raffaele's from 8.42 p.m. to 6.02 a.m. The records also showed that Amanda and Raffaele both usually kept their mobiles switched on until late at night.

A detective called Raffaele on his mobile. 'Raffaele, we need you to come to the police station for some more questions,' the detective said.

'I'm having dinner with Amanda at a friend's place; I'll come when we've finished,' Raffaele said.

When the detective told Napoleoni what Raffaele had said, she exploded: '*Madonna mia*, these two are driving me mad! Shouldn't you drop everything when the police call you? Surely a dinner isn't more important than helping to track down whoever's done those awful things to Meredith? And the police are supposed to wait for Raffaele to have his dessert?'

The Homicide Squad had summoned only Raffaele but like the previous day – when they had summoned only Amanda – both of them turned up at the police station, at about 10.30 p.m.

Remembering that Amanda had complained repeatedly over the past few days that she was tired, Napoleoni told her she didn't need to stay. 'Look, you've had dinner, you can go and sleep. We'll call you if we need you,' she said.

'No, no, I'll stay. I'll wait for him here, it's no problem,' Amanda said. She looked tense.

Napoleoni told her she could sit by the lifts just outside the offices of the Flying Squad – she didn't want Amanda to overhear anything happening inside – and then led Raffaele in.

Amanda sat down and called Filomena.

'*Ciao* gorgeous,' Amanda said.

'*Ciao* gorgeous, how are you?' Filomena asked.

'Fine, I've had a good day without the police, but Raffaele was told to go to the police station so I'm there, waiting for him . . . What did you do today?'

'I went to my office to get some information about the contract [for the cottage] . . . and I've got an appointment with the estate agency at 9.30 tomorrow morning . . . Do you want to come too?'

'Ah, I've got to meet my mother at the station tomorrow.'

'OK, fine . . . We'll meet up afterwards and I'll tell you how it went.'

'Yes, and you can meet my mom.'

'Of course! If you need something, we can meet up, OK?'

'Yes of course, call me, OK?'

'OK gorgeous, say hi to Raffaele for me. Hey Amanda, stay calm, all right?'

Amanda took some books out of her bag and started reading.

At 10.40 p.m., Napoleoni and two detectives from Rome began questioning Raffaele in the office of the head of the Flying Squad.

The detectives sat on one side of the desk, Raffaele on the other; he kept rubbing his hands, and clasping and unclasping them.

Less than a half hour into the questioning, Napoleoni went out to fetch a bottle of water from the vending machine downstairs and was astonished to see Amanda doing the splits followed by a cartwheel. That she could even think of doing such a thing in a police station shocked Napoleoni. 'Amanda's attitude was always over the top,' Napoleoni said later. That night, detectives saw her do the yoga bridge position, lying on the floor on her back with her knees up, hands at her side, and arching her back upwards several times as she took slow, deep breaths. A detective reprimanded her, telling her a police station was no place for yoga.

In his statement to Napoleoni and her colleagues, Raffaele said that on the morning of 1 November, he had woken up at 11 a.m. and had breakfast with Amanda at his flat. She left and he went back to bed until lunchtime, when he went to the cottage. They saw Meredith there; she seemed to be in a hurry and went out at 4 p.m. Some two hours later, he and Amanda walked into the centre of Perugia, but he couldn't remember what they'd done.

At about 9 p.m., Raffaele returned to his flat on his own; Amanda had told him she was going to Le Chic, where she wanted to meet some friends. Raffaele sat at his computer for a while, and smoked a joint. At about 11 p.m., his father called him on the flat's phone; Amanda hadn't returned yet. Raffaele then surfed the Internet for another two hours, stopping only when Amanda arrived at about 1 a.m. He couldn't remember what he had for dinner, how Amanda was dressed, or whether they had sex that night.

They woke the next morning, 2 November, at about 10 a.m.; Amanda told him she wanted to go and have a shower at her house and change her clothes. She left half an hour later carrying an empty plastic bag, telling him she needed it to bring back her dirty laundry. Raffaele went back to sleep. At about 11.30 a.m. Amanda came back, having changed her clothes.

The couple sat down in the kitchen where they chatted and 'maybe' had breakfast. It was only then, according to Raffaele's account, that she told him what she had discovered that morning: 'Amanda told me that when she arrived at her house she found the front door wide open and traces of blood in the small bathroom. She asked me if I thought this was strange. I answered that yes, it was strange, and I told her that she should call her friends. She told me she'd called Filomena, but that Meredith wasn't answering her phone.'

At midday, the couple set out for Amanda's house and reached it ten minutes later. Raffaele saw the mess and the broken glass in Filomena's room. He saw that Meredith's door was locked, and the blood in the bathroom. 'I went into Laura's room and I saw that everything was all right. At that moment Amanda went into the big bathroom, next to the kitchen, and came out looking frightened. She hugged me tightly and told me that earlier, when she had taken her shower, she had seen excrement inside the toilet, but that now it was clean . . . At that point I asked myself what was happening.'

They went outside to try to climb the wall to Meredith's window, but Raffaele said it was too dangerous. Then they went back in to try to break down her door; Raffaele kicked it several times and tried forcing it with his shoulder several times, but without success. He called his sister, an officer in the *carabinieri*, and she told him to call them, which he said he did, before the postal police arrived.

Raffaele's statement contradicted his earlier accounts to police. Previously, he had said that Amanda had returned to his flat with him on the evening of 1 November; now he was saying that Amanda didn't return with him.

Napoleoni asked Raffaele why he was giving her a different version.

'I told you a lot of bullshit in my earlier statement, because she'd convinced me that her version of what happened was right, and I didn't think of the inconsistencies,' Raffaele replied.

It was the first time that Raffaele had distanced himself from Amanda's account.

★   ★   ★

Shortly after Napoleoni saw Amanda doing the splits and the wheel, a man went to sit next to her, saying he just wanted to chat. He didn't say he was from the police, but Amanda later guessed he was. She vented her frustration with him: it was ridiculous that the police called Raffaele and her in at ridiculous hours of the night and kept them at the police station for hours on end, with only food from a vending machine available.

The man asked her who she thought the murderer could be. How could she know, Amanda replied, she didn't know anyone dangerous. Soon several detectives joined them, asking the same questions again: 'Which men have been in your house? Who knew Meredith? Who do you think the murderer is?'

After a barrage of questions, a detective asked Amanda to come into the Flying Squad's offices; he said it would be warmer there. She asked where Raffaele was, and was told he would be done soon. At about 11 p.m., at the request of Chief Detective Inspector Rita Ficarra, a thin, slight officer from Sicily, Amanda looked in her mobile's address book and made a list of the names and mobile phone numbers of men whom Meredith had known, on a piece of paper she ripped from her notebook. She drew maps to show where they lived.

Among the men she mentioned were Patrick, an Algerian called Yuve who sometimes worked at Le Chic, 'Shaky' who worked in a pizzeria, and a short, black 'South African' who played basketball on Piazza Grimana and who had once been to the semi-basement flat when Meredith was there too.

Until then, Amanda had denied ever using drugs but she now admitted to Ficarra that she and Raffaele both smoked hashish. Raffaele himself had earlier confided to Amanda that he had in the past taken cocaine and acid, but said that now he limited himself to joints; Amanda added that he suffered from depression.

Earlier that evening at home, Mignini watched a crime programme on TV about Meredith's murder which focused on a North African man spotted washing his clothes and shoes in a laundry on the day of the murder and who had since disappeared.

The programme irritated the prosecutor; the Homicide Squad had first heard about the man on the evening of the day after the murder, and had quickly ruled him out as a suspect.

Exhausted after catching little sleep for three nights in a row, Mignini went to bed soon after 10.30 p.m., looking forward to a good night's sleep. He fell asleep immediately but only half an hour later the phone rang and he lost all hope of rest: Giacinto Profazio, the head of the Flying Squad, had also been bothered by the TV programme and worried that if the investigation kept going round and round in circles for much longer, it could even stall permanently. He had launched another round of questioning and asked Mignini to come to the police station.

Mignini didn't hesitate. Some of his colleagues kept the police at arm's length, simply giving them directions and then waiting for the results, but Mignini wanted to be as closely involved as possible; he carried out his job as if he was a detective himself.

'I think this one's also going to be a long night,' Mignini told his wife Cristina as he got out of bed.

Mignini's family had long become used to the long hours that kept him away from home. He never discussed the confidential details of an investigation with Cristina or his daughters, and they knew better than to ask. He once asked his daughters about the various bars Meredith went to. One, the Domus, was very close to where they lived. 'We've probably walked past Meredith in the street, the Domus is just around the corner from us,' he mused. But his family followed the case closely on TV and in the newspapers. They had seen dozens of students gather that evening for a candlelight vigil on the white and pink marble steps of the cathedral, and talked occasionally about 'Meredith' – like most Perugians, they called her by her first name, a sign of affection.

At the police station, Mignini found detectives bustling back and forth, despite the late hour. Profazio told the prosecutor that Napoleoni was questioning Raffaele next door and, together with other detectives, they discussed what had emerged from the investigation so far, trying to envisage every possible scenario for the murder.

20

It was now after midnight and Raffaele was still being questioned when Napoleoni suddenly slipped out to speak to the Flying Squad chief Profazio. She felt they were at last on to something.

'Listen, Raffaele isn't giving Amanda an alibi any more. He's admitted he told a pack of lies because of Amanda,' Napoleoni said.

With her boss's approval, Napoleoni instructed her colleague Ficarra: 'Question Amanda again, on the record. Something's not right here.'

At 1.45 a.m. in an office of the Robberies Unit, away from where Raffaele was still talking, Ficarra and two other detectives started questioning Amanda again with the help of an interpreter. During the questioning, detectives repeatedly went to fetch her a snack, water and hot drinks including camomile tea.

Asked why she hadn't gone to work at Le Chic on the evening of Thursday, 1 November, Amanda replied she'd received a message from Patrick at 8.18 p.m. telling her that the bar wouldn't open that evening because there were no customers, and so she didn't need to come to work.

Amanda said she hadn't replied to the message, but a detective showed her that her reply was still on the display of her mobile phone. '*Sure. See you later. Have a good evening!*' the message read. The message from Patrick was no longer in the mobile's memory.

When her message was shown to her, Amanda suffered what the interpreter later described as 'an emotional shock'. She lifted her hands up to her head and put them over her ears, hunched her shoulders forward and started crying.

'It's him! It's him! He did it! I can hear it,' she burst out. Shaking her head, she added: 'He's bad, he's bad.'

A detective asked Amanda: 'Why are you crying?'

'I remember that I was inside the kitchen,' she said.

Still distraught, and repeatedly putting her hands over her ears and shaking her head, Amanda now said she was in Raffaele's flat when she received Patrick's message, and replied at 8.35 p.m. 'I answered the message saying that we'd see each other straight-away, and then I left the house telling my boyfriend that I had to go to work. I have to say that in the afternoon Raffaele and I had smoked a joint and so I felt confused because I don't often use either light or heavy drugs,' Amanda said. 'I met Patrick just afterwards at the basketball court on Piazza Grimana and I went home with him. I don't remember whether Meredith was already there or whether she arrived a short time later. It's hard for me to remember but Patrick had sex with Meredith, he was infatuated with her, but I don't remember if Meredith was threatened first. I remember confusedly that he's the one who killed her.'

Ficarra abruptly ended the interview. With only a couple of sentences, Amanda had turned herself from witness to suspect, placing herself as she had at the scene of the crime.

Ficarra rushed to fetch Napoleoni out of the room where she was still questioning Raffaele. Out of Raffaele's hearing, Ficarra announced: 'Amanda's confessed, she says Patrick killed Meredith.'

Amanda's turnaround electrified Mignini and the detectives. Shattered and tense after so many sleepless nights, they urgently discussed what to do next, but couldn't agree on the best strategy. Chiacchiera, the deputy head of the Flying Squad, wanted to put Patrick, Amanda and Raffaele under tight surveillance, phone taps included, hoping they would say or do something that would incriminate them. Arresting them now wouldn't help the investigation, he insisted.

Napoleoni however argued that Patrick, Amanda and Raffaele should all be arrested. She was convinced Raffaele was lying, and so was Amanda; that was the reason why he and Amanda had never wanted to be separated over the past few days, she reasoned. Backed by several other detectives, Napoleoni argued that Amanda's involvement in the murder was certain – she was at the cottage, so she must have let the killer in, and there was the text message in which she told Patrick, in Italian: '*Sure. See you later. Have a good evening!*' For Napoleoni, '*See you later*' meant the two planned to meet. Several detectives were however less certain as far as Raffaele was concerned, objecting that the evidence against him was weak.

Mignini decided he had no choice but to arrest Patrick as soon as possible since Amanda had accused him of murdering Meredith – a team started work on finding out where he lived and seizing him there. The prosecutor also decided that he would hear Amanda himself. He was anxious to get what she had told the police on the record in his presence, in order to be able to use it against her in future; under Italian law, what Amanda had said as a witness could not be used against her, although it could be used against others.

While Mignini and the detectives talked, other officers brought Amanda buns and more hot camomile tea – they gave her so much it irritated Napoleoni, but she said nothing. Napoleoni asked Amanda whether she wanted a lawyer, but she refused. Then – surprising Napoleoni yet again – Amanda stretched out over a couple of chairs and fell asleep. Raffaele's questioning lasted almost five hours, until 3.30 a.m.

At 5.45 a.m., Mignini summoned Amanda. Speaking through an interpreter, the prosecutor asked if she was willing to make a statement. He opened a copy of the penal code and read out an article to her, which the interpreter translated. The law, Mignini explained, said that he couldn't ask her any questions and would limit himself to taking down her statement. 'You talk, and I listen,' Mignini said. He pointed out that from now on, anything she said could be used against her, and she was entitled to a lawyer. Amanda said she didn't need one. As he talked, Mignini noticed a red mark in the middle of her throat, but thought nothing of it.

Amanda wanted to speak, she explained, because she was deeply upset by Meredith's death and very afraid of Patrick, whom she had met at about 9 p.m. 'Patrick and Meredith went into her room, and I think I stayed in the kitchen. I can't remember how long they stayed there; all I can say is that at a certain moment I heard Meredith's screams. I was frightened and I put my hands over my ears. I don't remember anything after that; I'm all muddled up in my head. I don't remember if Meredith was screaming or if I also heard thuds because I was really upset, but I imagined what could have happened.' She wasn't sure whether Raffaele was with her that evening. 'But I remember that I woke up at my boyfriend's house, in his bed.'

Amanda stopped talking. She was in tears and Mignini, who had been scrutinising her carefully, broke his silence to dictate to the assistant transcribing her words: 'It is noted that Knox repeatedly raises her hands to her head and shakes it.' A detective put his arm around Amanda's shoulders to comfort her and spoke reassuringly to her.

Watching Amanda, Mignini had the impression that Patrick terrified her. He didn't doubt her sincerity; he thought she had unburdened herself in accusing him and had then cried with relief. The prosecutor hoped Amanda might tell them the rest of the story. 'Come on, go on talking. Tell us what happened, you can get this weight off your shoulders,' he said to her.

But Amanda refused to say any more. Mignini saw he could do nothing but wait; she might talk some more if she got some rest and if he and the detectives managed to win her trust. 'You're tired, why don't you get some sleep?' he suggested.

Mignini gave her a copy of her statement; the interpreter translated it for her, and Amanda signed it. When Mignini said goodbye to her, she had an absent, blank look on her face. What Amanda revealed fitted Mignini's theory that someone inside the flat had let an outsider in who first sexually assaulted Meredith and then killed her. Mignini wasn't sure whether Amanda had been directly involved in the murder itself, but he believed she had been in the cottage at the time and had helped Patrick in some way. 'Amanda may be a fresh-faced beauty, but she's also an actress, very calculating and a shameless liar,' Mignini commented.

That morning, Mignini made up his mind. He decided to arrest all three suspects, worried they would otherwise flee or tamper with the evidence.

Mignini was confident that Amanda's account was more than enough to enable him to take her in. The law required serious circumstantial evidence to hold a suspect in preventive custody – proof of guilt was not necessary. He had no proof as yet but the collapse of an alibi was seen as serious evidence of guilt, and this in his eyes applied to both Amanda and Raffaele. The prosecutor was worried that Amanda might flee abroad; her mother Edda was on her way to Perugia and there was nothing to stop her taking her daughter straight back to America on the first flight home. As for Raffaele, his family was wealthy and might well decide to suddenly spirit him away to Australia for all Mignini knew.

He consulted his superior – Perugia's chief prosecutor – who gave him the green light, then started work on drafting the three arrest warrants and drawing up a concise list of the grounds for their arrests. There were the contradictions in Amanda's statements and her accusation against Patrick; Raffaele's surprise retraction of the alibi he had given Amanda in saying he had spent the whole night with her; and the fact that Amanda and Raffaele's mobile phones had become inactive at virtually the same time in the evening. The prosecutor also listed Patrick's text message to Amanda and her reply.

Two pieces of evidence the investigators had found could incriminate Raffaele. One was a shoe print, size 42.5 (size 9 in the UK), discovered under the quilt which covered Meredith's body and which the local forensic police said could have been left by a pair of Nike Air Force 1 shoes similar to the ones owned by

Raffaele. The other was a jackknife with a blade just over three inches long and almost an inch wide, which detectives had found in his pocket that morning, and which Mignini wrote could have caused Meredith's fatal wound.

Amanda, he concluded in the warrant, had '*demonstrated herself particularly unscrupulous in lying repeatedly to investigators and in involving the young [Raffaele] Sollecito in such a serious affair.*' He accused Patrick, Amanda and Raffaele of aggravated murder and aggravated sexual violence, and ordered them to be held in isolation without access to lawyers. The crime of sexual violence carried a sentence of five to ten years; that of aggravated murder, a maximum sentence of life in jail.

At his home in a block of flats on Perugia's outskirts, Patrick was woken up before dawn by his eighteen-month-old son crying. Patrick got out of bed, went to fetch the baby and carried it to the kitchen where he prepared some milk. When the milk was ready, Patrick switched on the TV, put a cartoon on for the baby and started to feed him.

Patrick heard a knock at the door. He thought it must be a neighbour complaining about the noise of the TV, so he lowered the volume. There was another knock. Patrick went up to the door and asked 'Who's there?'

A woman's voice replied: 'Open the door.'

Keeping the security chain on the door, Patrick opened it a fraction and looked out into the hallway. He saw the word 'POLICE' on the dark jackets of several people outside.

'Police, police, open the door,' one of them said.

'There's a baby, wait just a moment,' Patrick said before opening the door.

The officers swept in and handcuffed him in front of his baby son; he estimated later that there were about ten of them. 'What's happening, why?' Patrick asked as the baby started crying again and his pretty Polish girlfriend, Aleksandra Beata, rushed in from the bedroom.

'You know what you did,' an officer replied.

'What did he do?' Aleksandra asked.

'He knows,' was the only reply.

Patrick was taken to the police station, where he kept thinking that perhaps the police had been looking for someone called 'Patrick' and had got the wrong man. He asked the officers: 'But are you sure I'm the person you're looking for?'

21

Before arresting Amanda and Raffaele, the Homicide Squad made a search of their homes. At the cottage, where the forensic police had completed its work only the previous day, Napoleoni seized three diaries belonging to Amanda as well as her Toshiba laptop. She ignored some knives in a suitcase under Amanda's bed – the suitcase also contained kitchen utensils including saucepans for making pasta – because they were new and still in their plastic wrappers. The detectives failed to find Meredith's keys – both to her room and to the front door – and her wallet.

At Raffaele's one-bedroom flat, detectives noticed a strong smell of bleach when they walked in. Armando Finzi, a veteran investigator with thirty years' experience, opened a cutlery drawer in the kitchen. Only one knife attracted his attention: made by the Italian firm Marietti, it was twelve inches long, including the black handle. The stainless steel blade was six-and-a-half inches long.

Finzi pointed it out to Chiacchiera: 'Boss, could this knife be the one we want?'

Chiacchiera glanced at it. From what he knew of the wounds on Meredith's neck, it was worth taking a closer look at – the blade seemed big and sharp enough, and only one side of it was sharp, and smooth edged.

'Take it,' Chiacchiera replied. Finzi put the knife in an evidence bag.

Chiacchiera went up a couple of steps into Raffaele's bedroom and leafed through some comics. He was shocked by their content, 'a mix of pornography and horror' as he described it later. The comics had titles like *Blood: The Last Vampire*, and *MPD-Psycho: In the Labyrinths of the Mind*; he found out later they were Japanese manga. He ordered them to be seized because they seemed so strange to him.

The detectives also took two local newspapers dated 3 November, the day after Meredith's body was found – the *Corriere dell'Umbria* and *La Voce di Perugia Nuova*. 'KILLED IN THE BEDROOM WITH HER THROAT SLIT', ran the front-page headline in the *Corriere*; 'STUDENT KILLED IN BED – BOYFRIEND AND FRIENDS ARE SUSPECTS' said *La Voce*. Amanda and Raffaele's fingerprints were found later on both of them. The newspapers were probably the ones which the journalist Kate Mansey had given Raffaele when she met him by chance in the street.

Back in the offices of the Flying Squad, the detectives handed the evidence bag containing the kitchen knife to Officer Stefano Gubbiotti who – worried that someone might get injured if the point of the knife pierced the bag – took it out and put it in an empty cardboard box that had previously contained a large diary, and sent it to the forensic police in Rome.

Later, Mignini noticed that among Raffaele's manga comics was the story of a heroine who lived in an American military base in Japan and whose task was to kill vampires who hid among students at a nearby school. On Halloween night, the prosecutor remembered, Meredith had dressed up as a vampire. Mignini also came across a picture of a murdered young woman – the position of the body was very similar to that of Meredith's.

Amanda was arrested at midday in the offices of the Flying Squad, her arrest witnessed by Napoleoni and thirty-five other officers who had worked on the Kercher case – it was standard practice in the squad for all officers involved in an investigation to sign as witnesses to an arrest. When Amanda discovered what she was accused of, she burst out: 'You used me, you stressed me out, you yelled at me and now you put me in prison accusing me of having killed my friend? But I could be dead now! And you tell me I'm a murderer?' She asked the detectives to tell her mother what had happened to her.

Detectives seized a diary with a light green cover that she had begun in August and which they found in her bag; the last pages, from early October onwards, had been ripped out. The pathologist Lalli was called and, helped by a woman doctor, made a physical examination of Amanda, taking samples of her DNA, her saliva, hair, pubic hair and urine.

Mignini suspected that on the night of the murder Amanda and Raffaele had taken drugs stronger than the marijuana they had admitted to; maybe cocaine, he thought. But no such traces were found in either Amanda or Raffaele's hair.

When the three arrests had been carried out, the Perugia Police Chief Arturo De Felice held a triumphant news conference. He announced the arrests and declared that the investigation was 'substantially closed' – a choice of words that dismayed many investigators who knew they still had much to discover about the murder. '*Mamma mia!* How could he say such a thing?' one senior investigator asked.

As detectives prepared to take Amanda to prison, she asked Ficarra – the woman detective she had told Patrick killed Meredith – for pen and paper. 'I want to give you a present,' Amanda said. 'All the detectives should read it,' she added.

Ficarra gave her what she had asked for, and Amanda started writing. She took so long that Napoleoni burst out impatiently to Ficarra: 'Let's go; she'll finish writing in prison.'

But Amanda insisted she wanted to finish before they left, and the detectives agreed to wait. When she finished, she handed the papers to Ficarra who told her she would have it translated into Italian and then pass it on to Mignini.

In her handwritten account, Amanda wrote that she spent the afternoon of 1 November watching the whimsical film *Amélie* – a romantic comedy starring Audrey Tautou as a shy Parisian waitress who decides to change the lives of those around her – until she received Patrick's message and replied to it. She couldn't remember what had happened afterwards because of the marijuana she'd smoked. She couldn't remember whether she had sex with Raffaele, but she did remember having a shower with him, having dinner with him at home at about 11 p.m. and seeing blood on Raffaele's hand, which may have come from fish they ate. They had gone to bed late and got up at 10 a.m. the next morning.

As for the 'confession' – as she herself called it – that she made the previous night, she wrote: *'I'm very doubtful of the entity of my statements because they were made under the pressures of stress, shock and extreme exhaustion. Not only was I told I would be arrested and put in jail for thirty years, but I was also hit in the head when I didn't remember a fact correctly.'*

It was under this pressure and after *'many hours of confusion'* that she saw Patrick *'in my mind in flashes of blurred images'*: she saw him near the basketball court, and at the front door of the cottage. She also saw herself *'cowering in the kitchen with my hands over my ears because in my head I could hear Meredith screaming.'*

But, she explained: *'These things seem unreal to me, like a dream, and I am unsure if they are real things that happened or are just dreams my mind has made to try to answer the questions in my head and the questions I am being asked. But the truth is, I'm unsure about the truth.'*

All Amanda knew for sure was that she didn't kill Meredith. She then returned once again to Patrick: *'In these flashbacks that I'm having I see Patrick as the murderer, but the way the truth feels in my mind, there is no way for me to have known because I don't remember FOR SURE if I was at my house that night.'*

Later, when Mignini read through Amanda's writings again and again, he thought that Amanda might have a dissociated personality: why else did she write that she might have been at the cottage on the night of the murder, but that she might also have been at Raffaele's flat? The prosecutor considered appointing a psychiatrist to analyse Amanda, but quickly dismissed the idea; such analyses were rare in Italian courts and besides, he had no reason to think that Amanda was suffering from diminished responsibility at the time of the murder.

The squat, cream-coloured blocks of the Capanne prison, a half-hour drive south-west of Perugia, and its grounds sprawl across an area as big as fifty soccer fields. Opened only two years earlier, Capanne is a 'medium-security' jail with separate wings for 235 men, mostly North Africans and Eastern Europeans convicted of drug offences and robbery, and forty women, many of whom are African prostitutes or Latin Americans who have ferried illegal substances to Italy and are being weaned off drugs themselves.

Amanda was taken to Capanne with only the clothes she had on – a pair of jeans and a blue woollen Disney Store sweater bearing the American flag above the name 'MICKEY'. When Ficarra handed her over to the prison guards, Amanda kissed her goodbye on both cheeks. Like Patrick and Raffaele, who were also taken to Capanne that afternoon, Amanda was searched, then handed over to one of the prison psychologists whose job it was to assess whether there was any risk of her committing suicide or being attacked by other prisoners.

Led through two sets of double-entrance security doors and a series of steel gates, then down endless, spotless corridors of pink granite floors, yellow walls and pastel-green steel doors, Amanda was locked into an isolation cell that was damp and cold. The cell had its own shower room and toilet; spyholes allowed guards to check on her there too. She had a reading lamp but wasn't allowed any books or TV.

The view through her barred window had none of the beauty of the one from the cottage she had loved so much – the grey blocks of the prison, the busy road which runs by it, bare fields and in the distance, dark low hills. The only sounds were those of people walking down the corridor, the jangling of metal keys, steel doors slamming shut and – from outside the prison – traffic on the road and the occasional church bell from a village she couldn't see.

*   *   *

On her arrival in Perugia, Amanda's mother Edda had planned to meet her daughter at the station; they would then go together to a flat in the city centre where they would both be staying. The mayor, who wanted to give Edda a helping hand because Seattle and Perugia were twinned cities, had found the flat for them. But when Edda's plane landed after the long flight from Seattle, she discovered that her daughter had been arrested.

Later that day, Daniela Borghesi from the mayor's office called Luciano Ghirga, one of Perugia's most prominent lawyers who was also a close friend of the mayor, to ask: 'Have you heard about the Meredith Kercher case?'

'Yes, of course,' replied the sixty-three-year-old Ghirga, a heavily built, silver-haired figure with sharp, blue eyes and the typical Perugian temperament – good-natured but often diffident and uncommunicative, and fiercely proud of his city.

'Would you be ready to defend the young American, Amanda Knox?'

Ghirga had only come back to work ten days earlier after a tough hip operation, and felt snowed under, but this was a request no lawyer could refuse. 'Fine, of course I am,' he said.

A printer's son, Ghirga had become a local celebrity at the age of sixteen when Turin's First Division Juventus team bought him to play first as a full back and then as a sweeper. After a few years he moved back to Perugia to play for the local team, before turning his back on football to study law. During his thirty-five-year career, he'd defended public officials and businessmen accused of corruption and worked on twelve murder cases – defending Mafiosi accused of shooting a clan boss near Perugia, and of hanging a prisoner in jail.

All Ghirga knew about the Kercher case was what he'd read in the newspapers. He'd been horrified by how ugly and how big the fatal wound was. The killer or killers had almost severed her throat, he thought, something completely foreign to the Perugia he knew and to its community of youngsters. It had to be a crazed act, a murder committed on impulse by someone who'd lost their head, and didn't know what they were doing.

Meredith's friend Sophie felt nothing when she saw the news of Amanda's arrest on the television. She wasn't surprised. Her father had been the first to say to her that Amanda might be guilty when she'd told him three days earlier about Amanda's behaviour at the police station.

What Sophie learned from news reports about Amanda's role made sense to her – part of Amanda's statements to investigators had been leaked immediately by the media. But she still didn't understand how or why Meredith had died. Patrick's arrest however did shock Sophie; she'd read about his girlfriend and his young son, and to her he didn't seem to fit in.

When the police finally told Sophie she could leave, she flew home with her parents. She had decided to cut short her year in Perugia; she simply couldn't face staying on.

22

Woken in her cell in the Capanne prison at 7.30 a.m., Amanda ate only a little of her breakfast of bread and coffee. She spent much of her first full day in jail stretched out on her bed, thinking for hours at a time, sometimes in tears. She found some relief writing in a large notebook she had requested.

On the first page, in black ink and tall, neat letters, Amanda wrote: '*My PRISON DIARY*'. She put down her home in Seattle – not the cottage, or the prison – as her address and wrote: *I'm writing this because I want to remember.*

'Good morning, I'm Father Saulo. How are you?' the meek-looking, grey-bearded priest Saulo Scarabattoli, the chaplain for the women's section, greeted Amanda. He shook her hand awkwardly through the bars of the cell door.

'OK thanks, how are you?' Amanda replied.

'Would you like to talk to a Catholic priest?'

'Yes.'

Father Saulo thought she would probably have said 'yes' to anyone who offered to talk to her, she looked so desperate.

A guard unlocked the cell door and escorted Amanda across the corridor to a room that was bare apart from a desk and two chairs and she sat down opposite the priest. The guard left the door ajar and stood nearby; the rule was that the door would be closed only when the priest was hearing confession.

To Father Saulo, who was in his mid-sixties and invariably dressed in navy blue, the look in Amanda's eyes was typical of the dozens of new arrivals he had met over the past twelve years he'd worked as prison chaplain – the lost look, as he described it, of someone who had been thrown into a pool of icy water and, struggling to remain afloat, was desperately seeking something to hold on to.

As a priest, Father Saulo saw his role first and foremost as a mission – that of trying to bring hope to the prisoners. He liked to quote St Paul to them: '*And we know that all things work together for the good of those that love God.*' But beyond his faith, he couldn't help feeling sympathy for each and every one of them, whatever the crime they were accused of; he offered them a helping hand and did them favours when he could, like calling a relative for them.

Usually Father Saulo knew nothing about new prisoners when they arrived at the jail; he always skipped the crime stories in the local paper. He never asked a prisoner what she'd done; he asked her instead what she was accused of. He compared his task to that of a doctor; his job was to heal people who'd had an accident, not to find out how the accident happened. But like everyone else in Perugia, he'd heard about the Kercher case; he'd glanced at the newspaper placards, and people chatted about it when he stopped for coffee in a bar.

As he talked to Amanda, Father Saulo was careful not to mention Meredith's murder. Amanda didn't mention it either. He asked Amanda about herself and her family, and she asked if she could go to Mass in prison; he said yes, of course. Father Saulo found it impossible to imagine Amanda murdering Meredith. She looked like a babe in arms to him; her manner and the way she spoke strongly marked her out from the other prisoners, most of whom were from deprived backgrounds.

Early that morning, after first walking his dog, a still-exhausted Mignini walked along the main Corso Vannucci as he did every morning, and took the escalators that lead down through the dungeon-like foundations of the Rocca Paolina, a sixteenth-century fortress built by Pope Paul III, to reach his office in an austere, grey stone building downhill from the centre of Perugia. As usual, before going in to work, the prosecutor had dropped in on his elderly mother who lived close by.

On the walls near his desk, which was cluttered with leaning piles of case files, he'd hung a small crucifix, a copy of the Renaissance *Madonna delle Grazie* from Perugia's cathedral and a photograph of Giovanni Falcone and Paolo Borsellino, two Sicilian anti-mafia prosecutors who were assassinated in 1992. Near his desk was a small stack of CDs – when alone, he liked to work while playing Wagner's thunderous opera *The Valkyrie*. As a boy, he'd stand in front of a mirror, two paintbrushes in his hands, and conduct an imaginary orchestra while Wagner's music resounded through his home.

The prosecutor showed Meredith's father John into his office. John looked crushed, and Mignini couldn't help thinking of his own daughters.

'When did you last see your daughter?' the prosecutor began, questioning John as a witness.

'I think in late September or early October, when Meredith came to us to get her winter clothes,' John replied.

'Did you talk often with your daughter?'

'I spoke to her every evening, or at the most every two days.'

'Did your daughter ever mention to you being worried about something, or that she'd had any unpleasant encounters?'

'No. My daughter has always been untroubled and happy and she never talked to me about having problems with other people.'

'Did she ever talk about the friends who lived with her?'

'Meredith once spoke to me about Amanda in a joking way, as a girl who was very sure of herself and a bit eccentric. Amanda boasted about being a great singer, she said that if she'd had a guitar she'd have shown Meredith her talent.'

'Did she ever talk to you about Amanda's boyfriend, Raffaele Sollecito?'

'All that Meredith said was that Amanda had been there just a week and she already had a boyfriend.'

'Tell me about the last evening you spoke to Meredith.'

'It was on 1 November at 2 p.m. [3 p.m. in Italy] and we were on the phone for about two minutes. She called me at 2 p.m. that day; we didn't talk long so as not to make her spend too much. When we talked, Meredith would tell me what she'd done that day, including the time she spent with her friends. Meredith always called me in the evening, partly because it cost a bit less.'

'That day, did you try to call her again?'

'No, not as far as I can remember. I called her only on Friday . . . when I found out about the death of an English girl in Perugia, but at first the number couldn't be reached, then it rang but there was no answer. I repeat, Meredith was a sunny, cheerful girl, and she never had any problems with anyone and she loved her family very much, especially her mother also because of her illness.'

After he'd heard John, Mignini also questioned his ex-wife Arline and Meredith's sister Stephanie. Stephanie told the prosecutor that Meredith had never talked to her of the men she had met in Perugia, and had never mentioned either Patrick or Raffaele. 'I can only say that my sister had a lot of common sense, she was careful,' Stephanie said.

In his meetings with Meredith's family, Mignini got the impression that what mattered to them above all – more even than finding the murderer or murderers, and more than seeing them punished – was to find out the truth about her murder. They seemed to feel no hatred for whoever had killed her.

Later, as he briefed the Kerchers' lawyer, Maresca, about the investigation, Mignini told him: 'This murder is typically Perugian.'

'Why's that?' Maresca asked.

'It's a feeling I've got about the way the killers fled the cottage. It's as if this murder could only have happened in Perugia because the city is so small – the killers moved quickly from one part of the city to another, they probably got to their homes in just a few minutes. And no one saw them. That couldn't have happened in a big city like Rome,' Mignini said.

Maresca kept in close touch with Mignini so that he could keep the Kerchers informed about the investigation; the lawyer briefed the family – mainly Stephanie and her brother Lyle – every day, by phone or by email. The more time passed, the more the family wanted to know why everything was so slow. They wanted Meredith to be flown home as soon as possible, but Maresca told them they must wait for a judge to decide whether or not another autopsy was needed to establish the cause and time of death. The wait was hard on the Kerchers. They emailed Maresca, the bluntness of the message surprising him: '*When do you think we can have the body?*'

While Meredith's family was talking to the prosecutor, Amanda's mother, Edda, was with the lawyer, Ghirga, at his office behind the cathedral. Edda was so upset she started crying as soon as she sat down opposite him at his large, rustic wooden desk. Through her tears, and with a friend of Ghirga's acting as an interpreter, Edda repeated again and again: 'Amanda is innocent, Amanda is innocent.'

Edda told Ghirga about Amanda's phone calls and her long email, and said she was completely convinced that her daughter was telling her the truth.

'I know my daughter. She would never do a thing like that, not even in a fit of madness. My daughter is innocent; please defend her,' Edda said.

The meeting was brief, because Edda was too distraught to talk about Amanda or her time in Perugia in any detail. Ghirga promised he would do the best he could, and took on his thirteenth murder case.

In her cell, Amanda wrote over two pages her most detailed account so far of the night of Meredith's murder. '*Oh my God!*' she began, '*I'm freaking out a bit now because I just talked to a sister (nun) and I finally remember. It can't be a coincidence. I remember what I was doing with Raffaele at the time of the murder of my friend! We are both innocent! This is why.'*

Amanda and Raffaele had gone to his flat at about 5 p.m. She checked her email on his computer, read Harry Potter aloud to him in German, and watched *Amélie*. She told him her friends thought she was like Amélie *'because I'm a bit of a weirdo, in that I like random little things, like birds singing, and these little things make me happy.'* She received the message from Patrick saying she didn't have to work that evening. She replied: '*Ci vediamo. Buona serata.*' (See you. Have a good evening.) After dinner, she gave Raffaele a back massage while he did the washing up. The pipes under the sink suddenly came loose and water flooded the kitchen floor. Raffaele was upset but she told him not to worry, they would clean it up the next day with a mop she would bring from the cottage.

Raffaele rolled a joint to calm himself down, and Amanda watched him quietly as she lay in his bed. They had a heart-to-heart conversation, with Raffaele talking of the cocaine he had taken in the past and of his mother's death, and Amanda reassuring him. *'After our conversation I know we stayed in bed together for a long time. We had sex and then afterwards we played our game of looking at each other and making faces ... We fell asleep and I didn't wake up until Friday morning.'*

Then, for the first time, Amanda apologised for what she'd told the police: *'I'm sorry I didn't remember before and I'm sorry I said I could have been at the house when it happened. I said these things because I was confused and scared.'* She hadn't lied when she said she thought Patrick was the killer: *'I was very stressed at the time and I really did think he was the murderer. But now I remember I can't know who was the murderer because I didn't return back to the house.'*

Amanda handed the two pages to a guard, who gave them to the prison governor; they were then sent to Mignini.

From Amanda's prison diary:

I was in my cell thinking and thinking and thinking and thinking, hoping I would remember . . . Perhaps a minute [after the sister left] I sat down again to write and try to remember and then it hit me. Everything came back to me like a flood, one detail after another until the moment my head hit my pillow and I was asleep the night Meredith was murdered. I cried I was so happy.

23

Mignini lost all hope of Amanda ever cooperating again with him as soon as he saw her in the Perugia law courts at a hearing held to decide whether or not she should stay in prison. Amanda avoided the prosecutor's gaze and huddled with her lawyers, talking intensely to them. To all appearances, she was already building a close relationship with them. Her family had hired both Ghirga and the Rome lawyer Carlo Dalla Vedova, who had worked with the US Embassy in the capital.

Amanda hadn't met her lawyers before the hearing and they had their first chance to talk to her when the judge, Claudia Matteini – nicknamed 'the Iron Lady' by one local newspaper for the rigorous way she applied the law in Perugia's most serious criminal cases – suspended proceedings for an hour in order to give them time to photocopy and study what documents were available. Ghirga realised immediately that Amanda had no idea what the hearing was about, just as she had no idea what awaited her in the coming weeks or months as far as the Italian judicial system was concerned. To make things worse, Amanda's Italian was fine for ordering a meal in a restaurant, but legal jargon was a complete mystery to her.

When the hearing began again, Amanda simply declared she was innocent and refused to answer questions.

Unlike Amanda, Raffaele agreed to answer questions when he appeared before Judge Matteini shortly after her. He began by turning against his former girlfriend. 'I don't want to see Amanda any more,' Raffaele said when asked about their relationship.

Raffaele described himself as 'a worrier'. He added: 'I smoke cannabis and I smoke every weekend or holiday and every time I feel I need to,' Raffaele said. He couldn't remember how many joints he'd smoked on 1 November, the day on which investigators believed Meredith was murdered, but 'definitely one at Amanda's house and at my place every time I felt like it.'

He then changed the version of events he had given to Napoleoni at the police station three days earlier. He had told Napoleoni that he returned to his flat alone at about 9 p.m. after walking around town with Amanda on 1 November. But today, he said that he and Amanda went back to his flat together. Previously, he had also told Napoleoni that his father called him at about 11 p.m. on the flat's phone; now he said he couldn't remember whether the call was on that phone or on his mobile. Phone records showed his father had called him at 8.42 p.m. and then sent him a text message which read simply 'Goodnight' at 11.14 p.m.; Raffaele got the message only at 6.02 a.m. the next day.

Raffaele said he had lied when questioned by Napoleoni. 'I was under pressure and I was very upset; I was shocked and I was scared. I spent the night of 1 November with Amanda . . . I remember that Amanda must have come back home with me, I don't remember if she went out that evening.' He had worked at his computer until midnight, smoking joints.

He denied the shoe print the forensic police had found in Meredith's bedroom was his, because he wasn't wearing shoes like that on the day she died. 'I completely rule out having gone into the room where [Meredith] was found,' he insisted.

Asked about the knife the Flying Squad had found on him, Raffaele replied that he always had a knife on him; he liked to make cuts on trees. 'I've got a collection of knives [back home] in Giovinazzo; I've also got unsharpened swords. Knives are a passion of mine. I've always had a knife in my pocket since I was thirteen,' he said. He changed the knives he had on him according to the clothes he wore.

After Raffaele, it was Patrick's turn to go before Judge Matteini. He insisted that he had an alibi: he had been working at Le Chic the whole evening of 1 November. He arrived at the bar between 5.30 and 6 p.m. and because it looked like a quiet evening, he texted Amanda at about 8.30 p.m. telling her not to come. He served drinks to some sixteen customers that evening, including a Swiss professor – he couldn't remember the professor's name, but he did remember he was staying at the Hotel dei Priori in the centre of Perugia.

Patrick didn't see Amanda that evening. He closed the bar after midnight and went straight home. Asked why the first receipt from his till was timed 10.29 p.m., Patrick sat in silence for a few minutes. He then said that when there were few customers in the bar, he asked them to pay only when they were leaving.

He had never quarrelled with Amanda, they had a good relationship. He had never told her that he was attracted to Meredith; he wasn't, and had never flirted with her. 'I didn't go to Amanda's house. I didn't kill Meredith. I'm innocent and God knows it,' Patrick said.

Patrick, like Amanda and Raffaele, was escorted back to prison after the hearings. Patrick thought of his father, who had been politically active in Zaire and who had been seized when he was nine years old. His family had never had any news of him. Patrick feared he would never hug his baby son again.

9 November 2007

In her ruling, Judge Matteini picked through what she saw as contradictions in the accounts of the three accused, and attempted to reconstruct what they did on 1 November, and Meredith's last moments.

Amanda and Raffaele, the judge wrote, spent the entire afternoon smoking hashish together. At about 8.30 p.m., while she
was at Raffaele's flat, Amanda received Patrick's text message.
Amanda and Patrick had given contradictory accounts of the
message. According to Amanda, Patrick told her the bar would
stay closed that evening so she didn't need to go to work. According
to Patrick, he told Amanda he didn't need her help because there
were few customers.

Rather than simply telling Amanda not to come to work, the
message confirmed an appointment they had for that evening –
the two had 'evidently' agreed earlier that Amanda would help
him meet her friend Meredith. After Amanda's reply – *See you
later* – she and Raffaele left his flat together; Raffaele was bored
with evenings that were all the same and he wanted to feel 'big
thrills' as he'd written in a blog and as he'd confirmed to the judge
herself.

At about 9–9.30 p.m., the two met Patrick in Piazza Grimana
and walked to the cottage. More or less at this time, both Amanda
and Raffaele switched off their mobile phones; they turned them
on again only the following morning. Meredith returned to the
cottage shortly afterwards, or was already there when the three
arrived. Meredith went to her room with Patrick after which, the
judge wrote, 'something went wrong – in the sense that [Raffaele]
probably intervened too and the pair started to demand something which the girl refused to do.' Meredith was threatened with
a knife, which Raffaele always carried with him. She was then
stabbed in the neck.

The bruises and grazes on Meredith's lips, as well as on her
gums and on her left check and chin, were compatible with her
being held forcibly with her face downwards and pressed hard
against the floor. The bruises to her anus, and the fact that it
was amply dilated, could be due to constipation but also to anal
intercourse. The bruises on Meredith's neck, compatible with
the pressure of an attacker's fingers, indicated that she was held
by the neck. The bruises inside her vagina that were due to lack

of lubrication indicated that Meredith was also held down on her back for sex, which was either hurried or against her will. The judge concluded that Meredith was the victim of sexual violence.

Taking into account the fact that Meredith had had dinner early in the evening, the judge estimated she died between 8.30 p.m. and 10.30 p.m. Afterwards Amanda, Raffaele and Patrick created chaos in the flat, staging a fake robbery and dirtying the floor and the sink in the bathroom with blood as they tried to clean themselves. Then they fled, taking Meredith's mobile phones before getting rid of them.

As for the reason why Meredith died, the judge wrote that at first the three attackers – especially Amanda and Raffaele – wanted 'to experience some new sensation'. Patrick wanted sex with a girl he fancied. Meredith refused, the attackers tried to bend her will by using Raffaele's knife and the sexual violence turned into murder. Meredith died because an attacker or attackers wanted to have sex with her, which she refused. The motive was, in the judge's words, 'completely futile'.

When the postal police arrived at the cottage the following day, Amanda and Raffaele lied in telling them that they had already called the *carabinieri* because they had been surprised at the house and wanted to justify their presence there. The judge pointed to phone records which timed Raffaele's two calls to the *carabinieri* – the first at 12.51 p.m., the second 12.54 p.m. – *after* the postal police arrived.

In his statement to police, Patrick had failed to explain why he said he'd opened Le Chic between 5 and 6 p.m. on the evening Meredith died, while the first receipts were timed from 10.29 p.m. onwards. Nor had he identified precisely any customers who could say that he was at the bar during that time: he had named simply as 'Usi' a person whom he said had entered the bar at 8 p.m., but he didn't have a phone number for him even though he called him a friend. Patrick had probably intended not to open the bar because he thought he could spend the night with Meredith, but after the murder he decided to open it to create an alibi for himself.

Judge Matteini ordered Amanda, Raffaele and Patrick to be jailed for a year as they awaited trial. During this time Mignini would finish his investigation and then it would be up to him to decide whether to request that the accused stand trial, or whether to shelve the case and request they go free.

Amanda was handed a copy of the ruling in her cell shortly before midday. She wrote in a letter to her lawyers soon afterwards: '*It says I must remain here in prison for one year. I'm assuming this means only if they can't prove I did it or not. So I'm not so sad, I just have to wait until they prove I'm not guilty, and that I wasn't there.*'

24

When Raffaele's lawyers, Luca Maori and Marco Brusco, visited him for the first time in prison on the morning of 9 November, they were struck by how young and frightened Raffaele seemed. Brusco, a cheerful figure with a goatee beard, had followed the case in the papers and on television and he thought Raffaele was probably guilty in some way. The shoe print looked like quite strong evidence. He believed the case against Amanda was even stronger.

Despite the look of fear on his new client's face, Brusco decided to be frank with him: 'Listen Raffaele, as I see it there are three possibilities. One, you killed Meredith. Two, you didn't do anything. And three, perhaps you arrived on the scene at a later stage to help Amanda and others clean up. Whichever one it is, you should tell us. And if it's number three, you'd better tell us immediately because we're going to have to move fast.'

Raffaele listened in silence, his gaze fixed steadily on his lawyer. He replied without hesitation: 'No, I wasn't there that evening. And I didn't get involved afterwards.'

'And Amanda? Look, let's be frank; she's in it, isn't she?' Brusco asked.

'I'm interested only in my position but I don't think Amanda has anything to do with it either,' Raffaele said calmly.

Soon afterwards, in a written interview with the author, Raffaele stuck to his version of events which backed up Amanda's. '*I spent that whole evening at my home, having fun at the computer until I went to bed, at about 3 a.m. Amanda slept with me and it was only the next morning that we discovered what had happened at her house. I went to Meredith's home with Amanda and after seeing the chaos there I became alarmed and I called the police,'* he wrote.

From the moment Meredith's body was found, Raffaele had lived through '*hell*' with exhausting interrogations and now prison. '*All I can say is that I am a simple and honest student, who cannot celebrate his graduation with his own family and who finds himself in prison on he doesn't know what charge.*'

To his lawyers, who questioned him about the sex he had with Amanda, Raffaele replied: 'We made love in the traditional way.'

10 November 2007

Shortly before 8 a.m., dressed in a heavy brown coat with a hood that she pulled over her head to hide her face from photographers, Edda queued with relatives and friends of other prisoners outside the Capanne prison. After a long wait, she was shown into a small visiting room with a window too high to see out of. The room felt even smaller than it really was because almost all the available space was taken up by an L-shaped table, chairs and a filing cabinet. There was barely space to open the door. A guard told Edda to sit on one side of the table; Amanda would sit opposite her. As she waited, Edda looked up to the ceiling and saw what she thought must be a microphone in the overhead light; wires ran out of the light and across the ceiling. It made her feel even more apprehensive.

Amanda was led into the room; mother and daughter cried as they hugged each other. Hardly stopping for breath and gripping Edda's hands tightly on the table, Amanda started to explain what had happened: Raffaele had changed his version, contradicting hers, and the police were accusing her of lying, but she was so stressed out she couldn't remember anything of what happened. She'd been at Raffaele's house that evening to watch a film and then she'd sent a message to Patrick. She'd been hit twice by a policewoman – a claim later denied by police.

As they talked, Edda saw prison guards outside the room keep looking at them through a glass panel in the door. She told her daughter as calmly as she could that she had spoken to her lawyers, and they wanted her to ask Amanda why she had changed her version of events.

Because the police threatened her, they told her that if she didn't tell the truth she would go to jail for thirty years, Amanda replied. She told the police she wanted to help but she didn't know what happened exactly. 'I'm not a liar,' Amanda said. 'I'm sorry about Patrick. Perhaps it's my fault he became involved, but it was the first name I thought of when I was pressed by the police.'

Edda asked her about her days in jail. Amanda told her about the food and about the priest Father Saulo, but she then started crying again, saying how sad she felt at seeing her mother in a place like this.

Amanda again mentioned Patrick. 'I didn't intend to lie when I mentioned Patrick. I simply imagined that . . . I was so scared because they told me I would go to jail immediately, telling me: "Give us a name, give us a name!" And I told them: "I don't know it." And they told me: "No, you know it! No, you know it! No, you know it!" '

But despite everything she was calm now, she insisted, because she wasn't guilty of anything. Today, she'd tried to remember when she last saw Meredith. She really liked Meredith; Meredith was a friend. How could they think she'd killed her? 'Why would I have done it? There's no reason why I should have done it! Why?' she said.

When this was all over, Amanda said, she would ask the police to apologise to her. She planned to write a book about it all and all the 'bullshit' that had come out, even if she knew she couldn't give some details because she didn't know them. Amanda told Edda more about her life in prison. She was being held in isolation, and wasn't allowed to watch TV. So she spent all her time in bed, crying and trying to remember.

Amanda cringed visibly when a guard opened the door and announced that the hour-long visit was over. Mother and daughter said goodbye and as Edda left the prison, she again pulled the hood over her face and kept her head down with her eyes on the ground.

She ignored the waiting journalists and got into a car which drew up just outside the prison gates. From then on, Amanda's family were allowed two hour-long visits a week and began alternating with each other to make sure someone was always there for her. Later, Edda said of her visits to Amanda in prison: 'Walking away is just the hardest thing. Leaving her there is unbearable.'

11 November 2007

For the first time in her career, Napoleoni found herself leading a major investigation when her boss Chiacchiera, who had argued against arresting Patrick, Amanda and Raffaele, dropped out of it – officially because he was too busy with other cases. Working now under Mignini's authority and in daily contact with him – the prosecutor appreciated and trusted her – Napoleoni took the Kercher case to heart more than any other she'd come across. One of her two daughters was almost the same age as Meredith had been and Napoleoni talked to them both about the case. Once the teenage daughter was watching a TV report about the accused when she exclaimed: 'Look at them, they say they're innocent!' Napoleoni retorted: 'What they say isn't important,' before explaining the evidence against them.

After Amanda accused Patrick of killing Meredith, Napoleoni tried to find out what precisely he had done on the evening of 1 November. Among the first witnesses she came across in her search were two Belgian students who said they'd seen Patrick working at Le Chic from about 10 p.m. to about midnight. But Patrick still had no alibi for the early part of the evening.

Then, an Italian–Swiss schoolteacher, Raffaele Mero, called the Perugia police from Zurich to say that he wanted to talk about Patrick. He agreed to come to Perugia and was questioned by Mignini and Napoleoni at the police station. Both the prosecutor and the detective were impressed by Mero's memory; he could remember where he had eaten, what he had eaten and how much he had paid for it, for each of his meals during a stay in Perugia which had ended on 2 November.

The day before leaving, he went to Le Chic at about 8.30 p.m. and stayed there until 9.55 p.m. When he arrived, Patrick was the only person in the bar – Mero had been there several times over the past few days and knew him. 'Patrick was behind the counter and doing absolutely nothing. I asked myself why the bar was empty. The more I stayed the more I was struck by the fact that it was empty. I didn't ask him about it because I didn't want to offend him,' Mero said. The two talked about Patrick's decision to rent the bar out, and about politics in Congo, his homeland.

Mignini and Napoleoni faced a major setback: Patrick's alibi seemed to be genuine. If so, he would of course have to be released despite the embarrassment it would inevitably mean for all the investigators. But if Amanda had lied, why had she done so?

That day, Meredith's mother Arline turned sixty-two. There was no family celebration. The chocolate presents Meredith had bought for them stayed in the suitcase she had placed under her bed, in the bedroom where the dried blood turned darker and darker as the days went by.

Meredith's body was flown home the next day. 'We're pleased that Meredith will be back in the UK with her family,' her father John told journalists. He said he hoped to hold the funeral in two weeks' time. In fact, the family had to wait an agonising six weeks while the investigation was carried out.

25

Amanda's prison cell was so cold that she spent much of her days in bed, under a blanket. After lunch, she would sleep for a while, then try to read Italian literature and other books. Sometimes she was allowed out into a small yard, for an hour or so, and walked around stretching and doing other exercises. Guards always kept her away from other prisoners.

At her first meeting with Ghirga and Dalla Vedova in a room reserved for prisoners and their lawyers, Amanda instructed them: 'Look, try to do your best. Make sure that I get out of here one day. Make sure that it happens . . . Remember I'm innocent!'

Amanda told her lawyers her life was in their hands. She was only twenty years old and they were the ones who could decide her fate. Ghirga replied that her case was very important to him, precisely because she was twenty and because she was innocent.

'Let's see how we can help you,' Ghirga said briskly. Amanda and her lawyers agreed that the first step would be to lodge a new appeal for her release with a special panel of three judges, which they did a few days later.

Amanda told her two lawyers that she'd been hit by the police during her questioning on the night she accused Patrick, but Ghirga didn't see anything worth making a fuss about. 'Amanda wasn't ill-treated,' Ghirga said later. 'A policewoman just said to her, "Come on, tell the truth. It's in your interest; otherwise you'll get thirty years." It was just a cuff on the head, which in

Italy is something a father would give his son. It's all completely understandable.'

Ghirga was taught early in his career never to ask a client if he or she was guilty, and he'd always stuck to that rule throughout the three decades that followed. He believed almost all the clients he had defended were innocent; only in two or three cases had he realised the person he was defending was guilty and had suggested at least a partial confession to avoid a heavy sentence. But what a lawyer thought about his client didn't matter much; Ghirga believed his job was to guarantee the accused's presumption of innocence, full stop. Ghirga never did ask Amanda outright whether she was guilty or not, and he always insisted both publicly and privately there was nothing in the investigation to prove that she had killed Meredith.

Ghirga grew fond of Amanda. He thought she was a wonderful young woman, who had become drunk on the freedom she had found in Perugia. She had made mistakes, but then so had thousands of other kids who smoked joints, or who met someone in a nightclub and had sex with them that very night. Ghirga knew what kids got up to – one of his children was a year younger than Amanda, and the other a year older – and he admitted that he felt like a father to her. 'Amanda is pretty, she's intelligent, I'd love to have her as my own daughter,' the lawyer confided to a friend.

It irritated him the way witnesses like Amanda's flatmates and Meredith's English friends judged her. The way they talked, it was fine for Meredith to 'make love' with Giacomo who lived in the semi-basement flat, but Amanda was little more than a prostitute for 'having sex' with a man whom she'd met in a nightclub.

13 November 2007

In a visiting room of the Capanne prison, Edda and her ex-husband Curt, who had flown from Seattle to join her, exchanged only a few words in low voices, deliberately avoiding any serious conversation that might be picked up by microphones, as they waited for their daughter. Curt asked Edda how to pronounce 'Perugia'; Edda wondered whether Amanda was doing yoga in prison.

Amanda was shown in, wearing socks but no shoes. They kissed and hugged each other, and Amanda explained that her shoes had been taken away for the investigation. Edda said she had brought her a pair of slippers, some knickers and comics. Amanda described her days in jail – she had been told to clean the bathroom and to do her own washing in the basin. She had been allowed outside for a bit after lunch that Sunday but wasn't allowed to talk to anyone.

Curt interrupted her to pass on a warning from her lawyers; there were probably hidden microphones in this room, and perhaps also spies inside the prison. She shouldn't talk to anyone anyway.

Edda tried to reassure her daughter. The legal section of the US Consulate had said it would take at least two to three weeks to get Amanda out of jail. Amanda said she'd been told that too; the idea that she would have to stay in prison had stunned her. But on the other hand, she comforted herself, if the Italian authorities weren't rushing things, they must be looking for objective evidence and that could only be good for her. Otherwise, she risked staying in jail for the rest of her life.

The time she had spent at the police station had been the worst of her life, Amanda said. She had told a man from the US Consulate that the police had beaten her, and he had been amazed to hear this.

Edda cautioned Amanda: accusing the police of intimidating her would be counterproductive right now, especially given that there were no visible signs of violence. It would be hard to prove.

The police had treated her in different ways, Amanda said: one woman had beaten her, then the police had been nice to her when they took her to prison, and then they'd accused her. She felt very confused; when Edda had told her she was flying over, she had been looking forward to introducing her to Raffaele. And instead . . .

Amanda told her parents about Raffaele; he was very sweet with her, hugging her all the time. She didn't understand why he hadn't told the truth like her. It wasn't fair; there was nothing to be scared of. He must tell the truth, because then she could get out.

As Amanda talked, Curt suddenly interrupted her, pointing to what looked like a tattoo on her skin. 'What's that?' he asked.

'It's a fake tattoo Meredith gave me,' Amanda replied.

Edda mentioned the lawyers again; they wanted to be sure that Amanda wouldn't cover for Raffaele.

'No, I mean that I fell asleep in his arms and I woke up the next morning. Of course I don't remember when I fell asleep, sorry, but I didn't look at my watch!' Amanda said. 'The police are wasting their time, my time and my life.'

She was sorry for what she had done to Patrick. 'I feel so bad about Patrick, so bad! I screwed his life up!' she exclaimed fervently.

Edda interrupted: yes that was true, but the police had screwed up her life and Raffaele's.

'Yes, but even so I want to get down on my knees and tell him I'm so sorry!' Amanda said, again in passionate tone. He's a good man, she said, but she had been scared by the police questioning and she'd thought then that he could have killed someone.

She said it once more, strongly emphasising each word: 'I was so scared!'

Trawling through the students whom Raffaele knew, Napoleoni found a witness who flatly contradicted him. Raffaele had told detectives that he'd returned to his flat at 9 p.m. on the evening of 1 November, after walking around town (to Napoleoni he said he went home alone; then to Judge Matteini he said he went home with Amanda).

But Jovana Popovic, a Serbian medical student and a friend of Raffaele's, said that at about 5.50 p.m. that day – she remembered the time because she had a violin lesson at 6 p.m. – she went to see Raffaele to ask him if he could do her a favour. Jovana's mother, who lived in Milan, wanted to send her a suitcase on a bus that would arrive at the station at midnight. Jovana needed Raffaele to help her fetch it in his car.

Jovana pressed the buzzer and Amanda opened the door. Amanda, who had been writing at the computer, told her that Raffaele was in the bathroom. The two talked briefly in the small flat until Raffaele joined them; when Jovana asked him the favour, he glanced at Amanda and then said in a cold tone that he would accompany her to the station. Jovana was surprised by his manner; he was usually very friendly towards her. She thought that perhaps he had been embarrassed by Amanda's presence, or because Jovana had come to his home.

At about 7 p.m., Jovana's mother called to say she had tried to give the suitcase to the bus driver, but he had refused to take it. After her violin lesson, Jovana went back to Raffaele's flat to tell him she no longer needed his help. Jovana arrived at the flat at about 8.40 p.m. and a very happy-looking Amanda – she smiled at everything Jovana said, and laughed – told her Raffaele was in and invited her in. Jovana stayed outside, asking Amanda to tell Raffaele that she no longer needed his help. Jovana thanked Amanda and left.

From another young witness, Luis Temgoua, Napoleoni learnt that among the men who played basketball regularly at Piazza Grimana was a young coloured man called Rudy. Napoleoni had nothing else on him.

26

Mignini found out about what he immediately saw as a major breakthrough while sitting enjoying a brief after-lunch siesta in an armchair in his mother's house – the house where he was born. A detective called on his mobile; the biologist Stefanoni from the forensic police in Rome had found traces of Amanda's DNA on the handle of the kitchen knife seized from Raffaele's flat, and traces of Meredith's DNA on the blade.

The blade was spotless when Stefanoni first looked at it; it had apparently been cleaned and there didn't seem to be anything of interest on it. But when she looked closely, she noticed there were some scratches and thought that if there was a minute biological trace on the blade, there was a good chance it could have lodged itself in the tiny groove of a scratch. It was in just such a groove that Stefanoni found Meredith's DNA.

Amanda's DNA was on the part of the handle where the hand butted against a small prominence which prevented it from slipping onto the blade; it was the most likely point where the knife would be held in a stabbing action.

Tests showed the two traces were not human blood, but the negative result could be due to the tiny size of the samples. Stefanoni thought the trace on the handle was probably from Amanda's skin as this was the point where a person would hold the knife; she didn't make a guess as to what Meredith's trace could be.

As he took in the news, Mignini thought of the quilt that had covered Meredith's body; from the very time he'd looked into her bedroom his hunch had been that only a woman could have been so shaken by the sight of the victim as to seek to hide the body.

The DNA finding quickly became public, and a senior prison officer showed Amanda a newspaper article about it. 'How do you feel about this?' the guard asked.

'I don't understand,' Amanda replied.

Soon afterwards, Father Saulo marvelled at Amanda's calm manner. The chaplain visited the women's wing five days a week, celebrating Mass there on Saturday afternoons. He would greet Amanda briefly at the cell door, and once a week they usually spent up to half an hour talking in the room opposite her cell.

A prisoner had once told Father Saulo that to hide her desperation at life in jail, she effectively put a mask on in the morning when she got up for the benefit of her cellmates and the guards, and would take it off only when she went to bed, often crying herself to sleep. But Amanda didn't appear to be like that. Father Saulo was impressed by her strength, by her self-control: she never seemed anguished, she was never in tears, and he was told that she didn't need tranquillisers to enable her to sleep, unlike several other prisoners. In just a few days, she had lost the look of desperation she'd had when she first arrived.

To the priest, whom she affectionately called just 'Saulo', Amanda often repeated: 'I'm calm because I didn't do anything.'

In Father Saulo's experience, most prisoners confessed to the crime they were accused of. He believed Amanda was sincere when she said she was innocent. But he refused to make up his mind on whether she was in fact innocent or guilty. He was certain that even if he read the thousands of pages of the investigation, he still wouldn't be one hundred per cent certain either way. He preferred not to allow himself to judge any of the prisoners.

'I believe what you say; I believe in everything that the others tell me until proven otherwise,' Father Saulo told Amanda.

Amanda smiled and told him she was happy he believed her.

As with all the other prisoners, Father Saulo spoke mainly about the Bible when he talked to Amanda – she told him she wasn't a Catholic, but he hoped she might convert one day and gave her a copy of the Bible.

'I hope that one day you can feel the truth of these words, and feel the beauty in them,' he told her.

She replied that rationally she could only go part of the way towards believing in God. She told him she wasn't very religious, even if she had studied religion at high school. But she respected religion.

Father Saulo and Amanda talked many times about, as he put it later, 'the meaning of life – including where do I come from, where am I going, love, good and evil, and right and wrong.' She would read a passage of the Bible before his visit, and they would then talk about it together.

Once, when the murder came up in their conversation, Amanda told him firmly: 'I don't want to talk about that.' She mentioned Meredith only a couple of times, saying she was sorry about what had happened to 'my friend'. On one occasion, she and the priest talked about forgiveness.

Mignini and Father Saulo knew each other well and were on friendly terms – Father Saulo had been his mother's parish priest. But they didn't see eye to eye on Amanda. Mignini would discuss what was publicly known about the case with the priest, but the latter refused to accept that Amanda was guilty. However hard Mignini tried, Father Saulo refused to be convinced. Mignini was fond of him but he thought Father Saulo saw Amanda and the other prisoners in his care 'through a priest's eyes' – he was a good man but too ready to see good in others.

Father Saulo thought the courts didn't always succeed in establishing the truth behind a crime.

'Giuliano, I pray for you to be enlightened in your task,' the priest told the prosecutor.

The two agreed to leave it at that.

16 November 2007

A second breakthrough for Mignini and Napoleoni in just two days came at lunchtime as they waited in Raffaele's narrow street with a team from the Homicide Squad ready to enter his flat for a fresh search. A senior detective drove up to where they stood and reported that the forensic team in Rome had made another discovery: a fragment of a bloody palm print on the cushion which had been found under Meredith's body belonged not to any of the three accused but to a twenty-year-old man born in the Ivory Coast, Rudy Guede.

Mignini quickly issued a warrant for Rudy's arrest. Detectives soon found out that he lived in an old yellow house, almost round the corner from Raffaele, in a bedsit on the ground floor. But when they arrived at his home, he was nowhere to be seen. Rudy's landlord told them he had gone away a few days after Meredith's murder.

That evening, three detectives tracked down Rudy's father, Roger, to a house in which he lived with other immigrants on a busy road south of Perugia. Again there was no sign of Rudy himself. Roger, a labourer whose son was born when he was only nineteen, explained he hadn't seen him for three years; he didn't even know his address. Rudy's mother, Roger said, had abandoned her son when he was a baby. Roger had married again, but his second wife had left him too.

Napoleoni's team found out a little more about Rudy from the *carabinieri* in Milan. They had detained him at a kindergarten in the city on 27 October – six days before Meredith's murder – and accused him of attempted robbery. Rudy told officers that he had gone there to spend the night, but the head of the kindergarten said he had forced her locker and tampered with her computer.

In Rudy's rucksack, officers found a big kitchen knife he had

taken from the kindergarten, a hammer of the kind used for breaking windows on trains in emergencies, as well as a laptop and a
cell phone they said he had stolen from a lawyer's office in Perugia
in mid-October.

Meredith's friend Sophie flew back to Perugia from London to
fetch the things she'd left behind in her flat when she'd left the
city a little more than a week earlier. She arranged to meet several
English students who'd stayed on in Perugia, at the Merlin Pub.
But as soon as she walked in she started crying; it had been one of
Meredith's favourite spots.

   She had a drink with her friends and then walked back alone to
the flat on Via del Lupo. On the way, she came across a group of
people sitting on some stairs; they were only talking to each other,
but the sight terrified her. She walked on to the flat, relieved she
had decided she could no longer live in Perugia.

27

Amanda had been moved to a new cell, which she shared with one other prisoner, and was now allowed to watch the television. As soon as she saw her parents in the visiting room at the prison on the morning of 17 November, she started telling them what an awful time she'd had the day before. The TV news had described her as a liar because she'd given two different versions of what happened on the night of Meredith's death. She insisted again that she had done nothing. The news had made her cry a lot, and she'd felt very cold.

Edda tried to reassure her daughter: it was just as her lawyers were saying, people were trying to scare her by feeding lies to the media. That's all they were, lies. People wanted to pressure her into revealing something else. The lawyers said that whatever Amanda did, she must stay calm and not say anything to anyone.

'It's stupid, because I can't say anything else. I was there and I can't lie about this, there's no reason to,' Amanda said.

Don't talk to anyone, Curt insisted. Was she receiving any letters?

Thousands, from admirers, Amanda replied.

Don't write to anyone, the parents insisted, don't say anything.

Her cell was so cold. And she missed her music so much. But going out into the courtyard made her feel better: she was free to move around there, she could sing at the top of her voice and she could also scream and shout. It was good, too, to be in the sun;

the electric light was on most of the time in the cell. She was even getting a bit of a tan.

Amanda mentioned the knife, which according to the forensic police had her DNA on the handle and Meredith's on the blade. 'It makes no sense, because I never took a knife from Raffaele's house to my house!' she exclaimed.

Edda asked her daughter whether it was true Raffaele always carried a knife on him.

Amanda said yes, adding that DJ – her Seattle boyfriend – did too. She told her parents that Raffaele's lawyers wanted the two of them to appear together before a judge but she would probably refuse.

'Basically, if you two went back to the original story, before they started hitting you and all the rest—' Edda said.

Amanda interrupted her: 'When they said that I'd have been sent to prison for thirty years, and I didn't know what was happening . . .'

Amanda exclaimed that actually she could be dead right now! She could have been in the cottage when the thing happened!

Edda agreed: she thought of course of Meredith and her family, but she had to say that things could have gone worse.

Soon after finding Rudy's palm print on the cushion in Meredith's bedroom, the Rome forensic police uncovered more evidence placing him at the crime scene: Rudy's DNA was found on Meredith's vaginal swab, on toilet paper in the lavatory which had been left unflushed in the big bathroom, mixed with Meredith's DNA in bloodstains inside her shoulder bag on her bed, and on the left sleeve of her blood-soaked sweatshirt. Experts appointed by Mignini concluded that a shoe print found in Meredith's room, under the quilt that covered her body, was compatible with Rudy's Nike Outbreak 2 shoes – they ruled out a previous finding that the shoe print had been left by Raffaele's Nike Air Force 1 pair.

The forensic police reported that of the 108 fingerprints, handprints and footprints it found in the flat, it had managed to identify forty-seven. Of these, seventeen were Meredith's, five Raffaele's, just one Amanda's – the print of her right index finger on a glass on the sink in the kitchen – fifteen Laura's and five Filomena's. Raffaele's fingerprints were found on the outside of Meredith's bedroom door, on the inside of the door to Laura's room, and on the inside of the fridge door.

The Homicide Squad still had no idea where Rudy was. From Giacomo Benedetti, a twenty-year-old student from nearby Assisi who was his closest friend, detectives learnt more about Rudy. The two had already known each other for ten years before going to secondary school together.

According to Benedetti, Rudy had had a very unhappy childhood. His mother abandoned him when he was only a few days old; his parents divorced when he was ten and his father then remarried. The Perugian social services entrusted him to one foster family after another. Rudy had a habit of vanishing when he had a 'problem', according to Benedetti, but he would usually call his friend. But not this time. Benedetti had no idea where he was, and nor did his former foster families.

Detectives found Rudy's Internet blog, on which he'd posted a year earlier an autobiographical account, entitled *A House Without a Roof is Like a Child Without a Father*. Rudy wrote that he'd been raised by an aunt after being robbed of a mother, and effectively of a father too. He wrote about himself in the third person and said he'd grown up '*with a thousand difficulties, a thousand anxieties . . . at one point he wanted to commit suicide because he couldn't bear it anymore.*'

His aunt kept moving from town to town in the Ivory Coast, so he never made true friends. '*But one day, while he was sitting quietly under a tree, in the shade on a hot day, a puff of wind caressed his face and he saw a woman next to him who stared at him, her eyes full of tears of happiness. She was none other than his mother, the mother he had never seen before and so he didn't know what to do, whether to run away or hug her. In the end his heart told him what to do.*'

Rudy and his mother became inseparable: '*the boy had a mother all for himself at last, now his life had a meaning. He had a bit of affection and he no longer felt alone. He didn't leave her for a second, they were always together. But one day the woman went away while he was playing with friends, she didn't even say goodbye.'* When Rudy started school some time later, his aunt was busy at work and he walked to it on his own. *'How awful it was to see the other children with their mothers while you're there alone like an orphan – but yours is somewhere or other.'*

From Rudy's friends and the families who'd cared for him, detectives learnt that when he was fifteen and living in Perugia, his father Roger flew off to the Ivory Coast, leaving his son with a girlfriend he didn't like. The social services intervened and placed him with a foster family. Later, Roger claimed: 'I didn't abandon Rudy; they took him away from me. They said I wasn't a good father.'

Two months later Roger came back, but Rudy refused to go back to him. He was living with the wealthy Caporali family who owned the Liomatic Perugia basketball team. Rudy became a keen basketball player and even played with the team. But he failed to settle down, dropping out first from a hotel management school, then a computer studies course. The Caporalis had a farmhouse bed and breakfast and in the spring of 2007 they took him on as an assistant gardener. He worked hard for a couple of months, playing basketball on the Piazza Grimana in the evenings with, among others, two of the students who lived in the flat below Meredith's. That summer however he fell ill, failed to send his employers a medical certificate, and was sacked.

One witness, Christian Tramontano, co-owner of the Coffee Break bar, told Napoleoni that at six o'clock one morning in early September, he'd surprised a young black man rummaging through his flat. Tramontano had jumped out of the bed where he'd been sleeping with his girlfriend and tried to chase him out of the flat.

The intruder, finding the front door locked, grabbed a chair to keep Tramontano at a distance and brandished a jackknife. He spoke good Italian and Tramontano was close enough to smell wine on his breath. Tramontano turned, fled back to his girlfriend and called the police. Shortly afterwards, the intruder left the flat, having stolen a five euro banknote (worth just over four pounds) and three credit cards. That evening, Tramontano recognised the thief at the Domus nightclub: Tramontano said his name was Rudy Guede. Tramontano went to the police station to report the theft, but gave up after three trips to the police station because the queue was always too long.

This was about the same time that Rudy went to Le Chic after he was handed a leaflet advertising the bar's opening. Amanda was working as a waitress that evening. She went up to Rudy and asked, in English, if he wanted to drink something. Rudy asked for a sangria and the two chatted briefly. Amanda told him she came from Seattle, and Rudy mentioned a student friend of his came from there too – did she know him? Amanda said no, and their chat ended there.

Since vanishing in early November, Rudy had only been in touch with Gabriele Mancini, a friend of his from one of the foster families. Twelve days after Meredith's murder, Rudy tried to contact his friend through his Messenger account. Mancini sent Rudy two messages, but received no reply. Then Mancini sent Rudy a third message, telling him off for disappearing yet again.

This time, Rudy replied. '*I can't,*' he wrote.

'*What do you mean, you can't?*' a surprised Mancini asked.

'*You know,*' Rudy messaged back.

'*What am I supposed to know?*' Mancini wrote, even more surprised.

Rudy disconnected himself.

On 13 November, Rudy sent a brief message to a German student he'd played basketball with: '*Hey, I'm in Sweden now.*'

As they searched for clues to Rudy's whereabouts, detectives went through the statements they'd gathered so far. Amanda had mentioned a man she described as a short 'South African'. She'd said he played basketball on Piazza Grimana and had once been to the semi-basement flat when Meredith was there too. Stefano Bonassi, one of the students in the flat, had said the 'South African' was so drunk on a visit there that he had fallen asleep on the toilet without flushing it – a detail that had reminded Napoleoni that someone failed to flush the toilet in Meredith's flat around the time she was killed. Bonassi also said the 'South African' was very attracted to Amanda.

Several of the young men who used to play basketball with Rudy told detectives that he liked 'white girls, not black ones' and that he often went to the Merlin Pub – Meredith's favourite. Rudy sometimes drank too much and danced on the tables. One acquaintance said people didn't like dancing too close to Rudy because when he got sweaty he stank.

Another friend of Rudy's, an Australian student called Alexander Crudo, had met Rudy in the centre of Perugia on the afternoon of 2 November, the day after the murder. When Crudo mentioned Meredith's death, Rudy told him she was the girl they'd seen watching an England–South Africa rugby match at a pub some three weeks earlier. He also told Crudo he was leaving for Milan to go dancing there. That night, Rudy was seen dancing at the Domus nightclub long after midnight.

In a video he'd posted on the web some time ago, Rudy is sitting in front of the camera pulling faces, rolling his eyes and his tongue, and groaning and giggling. He ends with the words: 'I'm a vampire. I'm Dracula. I'm going to suck your blood.'

Mignini signed decrees ordering phone taps on many of Rudy's friends, but they yielded no clues to where he was hiding.

28

On a Sunday afternoon, Amanda's lawyer, Ghirga, had agreed to see a couple of journalists with her father, Curt, at the Caffè Turreno opposite the cathedral. The old-fashioned bar, once popular with anti-fascist partisans during the Second World War, was Ghirga's favourite haunt. He had a rigid routine and every day at 8 a.m., after taking his daughter to school, again at midday and then at 7 p.m. he would go there for a chat with friends and clients.

But both Ghirga and Curt were completely unprepared for what they saw when they arrived at the *caffè*: a mob of journalists, photographers and what felt like a hundred TV cameras were waiting outside it. It was the first time Ghirga realised how fascinated the media was with the Kercher case, and with Amanda in particular.

Ghirga was no publicity-hungry lawyer and to him the media interest was an act of aggression. He turned down a flood of interview requests that he received from the world's media, declining TV talk shows and true crime programmes. He was even offered £9,000 merely to ask Amanda five questions and write down her replies. He rejected such offers out of hand, and when journalists and TV crews mobbed him as he walked out of a hearing he would sometimes curse loudly as he strode away.

He saw it as a question of self-respect, convinced that right now silence was truly golden, even though he believed investigators were leaking confidential information to the newspapers. Now wasn't the time to rock the boat; there would be plenty of opportunity to challenge the investigators if the case ever came to trial. Journalists were always stalking him at the Caffè Turreno. Ghirga often bought a round of *aperitivi* but when they steered the conversation to Amanda, he'd often clam up and they would end up doing most of the talking.

Ghirga and his colleague Dalla Vedova were not only concerned about journalists. They warned Edda to be very careful whenever she talked about sensitive aspects of the case. She must assume that her mobile phone was bugged, that her emails were being intercepted, that mikes might be hidden in her car and even in the flat where she was staying. They often asked her to go for a walk in the open air with them when they needed to talk – even when she was staying in a cottage in the middle of the countryside.

19 November 2007

From Amanda's prison diary:
I received twenty-three 'fan letters' today . . . The majority comment on how beautiful I am. I've received blatant love letters from people who love me from first sight, a marriage proposal, and others wanting to get to know 'the girl with the angel face'
. . . If I were ugly, would they be writing me wishing me encouragement? I don't think so . . . And jeez, I'm not even that good-looking! People are acting like I'm the prettiest thing since Helen of Troy!

With still no clues as to where Rudy had fled, the police decided to recruit his closest friend, the student Giacomo Benedetti. He agreed to keep trying Rudy on his mobile phone, but it had apparently gone dead. Benedetti also tried contacting him on the web, through the MSN Messenger service. At about 6 p.m., Benedetti logged on to the service and saw that Rudy was online.

Benedetti immediately phoned his police contact, a detective from Rome who had been sent to Perugia to work on the Kercher case. 'Is it you or him?' Benedetti asked, thinking the detective was using Rudy's account to get to his friends, and that's why Rudy was coming up as online.

'No, it isn't us, so it's him. Try to keep him talking, we're coming over. Try to set up a meeting with him; say you could give him some money,' the detective said.

Detectives raced to Benedetti's flat and guided him as, after switching to instant messaging on the Skype network, he quizzed Rudy.

'*hey rudy, where are you? feel like talking?*' Benedetti typed.

'*I've got fuck all to do with this thing but i'm scared,*' Rudy replied.

'*you've got to stay calm.*'

'*i was there when it happened. I've got fuck all to do with it.*'

'*but where are you now?*'

'*i tried to help her but then i fled.*'

'*i can help you if you try to explain things to me better. but you've got to stay calm.*'

'*i'm not in italy now.*'

'*so where are you?*'

'*it's not that i don't trust you but i can't tell you now. i'm sorry but i'm afraid.*'

'*what of?*'

'*the funny thing is that i tried to help her. it happened while i was in the bathroom having a shit. but he fled.*'

'*who he?*'

'*Amanda doesn't have anything to do with it.*'

Slowly, Benedetti and the detectives prised Rudy's account out of him. Rudy said he went to the cottage after Meredith agreed to see him there. They started having sex – '*we both wanted it*' he said – but they didn't go all the way. Rudy went to the bathroom and, while he was there, he heard a scream. He rushed out of the bathroom and was attacked by a young Italian man. He thought the man was Raffaele, but he wasn't sure because he didn't see his face. Patrick had nothing to do with it all; neither did Amanda, but he wasn't as sure about her as he was about Patrick.

Right now, Rudy needed money. Promising to send Rudy £100, Benedetti found out that he was hiding in Düsseldorf. They agreed that he would pick money up from the Western Union branch there, using the name of Kevin Wade and the codeword 'basket'.

'*please don't betray me,*' Rudy typed.

'*I wouldn't dream of it,*' Benedetti replied.

After saying goodbye to Rudy, the detectives rushed Benedetti to the offices of the postal police where they arranged the money transfer. He then called Rudy and the two chatted, this time on the phone.

Rudy insisted repeatedly on how loud Meredith's screams had been. 'She yelled really loudly, she yelled so loudly that if someone had been passing by, they'd have heard it,' Rudy said, adding that the time was between 9.20 and 9.30 p.m.

He had run out of the bathroom in such a hurry that he didn't even stop to pull up his trousers. He saw the wound on Meredith's neck, and fetched a towel, which he tried to hold against it. 'She was holding me tightly, tightly . . . I don't know why I didn't call the ambulance because I was the only one then, the only one . . . I was all filthy with blood and I was scared I would get all the blame,' Rudy said. He fled the cottage.

Rudy wanted to send his friend a statement about Meredith's murder for him to give the police. Benedetti tried to persuade Rudy to come back to Italy. He urged him to take a train to Milan; they would meet at the station in the early afternoon the next day and consult a lawyer he knew. Prompted by the detectives, Benedetti advised Rudy to wear a hat and scarf so that the German police wouldn't recognise him – the Italians wanted to seize their man themselves.

Rudy finally agreed. 'I'll be seeing you. In any case, as soon as I get there they'll throw me into prison,' he said.

'Come on, come on,' Benedetti said. 'I'll sort things out. I won't make you go to prison, don't worry.'

That evening Napoleoni and a couple of other detectives rushed out of Perugia, racing up the motorway. She hoped to arrest Rudy as he crossed the border into Italy.

Mignini signed a warrant for Patrick's release from jail; the case against the owner of Le Chic had clearly collapsed. In his warrant, the prosecutor wrote that Amanda may have blamed him for the murder in order to protect Rudy. As far as Mignini was concerned, he had done his job. The law demanded that a prosecutor should be impartial, looking for evidence both against a suspect and in his favour. He must also be ready to free a suspect if new evidence came to light to clear him. Mignini had been convinced that he had no choice but to arrest Patrick after Amanda's accusation, and now, when the investigation showed Patrick's alibi had been backed by several witnesses, he released him.

29

At 6 a.m., as the Intercity 2021 heading south from Hamburg sped along the river Rhine between Koblenz and Mainz, a ticket inspector asked Rudy for his ticket. Rudy didn't have one and only had four euros (just over three pounds) on him so the guard detained him. A routine check revealed an international arrest warrant had been issued, and he was taken to a prison in Koblenz.

Rudy told prosecutors in Koblenz that he'd been in the country for two weeks. He'd left Perugia with forty-five pounds, three pairs of jeans, three sweaters, three T-shirts, a thick sweatshirt, a woolly hat, two combs and a small towel wrapped around his toothbrush. Investigators found out later that Austrian police had already stopped him once, and the German police three times – on 4 November in Munich, on 6 November in Stuttgart and on 7 November in Karlsruhe. There was no warrant out for his arrest at the time, so he was simply booked for not having a residence permit, and left free to go on his way every time. He was on his way to meet his friend Benedetti in Milan when he was arrested.

Rudy told the German prosecutors a similar story to the one he gave his friend Benedetti. He said that he had tried to stop Meredith's bleeding, fetching first one towel and then another after the first became drenched with her blood. Meredith was still alive, and dressed – blue jeans, a white pullover and a dark jacket – when he fled the cottage.

'She was very strong and she was still breathing. In that moment Meredith lay diagonally across the floor . . . close to the cupboard. When I tried to stop the blood with the towel, she was still moving. I can't say for sure if she was conscious or not when I left,' Rudy said.

He'd read about the supposed burglary in the newspapers. But when he and Meredith went into the cottage, Filomena's window wasn't broken, he said. When he ran away home, he left Meredith's door open.

Rudy's long-estranged father, Roger, found out about his son's arrest watching the TV news that lunchtime, and immediately burst into tears. 'Rudy is a very gentle, good-hearted boy; he loved everybody and he loved to have fun,' Roger said. 'I love him as a son.' Did he feel at all to blame after allegedly abandoning Rudy when he was sixteen? 'No, no, I don't feel guilty because he was taken from me and given to another family.' His son's arrest was just racism: 'They found a first black man, then they had to let him go, so now they've grabbed another one.'

Roger knew nothing about his son's friends or girlfriends. But surely he'd had news of his son over the past few years? 'Since Rudy was sixteen and went to live with other families, I've heard nothing from him,' Roger said. He did however bump into his son on a bus that summer. 'Rudy said hello to me. I asked where he lived and he told me in the centre of town, that he worked as a gardener during the day and that he made pizzas in a restaurant in the evening. He got off at the next stop,' Roger recalled. Rudy clearly had nothing to say to his father.

Delighted that Rudy had been caught, but frustrated that she hadn't been the one who arrested him, Napoleoni and her colleagues turned their car round and headed back to Perugia.

Amanda's father sounded an optimistic note as he greeted her in the visiting room. Curt said he was hopeful she would get out of prison soon, because investigators were seeking a suspect he called 'the fourth man' – Curt didn't yet know that Rudy had been arrested three hours earlier.

'Ah yes, because this fourth man ... I know him, but not well ... I'm not sure, but I met him through ... I saw him first with the neighbours,' Amanda said.

Curt asked whether she meant the male students who lived in the downstairs flat.

'Yes ... And also one evening when I was with the neighbours in town ... we bumped into him ... And then I saw him once in the basketball court, and I think I saw him once when I was at work ... but the fact is I barely knew him ... I don't know his phone number ... I don't even know his name because I've forgotten it, simply because I've never spoken to him; I don't even know him. And the lawyer told me the police says I phone him or something ... but I don't even know him.'

Curt passed on the news he'd got from the lawyer: first of all they were looking for this person ...

Amanda interrupted: 'Oh yeah? Why?'

'Because there's his palm print on the cushion which was under Meredith ...'

Amanda interrupted again: 'And it's his?'

'Yes, it's his, and it was established that it was his palm print because he's apparently from the Ivory Coast and he was adopted by an Italian family ... so his prints are on file and—'

'Oh my God!' Amanda cried out.

'Yes, so they're looking for him because apparently he's disappeared ...'

Her tone incredulous, Amanda commented that this whole affair was in a way 'unreal' for her, it was as if it wasn't really happening to her; she was in prison but at the same time she wasn't there, because she was always thinking about when she'd get out. 'I mean, just the idea of knowing who might have done it ... I mean I know him, I saw him before, I spoke with him a bit before ... oh my God!'

'Yes, but it seems that ... this is what I heard, it seems there's that imprint on her cushion and some other imprints ... one in the bathroom ... I don't know, so—' Curt said.

Amanda interrupted once more: 'Oh my God! What a bastard!'

'I don't know . . . I don't know who it is.'

'I know, I know . . . I mean . . . I'll have met him, but it's pretty strange that . . . him just there, because I never invited him to the house before,' Amanda said.

Asked about her latest meeting with the lawyer Ghirga, Amanda said they had talked about 'the knife with Meredith's DNA' – she made no mention of her own DNA on it. 'I don't understand how Meredith's DNA can be on it because I never took it to my house for anything . . . so it's a mistake . . . or Raffaele brought it home . . . but I think that can't be either, because he was with me in the house . . . so there must be a mistake . . . and [Ghirga] told me: OK, we'll say it was a mistake.'

Amanda continued: 'And then [Ghirga] asked me at what level I know this other man . . . this Rudy. Is that his name, Rudy?'

Curt replied no one had said anything yet about his name.

Amanda told him the TV had given his name.

From Amanda's prison diary:

Updates about me: my lawyers are optimistic that they can get me out of here within the next two weeks. Yeah! Granted, it will be probably a transfer to house arrest, but I'll be able to see Mom and Dad as much as I want and play [the] guitar . . .

. . . Patrick got out today! Finally! Something is going right! Me next! Well, most likely Raffaele before me, but soon! I'm so happy!'

30

22 November 2007

In her prison diary, Amanda wrote that a doctor had told her that test results showed she had the HIV virus. The doctor told her not to worry, that it might be a mistake; a new test would be carried out the following week.

Amanda described this as the: *worst experience of my life. I'm in prison for a crime I didn't commit and I might have HIV.*

I don't want to die. I want to get married and have children. I want to create something good. I want to get old. I want my time. I want my life. Why why why? I can't believe this.

Amanda listed seven men she has had sex with, and concludes she could have been infected by three of them.

Oh please please let it be a mistake. Please oh please let it not be true. I don't want to die.

23 November 2007

Antioco Fois, a slight twenty-nine-year-old with a deceptively mild manner, was one of the youngest reporters on the local *Giornale dell'Umbria* newspaper when Perugia's biggest crime case in years, if not decades, began virtually on his doorstep. Fois lived at the bottom of Corso Garibaldi, the same street as Raffaele's and only a couple of minutes walk away from the cottage.

Fois had started out as an intern only three years earlier. What he loved the most about his job was investigative journalism – in-depth investigations that exposed facts or even crimes that his targets preferred to hide. He'd sometimes hidden his true identity to get a news story; once he pretended to be an MP's assistant to show how easy it was to jump hospital waiting lists, and another time he posed as a customer to find out whether arson attacks on shops were the work of an extortion gang.

Following Meredith's murder, Fois spent hours at a stretch chatting to as many neighbours and shopkeepers as he could find to discover whether anyone had seen or heard anything that night. The more he thought about Meredith's murder, the more he thought of Alfred Hitchcock's 1954 film *Rear Window* starring James Stewart and Grace Kelly, in which a photographer, confined to a wheelchair, uncovers a murder by spying on his neighbours through his flat's rear window. Fois thought that no one had seen Meredith killed, but someone must have seen something before or after the murder – something that they would dismiss as unimportant, but could in fact be significant.

After three weeks of digging, Fois discovered from an acquaintance that the schoolteacher's widow Nara Capezzali, who lived across the car park from the cottage, had confided hearing a heart-rending scream on the night of the murder. Fois found out Capezzali's address, timed his visit for just before lunchtime when he expected her to be at home, and pressed the buzzer to her flat.

A homely, plump figure in a dressing gown, Capezzali appeared a bit wary of him at first but soon described what she had heard, as if it was a relief for her to unburden herself: the long, piercing woman's scream on the night of 1 November which, she said with her eyes moist and her hands pressed against her chest, 'was like a scream of pain, and like a call for help'. At the time she'd been walking past the dining-room window which gave out on the cottage. And then the sound of someone running on the iron staircase that led up from the car park, and one or more people 'scurrying' along the cottage drive.

Moved by her account, Fois told her his story would come out the next day and he'd leave her name out of it. As he was about to leave, Capezzali mentioned the scream once more. Every time she walked past the dining-room window she had the impression that she could hear that scream again. 'It was so ghastly, it must have been the scream of someone who'd been wounded to death. I heard her in the moment she was dying. Poor girl, poor dear, what did they do to her?'

In her prison diary, Amanda wrote that a senior guard had told her that her cellmate was telling people she had HIV. The doctor came back to Amanda and this time told her that the first result was 'absolutely unsure'; the second test, he added, would almost certainly be negative.
Amanda wrote:

> He had a weird way of showing his support however. He said that he would most definitely have sex with me right now he was so sure that I had nothing to worry about.
>
> ...The TV said Rudy said something about being at my house that night with another guy, and it was the other guy who killed Meredith. I don't know what to think. I mean, could be true, could be not, but I know better than to trust publicity.
>
> All in all I'm glad something is being figured out. It means finally the creep who did this will go to jail and I'll get to go free. I might even be able to see my family at Christmas!
>
> ...I want to get another tattoo – the words 'Let it be'. They mean so much to me now. I don't know where, I just want them.

Several days later, the fresh test established that Amanda definitely wasn't infected.

24 November 2007

Fois's interview made the front page of the *Giornale dell'Umbria*, with the story headlined 'A HEART-RENDING SCREAM, THEN

SEVERAL PEOPLE FLEEING'. The question was, Fois ended his story, why none of those who had heard the scream – he reported that a female student had also heard a scream from the cottage – had called the police. Fois quoted a local shopkeeper: 'In this area, hearing screams at night is something which is completely normal.'

As he'd promised, Fois didn't name Capezzali in the story. But he gave her name to Mignini and the prosecutor questioned her soon afterwards. For Mignini, there was no doubt the scream was Meredith's and had been prompted by the last, fatal blow to her throat. The prosecutor estimated that Meredith had died after 10 p.m., most likely between 10.30 and 10.40 p.m., killed by the people who had run away just after her scream.

Another witness helped Mignini estimate the time of the murder. Shortly before 8 p.m. that evening Alessandra Formica, a surveyor in her mid-twenties, and her boyfriend parked in the car park opposite the cottage. Formica had booked a table for 8 p.m. at the restaurant Il Settimo Sigillo, at the top of the steep street that leads from Piazza Grimana to the cathedral. The restaurant was so crowded they would have to wait a long time for a table so they took a walk down the Corso Vannucci despite the cold night.

After dinner, they walked back out into the cold and down towards Piazza Grimana. At 10.30–10.40 p.m., they reached the bottom of the stairs on the edge of the square, with the basketball court on their left when, Formica said, 'a coloured man who was running bumped violently into my boyfriend'.

The man, who was coming up the stairs – away from the cottage – had his head down and bumped into her boyfriend with his shoulder; he was young, well built but 'not tall' and wore a heavy jacket. He ran on without stopping or apologising.

'This area's really full of good-for-nothings; he didn't even say sorry,' Formica complained to her boyfriend.

Amanda confided to her father Curt in the prison visiting room that she was worried about what Raffaele was going to tell the court, which would soon hear a new appeal for their release.

'Apparently, Raffaele seems to be saying that I'm innocent: OK, great! But I don't know if that's true. Yesterday I spoke to Luciano [Ghirga, her lawyer], who told me that Raffaele wants to say I'm innocent, while his lawyer wants him to say I'm guilty,' Amanda said.

Ghirga had also told her the previous day that the police wanted to portray her as a girl with an angel face and the devil inside her. Everyone in the jail knew that an Italian newspaper called her 'Amanda, angel face', and the police was saying that yes, she had an angel face, but she also had the soul of a devil.

Amanda burst out laughing. Curt said this was the first he'd heard of it, as he didn't speak Italian. Better that way, Amanda said as she laughed again, it was all crap anyway.

Amanda laughed again and again as Curt described driving around the Umbrian countryside to find a mail-delivery office, and how he'd left Ghirga's office 'walking like Dracula', as he put it, to avoid waiting journalists and get to his small red Fiat.

Amanda told Curt she was reading the New Testament in Italian, which the chaplain had given her. She didn't talk about personal things with the priest, but even though she wasn't religious she found their conversations interesting.

She told Curt she'd again been moved to a new cell. Two of her new cellmates were in their forties, and the oldest was fifty-five years old. Amanda felt like a little girl in front of them; in fact, in prison she felt like a little girl. Her new cellmates had taught her how to clean the bathroom and how to do her laundry in the bidet.

While Amanda worried about what Raffaele would say in court, her former boyfriend tried to work out, as he put it in a letter to his father, what her role had been '*in this affair*'. He had known her only a week, and for all that time Amanda had been '*slippery*'.

He wrote: '*I think she was living on another planet. She lives life as if it was a dream, she can't distinguish between dreams and reality ... The Amanda I knew is an Amanda who lives life in a thoughtless way.*

All she thinks of is seeking pleasure all the time. But it's impossible to even imagine that she's a murderess.'

In a self-critical note, Raffaele blamed himself – to a limited extent – for Amanda, Rudy and him being arrested: '*I realise that if we've all ended up in prison it's also because of my irresponsibility concerning what happened that evening. And also because of the fact that we smoked such a lot of joints and I'm very sorry about that ... I'm paying the price for my superficiality, and this time I'll pay everything, down to the last penny.'*

31

At the Forensic Medicine Institute of the University of Perugia, forensic pathologists appointed by Judge Matteini, Mignini and lawyers representing Amanda and Raffaele met to study body parts taken during Meredith's autopsy, including parts of her neck, lungs and pelvis area. They would then study photographs and films taken at the time to try to establish how and when Meredith died.

The three professors appointed by the judge – Anna Aprile, Mariano Cingolani and Gian Carlo Umani Ronchi – quickly agreed there was no need to carry out a new autopsy. This was a relief to Meredith's family, who had been waiting for a decision before planning the funeral; there would have been nothing worse for them than burying Meredith only to have to exhume her just a few days later. But the family faced a long wait; it would take the professors several months to complete their report.

From Amanda's prison diary:
To all those who believed I was a criminal mastermind and a murderer:

I forgive you. How could you have known? You believed the recycled rumours of newspapers . . . Heck, if I were in your shoes, I would do the same thing . . .

Who wants fifteen minutes of fame for being accused of murdering a friend? Meredith was my friend and I'll never forget how wonderful she was. How is anyone else supposed to know what it feels like to feel like your own death was just as close? It was my home after all, and I could have just as likely been found there with my own throat split like no one's should ever be.

28 November 2007

In a report the Rome forensic police sent Mignini, it described the DNA evidence it had found following its three-day survey of the cottage after Meredith's body was discovered. The most significant in the prosecutor's eyes were mixed traces belonging to both Amanda and Meredith in blood on the bidet. At Raffaele's flat, traces of Amanda and Raffaele's blood were found on a dishcloth and on a sponge.

With every new bit of bad news for Amanda – the DNA on the knife, and now the mixed DNA traces of both Amanda and Meredith – her lawyer Ghirga assured her there was still everything to play for. The more Ghirga studied the case files, the more he became convinced there was nothing to prove she was in the cottage at the time of the murder.

'I'll save you because there isn't any proof against you in the files,' he told her.

He thought a trial was likely given the gravity of the charges against Amanda, Raffaele and Rudy, and he started to plan his strategy. What he saw as the lack of direct proof would be his main card. The law stated clearly that without it, circumstantial evidence should be considered to be direct proof only when it was certain, of sufficient gravity and when the various elements pointed to the same conclusion – Ghirga would therefore fight to demolish whatever circumstantial evidence the prosecution put forward, challenging the methods and findings not only of the investigators but of the forensic experts as well.

29 November 2007

Three weeks after her arrest, detectives searched Amanda's cell and seized a diary with a pink cover. Inside were two handwritten sheets of paper, which included a repeat of how she said she had spent the evening of 1 November with Raffaele, and a passage in which she wrote that both when she was alone and when she was with the police, '*I fear my mind.*' She described how she imagined '*the horrors my friend must have gone through in her final moments*':

> *I know my friend was raped before she was murdered. I can only imagine how she must have felt at these moments, scared, hurt, violated. But even more I have to imagine what it must have felt like when she felt her blood flowing out of her. What must she have thought? About her mom? Regret? Did she have time to come to a moment of peace or did she only experience terror in the end?*

At the bottom of the second page Amanda drew a castle, two girls smiling and holding hands, and a smiley face behind a smiling mask.

30 November 2007

Amanda and Raffaele's hopes of freedom – a fortnight earlier both had made a new appeal for their release – were drastically dashed by a panel of three judges headed by Judge Massimo Ricciarelli. The judges endorsed much of Mignini's reconstruction of the murder and decreed they should stay in prison.

Their ruling was scathing in its analysis of Amanda. She had 'a many-sided personality – self-confident, shrewd and naïve, but with a strong taste for taking centre stage and a marked, we could say fatal, ability in putting people together.' She acted on her desires 'even when they can lead to violent and uncontrol-lable acts.' As for Amanda's statements since Meredith's death, they were a 'constant attempt to do and undo, to say something and then immediately deny it, as if she wanted to please everyone. Such behaviour seems to be the result of slyness and naïvety at the same time.'

For the judges, there was no burglary at the cottage. Only Spiderman, they said, could have entered the cottage through Filomena's broken window. Why would a thief have got rid of Meredith's mobile phones so soon after the crime? And why would a killer take the phones with him in the first place, only to abandon them a short distance away? Meredith's killers had taken them from the cottage, the judges surmised, because they didn't want the phones to ring there. The killers needed to pretend to call Meredith after her death, and they didn't want their call to help track her down to her room.

'The killer did not have to exercise any type of violence in order to enter the house, having used the keys or having been allowed in by the victim herself,' the judges said. Meredith was killed by someone she knew, and probably by more than one person.

Raffaele had lied in claiming to have called the police before they arrived at the cottage. Nor had he gone to bed the previous night at about midnight or 1 a.m. He had spent a turbulent night, so much so that he had switched his mobile on again very early and received a message from his father at 6 a.m. – it was a goodnight message, clearly sent when the mobile was switched off and for that reason had reached him only the next morning.

The judges mocked Raffaele for claiming he could recall spending a long time at his computer as well as smoking joints on the evening of 1 November. Appearing before the judges themselves a few days earlier, he'd given new details of his time at the computer which, they remarked, 'clearly conflict with the pitch darkness that would have reigned in his mind after taking the drugs, unless he suffers from a particular pathology – the selective loss of memory.'

An expert's analysis of Raffaele's laptop showed there had been human activity between 6.27 p.m. and 9.10 p.m. when the film *Amélie* was screened. There was no trace of human activity between 9.10 p.m. and 5.32 a.m. – 'a formidable corroboration of Raffaele's involvement' as the dawn activity, they said, pointed to a virtually sleepless night.

In his blog, Raffaele had failed to distance himself from serious criminals – he'd praised a convict who killed two boys – and above all he'd proclaimed his desire for 'big thrills'. The judges also mentioned the photograph of him in which he brandished a cleaver. Violence, they concluded, attracted him. Both in his behaviour and in his wavering statements, which often fell into line with Amanda's 'dream-like' accounts, Raffaele had shown himself to have a fragile temperament, 'exposed to impulses and outside influences of every kind'.

32

After he was extradited to Italy, Rudy gave his most detailed account yet of the night of Meredith's murder to Judge Matteini, the judge who a month earlier had ordered that Amanda, Raffaele and Patrick should stay in prison.

In a room at the Capanne prison, with Mignini as a silent observer, Rudy first described how he knew Amanda. After meeting her for the first time at Le Chic in early September, he saw her again a month later when the students in the semi-basement flat invited him there. Rudy and the students had been drinking and made some raunchy comments about Amanda, because she was pretty. 'One of us imagined her in bed, another said he'd give it to her this way or that way,' Rudy said. Amanda was a slut, the students told him, and she often came to their flat to smoke joints. Rudy said he'd never seen Raffaele and didn't even know he was Amanda's boyfriend.

When Amanda came into the flat, the young men looked at each other and burst out laughing because they were still talking about her. Amanda sat down and they all smoked cannabis for the rest of the evening. Then Meredith came in.

'I admired her beauty, I mean I looked at her because she was a beautiful girl,' Rudy said. He noticed her English accent and said to her: 'There isn't anything English about you.' Meredith told him about her parents, saying she was of mixed blood. According to Rudy, they talked the whole evening.

He saw Amanda a few other times in the street 'but it was "*Ciao!*" and that's it.' He also met Meredith again in the street, and in bars including the Shamrock where he had gone to watch an England–South Africa rugby match. Meredith was with some English friends and they greeted each other; he supported the South Africans and he pulled her leg after his team won.

On Halloween night, Rudy went to a party in the flat of some Spanish friends near the Corso Vannucci and at about midnight a girl dressed as a vampire approached him. It took him some time to recognise Meredith, and he said to her: 'What do you want to do? Do you want to suck my blood?' – he was pulling her leg because of the South African rugby victory. They talked a lot together, and kissed each other on the mouth. They agreed to meet the following evening at 8.30 p.m. Rudy left the party at 2 a.m. and went on to the Domus nightclub, but he didn't see Meredith there.

On 1 November, he met Meredith at the cottage at about 9 p.m. At one point she went to her room and he heard her complaining about something; he went to see and she said she couldn't find her money. She started complaining about Amanda, and went into her flatmate's room and opened a drawer there. 'That bloody drug addict,' Meredith said.

Rudy managed to calm her down and they started to flirt in the sitting room. 'We started touching each other. She asked me if I had a condom but I didn't have one, so I realised we should stop . . . We'd both lowered our trousers,' he said. He also touched her bra.

Rudy then went to the bathroom; he needed to go to the toilet because of the kebab he'd eaten earlier. He listened to his iPod, heard the doorbell ring and listened to two and a half songs. He'd put the volume up high but he heard a scream; he went out of the bathroom and in Meredith's bedroom he saw a man a little shorter than him with chestnut hair. Meredith's body was on the floor. He saw that blood was coming out of the left side of her neck; she was wearing blue jeans and a white woollen top.

The man struck Rudy on the left hand with a knife and Rudy backed away, throwing a chair at the attacker before the latter made for the front door. Rudy heard him say in Italian: 'He's black, the culprit's been found. Let's go,' and then the steps of two people walking away on the gravel outside the cottage.

Rudy went back to Meredith. 'I'd never seen so much blood. It was on the floor, the blood was coming out of Meredith and her shoulder was all drenched,' Rudy said. 'I didn't know what to do but I went to the bathroom, I took a small towel and I tried to pack the wound but it got soaked straight away so I went back to the bathroom and I took another towel.'

At that moment, Meredith tried to speak: 'She wanted to tell me something but there was a lot of blood coming out of both her neck and her mouth, I was kneeling next to her and I heard her say "af . . .", "af . . ." I tried to write these letters on the wall.

'Meredith took my hand as if to tell me I mustn't leave her; but I was scared. I don't remember how I could have touched the cushion and I don't know how the print of my palm could have ended up on it,' Rudy said.

Why didn't he call an ambulance? Judge Matteini asked. 'I didn't call the ambulance because I didn't have my mobile phone. In that moment I wasn't lucid, I wanted to call the ambulance but I was scared; my hands and feet were dirty with blood and I started to think things out – who would believe me?' Rudy replied.

He fled the cottage at about 10.30 p.m. after hearing the noise of a chair or table being moved in the semi-basement flat. He fled through Piazza Grimana, trying to hide his trousers and hands dirty with blood. When he got home, he washed his hands, undressed completely and dumped his dirty clothes on the floor of his room.

'I was confused, I couldn't stay in the flat because I couldn't get the sight of the blood out of my head and when I'd touched Meredith I'd touched her neck, I could still smell the smell of blood which was nauseating.' At about 11.30 p.m., he went to a friend's house and tried to act normal even though 'I was on another planet'. Later he'd followed his friends to the Domus and then to the Velvet nightclubs, going home at about 4.30–5 a.m.

On the night of 2 November, Rudy again went dancing at the Domus with three female American students he'd met in another pub. Judge Matteini took Rudy to task for going out clubbing after witnessing Meredith's death. 'You were dancing, you were having fun,' Judge Matteini said.

'Well, it depends how you look at it.'

'Well, as far as I'm concerned when you go to a nightclub and you dance you don't go there to cry.'

'Yes yes, but in that moment I was trying to be normal.'

'Your try was jolly good,' the judge snapped.

As Rudy was dancing at the Domus on the night of 2 November, the disc jockey asked for a minute of silence in Meredith's honour. The young people who had been dancing until a moment earlier suddenly froze and stood still, some with their heads bowed. Rudy froze too, his face impassive.

'I respected the minute of silence,' Rudy said.

'You respected the minute of silence but didn't you say "poor Meredith" or anything like that?' Judge Matteini asked.

'I didn't express it out loud, but there was something inside me,' Rudy replied.

The judge showed Rudy pictures of Meredith's body. Rudy remained impassive.

For Mignini, there was no doubt Rudy was lying: he couldn't deny his presence in the cottage, or his sexual contact with Meredith, given the evidence showing he was there at the time of the murder. So instead he'd decided to claim that Meredith had agreed to see him and invented a flirtation with her. There was no trace at the cottage of the letters 'AF' which Rudy said he'd tried to trace on the wall. Mignini didn't believe that Meredith had said the letters to Rudy, or that he'd tried to trace them; the prosecutor suspected Rudy wanted investigators to think that she'd been trying to say Raffaele's name.

Since her aborted trip to the German border to arrest Rudy, Napoleoni had focused on verifying Rudy's story. The detective found that his claim to have met Meredith on Halloween in the flat of some Spanish friends didn't stand up because Meredith's friends said she didn't go anywhere alone that night – they had photographs of them all together and nowhere near that flat. They also denied that she knew Rudy; she'd never talked about him and they'd never seen him near her.

Napoleoni questioned two female Spanish students who lived in the flat above Rudy's bedsit. They said they'd spent Halloween with Rudy and other friends, dancing at the Domus nightclub from 1 a.m. until it closed at 5.30 a.m. The only girl they saw him talking to and dancing with had 'long, straight blonde hair' – Meredith had dark hair.

Napoleoni also talked to a friend of Rudy's, a Somali in his early twenties who like him had settled in Italy as a child. Rudy and Mohamed Barrow Abukar had been friends for the past six years; they played basketball on Piazza Grimana, and went drinking together. Barrow Abukar told Napoleoni: 'I've never liked the way Rudy behaved, especially when he got drunk. And when he took drugs (cocaine and other stuff), he bothered people, especially the girls. He'd overpower them and try to kiss them. A lot of people disliked him and I heard he'd got into trouble for molesting girls before.' He added that Rudy often lied.

14 December 2007

Six weeks after she died, Meredith's family held the funeral service for her at the medieval Croydon Parish Church next to the Old Palace School where she had studied. One television channel offered the Kerchers more than £500,000 for exclusive coverage of the funeral. 'How disgusting. How could they?' Stephanie burst out when told about the bid. Meredith's father John, himself a journalist, was the most sickened by the cheque-book journalism and insisted that the family shouldn't talk to the media. 'The pain is only ours, and we'll talk when we've decided to, not when it suits other people,' he told his lawyer Maresca.

At the church, yellow flowers by the coffin spelt out Meredith's nickname, 'Mez'. Sophie, Amy and Robyn – Meredith's friends from Perugia – gave her parents a photo-album of pictures they'd taken with her. Her family were stunned to see more than 500 people come to the church, with friends flying in from as far away as Canada and Japan. Stephanie read a poem she had written in Meredith's memory. Her brother Lyle made the congregation laugh as he told some funny anecdotes about Meredith. Her friends and teachers would guarantee that Meredith was a bad timekeeper, Lyle said: 'You could set your watch by her, granted that she would always be twenty minutes late. That's just the way she was. It was a family trait.'

A choir from Meredith's old school sang a requiem and mourners then listened to her favourite song, 'With or Without You' by the rock band U2. Meredith's other brother, called John like their father, read out a passage from the Bible:

> *And I saw a new heaven and a new earth: for the first heaven and the first earth were passed away; and there was no more sea.*
>
> *And I John saw the holy city, new Jerusalem, coming down from God out of heaven, prepared as a bride adorned for her husband.*
>
> *And I heard a great voice out of heaven saying . . . God shall wipe away all tears from their eyes; and there shall be no more death, neither sorrow, nor crying, neither shall there be any more pain: for the former things are passed away.*
>
> *. . . He that overcometh shall inherit all things; and I will be his God, and he shall be my son.* (Revelation 21)

The passage which Meredith's brother read out stopped just short of the following:

> *But the fearful, and unbelieving, and the abominable, and murderers, and whoremongers, and sorcerers, and idolaters, and all liars,*

shall have their part in the lake which burneth with fire and brim-
stone: which is the second death.

The Rev Colin Boswell, vicar of Croydon, said after the service: 'It is important at a funeral like this that we try to remember
things that are happy and good, or else only evil and not very creative things take over and we have got to try and rise above that.'

Meredith was buried at Mitcham Road Cemetery, near
Croydon.

Some time later, Amy, Robyn and Sophie had lunch with
Meredith's parents – they'd had little chance to talk at the funeral.
The three wanted to answer any questions Arline and John might
have for them.

'If you want to ask us anything . . .' they gently prompted Arline
and John.

But Meredith's parents didn't have any questions; they just
talked about their dead daughter, telling stories about what she'd
been like as a little girl.

Sophie kept in touch, especially with Arline. When Sophie told
her to take care, Arline replied gently: 'You look after yourself. I'm
sorry for what you've been through.'

Not a day passed without Sophie thinking of Meredith. The first
thing she did every morning was to check the news by going
on Google and typing the name of her dead friend. Depressed,
Sophie spent most of her days on the sofa in her sitting room. Day
in, day out, there was nothing she wanted to do. Bristol University
allowed her to put her studies on hold, and she simply stayed at
her home, east of London.

One thought tormented Sophie, and she talked about it again
and again with Meredith's other friends Amy and Robyn: was there
anything they could have done that last night to prevent Meredith
being killed? Sophie, Amy and Robyn all blamed themselves.

'Why didn't we tell Meredith to stay with us that night? Why didn't we ask her who was in the cottage?' they asked each other. 'Why didn't I call her to see if she got home OK?' Sophie said.

And, for Sophie, the hardest question of them all: 'Why didn't I walk her all the way home?' But Sophie had never walked Meredith all the way home after a night out; she'd accompanied her to the cottage only once, when Meredith had wanted to change her shoes before going clubbing.

At the end of the day, Sophie reasoned, why should that last night have been any different? Rationally, Sophie knew that Meredith's death wasn't her fault, but the sense of guilt haunted her.

33

Shortly before 11 a.m. in a cramped room of the Capanne prison, Mignini sat down opposite Amanda and her lawyers Ghirga and Dalla Vedova, and began questioning her in a steady, neutral tone. Amanda had agreed to be interrogated – her lawyers insisted she had nothing to hide – and the prosecutor had carefully drafted a long list of questions, which he expected would take all day to get through.

Mignini had thought long and hard about the best way to tackle Amanda. Her greatest strength, he thought, was her intelligence; her greatest weakness was her fragility. He started by asking Amanda about her return to the cottage on the morning of 2 November, when she took a shower despite finding the front door open and blood in the bathroom. 'Were the doors of the rooms open or closed?' Mignini asked.

Speaking in English with an interpreter translating what she said into Italian, Amanda replied in as steady a tone as the prosecutor's. 'No, they were all closed. Filomena's was closed, Meredith's was closed and Laura's, I think, was a bit ajar,' she said.

'Did you try to open them, to knock?'

'No.'

'Why didn't you try? There was the blood, the open front door . . .'

'I didn't see any reason to.'

'I beg your pardon, but you find the front door open, you find the blood in the bathroom and you take a shower all the same. If you'll allow me this is rather strange, there could have been some-body dangerous in the house,' Mignini insisted.

'In my whole life nothing remotely like this ever happened to me; I didn't expect to go home and find something wrong.'

Mignini pressed on: 'You found the excrement in the bath-room, which was a sign that an outsider was there, but you didn't feel the need to call the police?'

'No, because if you go into the house and there's nothing miss-ing usually that means no outsider came in.'

'Yes, I understand but there was the blood . . .'

'There was only a little . . .'

'Did you check there was nothing missing?'

'I didn't really check, but the computer was still in my room and that was a big clue, and in the rest of the flat everything was fine.'

Mignini next tried to pick apart Amanda's account of how she had arrived at Raffaele's flat at about midday, but didn't imme-diately mention what she'd discovered at the cottage. She helped Raffaele clean up the water which had leaked from the kitchen sink the previous evening, and it was only after about an hour, when they sat down to have breakfast, that Amanda told him.

'What did you tell Raffaele when you arrived at his flat?' Mignini asked.

'At first I didn't tell him anything because I didn't know what to say to him. I didn't know yet whether there was something strange . . .'

'What did you think? Can you please explain this to me, because quite honestly it's a version which . . .' Mignini trailed off.

'I was trying to understand what it all meant . . . At first I didn't tell Raffaele because I didn't know if there was something really serious . . . I'd realised there was something strange but I didn't know whether it was serious.'

'But . . . at one point you told me "blood, open door, excrement etc. I became worried" and now you tell me "I wasn't worried" . . . I mean, really, explain yourself because it's not at all clear.'

'It seemed strange to me but not that worrying or alarming because the flat was exactly as it should be except for those small things,' Amanda said. Her first words to Raffaele about this were: 'Hey, listen to the strange things that happened to me this morning.' He told her to call her flatmates.

Amanda said she had called her flatmate Filomena from Raffaele's flat. But Mignini pointed out that according to Filomena, Amanda had told her in that first phone call that she planned to call Raffaele – which meant she had called Filomena before talking to him.

'What I remember of that morning is that the first time I called Filomena I was at Raffaele's flat . . . So what may have happened is that I've forgotten I called Filomena or that we didn't manage to communicate because she doesn't speak English well and I don't speak Italian well,' Amanda said.

Mignini now pressed Amanda on what she had known of Meredith's death on the day the body was discovered. Amanda said neither she nor Raffaele, who were in the sitting room at the time, had seen into Meredith's bedroom when the door was kicked open.

'I only remember Filomena saying: "A foot! A foot!" We were all pushed outside, I sat down on the ground and I couldn't . . . I was in shock and I didn't understand what had happened,' Amanda said.

At the police station that evening, Meredith's friend Natalie had said: 'Let's hope she didn't suffer.' Mignini asked Amanda why she'd said: 'What do you think? They cut her throat Natalie. She fucking bled to death!'

Amanda replied: 'The police had told me that her throat had been cut and as far as I know it's terrible; I've heard it's an awful way of dying.'

'But we found that out afterwards, not straight away.'

'The police told me her throat had been cut,' Amanda insisted. She said it had 'probably' been a police officer who acted as an interpreter.

Mignini turned next to Amanda's accusation against Patrick. The prosecutor was convinced that Amanda had wanted to conceal from herself her own role in the murder, and that she had done so again in her writing – just as she had done in covering Meredith's body with the quilt. Mignini asked Amanda why she had accused Patrick of murdering Meredith after having sex with her in the cottage – a charge she had then gone back on. Mignini reminded Amanda that she had cried when she made the accusation.

'I was scared, I was confused, I'd been with the police for hours. I thought they were protecting me but instead they were putting me under pressure and they were threatening me,' Amanda replied.

'Yes, go on.'

'The reason I thought of Patrick was that the police were shouting at me about Patrick, they kept talking about the message, that I'd sent a message to Patrick. That was the worst experience of my life. I was never as confused as I was then.'

Mignini was convinced the real reason was that when the police mentioned Patrick, Amanda had seen it as an opportunity to accuse him and protect herself.

'But in the text you wrote afterwards, before going to prison, you didn't deny that accusation. You write that you find it difficult to distinguish between a dream and reality, I think you write: "I still see this image in front of me": you hear Meredith's screams and you put your hands over your ears. Why do you have this image? Why the hands over the ears? Why the scream?'

Amanda's lawyers had remained virtually silent but now one of them intervened. 'But she says she was very confused. She was under a lot of stress,' the lawyer said.

'Yes, I imagined these things. I was so scared and confused that I tried to imagine what could have happened. The police told me I probably couldn't remember very well. So I thought of what might be another answer and so I imagined it,' Amanda said.

Mignini was convinced that Amanda hadn't 'imagined' the moment of the murder – she had lived it and it had shocked her, which was why she had broken down in tears in front of the police. He decided to keep pressing Amanda, in the hope that she might again break under pressure and even confess.

'But you made no mention of Patrick in your previous statements, on the second of November nor on the third, so how come this Patrick emerges all of a sudden?' he asked.

'They were saying to me: "Why did you send this message to Patrick, this message to Patrick?" ' Amanda replied.

'It's true you sent messages to each other a few hours before the crime so it's normal that the police should want to know why, and what it meant. But why did you make such an accusation?'

'Because I thought it could be true,' Amanda said.

Mignini was so stunned by her reply all he could do was repeat it. 'It could be true?' he asked.

Amanda's lawyer Ghirga intervened, the voices overlapping each other. 'Why?' he asked.

Amanda: 'When I was there feeling confused—'

Mignini, irritated by Ghirga's meddling: 'No, no, excuse me. The lawyers can address me but the suspect—'

Ghirga, to Mignini: 'But you didn't ask a question.'

Mignini ignored the lawyer: 'It could have been true. Which means—'

Ghirga, interrupting again: 'You didn't ask a question.'

Mignini: 'What? I'm asking the question now.'

Ghirga: 'Well, ask it then.'

Mignini: 'What does it mean, how could it have been true? What were you talking about?'

Ghirga interrupted him again, and the question remained unanswered.

After yet another clash between Mignini and Ghirga, which Amanda followed with her head bowed, looking from one to the other and back again, the prosecutor managed to ask her: 'Why did you imagine it?'

Amanda hesitated. 'Why? . . . Because I was under stress. I was scared, it had been so many hours and it was the middle of the night . . . And they were telling me I was guilty . . .' Her voice began to tremble.

Mignini: 'Who was saying it? Who was guilty?'

'After hours—' Amanda said and then broke off. She brought her hands up to her head and covered her ears – that gesture again, Mignini thought to himself – and started to cry.

As Amanda wiped the tears away with her fingers, Mignini immediately made a point of requesting that her tears be noted for the record. Amanda continued to cry but he pressed on: 'Why did you accuse Patrick and not anyone else? How many people did you know who could have—'

Amanda, her voice still wavering: 'Because they were shouting Patrick's name at me.'

'What were the police telling you?'

Amanda, still in tears but in a steadier, forceful tone: 'The police were saying to me: "We know you were in that house, we know you were at home," and just before I said Patrick's name, someone was showing me the message I sent him.'

'But that's normal. I beg your pardon, I beg your pardon . . . the police wanted to know about the relationship between you and Patrick. And that's normal,' Mignini said.

'I couldn't understand why they insisted I was lying, they kept saying I was lying.'

Mignini noted aloud, for the second time, that Amanda was crying: 'But why did you accuse . . . ? You're crying again a long time, I mention it for the record, I mention it for the record, you've been crying for ten minutes. Why did you accuse a person whom you say today is innocent? You told us earlier "it could be true"; what does that mean?'

Ghirga: 'Can we suspend this please?'

Mignini: 'Eh . . .'

Ghirga, addressing Mignini: 'We request a suspension . . . she's calm, you say she's crying but it doesn't seem so to us.'

Mignini: 'I mention it for the record because I saw the tears, she cried and we could all hear her.'

Mignini agreed to suspend the interrogation for a few moments. When it restarted, Ghirga asked for permission for him and Amanda's other lawyers to speak with their client privately for ten minutes. Mignini tried to brush him aside, saying the lawyers could talk to her after the interrogation was over.

But Ghirga then played his last remaining card: he asked Mignini to ask Amanda whether she wanted to stop the interrogation completely, as was her right. Mignini had no alternative but to put the question to her.

'I prefer not to answer any more,' Amanda replied.

For the record, Mignini noted that she had stopped the interrogation – after almost five hours – at her lawyer's suggestion.

Mignini was still seething as he strode out of the prison. He had never carried out such a tense interrogation. He was convinced Amanda had decided to grab the lifeline thrown by her lawyer and stop the interrogation to get herself out of a tight spot. The prosecutor always attached a great deal of importance to the body language of suspects he confronted – it revealed things they would never want to admit – and what with her tears and that gesture of covering her ears with her hands, Amanda was an open book. The gesture meant she was trying to blot out the screams she really *had* heard, he was sure of that. She was desperate to forget what had happened at the cottage – she was trying to deny to herself that it ever happened – but it kept coming back to her and her tears were tears of frustration.

How could Amanda say that the possibility that she was at the cottage and heard Meredith's screams as someone killed her 'could be true'? Simply admitting this was a confession that she had been at the scene of the crime. Mignini was convinced that her decision to stop the interrogation was a further sign of her guilt.

Ghirga was just as angry after the interrogation as the prosecutor was. Amanda had simply wanted to defend herself by answering questions but she'd been prevented from telling her story calmly. The exchange had become so tense he'd felt compelled to interrupt the interrogation.

34

For the first time in more than a month, Mignini returned to the cottage on a cold morning to watch a fresh survey by the Rome biologist Patrizia Stefanoni and her forensic team. Amanda's lawyer Ghirga, Raffaele's lawyer Maori and the prosecutor climbed into a Volkswagen camper van parked outside the cottage. The police had set up a big flat-screen monitor, which would allow them to follow the forensic team on a live relay without entering the flat. Napoleoni however, dressed in white overalls like her forensic colleagues, walked inside with them.

As the first images of the flat appeared on the screen, the two defence lawyers began to protest loudly. Why on earth, they asked, was Meredith's mattress no longer on her bed but now on its side in the kitchen? And why was Meredith's room itself a scene of chaos, as they called it? Clothes were crumpled up on Meredith's bed, both cupboard doors had been dismantled and were now leaning against a wall and – most shocking of all for Ghirga – the cushion found under the body with the bloody imprint of Rudy's palm had been stuffed inside the cupboard. Mignini dismissed the lawyers' protests as theatrics; detectives were notorious for making a mess of crime scenes once forensic police had done their job.

Standing just outside Meredith's bedroom, Napoleoni watched in silence as officers slowly searched it. Suddenly, one of them, pointing at the floor, exclaimed: 'Ah, here's the bra clasp.'

After no fewer than forty-six days, the clasp from Meredith's bra that had first been spotted by the Perugia forensic police on the day after the murder, then overlooked by their Rome colleagues, had at last been found. The clasp was under a rug near the desk, a little over a yard away from where it had first been found on the day after the murder under the cushion placed below Meredith's body. Stefanoni seized the clasp, examined it briefly and then put it away carefully in an evidence bag.

At her office in Rome some time later, Stefanoni found DNA traces of Raffaele and Meredith on the clasp, and DNA traces of Rudy on a bra strap, close to where it had been cut from the rest of the bra. The clasp was to become one of the key – and most fought-over – pieces of evidence in the Kercher case.

In the eyes of the investigators, the forensic team found more new evidence placing both Raffaele and Amanda at the scene of the crime after spraying the floor with Luminol, a chemical that gives a striking blue glow when it reacts with the iron in red blood cells and bleach among other substances; the chemical can detect traces which are invisible to the naked eye.

Experts attributed four bare footprints allegedly stained with blood – they spoke of 'probable identity' – to Amanda and Raffaele. Amanda's were in her bedroom, pointing to her door, and in the corridor in front of Meredith's room, pointing towards it. Raffaele's were on a bathmat in bathroom next to Meredith's room, and in the corridor outside her room, also pointing towards it. A shoe print on a cushion under Meredith's body was seen as being of a woman's small shoe size, possibly Amanda's.

On the floor in Filomena's room, the Luminol test revealed two bloodstains. One had Meredith's DNA; the other, closer to the doorway, had both Meredith's and Amanda's DNA.

That afternoon Francesco Camana, in charge of the ballistics section of the Rome forensic police, carefully measured and photographed the twenty-seven traces of blood he found on one of the cupboard doors, which would enable him to carry out a Bloodstain Pattern Analysis with the aim of establishing Meredith's position at the time she was stabbed.

In a report he sent Mignini later, Camana established with what he said was a certainty of more than 65 per cent that, based on the bloodstains on the cupboard, Meredith's neck at the time the blow or blows were inflicted was some sixteen inches from the floor, some twelve inches from the wall and some thirteen inches from the cupboard.

Camana came up with three alternative positions Meredith could have been in when she was stabbed. In the first, Meredith lay on her back, her elbows on the floor and her chest raised, with her head back and turned towards the window; it suggested she was moving backwards in a defensive position – her attacker facing her.

In the second, Meredith lay face downwards, her hands and pelvis on the floor, her chest raised and her face turned towards the cupboard, before falling to the floor when she was knifed – her attacker behind her.

The third scenario, Camana wrote, explained better than the other two some of the traces found on the floor: Meredith was face down as in the previous scenario, but this time she was on her hands and knees.

Camana deduced that traces on the floor indicated that Meredith had dragged herself, or had been dragged, to the point where she was found. The many bloodstains on her left hand, especially on her index finger, indicated either that the hand was already close to her neck when the fatal wound was inflicted, or that she had touched it soon afterwards.

Spurts of blood in the middle of Meredith's chest and other bloodstains indicated that she was wearing her blue sweatshirt – it was more bloody on the right side, corresponding to the fatal wound, than on the left – and white T-shirt at the moment the wound was inflicted. The T-shirt and sweatshirt had been rolled up towards her shoulders.

24 December 2007

On the morning of Christmas Eve, Ghirga left his family to go and see Amanda in prison. Usually calm and smiling when he came, she broke down and cried, talking to him about her family: it was the first Christmas she had ever spent away from them. Ghirga tried to give her something to hope for, telling her that he would soon be making a new appeal for her release, this time to the Supreme Court, Italy's highest.

Amanda's mother Edda also spent a tearful Christmas. 'If I didn't have [Amanda's sister] Deanna and the rest of my family, I don't know that I would get out of bed,' Edda confided. Going to work got her mind off 'it' for a little while but the nights were the worst: 'I don't sleep, I sleep in chunks. A few hours and then I'm up, another few hours and then I'm up again. I was always very fit – I played for two soccer teams – and my blood pressure was fine but now I have to take medicine to keep my pressure down. I lost twenty-five pounds in two months, I have this constant sick feeling in my stomach because my child is suffering and there's nothing I can do about it.'

Amanda cried again early in the New Year when Curt went to see her. He held her in his arms, doing his best to calm her down but she kept crying for half the hour-long visit. Over and over again, Amanda said she couldn't understand why she was in there when she hadn't done anything. Guards looked in repeatedly as she wept and when the visit ended, several of them – Curt noticed one had more stripes on his uniform than the others – came up and asked him: 'What can we do for her?'

They took Amanda into another room nearby, shutting the door on Curt and leaving him on his own. That had never happened before. Curt thought angrily to himself: 'Do they think they're going to get her "confession"?'

After a short Christmas break spent with their families, Mignini and Napoleoni pursued their investigation. A police officer

called Fabio D'Astolto, whom Amanda had said was 'probably' the officer who told her Meredith's throat had been cut,
said that all he knew when he was acting as her interpreter
was that the body of an English girl had been found at her
home. It proved impossible to find an officer to back Amanda's
version.

During a new search of Raffaele's flat, detectives seized an
inventory of the contents drawn up by his landlady. The list of
cutlery included the knife, which investigators believed was the
murder weapon. Mignini immediately thought this explained why
the knife had been placed back in the drawer after the murder – its
absence would have been noticed.

In late January, a thirty-three-year-old Albanian farmhand,
Hekuran Kokomani, asked to give a statement to Mignini.
Kokomani told the prosecutor that on Halloween or on the
evening of 1 November – he remembered it was raining – he had
been driving past the cottage when he saw what looked like a
black bag in the middle of the road. Kokomani sounded his horn
but the 'bag' didn't move. He moved forward slowly and touched
the 'bag', which he now realised was actually a young man and
woman who suddenly stood up. The woman had a black scarf
around her neck that partly covered her face, and the man wore
some kind of hat.

The man stood in front of the car while the woman walked
towards him, threatening him with a long knife which she held
up in both her hands, shouting in Italian: 'Get out of here or I'll
show you!' The knife was about twelve inches long, and the blade
an inch wide.

Kokomani lowered his window and told them to fuck off.

'Forget it; what can a girl do to you?' the man said.

Further ahead and outside the cottage, Kokomani saw a young
black man. He heard the woman tell the other two not to show
their faces but he had already seen all three of them. Kokomani
recalled that the next day was a holiday and that he slept late. He
recognised Amanda and Raffaele 'without a shadow of a doubt'

when he saw their photographs in the newspaper a few days later, and Rudy too when his picture also appeared. He had failed to speak out before now because he was scared of 'getting caught up in such a serious thing'.

35

The young local journalist Antioco Fois kept digging for a story for his paper in the area around the cottage – his own home was only a stone's throw from the university – and in January 2008 he struck lucky. A shopkeeper told him that Antonio Curatolo, a tramp who spent much of his days, and most nights, on a bench on Piazza Grimana, had apparently been heard muttering after the arrests: 'If those two get off, I'll talk. I saw them that evening.'

Fois had no difficulty finding Curatolo. He knew the tramp by sight, and spotted him sitting on his usual bench by the news stand on Piazza Grimana. Sixty-one, with a scrawny, weather-beaten face, flowing white hair, long beard and sharp, black eyes, Curatolo had lived as a tramp in Perugia for the past two decades. He was a cheerful figure, who liked to chat with students who stopped by his bench in the square.

The morning Fois went up to him for the first time, Curatolo was dressed warmly against the cold, a gaily coloured woollen hat on his head. Next to him on the bench was a big plastic bag full of his belongings, among them the news magazines he liked to read from cover to cover. Fois introduced himself and offered Curatolo a cigarette. They started talking.

Fois waited a while before putting his question. 'Look, I'm working on this awful story, the English girl who was killed. Did you see or hear anything that evening?'

Curatolo replied without any hesitation: 'Well, I saw the two of them.'

'Which two?'

'Those two – Amanda and Raffaele.'

Fois worried this was too easy. 'Are you sure it was them?' he asked.

'Yes, I'm sure. I'd seen them around before and I recognised them in the papers afterwards. I was sitting here on this bench, I was smoking. They were hugging and kissing each other. It was at night, between eleven and midnight.'

'But didn't the police ask you about the night of the murder when they went round the neighbourhood?'

'Yes, the *carabinieri* asked me the morning after whether I'd noticed anything strange. But I only realised what I'd seen when I saw the pictures of Amanda and Raffaele in the paper a few days later.'

Wary of irritating Curatolo with a police-style interrogation, Fois stopped questioning him; he could always ask for more details another time. Fois reported back to Giuseppe Castellini, his editor at the *Giornale dell'Umbria*, and started to tell him that a witness had seen Amanda and Raffaele near the cottage on the night of the murder. Castellini's eyes shone at the news, but he looked rather disappointed when Fois told him the witness was a tramp.

'OK, here's what we'll do: we'll bring him to Mignini so he can give a statement. That way the prosecutor can establish whether he's reliable or not. In the meantime, go back to him, ask him all the questions you can think of, see if he contradicts himself,' Castellini said.

Castellini decided to hold off publishing until Curatolo had met Mignini. The editor thought it was his duty as a citizen to contribute to the investigation. Besides, if the newspaper published the story the tramp might get scared by the publicity, deny it all and refuse to meet Mignini.

Fois went back to Curatolo again and again and the tramp gradually told him the full story as they sat side by side on 'his' bench. He'd seen Amanda and Raffaele until sometime after 11 p.m., when the last buses taking people to nightclubs outside Perugia had gone. The pair sat on a low wall in the corner of the basketball court closest to the cottage. They talked, hugged and kissed each other. Every so often, one of them would get up, walk to the railing a few yards away and look towards the gate of the cottage.

'I had the impression they were checking on something,' he said. Their manner was sometimes agitated. They left shortly before midnight, walking down the staircase that leads to Via della Pergola and the gate of the cottage a few yards across the street. Curatolo himself left the square a short time after.

'How do you know it was the night of the murder?' Fois asked.

'Because it was a holiday, the buses on the square were waiting to take kids to the nightclubs,' Curatolo said.

'But there are buses on other nights too,' Fois pointed out.

'Yes, but I remember that the next day the *carabinieri* asked me if I'd seen something strange the previous night,' Curatolo said.

Fois made some checks on Curatolo. He found out that the tramp had paid several visits to a centre for drug addicts just behind the university and sometimes got drunk. But Fois was convinced that he'd seen what he described. Together with his editor Castellini, who wanted to make sure for himself that Curatolo was reliable and not just a crank, Fois kept on going back to talk to him.

When Castellini, impressed by the precision of Curatolo's account after a few meetings, was satisfied that the tramp was speaking the truth, he told him: 'I believe you. But you've got to talk to the prosecutor, it might be important.'

Curatolo grimaced. 'I want to stay out of this. Besides, I'm a tramp. No one will believe me.'

'If you tell the truth, no one can prove you wrong. It's important: a girl was killed,' Castellini insisted.

But Curatolo feared for his own skin: 'I could get killed. I'm out here on the street; it's easy to kill me.'

Castellini reassured him: 'If you talk to the prosecutor, you'll become an official witness. That will protect you more than if there's just a rumour flying around, as there is now. Making a statement to the prosecutor would be like taking out an insurance policy.'

But Curatolo was worried, and it took almost a month to persuade him. 'Amanda and Raffaele say they weren't there, but a girl died and I saw them,' Curatolo said when he agreed to go at last. He then asked how long it would take.

Fois pulled his leg: 'What's the problem Antonio, have you got a business appointment?'

Castellini tipped off Mignini, and they agreed Curatolo would go to him on a Saturday, because the prosecutor's offices would be almost deserted then. The editor told Mignini the story was ready to run in his newspaper, but agreed to wait until Curatolo had talked to him.

2 February 2008

On the day Curatolo was due to meet the prosecutor, Castellini, Fois and the paper's crime reporter, Francesca Bene, spent much of a rainy, cold morning looking for him, afraid the tramp had pulled out at the last minute. They finally found him in a shelter for down-and-outs; Curatolo complained he hadn't slept the previous night and was aching all over.

The journalists drove Curatolo to Mignini's office. They first watched in amazement and then laughed as Curatolo kept setting off the alarm, obliged to pass several times through the metal detector in the lobby of the prosecutors' building, and making a small pile of the metallic belongings he reluctantly pulled from the many pockets of his big army surplus jacket: a penknife, keyrings, even a couple of chargers for mobile phones and other odds and ends. Curatolo became more and more irritated each time the detector beeped. Then a security guard asked him to take his boots off because they had metal buckles.

'*Basta!* I'm leaving!' Curatolo burst out.

The journalists managed to persuade him to stay; Castellini worried about the tramp's smelly feet. The problem was solved when it was agreed an assistant of Mignini's would accompany Curatolo upstairs, with his boots on.

Shortly before midday, Curatolo sat down opposite the prosecutor, ready at last. Asked for his address, he replied without hesitation: 'I live in Piazza Grimana in Perugia and I sleep in the open, near the news stand.' Curatolo said that on the evening of 1 November he'd seen on Piazza Grimana a young couple he had seen several times before at the bar on the square.

'Every so often, Raffaele would lean on the iron railing and look out towards Via della Pergola, as if he was waiting for someone. The girl would also look out from the railing, and then they would go back and sit on the wall,' Curatolo said.

He didn't see the couple leave, but they'd gone by the time he left at about 11.30 p.m. or midnight to go and sleep in a nearby park. That evening, he also noticed young men and women wearing masks or dressed in black costumes with several women dressed as witches. The next day, *carabinieri* officers came to Piazza Grimana asking if anyone had seen anything related to Meredith's murder the previous night. Curatolo told them he hadn't; he recognised the couple as Amanda and Raffaele only when he saw their pictures in the newspaper a few days later.

After Curatolo had finished, an assistant of Mignini's went up to Castellini and asked him to hold off publishing anything about the tramp for a couple of months; the prosecutor needed to check his account and an article could jeopardise that. The request frustrated Castellini – it was a first-class story, and it was exclusive – but he promised to wait.

Wary after seeing much of his work leak to the media over the past three months, Mignini formally classified Curatolo's statement as secret, and locked it in his safe. He then reached to the shelf behind his desk for an air-spray and sprayed some disinfectant in the air, which had grown heavy with the tramp's smell.

A month after Curatolo met the prosecutor, Castellini was having lunch in a restaurant when one of Rudy's lawyers went up to his table and asked: 'What's this about a tramp? Is it true?'

Swearing inwardly, Castellini mumbled something incomprehensible and rushed back to his office. He called Mignini and told him word had leaked out; he would publish the story the next morning.

The editor splashed the story across the front page of the next day's *Giornale dell'Umbria*. The headline read 'HERE IS THE SUPER-WITNESS.' A smaller one proclaimed 'The Perugia Murder' – there was no need to specify which one – and with more than a touch of pride: '*We tracked him down.*'

36

Amanda's first winter in prison was weighing heavily on her. From early March onwards, she complained repeatedly to Edda and Curt about one of her cellmates, Rosa, who at twenty-three had already served five years in jail and had another seventeen to go. Rosa was more lesbian than heterosexual, Amanda said, and when they were first assigned a cell together Rosa had thought she was too. Rosa had made 'advances' to her, but Amanda had rejected them.

Rosa was obsessed with cleanliness and made Amanda clean everything in the cell, even parts of the washbasin no one could see – for six hours on one Saturday and for another five hours the next day. As Amanda scrubbed away, Rosa would follow her every move, finishing off with a sponge. Rosa even insisted on cleaning the walls and the windows, and Amanda showed her parents the red blotches on her hand she had as a result of all the cleaning. Even when she just washed her hands, Rosa made her wash the basin immediately. To survive life in jail, Amanda explained, Rosa had convinced herself that the prison was her home.

Amanda had her own strategy for coping with life in prison. She was studying five foreign languages – German, Italian, French, Chinese and Russian – trying to spend forty minutes every day on each. She had chosen Chinese because she wanted to use it to communicate with her Seattle boyfriend DJ – she often wrote to him – who was learning it on his long stay in China. Her sister Deanna had started Russian before Meredith's death, and Amanda wanted them to have a language they could talk together 'that no one else would understand'.

Amanda said she felt exhausted. She tried to stay in shape doing exercises in her cell – using bottles full of water as weights when she swung her arms – but she was putting on weight all the same. She often had dizzy spells and her vision was getting blurred, so much so she had trouble seeing people some distance away. She had blood tests done but the results were normal. Curt told his daughter she must be straining her eyes doing so much reading. She had just turned vegetarian, so he urged her to eat more proteins, such as eggs and beans.

When in mid-March detectives searched her cell, seizing some of her clothes, her Italian notebooks and a few books – a novel of the fantasy Dragonlance series, two romance novels, Yann Martel's *Life of Pi*, about a lost boy's wanderings and animals slaughtering each other on a lifeboat, and a comic called *I'm Ready for my Movie Contract* – Amanda lost her temper and wept with rage. She told Curt afterwards that she'd felt like shouting '*Vaffanculo!*' (Fuck off!) at them, but had thought better of it. What mattered to her wasn't so much the things they'd taken away, but the feeling that it was her life they were taking away.

A week later, when Edda visited on her own, Amanda told her about the service marking the Last Supper which she'd attended in the prison chapel. She was stunned when it came to the ritual washing the feet and the Bishop of Perugia chose to wash hers and even kissed them – she was a nobody. She had volunteered for the washing of feet part when the chaplain Father Saulo mentioned it to her before the service, even though she'd said she wasn't a Catholic. She had played the guitar during the ceremony.

25 March 2008

Amanda complained to Edda that Rosa had been in a foul mood all week, forcing her to clean the cell on Easter Sunday, even though they'd already cleaned it the previous day. Rosa had criticised Amanda for being cold and unfriendly, insisting she wanted to be her friend.

But Amanda had no intention of becoming friends with anyone, especially inside the prison, because she didn't trust anyone. The other prisoners must think she was unfriendly, but she didn't care what they thought: all she wanted was to mind her own business. She never chatted with anyone and she just stayed on her own, crying or writing. She was so sick of prison.

Amanda told Edda how much she enjoyed writing and wanted to write a book one day. She realised it would be difficult to promote but she was sure someone would do it for her. She complained that the police had seized some notes of hers.

Amanda suddenly put her head back and looked up at the ceiling, mocking any hidden listener: 'I'm innocent. Thanks very much. I'm innocent, I'm innocent, I'm innocent.' She then pulled a face.

26 March 2008

Rudy proved very talkative when Mignini questioned him at the Capanne prison. Asked about his attraction for Amanda, he stunned the prosecutor by saying: 'Yes, I'd like to – sorry about this – do her.' Mignini was amazed that Rudy had used the present tense.

Early on in the questioning, he again denied ever meeting Raffaele. He was anxious to correct a mistake he had made before a judge, when he'd said that he'd kissed Meredith at the home of Spanish friends of his on the night of Halloween. The truth was, he told Mignini now, that he'd kissed her at the Domus nightclub later that night.

'We talked and talked. I gave her a kiss but it wasn't a passionate kiss, it was a so-so kiss, and afterwards I told her how much I liked her and I asked if we could meet the next day and she said yes,' Rudy said.

At about 9.20 p.m. the next evening, 1 November, Rudy said, he'd met Meredith, who was wearing jeans and a white top, at the cottage. He was drinking some fruit juice in the sitting room when he heard her complaining angrily about something down the corridor. He went to see what the matter was and she pointed at a drawer in her bedside table, saying money she had put there had disappeared.

Meredith started to accuse Amanda. 'That bloody drug addict, I can't bear her anymore,' she exclaimed. She was sick of Amanda bringing men home.

Rudy tried to calm her down with a joke. 'Don't get angry or you'll get wrinkles,' he said.

The two went to sit down in the sitting room and Meredith gradually calmed down. Rudy started to talk about himself, telling her that he didn't know his mother from Adam but that he considered himself lucky 'because I've got so many mothers'.

Meredith looked sad. 'You've got lots of mothers but I've got only one and I'm scared of losing her,' she said.

'What do you mean?' Rudy asked.

Meredith told him about her mother's illness, but Rudy's English wasn't perfect and he didn't fully understand what she said; he understood that her mother had a cancer of the kidney.

After talking for a half hour or an hour, Rudy leant forward and kissed Meredith on the mouth. They caressed each other, but stopped when Meredith asked him if he had a condom. He didn't have one, and they stopped. Rudy went to the bathroom – he had eaten a kebab earlier and needed to go to the toilet. Rudy was still there when he heard the doorbell ring.

He heard Meredith call out, 'Who is it?' He then heard Meredith say in English in a tense tone of voice: 'We need to talk.'

A woman's voice – Rudy thought it was Amanda's – answered in English: 'What's happening?'

This was the first time Rudy had accused Amanda.

Rudy didn't follow what Meredith and the other woman said next. He took his iPod out of his pocket, put the headphones on and listened at a high volume to one hip hop song, then another, and then another. The third song was halfway through when he heard a scream over the music. He rushed out of the bathroom without stopping to flush the toilet.

The light in the sitting room had been turned off but he saw a man with his back to him standing by Meredith's room, where the light was still on. There was no sign of anyone else in the flat.

'What's happened?' Rudy asked. He looked in and glimpsed Meredith on the floor between the bedside table and the cupboard. The man turned quickly and Rudy saw he had a knife in his left hand.

Rudy instinctively raised his right hand up to protect himself and backed away but the man came after him, jabbing at Rudy's hands with his knife. Rudy hadn't done up his trousers properly in his haste to rush out of the bathroom; they suddenly dropped down and he fell to the floor near the fridge but then managed to grab a chair and throw it at the attacker, who fled from the cottage. The attack lasted just a few seconds – Rudy had previously said that it lasted some five minutes.

Asked to describe the attacker, Rudy said he was white, a bit shorter than he was and probably the same age, with sharp cheekbones and a slight double chin. He wore a white woollen hat.

As the man fled, Rudy heard him say in Italian, apparently to someone else: 'He's black. I've found a black guy, I've found the culprit. Let's go.' He heard the sound of 'more than one person' walking on the gravel in the drive, went to a window and recognised Amanda who was running away.

Rudy went back to Meredith. Still wearing the jeans and the white top, and shoes, she lay on her back on the floor with her face turned upwards, bleeding from the left side of her neck.

'I'd never seen anything like that in my life. My first thought was to go to the bathroom and fetch a towel. I put it on her neck but it got soaked very quickly and I went back and got another one and held that against her neck,' Rudy said.

Meredith was still moving and repeating something again and again, but blood was coming out of her mouth. All Rudy could make out was 'af . . .' His hands were covered in blood and he tried to write the letters on the wall above the bedside table.

Asked to describe the state of the room he said it was tidy; the bed was made, with a red quilt on top of it.

'When did you decide to leave?' Mignini asked.

Rudy stumbled repeatedly as he answered: 'When Meredith didn't have ... at a certain point she ... as I don't know how to define it ... she had a bit like ... at a certain point she sort of passed away.'

He had no idea what to do. Should he run out into the street and scream for help? 'I panicked because I said to myself: "No one's going to believe me." My hands were dirty with blood, I'd kneeled down ... when I put the cushion down, part of my left foot, part of my left knee had got soaked because I'd crouched down close to her, I was trying to help her.' He then ran out of the house to his own home.

On the following day, he decided to go and see an aunt, who had raised him as a child, in the city of Lecco on Lake Como; he would tell her everything. He got as far as Milan, but then took the wrong train and ended up first in Austria, and then in Germany.

As the questioning drew to an end after three and a half hours, Rudy said he had one last thing to say: 'I'm to blame because I could have called the ambulance, I could have gone out into the street and screamed and called someone. I say just this: if I have to do God knows how many years in prison because I didn't save someone's life I'll do it, no problem. But I don't see why I should do even one day in prison because people think I killed someone.'

Mignini didn't believe a word of Rudy's account. For one thing, Meredith's friends, who were with her the whole time she was at the Domus on Halloween, said that no coloured man had approached her there. The prosecutor believed that Rudy was still very attracted to Amanda, and suspected that on the night of the murder he'd been more interested in Amanda than in Meredith.

And yet Mignini felt sorry for Rudy, whom he saw as the most helpless of the three accused. Amanda and Raffaele had their families behind them; Rudy had no one. He'd been abandoned by his family and had a wretched life. The prosecutor hoped that Rudy would one day come clean and tell the whole truth, but so far he'd done nothing to help himself by continually changing his story.

37

28 March 2008

Part of Rudy's story, and his accusation against Amanda, was swiftly leaked to the media. Two days after Rudy talked to the prosecutor, Amanda confided to the chaplain Father Saulo that she felt upset and indignant after what Rudy had said.

That was understandable, Father Saulo said, adding: 'You at least have been sincere!'

Amanda replied firmly: 'Yes, because I haven't done anything!' She was happy, she said, that someone believed in her sincerity.

'Sometimes, people don't know what the truth is, even when they're sincere,' Father Saulo remarked gently.

'Father Saulo, I know I wasn't in that house that night!'

'Bless you, my girl.'

29 March 2008

The following morning at the Capanne jail, still shaken by Rudy's version, Amanda told Edda she was worried he had ruined her hopes of being granted some form of house arrest – perhaps a local hostel run by a charity – which her lawyers had formally requested.

'I was indignant, because . . . if Rudy was there, he's just saving his arse now,' Amanda said.

'But he's not saving his arse. The problem is that he's pointing the finger. But how do you explain all this shit? There isn't any evidence that you were there,' Edda said.

'And if he tries to explain it all by saying for example that he was protecting me, that would be bullshit because he doesn't know me . . . I'm so mad now, nothing could have been worse. What's worse than this?'

Amanda addressed Rudy as if he was in the visiting room with her: 'You know something? You're breaking my balls!'

Far from comforting her, Amanda's cellmate Rosa had made things worse for her: 'She came up to me telling me that I'd spend the next thirty years in prison, and that the best thing would be to lie and say that I had something to do with it . . . Which is simply bullshit!'

As Amanda talked of Rosa's twenty-five-year sentence, she bent down to rest her head on Edda's breast, saying she wanted to feel closer to her. Edda tried to distract her, talking of relatives who would be coming to visit but Amanda fell silent for a while. Edda urged her to be patient and wait for the house arrest ruling due the next week.

'Yes, I want to see what happens . . . otherwise, I'll have to get a bit better organised with a kitchen, a coffee machine, all that stuff . . .' Amanda said in a low voice.

That was no problem, Edda said, she would bring her everything she needed.

'Thanks, but the whole thing is a problem here,' Amanda said. She bowed her head, lost in thought.

Edda tried to cheer her up: 'You've survived injustice . . . You'll get out of all this, you're innocent. And you'll be alive at least . . . And the fact that you're such a strong person means you won't go crazy. You're doing everything you can to stay as busy as possible; everyone's been impressed by that.'

'Thanks,' Amanda said.

Stroking her daughter's hand and giving it little taps, Edda went on: 'Yes, because none of us have found themselves in a situation like this and survived. You've done it!'

'Thanks,' Amanda said again, smiling.

Edda started crying but managed to say: 'And you'll be fine!'

The cottage at 7, via della Pergola, where both Meredith and Amanda fell in love with the view over the rolling hills. 'I love it – I've never seen anything like it,' Amanda said when she discovered the view.

Amy Frost and Meredith. Meredith's friends remember her as fun, bubbly and quick-witted.

Above: The sight that greeted the first investigators in Meredith's room; her body lies under the quilt. They saw the fact that the body was covered as a revealing clue.

Above: Biologist Patrizia Stefanoni (centre) of the Rome forensic police, standing in front of the open door to Meredith's bedroom on the night after the murder. Stefanoni was to play a key role in the investigation and the trial.

Right: Police take Meredith's body out of the cottage. Her family faced a long wait before they were finally allowed to bury her.

Above: Observers were struck, and dismayed, by how often Amanda and Raffaele kissed and hugged each other after the murder. Amanda said she needed to be comforted.

Above: Amanda in the garden of the cottage. After the body was discovered, she complained repeatedly about police questioning her for hours.

A handcuffed Amanda is taken to jail. To her left is the detective Rita Ficarra, to whom she admitted being in the cottage on the night of the murder – which she later denied.

Patrick Lumumba is arrested a few hours after Amanda accused him of killing Meredith. 'But are you sure I'm the person you're looking for?' he asked the police.

Meredith's mother Arline, her sister Stephanie and her father John walk to the lawcourts on the day they testified at the trial. 'Why would anyone want to hurt her? Did she suffer?' they asked their lawyer soon after the murder.

Amanda's father Curt and her mother Edda by the cathedral. 'Be more on your guard. It's a foreign country you're going to,' Edda had told Amanda before she left Seattle.

Prosecutors Manuela Comodi and Giuliano Mignini. Like all investigators who worked on the Kercher case, it was to touch them more deeply than any other.

Amanda makes a cheerful entrance on the first day of the trial. Her behaviour – she smiled, chatted and laughed in court – stunned many observers.

Amanda shocked the court on Valentine's Day with a tribute to the Beatles, her favourite band – an oversize t-shirt stamped with the words: 'All you need is love'.

Raffaele in court. In a blog, he wrote that he wanted to find 'bigger thrills which will surprise me.'

A tomboy at the time, Amanda only reluctantly agreed to wear make-up and posed for her sister's photography assignment. Amanda posted this picture on a website.

Surrounded by four prison guards, Amanda smiles at Curt as she arrives for the start of a day in court. Her family ensured a relative was always in Perugia for her.

Amanda, moments after the appeal court announced her murder acquittal on the night of 3 October 2011.

Meredith's friends and many Perugian students hold a candlelit vigil for Meredith on the steps of the cathedral.

Amanda leant forwards towards her mother who hugged her. 'I miss you!' Amanda said, then sat for a while with her eyes closed, her head resting on her hand.

'That's why I feel so strong!' Amanda said eventually.

'Why?' Edda asked.

'Because I always miss you all,' Amanda replied, beginning to cry.

Amanda talked again about her cellmate. The previous Thursday, Rosa had been in an awful mood and Amanda had spent the whole evening trying to console her, hugging her and caressing her. At one point Rosa had whispered to her: 'Why don't we have sex?' Amanda had burst out: 'No! No! I'm not gay!' Amanda guessed that Rosa had said that because she was lonely, and because Amanda was the only attractive female to hand. Amanda was sure that Rosa would go round the bend if she stayed in prison.

Edda told Amanda she must stay strong for however long it took to get her out. She hoped this would happen sooner rather than later.

Amanda asked her point-blank: 'Do you think they could make me stay here for twenty years?'

'No,' Edda exclaimed, 'Carlo [Dalla Vedova, her lawyer] said you'll get out of here!'

It was their most emotional encounter in prison so far; both recognised that the possibility of a trial – and a verdict against Amanda – could no longer be ignored. When Amanda and Edda began to talk about a trial, Amanda said that would mean she would be interrogated by the prosecutor Mignini – 'the bastard', she said forcefully.

31 March 2008

After 11 p.m., and preceded by a warning to viewers that the next programme would include 'strong' content, the Telenorba 7 channel, a local network based in Raffaele's home region of Bari, broadcast a current affairs programme dedicated to the Kercher case. It showed footage from the video the forensic police had taken in Meredith's bedroom the day after the murder.

The two-and-a-half-minute extract left nothing to the imagination. Viewers saw the quilt covering Meredith's body, then an officer lifting it to reveal her near-naked body, from the head to the stomach, lying in a pool of blood. A close-up focused on her butchered throat; a mask covered her eyes. The film continued as investigators then turned the body over, exposing her blood-stained back and bottom.

The Kerchers' lawyer Maresca, who prided himself on his usually unflappable character, saw red as soon as he learnt of the broadcast – he could think of no more disgusting lack of respect for Meredith and her family. He called her siblings Stephanie and Lyle and urged them to sue the channel, which they agreed to do. A few days later, Maresca said in a TV interview that only Raffaele's lawyers had been authorised to copy the police video, implying that they had leaked it to the TV channel; they retorted that his comment was 'unfair and unfounded'. Police launched an investigation to try to find out how the channel had got hold of the film.

1 April 2008

Amanda's hopes of freedom before a decision on whether she should stand trial were wrecked yet again when the Supreme Court in Rome ruled that she, like Raffaele and Rudy, must stay in jail. The country's most senior judges ruled that Amanda was dangerous and must not be freed because of her 'negative personality', the possibility that she might flee to America, and the risk that she might seek to tamper with the evidence against her. As for Raffaele, he had a 'fragile' character and was a danger to society. Rudy's participation in the murder was 'obvious and indisputable'.

In what was effectively a reprimand for Mignini, however, the court ruled that the statement Amanda gave the prosecutor at 5.45 a.m. on 6 November – when she accused Patrick of the murder – couldn't be used against her or anyone else because although she had been formally placed under investigation she hadn't been given a lawyer. The prosecutor wasn't worried that this would weaken his case as Amanda had repeated her accusation in the text she wrote before going to prison, which the court ruled could be used against her and others.

5 April 2008

As Edda and her sister Christina Hagge, who had flown to Italy to join her, waited for Amanda in the visiting room of the Capanne prison, Christina looked around the room and wondered aloud if it was bugged.

'Who knows . . .' Edda said. She was silent for a time, then said in a low voice as she too looked around: 'Testing, testing, can you hear us? Testing, testing, I'm innocent. She didn't do anything.'

Amanda walked in and hugged her mother and aunt warmly. She said excitedly that she had jumped for joy that morning when guards gave her a Beatles CD, which Edda had brought her. She loved the book of Bob Dylan songs they had also given her and was copying them out in a notebook.

Edda mentioned the crime-scene video with images of Meredith's body broadcast by a TV station four days earlier. 'It's simply disgusting . . . Can you imagine Meredith's family?' Edda said.

'Oh . . . ! You mean they showed the film with Meredith? Oh my God! I didn't see it,' Amanda said.

Amanda was more astonished however when Edda told her about an article in an Italian magazine which said that Meredith had been drunk when she was killed. 'It's a huge thing, they're saying now she was almost in an alcoholic coma!'

Amanda looked stunned. 'Really?' she said.

Christina mentioned the blood alcohol level – 2.72 gr/l – and Amanda exclaimed, putting her hand over her mouth in surprise: 'Good God!'

'Yes, in an alcoholic coma,' Edda said.

'Really? Oh . . . what the heck happened?' Amanda asked.

'I don't know, and now they say that her friends said she'd had a beer, and so they checked the quantity [of alcohol],' Edda said.

'What the heck happened?' Amanda asked again. 'Good God! So that [quantity] of alcohol came out of the [autopsy] report?'

Edda said she had no idea.

The magazine report turned out to be untrue. Experts appointed by Mignini later established that the figure of 2.72 gr/l was mistaken and possibly due to an error in the preservation of the sample examined; the true value was a slight 0.43 gr/l.

Before Edda and her sister left, they asked Amanda what she would like them to bring her. Amanda said she'd like some knickers, because she'd been walking around without any on and people had been scandalised.

38

Meredith's mother Arline, along with Stephanie and Lyle, flew back to Perugia for the first time in six months to attend a closed hearing before Judge Matteini at which the three forensic pathologists the judge had appointed would analyse how Meredith died, basing their conclusions mainly on the results of the autopsy. In charge of preliminary investigations, Judge Matteini would later rule on the latest appeals for the release of Amanda, Raffaele and Rudy.

For the family, the hearing in Perugia's law courts near the cathedral would be the first time that they would learn the details of Meredith's death from court-appointed experts. They'd told their lawyer Maresca they were determined to come: they wanted to find out the truth about what Meredith had gone through – particularly whether she'd been raped or not – and how she'd died.

Meredith's brother Lyle took notes in a big notebook as the three pathologists presented their findings. They reported that Meredith had been 'involved in sexual activity' shortly before her death, but on the basis of biological traces alone, it was impossible to say whether she had been a willing participant or not. Meredith had died of asphyxiation caused by strangling and internal bleeding; it would have been impossible to save her life after the stab wounds were inflicted. They gave a wide range for the time of death: between 8.45 p.m. on the night of 1 November 2007 when she was last seen by her friend Sophie, and 12.50 a.m. that night.

When the first harrowing photographs of Meredith's body were shown on a screen – Maresca had warned them what to expect – Arline, Stephanie and Lyle asked to leave and were escorted by detectives to a small room across the corridor, away from the waiting media. But only a half hour later, to the surprise of many in the courtroom, both Stephanie and Lyle came back. This time they stayed, watching dry-eyed as more photographs of the crime scene, and of the autopsy, were screened.

During a break in the hearing, as Maresca briefed her on the experts' findings, Arline said to him: 'Francesco, it's not possible that they did this to my Mez; it's not possible. I don't believe it.' Arline especially refused to believe that her daughter had been raped, or involved in an erotic 'game'.

In court, as the pathologists discussed the time of death, Arline quietly asked the interpreter, again and again: 'How long did it take for Mez to die? Was it a few seconds or a few minutes?'

When one of the experts testified that Meredith's agony may have lasted as much as ten minutes, the Kerchers remained impassive. The hearing was the first time the Kerchers saw Raffaele, the only one of the three accused who chose to attend it; the Kerchers sat only a few yards away from him and ignored him throughout.

In a short statement issued during their stay in Perugia, the family gave a glimpse of their suffering. 'Almost six months since she died we are still coming to terms with the idea of never seeing our Meredith smiling and happy again,' the Kerchers said.

15 May 2008

Less than a month after the pathologists testified before her, Judge Matteini ordered that all three of the accused should stay in prison. The judge wrote in her ruling that Meredith was 'subjected to several violent acts characterised by extreme cruelty in a hideous crescendo, surely a sign of perverse personalities devoid of any inhibitions.'

The judge found that there was 'serious evidence' against Amanda, and expressed her 'dismay and apprehension' at Amanda's cold, detached manner after the murder; the judge was struck by a woman so young 'finding it so easy to govern her state of mind'.

20 May 2008

Back in Seattle, and increasingly frustrated by their daughter's fate, Edda and Curt decided to go on the offensive. They hired David Mariott, a public relations adviser and former TV journalist, and began giving interviews to the main American TV networks in which they criticised Mignini's investigation. In an interview with the author for the *Sunday Times Magazine* – the first they gave the British media – Edda, Curt and their daughter Deanna talked for more than three hours about the case. Sitting close together at one end of a long conference table in the office of their publicist in a downtown skyscraper, they made fresh attacks on the Perugian investigators.

Curt said Amanda had been 'abused physically and verbally'. She had told them that a police officer hit her in the back of the head. She had also said the police told her: 'If you ask for a lawyer, things will get worse for you.' The police denied this account.

Curt also accused the police of handling the crime scene in a 'shoddy' way. The police's own videos showed that the clasp of Meredith's bra was found in mid-December a few feet away from where it had first been filmed a month and a half earlier. The police had made such a mess of Meredith's bedroom that there could have been cross-contamination.

As for Amanda and Meredith's DNA traces on the kitchen knife, which investigators said could be the murder weapon – they simply didn't mean anything according to a forensic expert hired by Edda and Curt.

'Amanda cooks, so there's nothing surprising about her trace on the handle. But the expert told us the trace of Meredith was on the side of the knife, not the blade, and it had a very small chance of belonging to Meredith – he said it could belong to half the population of Italy!' Curt said.

Curt didn't trust either Mignini or the police. 'The approach has been to play the case out in the media rather than providing physical evidence. That blows me away. If this happened in the USA she would have been out months ago,' Curt said.

'It gets scary when you have the prosecutor accused of wrong-doing in another case,' Edda added. This was a reference to Mignini being due to stand trial on charges of misconduct in investigating a death connected to the serial killer known as the 'Monster of Florence' who murdered couples in the Florentine hills from 1968 to 1975. For Mignini, he had simply been doing his job, and was the victim of a vendetta.

Curt made a further attack on Mignini: 'The prosecutor's reputation is at stake. You don't make an international incident in the way this was done, the wild-sex-orgy-drugs scenario and then say, "Oops, I kept your daughter in jail for six months." I don't like it when people's reputations are at stake and it's them or a twenty-year-old kid.'

The family hesitated when asked if there was anything they would like to say to Meredith's family. Edda broke the silence: 'We're in a sticky situation because of what people have written about Amanda. We'd like to reach out, but what will they think if we say to them: "Your daughter was my daughter's housemate and we can only imagine your pain?" I can't imagine what they're having to live through.'

Over the weeks and months that followed, Edda and Curt's media offensive gathered speed with the support of American lawyers, private investigators and the writer Douglas Preston, co-author with the Italian journalist Mario Spezi of an investigation into the 'Monster of Florence' killings. A website called the 'Amanda Knox Defense Fund' displayed tributes from family and friends and details of how to donate money to her cause.

From Perugia, Amanda's lawyer Ghirga watched the publicity blitz with dismay; he was convinced that attacks in the media on Italian justice in general, and against Mignini and the police officers, weren't helping her cause in the slightest. For one thing, Ghirga couldn't accept the accusation that Amanda had been physically abused at the police station. He believed that attacking investigators in the media, as Edda and Curt were doing, would only antagonise all the people who really mattered: the police, the prosecutor, the judges and – if the case went to trial as he expected it to – the jurors who would decide Amanda's future.

24 May 2008

Giornale dell'Umbria splashed across its front page what it clearly believed was a sensational scoop: a drug addict and dealer in his thirties, his hands and shoes dirty with blood, had been heard shouting on Piazza Grimana the morning after the murder: 'I killed her! I killed her!'

The newspaper said it knew the addict's name but didn't print it, reporting that half a dozen people as well as paramedics passing through the area had seen him before Meredith's body was discovered. The article quoted one witness who said that the man's right hand was injured and that he washed it at a fountain. He then made a phone call from a public phone box, apparently talking to a woman and shouting, 'I'll kill you, you whore!'

Napoleoni checked the story. Maurizio Rosignoli, who owned the news stand on the square and was one of the sources for the article, told her that he saw a man go to a public phone box, and shout at someone he had called. What he said made no sense to Rosignoli except for the words: 'You ugly slut, whore, I'll kill you!' – or perhaps, 'In any case, I'll kill you!' Rosignoli said he had never said the man shouted, 'I killed her!' Nor had he said the man had blood on him.

Rosignoli's girlfriend Alessia Ceccarelli, who ran the news stand with him, told detectives later that the addict whom she knew by sight first came to her to change some money, and Ceccarelli noticed he had blood on the back of his right hand. He then made the phone call, shouting at a woman she presumed he had called. She heard him yell: 'I'll kill you, you whore!' She never heard him shout 'I killed her!'

Eventually detectives managed to identify the addict, and ruled him out of the investigation.

28 May 2008

As the attacks from Amanda's family, friends and supporters increased and Mignini prepared to request that the case go to trial, the prosecutor asked his boss for extra help; a second prosecutor, Manuela Comodi, was swiftly appointed to work alongside Mignini on the Kercher case from now on.

When she was asked to help take on Perugia's most high-profile case in many years, Comodi's first thought was a stunned '*Mamma mia!*' but she accepted immediately. The lively, smiling Comodi was notoriously independent-minded and let nothing stand in her way – not even the might of the Roman Catholic Church. Among her previous targets was a Naples cardinal she had accused of usury, placing hidden microphones in his residence – the cardinal was acquitted, but several other suspects were convicted.

In her mid-forties, more than ten years Mignini's junior, Comodi wasn't completely new to the Kercher case. Her office was three doors down the corridor from his, they got on well and she'd often talked to him, as well as to Homicide Squad detectives, about the investigation. She'd been intrigued from the start by what she saw as glaring contradictions in the stories of Amanda and Raffaele, and by their behaviour after the body was discovered.

Guided by Napoleoni, Comodi went to see Meredith and Amanda's flat early one afternoon. She wanted to see for herself what she had until then seen only in police photographs and films. Arriving at the cottage, she was struck by the beauty of the spot and the landscape, but also by its isolation; she thought to herself that she would never leave her two daughters – ten and twelve years old – alone in such a spot, even with a babysitter.

Inside, most of the shutters were closed and the electricity had been cut off so Napoleoni handed Comodi a torch and she walked slowly around, flashing the beam of light back and forth as she went in and out of the rooms and bathrooms – she wanted to understand the layout of the flat and how the rooms related to each other. Comodi did her best not to feel anything as she walked around; it was a form of self-defence for her, because she worried that if she did become upset in such situations her objectivity would go out the window.

The flat was dotted with pink and grey smudges especially around the door handles and light switches – the traces left by chemicals the forensic police had used to find fingerprints and other traces. What Comodi noticed was not so much the chaos in the flat – she was used to crime scenes that had been combed through by the police – as the atmosphere that still lingered of a typical, untidy students' home with its cheap furniture and decorations. She thought for a moment of the lives the four flatmates had led here, and then of the day when her own daughters might travel abroad to study for a while, perhaps in America. She checked herself and concentrated once again on the flat.

Comodi looked closely at Filomena's broken window, asking Napoleoni where precisely the stone had been found. Amanda's room was so tiny it felt claustrophobic; there wasn't even a light in the ceiling. The cottage looked spacious from outside, but inside it felt cramped – apparently the owner had wanted to cram in as many tenants as possible.

She stopped longest in Meredith's room, staring first at the bloodstains on the walls and then at the pool of dried-up blood on the floor. Napoleoni gestured across the stained floor to show her precisely where the body had been found. The defence lawyers had claimed the room was too small to contain four people, but this seemed absurd to Comodi. Students were used to cramped rooms, and the centre of the room was completely empty of any furniture. And in any case, a sex game with four people didn't require a huge amount of space – quite the opposite, she thought wryly.

Still staring around the silent room, Comodi then made herself run through how the three killers may have held Meredith before stabbing her. Comodi tried to imagine her last moments – only a few feet from where she now stood – but her feelings suddenly got the better of her. She sometimes suffered from claustrophobia, and now felt a tightening in her throat, almost as if she was being suffocated, so she walked briskly out of the room and out of the flat, into the fresh air.

Outside, she lit a cigarette to help her relax, drawing comfort from the beauty of the view. She didn't go back inside; she had seen enough.

39

Seven months after Meredith's murder, Mignini and his colleague Comodi signed the decree formally notifying Amanda, Raffaele and Rudy that they had finished their investigation as required by Italian law. The case files filled twelve volumes and 10,000 pages.

The two prosecutors accused Amanda, Raffaele and Rudy of both murdering and sexually attacking Meredith for 'futile motives'. The accused had tried to force her to take part in a sex game and, when she refused, they killed her by strangling and stabbing her. The accused also stole 300 euros (£270), two credit cards and two mobiles phones from Meredith, the prosecutors charged. Amanda and Raffaele were also accused of staging a fake burglary, and of illegally carrying a weapon in taking the knife believed to be the murder weapon from his flat to the cottage. Finally, Amanda was accused of slandering Patrick to cover Rudy.

If convicted, the three faced very heavy jail sentences – including a life sentence for the charge of 'voluntary murder with the aggravating circumstance of cruelty', and up to twelve years for sexual assault. Slandering Patrick could mean up to twenty years in prison for Amanda.

Less than a month later, Mignini and Comodi demanded that Amanda, Raffaele and Rudy stand trial, repeating their accusations against the three. A judge would hold a series of hearings after the summer to decide on the prosecutors' request.

★   ★   ★

That summer, Comodi took with her on holiday copies of several hundred pages from the investigation files. Under a beach umbrella on Italy's south-west coast, she steadily read her way through them as her daughters played in the sea. The more she read, the more she became convinced the prosecution case was solid.

Comodi saw Amanda as a narcissist, aware of her beauty and keen to show herself to others as free and uninhibited. Like many narcissists who were also insecure, she loved herself a great deal but also needed confirmation that the world loved her too – and this she obtained through sexual conquest. For Comodi, Amanda's one-night stands since her arrival in Italy were just more names on a list; she knew little about these men and cared even less.

Comodi tried again and again to reconstruct the sexual assault and the murder. Based on what she'd read of the characters of the accused and their relationships with each other, Comodi saw Amanda as the instigator. She was a charismatic figure, capable of influencing others, and she was the driving force who had drawn the group together, setting in motion the spiral of events with perhaps just a casual remark to Raffaele and Rudy: 'Come on, let's have some fun . . .' Raffaele was so devoted to her he followed her blindly; Rudy was a drifter, was easily influenced and fancied Amanda so he followed her too.

Comodi ruled out Meredith taking part willingly in the sex game; her character and her habits, as well as the bruises on her body, excluded it. The friends Meredith went out with were her English girlfriends, and she had just started a relationship with Giacomo from the flat downstairs. But try as she might, Comodi couldn't work out how the sexual assault had turned into murder. Her only certainty was that Amanda had held the knife, because of her DNA on the handle, and Meredith's on the blade.

27 August 2008

On the eve of the hearings which would decide whether Amanda, Raffaele and Rudy would stand trial, Raffaele's lawyers played a risky card. They wanted to prove that an intruder – they didn't say who outright, but it was clear they meant Rudy – could have broken into the cottage through Filomena's window and then murdered Meredith. To do so, the lawyers asked for permission to enter the garden of the cottage, which was granted.

Raffaele's team chose for the experiment Delfo Berretti, a bearded, long-haired lawyer who had the significant advantage of being more than six feet tall. Watched by Mignini and detectives of the Homicide Squad, Berretti took just a few seconds to climb up the wall and get a hold on Filomena's windowsill. But he could not pull himself up and hung there, stranded, and to avoid any further embarrassment a colleague called out hastily: 'That's enough, that's fine.' Berretti let himself fall back to the ground.

For Mignini, the experiment had backfired on Raffaele's lawyers. Rudy, who was shorter than Berretti, would have been unable to even touch the windowsill, let alone get in through the window.

15 September 2008

The Kercher family returned to Perugia for the start of the hearings. They knew it meant more painful revelations but they welcomed this new stage in the search for the truth about Meredith's death. At a press conference held in the hotel where Arline, John and Stephanie were staying, Stephanie read out a statement in the family's name: 'Each time we arrive in Perugia, we wish we were here for a different reason . . . Mez was such a significant part of so many lives. Mez was such a genuine person that when we think of her now and when we see her friends we don't need to say anything, we just need to smile.'

16 September 2008

On the very first day of the preliminary hearings, Judge Paolo Micheli, an elegant figure with nineteen years' experience who wrote songs in his spare time, accepted a request for a fast-track trial from Rudy's lawyers, which meant he would be judged differently from Amanda and Raffaele. Judge Micheli would rule not only on whether Amanda and Raffaele should stand trial, but also on whether Rudy was guilty or not. Under Italian procedure, the fast-track trial for Rudy meant he could hope to have his sentence reduced by up to a third if found guilty.

At the hearings, which were held behind closed doors, the Kerchers came face-to-face for the first time with all three accused. Sitting only a few yards away from them for hours on end, the family betrayed no sign of ill will towards them. 'Amazing. I'd have expected the Kerchers to say something rude to them at the very least,' a lawyer commented.

Among the handful of witnesses the court heard was the Albanian farmhand Kokomani, who claimed he'd seen Amanda, Raffaele and Rudy outside the cottage either on the night of the murder or the previous night, and some friends of Rudy's. After Stefanoni, the biologist from Rome's forensic police, had given her evidence, the two prosecutors, Mignini and Comodi, discussed what sentence they should demand for Rudy.

They both felt there was no choice: they must demand a life sentence as in Italy this usually meant twenty years in prison after reductions for good behaviour. Both were aware that such a sentence potentially meant wrecking the life of a twenty-one-year-old like Rudy.

But any doubts the two prosecutors had were dispelled at the mere thought of what they believed the three accused had done to Meredith. By refusing to come clean and explain precisely how she had died, Rudy had, in their opinion, thrown away his chance to be treated with some mercy. Comodi was sure he would never talk: rejected by his mother, drifting from one family to another for years, Rudy had developed a formidable resistance to hardship and an ingrained mistrust of others. She was convinced that he simply didn't believe that making a confession could help him in any way.

18 October 2008

In his final address ahead of the judge's verdict, Mignini gave his most detailed reconstruction so far of Meredith's last moments. The prosecutor had no doubt that Amanda and Raffaele – and very likely Rudy too – had been in a drugged state from late in the afternoon of 1 November.

Shortly after Meredith arrived home, Amanda let Raffaele and Rudy into the cottage. Meredith was tired, and she became angry with Amanda for bringing two men into the flat at a time when she just wanted to go to bed, and the two had a row.

Later that evening, Amanda asked Rudy, who was anxious to please her, to 'soften up' Meredith and prepare her for an erotic 'game' by sexually assaulting her, while Amanda 'dedicated herself' to Raffaele, Mignini suggested. Meredith refused to take part with such vigour that Rudy, Amanda and Raffaele became infuriated with her. All three threatened Meredith as she began to scream. They held her, cutting her several times, and at one point grabbed her by the neck and tried to strangle her – her neck was seized so violently that the hyoid bone snapped.

Meredith, the prosecutor continued, must have been kneeling in front of the cupboard in her room while Rudy holding her left arm by the wrist – his DNA had been found on the left sleeve of her sweatshirt – tried to rape her. Raffaele also tried to hold her still, seizing her right arm, while Amanda who was facing Meredith pricked her in the neck with the kitchen knife. Meredith tried to free herself and push away the blade with her right hand, but it cut her in the palm. Then, Mignini said: 'The situation precipitated and Amanda plunged the blade into Meredith's neck.'

As the last wound was inflicted and Meredith screamed for the last time, the three ripped the shoulder straps of her bra and cut the cloth next to the bra clasp. Raffaele's DNA trace on the clasp, according to the prosecutor, was a decisive piece of evidence as it not only nailed him to the crime scene but also showed he had had violent contact with the victim: the trace was believed to be from his skin and the hooks on the clasp were twisted. After the fatal blow, Meredith had been dragged, or had dragged herself, roughly a yard towards the bed, where she lay on her back.

After shifting the body and grabbing the two mobile phones and at least 300 euros, the killers fled – it was, according to Mignini, between 11.10 p.m. and shortly after midnight. Rudy went home where he washed himself before going to a nightclub, the Domus. But Amanda and Raffaele returned to the cottage to destroy the evidence. Mignini argued that the couple must have cleaned up in the cottage because only one fingerprint of Amanda's was found there, on a glass in the kitchen sink – something he said was implausible given that she lived there.

The quilt thrown over Meredith's body was a vital, psychological clue, the prosecutor said. 'It indicates a form of *pietas* [pity], of respect for the victim and a need to deny to oneself such a serious crime,' Mignini said. That meant killer and victim were acquaintances, or friends, and the killer was not a habitual murderer. An intruder who had entered the house to steal would have been used, perhaps, to committing violent acts and would have felt no need to cover the body. The quilt pointed to Amanda's involvement more than to that of Raffaele or Rudy 'because she, as a woman, couldn't bear that naked, mangled female corpse.'

The 'burglary' was no such thing; it had been staged by the only two people alive in the cottage on the morning of 2 November – Amanda and Raffaele. It would serve to 'justify' the call to the *carabinieri*, but the pair were caught by surprise by the earlier arrival of the postal police. Also that morning, Amanda and Raffaele had bought bleach – Raffaele's cleaner had never seen bleach in his flat before but police found several bottles there– to clean the blood off various objects including the kitchen knife.

Amanda – who according to her flatmates was by no means keen on housework – herself had told police that she brought a mop to his flat on the morning after the murder, saying at first this was to clean his bedroom and, in later questioning, saying it was to clean up after water had leaked from under a sink. Confirming that the two had indeed cleaned up, their DNA was found on sponges in a bucket at Raffaele's flat.

Mignini highlighted the couple's strange behaviour after Meredith's body was discovered. They displayed a 'morbid affection' for each other, embracing and kissing in the garden of the cottage and then at the police station – a warmth of feeling that contrasted with the 'ice-cold indifference' they had displayed over Meredith's death. As for Rudy, he had invented his account of sexual foreplay with Meredith; she never did kiss him in a nightclub or agree to meet him, and his story was baseless given her reserve, her serious character and her fidelity to her new boyfriend Giacomo.

What struck Mignini the most about Meredith's murder, he concluded before the court, was that, partly because of the violence shown on TV, in films or in comics like the Japanese ones Raffaele read, ferocious crimes once only committed by hardened criminals could today be committed by youngsters everyone thought of as 'the boy and girl next door' – as Amanda and Raffaele had been labelled in the media.

With his colleague Comodi, the prosecutor demanded a life sentence for Rudy, and that Amanda and Raffaele be sent to trial.

40

28 October 2008

After deliberating for almost twelve hours at the end of Rudy's fast-track trial, Judge Micheli found Rudy guilty of sexually assaulting and murdering Meredith, and sentenced him to thirty years in jail. He acquitted Rudy of theft, but ordered him to pay legal costs and damages of £1.8 million to each of Meredith's parents, and £1.3 million to each of her brothers and to her sister.

In line with the prosecutors' conclusions, Judge Micheli found that 'several' attackers had first agreed on a plan to 'satisfy [their] sexual instincts', threatened Meredith with a knife, and then murdered her in a spiral of escalating and then uncontrolled violence. The attackers had failed in their sexual intent only because of her desperate and extremely loud scream – which they cut off by stabbing her to death.

In Judge Micheli's reconstruction, Meredith was wounded in the neck while she stood near the desk and was then pushed to the ground, where she lay on her back. Rudy had then started sexually abusing her, part of a 'sex game', which involved the others as well. Rudy didn't deliver the fatal blow, the judge said, but he actively participated in the attack – the judge didn't speculate as to who did deliver it. When the attack became murderous, none of the attackers fled, tried to stop the others or called for help.

Rudy had told 'an almost endless series of lies' and believing him would require 'a superhuman leap of faith', Judge Micheli wrote in his ruling. Rudy had contradicted himself on where he was supposed to have kissed Meredith on the night before the murder, and his statement that he had heard Amanda ring the doorbell of the flat made no sense, as she had the keys to it. Nor was there any truth in Rudy's claim that Meredith had let him into the flat – the person who let him in 'could only be Amanda', the judge wrote. The three killers fled after the murder, and one or more of them returned later to stage a fake burglary.

When Amanda heard the judge announce that she would have to stand trial, she burst into tears. 'This is only the beginning, we have to keep fighting,' Ghirga told her and she quickly stopped crying. Raffaele turned to his lawyers and asked them: 'So can I go home now, when will I be free?' Rudy remained impassive; his lawyers announced they would appeal.

The verdict gave Meredith's family some relief. 'We're here because our sister was murdered, so "pleased" isn't an appropriate word. "Satisfied" is probably the best we can say,' Meredith's brother Lyle said.

15 November 2008

Just over a year after Meredith's murder, Antioco Fois of the *Giornale dell'Umbria* newspaper brought yet another witness to Mignini. Marco Quintavalle, a burly but quiet-spoken grocer whose supermarket was next to the journalist's home by the university, had confided to Fois that he'd seen Amanda in his supermarket early on the morning of 2 November – contradicting Amanda's statement that she was at Raffaele's flat at the time. He'd noticed how pale she looked and that she glanced around 'as if she was trying to hide'.

Was he sure, 100 per cent sure, it was Amanda? Fois asked.

'Not 100 per cent, no. I'd be sure only if I could see her in front of me,' Quintavalle replied.

At lunchtime on a Saturday – a time chosen to ensure as few people as possible would see them – Fois and his editor Castellini escorted the grocer to the prosecutors' office. Castellini was convinced the new witness nailed Amanda. 'This one's a bombshell!' he'd exclaimed when Fois first briefed him.

In Mignini's office, Quintavalle described how one evening a couple of weeks before the murder, he'd been surprised to see Raffaele walk into the supermarket with a girl he later found out was Amanda. Raffaele was a regular customer and was bizarre – 'always rigid, always wearing a scarf, he never laughed and he didn't chat to anyone,' Quintavalle said – and the grocer had never seen him with a girl before. He was so surprised he took a good look at Amanda's face.

On the morning of 2 November, the day after the murder, Quintavalle was pressing the switch to raise his shop's roll-up shutter when he saw a girl waiting to come in. She had blue eyes, he said; she wasn't tall and was wearing jeans, a grey jacket, a scarf and a hat. She looked at him out of the corner of her eye and went to the back of the shop where tins and detergents, including bleach, were kept.

'It seemed strange to me because it's very rare that youngsters come into the shop so early, especially on a day which was almost a holiday,' Quintavalle said.

The prosecutor asked about the girl's behaviour.

'Her manner was cautious, as if she didn't want to be recognised,' Quintavalle replied.

He said he didn't remember whether the girl had bought anything, but he saw her turn right out of the shop towards Piazza Grimana. When Amanda was arrested a few days later and her photograph was printed in the papers, he had the impression that the girl he'd seen early in the morning was Amanda, but he couldn't be certain because of the scarf and hat.

After Quintavalle had finished, Castellini switched his mobile phone off – he didn't want anyone calling to ask him about the new witness if word leaked out – and worked on the story that he would run the next day.

16 November 2008

'SUPER-WITNESS GETS AMANDA INTO TROUBLE' ran the front-page headline in the *Giornale dell'Umbria* under yet another 'exclusive' label. At Quintavalle's request, the paper didn't identify him, saying only that the witness had seen Amanda 'in a shop in the neighbourhood'. As they chased the story, journalists pestered shopkeepers throughout the area; several of them approached Quintavalle, but he told them politely he knew nothing. The last thing he wanted was to become a local celebrity.

The Homicide Squad was irritated that a potentially key witness had yet again emerged only thanks to the local paper, but it kept quiet. Two detectives had in fact shown photographs of Amanda and Raffaele to Quintavalle in his supermarket in the weeks after the murder, and the grocer had recognised them both. But he'd made no mention of what he'd seen on the morning after the murder.

Mignini thought the grocer's slowness in coming forward was typical of his fellow Perugians and their proverbial reserve. 'I hate to criticise my own people, but they've got a tendency to mind their own business when they should be helping the cause of justice. You've no idea how hard it can be to make people talk,' the prosecutor confided. 'Witnesses tell me, "But I didn't see them kill Meredith," and I have to explain that even so, what they've seen is important.'

The trial which was to decide the fate of both Amanda and Raffaele was to begin in the New Year. As Amanda waited for it to begin, she appeared calm and confident to those who saw her in prison. She told the chaplain Father Saulo repeatedly that she was confident she would prove her innocence at the trial. She began to play a more active part in prison life, attending aerobics and guitar lessons. Together with eleven other women, she acted in a show staged in the hall of the women's wing, called *The Last City* and described by its director as a 'fantasy journey' through the jail.

In a video of the show, Amanda looks straight at the camera and recites the soliloquy from Shakespeare's *Hamlet*:

> *To be, or not to be – that is the question;*
> *Whether 'tis nobler in the mind to suffer*
> *The slings and arrows of outrageous fortune*
> *Or to take arms against a sea of troubles*
> *And by opposing end them …*

Alessandro Riccini Ricci, the head of a Perugian film festival and one of the few people to see the film before it was withdrawn from circulation by the authorities, praised Amanda as 'a magnetic actress'. She had 'a personality which makes her stand out from the others, together with a strong stage presence.'

Soon, it would be the turn of a court to scrutinise not only the case against her but also her personality – and her 'stage presence' – before deciding her future.

Part 3
Trials

41

The strain of preparing for the trial weighed heavily on Mignini, the long hours spent combing through the files of the investigation day and night leaving him with heavy bags under his eyes. The day before it was due to begin, the prosecutor's voice became hoarse and he worried it might abandon him in court just as the proceedings got under way.

In his spare time – he had none now – Mignini loved reading history books, especially tales of great battles ranging from those in ancient times to the Second World War, and in some ways he saw what awaited him in court as a battle. At stake, for him, was justice for Meredith and her family. His weapons were the evidence he would submit to the court, and the witnesses he would bring before it. He would never go so far as to describe Amanda and Raffaele as his enemies – he believed they had killed Meredith, but to call them his enemies was too personal. But he knew their lawyers would challenge him at every turn, just as he would challenge any witnesses or experts whom they summoned.

Mignini worried that his case against Amanda and Raffaele had an Achilles heel – the fact that the members of the jury, like the ordinary man in the street, were used to being presented with a motive in every crime they saw on TV or read about in the newspapers. He had a theory that this reassured them. A wife finds her husband with a lover and kills him in a fit of passion; a Mafioso kills a rival for control of a clan. The jury would expect a rational explanation for Meredith's murder, but Mignini knew from experience that crime often had no motive. The prosecutor had described the motives behind the sexual attack on Meredith and her murder as 'futile', but he worried this might be a stumbling block for a jury demanding to know not only what had happened, but also why.

If Amanda's lawyer Ghirga worried about the trial, he didn't show it. He stuck to his daily routine despite constant pestering by journalists, paying his three visits a day to the Caffè Turreno opposite the cathedral. As he savoured his midday *aperitivo*, perched as usual on one of the terrace's high metal stools, on the day before the trial was due to begin, he briefly discussed the case with a couple of journalists. As he talked, he suddenly pointed a finger to simulate a knife and jabbed it an inch from the neck of one of the reporters.

'There, the knife goes in this way, and the killer moves it back and forth two or three times; that's how he makes that awful wound,' Ghirga explained in his booming voice, startling the journalists.

The *caffè's* regulars knew him well and didn't bat an eyelid.

A few days earlier, on one of his visits to the Capanne prison, Amanda had asked him: 'How come so many people who've read my case files don't believe I'm innocent?' It was as if the case against her, and the impending trial, seemed absurd to her – even though she had spent the past fourteen months in prison.

Through her lawyers, she gave a rare and theatrical statement to the media: 'Finally the hour of truth has arrived. I'm not afraid. In fact, I hope that the truth will come out once and for all because I've always been a friend of Meredith's and I didn't kill her.'

Raffaele's lawyers also proclaimed his innocence on the eve of the trial. They would boast the most heavyweight team in the courtroom, led by the Sicilian Giulia Bongiorno, whose previous clients included the former prime minister Giulio Andreotti. The

Supreme Court found he had forged links with mafia bosses, but acquitted him on the grounds that because the offence had been committed so long ago, he was no longer legally answerable for it. Bongiorno, vivacious and bespectacled, was not only a high-profile lawyer but also a conservative member of parliament, and head of its justice commission.

There was every reason to expect that Bongiorno would prove a formidable foe for Mignini, as she was tireless in picking any holes in a prosecution's case. In parliament, she'd thought nothing of fighting to prevent Silvio Berlusconi, the prime minister, from banning the use of telephone taps in investigations into various crimes. Bongiorno proved such a thorn in his side that he told his aides: 'Get her out of my sight!'

16 January 2009

The grandest courtroom in Perugia's Renaissance law courts is known as the Hall of Frescoes, but only parts of a couple of frescoes of the Virgin Mary and Child survive today, near the arched entrance. Across the hall, behind the raised platform where the court sits, Christ is again represented by a crucifix hanging on the wall – a symbol of man's violence to man.

The stone-walled, vaulted hall lies in the bowels of the law courts, two floors below the main entrance not far from the cathedral. It has been redesigned for the needs of justice with a typical Italian flair for style. Facing the judge are rows of smart, light-coloured wooden desks and comfortable swivel chairs of padded black leather with armrests. Even the large steel cage used for particularly dangerous offenders boasts a row of elegant, arrow-shaped tips along the top. Sleek, powerful lights hang from a grey metal grid that stretches right across the hall, hiding the top of the vaulted ceiling from view. 'The designer dungeon,' as one journalist called the courtroom.

At no time in living memory had Perugians seen so many journalists and TV crews descend on the law courts. Outside on a wet morning, a dozen TV vans waited to beam news over the ancient palaces lining the square. True to their parochial reputation, Perugians stayed away and only five mostly elderly locals bothered to turn up for the first day of the trial; for the citizens of Perugia, it was as if Meredith's murder had never happened.

In the narrow public gallery that ran the length of the courtroom below the frescoes, the tiny public audience was vastly outnumbered by reporters from across Europe and America. So many journalists massed inside the courtroom that police and *carabinieri* officers asked several to leave as there was no room for them. A dozen journalists promptly strode into the cage designed for the accused, and sat down there. The judge, Giancarlo Massei, had to be called in to dislodge them.

An experienced judge, the fifty-five-year-old Massei was known for conducting his trials – particularly when questioning witnesses or the accused – in a kindly, sometimes even shy manner. He never raised his voice. Short and bespectacled with wispy hair, he was in fact one of Perugia's most incisive judges. His attention never wavered and he would constantly reprimand lawyers if they failed to stick to the rule book. Married with three children, he was a practising Catholic and liked to duck into the neighbouring Church of Jesus to pray for a few moments before hearings.

The verdict would be decided not only by Judge Massei but also by a secondary judge, Beatrice Cristiani, and a six-member jury. Chosen at random by a computer programme, the three men and three women who made up the jury were between thirty-five and fifty-seven years old, and included a lawyer and a secretary in a primary school. Their verdict would be based exclusively on what they saw and heard in the courtroom, and on documents such as witness statements or experts' reports which the prosecutors and defence lawyers submitted. Under Italian law, they could convict only if they believed the accused were guilty 'beyond every reasonable doubt'. If they decided the evidence was insufficient, or contradictory, they would have to acquit them.

When armed prison guards led Amanda into the courtroom through heavy double doors only a few feet from the public gallery, the only sound was of camera shutters clicking open and shut as photographers took as many shots as they could. Dressed in jeans and a striped grey tracksuit top, with her straight brown hair drawn tightly back in a ponytail, Amanda had an oddly bashful expression on her pale face but she looked straight ahead, despite the flashlights. She smiled and nodded at Judge Massei as she was guided past him and then flashed a brighter smile at her lawyer Ghirga.

'What a lot of people!' a startled Amanda exclaimed to Ghirga as he briefly put his hand on her shoulder before she sat down in one of the black leather chairs in the front row. Ghirga and Dalla Vedova sat in their black lawyers' robes on either side of her, and two guards went to stand behind her, arms folded and bright blue berets on their heads.

Amanda looked relaxed, even cheerful at times. She turned to wave, smile and silently mouth 'Hi!' to her aunt sitting two rows behind her. She smiled at her lawyer, at the guards standing behind her, and at an interpreter who came to sit down next to her. The interpreter was rarely needed, as Amanda's Italian had become fluent in prison.

Raffaele, looking drawn and paler than Amanda, sat chewing his nails and his lower lip only a few feet away to her left, with only two lawyers separating them. But Amanda ignored him, and he ignored her. They were following their lawyers' instructions. 'I told Raffaele not to say hello to Amanda, and not even look at her, because otherwise you hacks would just blow it up out of proportion,' Raffaele's lawyer Maori confided later. They both sat still, staring intently as each of the six jurors, wearing sashes in the green, white and red of the Italian national flag, took their oaths, and as a clerk read out the accusations against them, describing in detail the wounds Meredith had suffered.

No witnesses were called that first day, which was taken up with procedural matters. The Kerchers' lawyer Maresca asked for the media to be banned from the trial. 'We request this to safeguard Meredith's memory and because witnesses will testify more freely if they're not required to do so in front of long lines of journalists and TV cameras. Meredith's family doesn't want excesses by the media to ruin the trial,' Maresca told the court. The last thing they wanted was for photographs or film of Meredith's body shown in court to end up in newspapers or on TV, as they had in March when an Italian channel had broadcast film of the crime scene.

Amanda and Raffaele's lawyers however argued justice would be best served by an open trial. They were quite willing to ban the media when pictures of Meredith's body had to be shown, out of respect for her. After withdrawing briefly to discuss the issue with the jury, Judge Massei announced that the trial would be open to the public and the media, but that he would order them out whenever images of Meredith's body were shown.

During breaks that day, Amanda's behaviour shocked many in the courtroom. She chatted to her lawyers or to her guards, gesticulating Italian-style, smiling and giving a few short laughs as she did so. '*Bravo!*' she exclaimed at one point, jabbing a finger towards the chest of one of the guards standing behind her.

One prosecutor put Amanda's behaviour down to her personality. 'Amanda's laughing because she feels the star of the show, and because she's confident things will go her way. She probably doesn't realise what she's risking,' the prosecutor confided.

Whatever the reason was, Amanda's smiles and laughs exasperated Maresca. 'Let's see if either of them will still be laughing when it's all over,' he remarked.

A few days later, the prison chaplain Father Saulo mentioned Amanda's behaviour in court to her. He told her that he'd heard she'd been smiling and laughing.

'It's my way of reacting. In a situation like that, I'm so nervous I can only laugh, or cry. I can't help it,' Amanda said.

Both Amanda and Raffaele faced a long and agonising wait for a verdict. Unlike murder trials in Britain or America, trials in Italy often last many months with long gaps between hearings. Judge Massei decreed that the next hearing would be in three weeks' time. From then on, the trial would take place on two days a week, three weeks a month.

6 February 2009

The Amanda who walked in to the courtroom on the second day of the trial had little of the cheery Amanda of the first day. She sat looking grim-faced and concentrated, her mouth turned down at the corners, fidgeting with her hair. During breaks, she chatted only a little with her lawyers; they confided later that they had warned her against appearing too relaxed in court.

Raffaele needed no such advice. He looked even paler than on the first day and sat nervously pinching his chin. When he got up to make a short statement before the first witnesses were called – with Judge Massei's consent, he and Amanda were allowed to do so at any time – he spoke in a weak, hesitant voice and coughed nervously. Amanda sat hunched forward, staring at him with a furrowed brow – the first time she had looked at him since the trial began.

The situation he found himself in felt 'unreal', Raffaele said, because he was innocent. 'I'm not a violent type and the thought of hurting someone has never crossed my mind. People who know me well know I have trouble even killing a fly.' He barely knew Meredith, and he had never met Rudy. He ended with a direct appeal to the court: 'I humbly ask you to examine everything that will be said with extreme care to establish what is in fact the truth.'

The prosecutors Mignini and Comodi called as their first witnesses the ones who could tell the story not only of how Meredith's body had been discovered, but also how Amanda and Raffaele had hugged and kissed each other in the hours that followed both at the cottage and at the police station when they were taken for questioning. They included the neighbours who had found Meredith's mobile phones on the morning after the murder, the postal police officers who had then gone to the cottage, and the student who had knocked Meredith's door down.

The jurors listened in attentive silence, one of them – a young lawyer – taking a stream of notes on his laptop as Mignini led his witnesses through what they had to tell. From two rows behind Amanda, her father Curt, who couldn't speak Italian, was silently struggling to understand what was going on. No one translated for him and he was left to stare at each speaker in turn for hours on end; Amanda's lawyers would brief him only during breaks.

Amanda stayed silent that day, but Raffaele got up a second time to say he was the one who had asked the postal police officers to come into the cottage. 'If I'd had something to hide, I wouldn't have asked him to go in. And besides, I wouldn't have been so stupid as to allow myself to be found there at that moment,' he said. It was true he'd been close to Amanda at the cottage and then at the police station, but this was only because she was very upset, and cold. 'Often she just stayed silent, she stared into space. I wanted to comfort her. I think that's normal; if someone thinks it isn't, that's their problem,' he said.

When the hearing ended, Judge Massei granted Amanda permission to hug her father.

'Be strong. Love you,' Curt told his daughter as he embraced her and kissed her on the forehead.

Both of them had tears in their eyes as guards led Amanda away, holding her firmly by the arms. She held her head down as she walked, looking at no one.

42

For the first time since the month Meredith was murdered, Sophie Purton flew back to Perugia. The following day she, Amy, Robyn and Meredith's other English friends were to testify at the trial.

Sophie believed that, as far as seemed possible to her, she had learnt to cope with Meredith's loss. Initially she'd given up on her studies and spent the first five months after the murder at home, going out only rarely. She saw a therapist at her local GP's a few times, but it was a week's holiday her parents took her on which gave her the impetus to pick herself up and look for a job. The job she found in early 2008 was a menial one – entering data into a computer for a utility company – but she felt that in a way it saved her; it got her out of the house. In September, she went back to finish her chemistry course at Bristol – she dropped the Italian course – and from then on stopped her daily search on Google for articles about Meredith.

But if Sophie saw an article about the case in the newspaper, she always read it. It annoyed her to see articles which were all about Amanda, and not Meredith, and which carried a photograph of Amanda, and not Meredith. *Why did people care what Amanda was going through?* Sophie wondered. No one seemed to remember Meredith; on TV and in the newspapers, she was just the person Amanda killed. Surely this was insensitive towards Meredith's family?

For Sophie, it was thanks to Meredith that she had managed to get on with her life. In the long months she'd spent closeted at home, she often thought that unlike Meredith she still had her life and that she shouldn't waste it. Doing nothing all day wasn't fair to Meredith.

But Sophie didn't think she would ever get over Meredith's loss. All she could do from now on, she thought, was remember Meredith. She thought of her every day.

Sophie believed Amanda was guilty, but she wasn't completely certain because she couldn't work out why or how Meredith had been killed, and she felt there wasn't enough DNA evidence against either Amanda or Raffaele. She couldn't decide whether Amanda was in the cottage when Meredith was killed, or whether Amanda was involved in some other way. Nor could Sophie understand why Amanda, Raffaele and Rudy had killed Meredith, because she simply couldn't imagine why anyone would carry out such a murder. What motive could prompt anyone to kill a person as lovely as Meredith?

But Sophie was certain that Amanda knew more than she was letting on. The fact that Amanda was in the cottage on the morning after the murder, the way she acted after the murder, and the way she had behaved in court all told her that.

Sophie's doubts didn't stop her hating Amanda. Even if Amanda were innocent, Sophie would hate her simply because of the callous way she had behaved at the police station and at the trial. Sophie knew she would never forgive her.

Sometimes, Sophie thought about what she'd say to Amanda if the two ever met again. She told herself she would beg Amanda to tell her the truth. Strange as it sounded, she felt that Amanda would break down and confess everything to her, because Sophie was Meredith's friend. But then again Sophie was afraid she'd just feel sick if she had Amanda in front of her, and wouldn't be able to say anything.

Now she was going to see Amanda in court the next day. 'Will

I be able to look at her?' Sophie wondered. The prospect of facing Amanda frightened her.

Called as a witness by both the prosecution and Amanda's lawyers, Sophie worried about what she would be asked to say. She wanted to give as accurate and fair an account as possible, and she was anxious not to be seen as someone who was there to have Amanda convicted. She hoped she wouldn't be reduced to saying 'Amanda did this' and 'Amanda did that'.

Before flying off to Perugia, Sophie had talked to Amy and Robyn about what lay ahead. Amy and Robyn were more certain of Amanda's guilt than Sophie was. The three had dissected what they saw of Amanda's behaviour after the murder again and again. They'd all been struck by what Amanda had chosen to wear on the morning after the murder – a white skirt, a blue sweater and thick grey socks which went up to her knees. The three friends all thought the socks and the skirt were a strange combination; why hadn't she just put some jeans on? Robyn guessed that she'd chosen the long thick socks to cover up scratch marks.

On the evening before their testimony, Sophie, Amy and Robyn, who were staying with their families at a hotel outside Perugia, were summoned to the police station. They were told they had to fill in their bank details on some forms in order to get refunds for their flights – the Italian State would pay for the flights, but not for the hotel nights.

At the police station, several officers spoke to Sophie and her friends about the case. They told them they believed Amanda had killed Meredith. One officer made unflattering remarks about the lawyers acting for Amanda and Raffaele, criticising the looks of Bongiorno, Raffaele's lawyer.

Sophie didn't want to know, and wished she could just fill in the forms and go back to her hotel. She felt uncomfortable and was sure it wasn't right for her to be in the police station on the eve of her testimony. She felt the police were trying to convince all the girls that Amanda and Raffaele were guilty.

13 February 2009

Shortly after leaving her hotel with her parents early in the morning, Sophie stood in the street talking to other English students who were also due to testify that day. A British photographer came close up to her and took a picture, his camera a few feet from her face. Sophie turned away and started crying.

'You haven't done anything wrong, why don't you want your picture taken?' the photographer asked her.

Sophie, Amy, Robyn and a couple of other students came across more photographers shortly afterwards when they left the Caffè di Perugia off Corso Vannucci, where they had been having a coffee, to walk to the law courts. Sophie, Amy and Robyn held hands and stared at the ground as they hurried through falling snow in silence, the photographers scurrying a few feet in front of them. Two detectives of the Homicide Squad walked on either side of the group of students but some distance away, not wanting to be photographed.

Sophie felt as if she and her friends were being paraded for the press by the police. It was strange that the detectives had forbidden their parents to walk with them, saying they would go back and fetch them afterwards.

Just inside the entrance to the law courts, Sophie saw Curt standing at the top of the stairs which led down to the Hall of Frescoes. She recognised him immediately as she had often seen him on television; now the sight upset her and nearly made her cry again. Sophie had long been sickened by the campaign waged by Amanda's family; she felt it was all about Amanda as the victim. To her, there seemed to be no thought for Meredith, the real victim, and no respect for Meredith's family.

Downstairs, Sophie and the other students were told to wait in a small room off a corridor leading into the courtroom. Sophie expected to be called first, because early on in the investigation the police had questioned her first as the last person to see Meredith alive. She felt pretty confident she would manage to answer questions properly. But to Sophie's surprise, Robyn was called first; Sophie felt nervous about having to wait.

Sitting at a wooden desk on the raised platform a couple of yards from Judge Massei, Robyn read the oath each witness had to take: 'I am aware of the moral and juridical responsibility that I assume in giving my testimony and I pledge to say the whole truth and not to hide anything that I am aware of.' In a quiet, forceful tone, she spoke of her friendship with Meredith, her friend's criticisms of Amanda's exuberant character and her failure to keep the bathroom clean, and Amanda's coldness after the murder.

Jurors listened almost open-mouthed as Robyn recalled Meredith's surprise at seeing Amanda leave her beauty case in the bathroom with a vibrator and condoms clearly visible, just after her arrival in the flat.

'Meredith said it was quite strange to leave these there where they could be seen. She found it quite uncomfortable,' Robyn said.

Dressed in jeans and a green woollen sweater, Amanda sat still as she stared fixedly at Robyn, her lips pressed tightly shut.

When Robyn described the last time she had seen Meredith at the dinner in her flat on the night of the murder, Amanda looked across at Raffaele, smiled and appeared to silently mouth the words '*Che palle!*' (What a pain in the arse!) at him.

Raffaele, who had been swinging slightly in his swivel armchair from side to side, grinned back at her.

During the rest of Robyn's testimony, Amanda glanced twice more at Raffaele, smiling at him and shrugging her shoulders.

After Robyn was dismissed, Ghirga announced that Amanda had something to say. Her cheeks a little flushed, she stood and hitched up her jeans. Because of her short size, the microphone used by her lawyers was too high for her and had to be lowered. The court hushed and Judge Massei, a stickler for the rules, asked her to give her name first.

Her voice was deep, clear and firm as she spoke in fluent Italian, gazing steadily at Judge Massei: 'Ah, Amanda Knox. Um, good morning, *Signor* Judge. I wanted to give a very brief explanation about the question of the beauty case which should still be in the bathroom at my house, I don't know.'

She continued: 'This vibrator *does* exist. It's a joke, it's a present a girlfriend gave me before I came to Italy. It's a small pink rabbit about this size . . .' she made a gesture to indicate it was about four inches long. 'Excuse me if . . . well, so, that's it. I also wanted to say I'm innocent and that I'm confident that everything will come out, everything will sort itself out, thank you. OK.'

She said 'OK' in a chirpy tone that sounded out of place in the courtroom. Amanda smiled as she finished, then sat down again with her head bowed, blowing air out through puffed cheeks, apparently to release tension.

Several lawyers looked at each other in disbelief – of all the things Amanda could have talked about, they wondered, why on earth had she focused on a toy vibrator?

The longer Sophie had to wait, the more tense she became. She felt worse when Amy was called in after Robyn, meaning she would have to wait even longer. While she and several of the other students were waiting, a police officer chatted to them in English, talking at length about the case. The officer boasted about how detectives had bugged a conversation between Amanda and her mother in prison. 'We put cameras in, we sat in the room next to them and listened to their conversation,' the officer said.

Sophie was called shortly after 3 p.m. She had waited more than five hours. By now, as she confessed later, she had gone to pieces. She had worried she would be frightened of Amanda but instead, when she walked into the court, she concentrated on getting to the raised platform and didn't think of Amanda, let alone look at her. Her voice hesitant and husky with tension, she found even saying her name and address a struggle.

'Did you know Meredith Kercher?' Mignini asked her – his very first question brought tears to Sophie's eyes again.

The prosecutor went on to ask about the tensions between Meredith and Amanda. One reason, Sophie said, was the way Amanda chatted about her sex life. 'Amanda was pretty open about her sex life and she left a beauty-case in the bathroom with a vibrator and some condoms,' Sophie said.

From time to time, Sophie would close her eyes as she remembered aloud Amanda's coldness when she hugged her at the police station, or Amanda telling her Meredith had died. She was vaguely aware of Amanda, sitting behind her and to her left, staring at her as she testified. But Sophie never turned to look at her.

As Mignini asked Sophie about the clothes Meredith was wearing the last time she saw her, he gave a clerk a photograph to show Sophie. 'Can you tell me if this sweatshirt corresponds to the one Meredith was wearing?' the prosecutor asked.

The photograph was in colour, and Sophie couldn't help seeing there was blood all over the light blue sweatshirt. The shock of seeing the blood – she had never seen that photograph before – made her cry. She could barely manage a nod in answer to Mignini.

Judge Massei asked Sophie if she wanted a break. 'No, I'm fine,' she replied.

Later, as Amanda's lawyer Dalla Vedova talked Sophie through the hours at the police station after Meredith's body was discovered, he asked: 'Do you remember if, among the young people who were there with you, there was someone who was particularly shocked, or who was crying? Was someone crying?'

'Everybody was crying except for Amanda,' Sophie replied. It wasn't the kind of thing Sophie had meant to say, because she hadn't wanted to sound as if she was accusing Amanda. But it was the first thing that had come to her mind.

'So Raffaele too?' Dalla Vedova asked.

'No, Raffaele wasn't crying,' Sophie said.

Dalla Vedova fired back: 'Neither was the police. It seems to me there are . . .'

Judge Massei cut short the lawyer to point out: 'We're talking about the group of young people.'

Sophie said nothing, but she was angry with Dalla Vedova. She felt he'd made her look stupid.

That afternoon, Sophie's friends told her what Amanda had said about the vibrator. Amanda was missing the point, Sophie thought. If it really was a joke one, why was it on show? Amanda must have put the vibrator, and the condoms, on display to show off. For Sophie, owning a vibrator didn't mean Amanda had killed Meredith, but showing off with it had struck Meredith as weird.

That day, none of Meredith's English friends looked at Amanda when they testified. The mother of one of them confided: 'The trial dragging out for so long makes it tough for the girls. For them it's as if everything keeps coming back to Meredith, all the time.'

14 February 2009

Although they quickly recovered their composure, neither the two judges nor the jury could hide their surprise at the T-shirt Amanda wore for St Valentine's Day – white, far too big for her slight figure, it had fat, red lettering all down her front: 'ALL YOU NEED IS LOVE'.

Some lawyers smiled at Amanda's tribute to The Beatles, her favourite band, but others shook their heads. Journalists in the press gallery forgot all about the Kercher case for a while and furiously debated the T-shirt's significance.

'She's behaving like a teenager – she's facing a life sentence but she wears a T-shirt like that as if she was going to a party!' one reporter said.

'No, she simply wants to be seen as a warm, loving personality. It's a cry for love – she's in prison and on trial, and she wants to be loved,' said another.

The court got a clear look at the T-shirt when Amanda got up to speak after witnesses including her former flatmate Laura, and the students from the semi-basement flat, had testified about her character and her relations with Meredith.

She spoke briefly, in Italian, as she had the previous day: 'Thank you to everyone, *Signor* Judge. I just wanted to say that hearing over the past few days all this testimony from witnesses including my ex-flatmates, I'm really and sincerely annoyed that after all this time some things are exaggerated, like about the cleaning.

'This has been extremely exaggerated,' she said. 'I wasn't . . . Yes, I talked to the girls, but it wasn't ever a cause of conflict, ever, in fact there were always good relations with these people. This is because I'm really annoyed, because really . . . It wasn't like that, so . . . Thank you.'

Once more, Amanda surprised many in the courtroom by singling out an issue that was to all appearances unimportant.

But what dominated the media in its reporting of that day's proceedings was Amanda, or rather her T-shirt – photographs of her wearing it appeared in newspapers from Rome to London to Seattle.

The sight dismayed the prosecutors. 'I wouldn't want it to be a message to Raffaele, in the sense of "let's stick together through this in the name of love",' one of them confided. 'What's for sure is that it points to Amanda as the driving force in all this, as a narcissist, as an actress and as someone who is unable to share the suffering of others. She thinks only of herself.'

The Kerchers' lawyer Maresca could hardly contain his anger. 'Amanda's gone too far. It's fine to declare yourself innocent all your life but there are limits. I can't stand this frivolous attitude, it's offensive to the court and it's especially offensive to Meredith's family. Let's remember we're talking about a girl who was stabbed to death,' Maresca stormed.

He was sure it would all backfire. 'I'm sure the judges and jury find it all offensive too. If I was Amanda's lawyer, I'd try to keep her in check,' he said.

Back at home in England, the sight of Amanda wearing the T-shirt made Sophie feel sick. It was so typical of Amanda, she thought. Surely if Amanda was innocent, she'd want to be taken seriously by the court and dress appropriately to help persuade it of her innocence. Sophie herself had thought a lot about what she should wear, and she'd been only a witness. How could Amanda think that wearing that T-shirt was the right thing to do?

'It's ridiculous. Amanda's crazy,' Sophie thought to herself. It was almost as if the trial was a joke to her.

When he next saw Amanda in prison, her stepfather Chris ticked her off gently for wearing the T-shirt, a present from a friend. 'You know, I don't think your lawyers are too happy about it,' he told her.

'I didn't think it would have such an impact,' Amanda replied. The T-shirt was one of her favourites, and she had thought it would be 'appropriate, a good thing' to wear on St Valentine's Day.

'Well, think of it next time,' Chris said. He didn't feel like rowing with her, what with all she was going through.

'Amanda's a goofball when it comes to that kind of thing,' Chris said later.

18 February 2009

If Amanda's Beatles T-shirt was a message for someone, it wasn't for Raffaele. Replying to letters he'd sent her on Valentine's Day and the following day – they were allowed to write to each other – Amanda dashed his hopes of the pair feeling for each other the way they did at first. She apologised for having '*steered myself back to the love that I knew and that was reborn in myself for DJ [her Seattle boyfriend]; because it means I can't give you what you want, I can't give you my heart completely.*' From then on, she made a point of signing herself: '*Your friend Amanda*'.

That day, Mignini returned to the cottage after police told him that intruders had broken in and ransacked Meredith and Amanda's flat. The break-in had been discovered by a passing patrol car. The first thing the prosecutor noticed was that the intruders had broken in through the glass door that gave on to the terrace – which he had always argued was the easiest way in. He saw it as further confirmation that no one had broken in through Filomena's window at the time of Meredith's murder.

Inside, the police had found a used candle and four big kitchen knives – one knife on a shelf near the front door, one on the kitchen floor on top of an empty police evidence bag, one on Meredith's bed, and one in front of her bedroom doorway, with the blade pointing towards it.

It might just be a stunt by some idiots, the prosecutor thought, but it might also be something more than that. He guessed it might be a coded message of some kind, but he had no idea what. Perhaps it had something to do with the fact that the detectives of the Flying Squad were due to testify at the trial in a few days' time.

27 February 2009

For her turn as a witness, the detective Napoleoni swapped the jeans and casual clothes she always wore on duty for her navy-blue police uniform. She had spent many hours following the trial in court over the past month, and was anxious to testify. For her, this was a chance to stand up publicly for her and her colleagues' work on the Kercher case after months of what she saw as mud-slinging by the defence lawyers who had virulently attacked the investigation.

The charge that had most rankled with Napoleoni was Amanda's allegation that police had beaten her at the station on the night she accused Patrick of murdering Meredith.

Asked by Patrick's lawyer Carlo Pacelli whether '*Signorina* Amanda', as he quaintly called her, had been beaten, Napoleoni replied firmly: 'No, absolutely not.'

'Was she by chance treated badly or threatened or insulted?' Pacelli asked.

'No, she was treated well. Obviously she was treated firmly, because it wasn't as if we were at the cinema or the circus, even if someone may have thought that's where we were,' Napoleoni said, in a clear dig at Amanda's yoga exercises at the police station.

Mignini's fellow prosecutor Comodi took advantage of Napoleoni and other detectives taking the witness box to show to the court the big stone which had been found on the floor in the room of Meredith and Amanda's flatmate Filomena, near the broken window. Several detectives had testified that it was too big and heavy to have been used in a 'burglary' – which they insisted had been staged after the murder.

In a not too discreet attempt to forge a direct relationship with the jurors, Comodi walked up to them, stone in hand, and handed it to each of them – and the two judges – in turn. She wanted them to touch it with their hands, to feel its full weight (4.5 kilos) and to see for themselves how absurd it was to claim that a thief would throw this at a window.

To her satisfaction, several of the jurors made comments along the lines of, 'God, it's so heavy.'

One woman juror turned to her neighbour and said: 'See, I told you it weighs four kilos.'

Over the past hearings, Comodi had been watching the jurors closely. Although they were clearly making an effort not to betray their opinion on the case, she noticed the women jurors nodding a couple of times when she or Mignini argued a point – something they never did when the defence lawyers spoke.

43

More than two months into the trial, snow fell again on Perugia, prettily dusting the statues of griffins in its squares as the first of the witnesses found by the local *Giornale dell'Umbria* newspaper took his turn in court. The grocer Marco Quintavalle, who had said he'd seen Amanda in his supermarket early on the morning after the murder – when she claimed she was in Raffaele's flat – spoke slowly and precisely.

But what Quintavalle clearly considered an ordeal unsettled him; his left eyebrow often twitched some half a dozen times in quick succession. Under questioning by Mignini, he described Raffaele as a 'very serious, very well-brought-up young man' who came to the shop as often as twice a day but never stopped for a chat.

What struck him about the young woman he had seen walk past him, only a couple of feet away from him, into his shop at 7.45 a.m. on the morning after the murder was how pale she looked – and her blue eyes.

'I can still see it today, she had a very white face, with these blue eyes it was very striking,' he said. 'She looked really exhausted but that looked pretty normal to me, because students who've been out dancing or to a party stay up all night.'

Some days later, one of the girls at the till who had been out for her coffee break came back and told him she'd heard that Raffaele had been arrested the previous day.

'It's not possible. Are you sure?' Quintavalle said. He asked her to go and buy a newspaper and when he saw Amanda's picture he immediately thought to himself: 'But that's the girl I saw the other morning.'

He told the court: 'I recognised the oval shape of her face, the nose which is very regular, this beautiful oval shape, with these very light-coloured eyes.'

Judge Massei interrupted Mignini's questioning. 'Excuse me. Do you recognise the girl you saw on that occasion in this courtroom?'

The courtroom went still; lawyers stopped tapping on their laptops.

Quintavalle turned to take a long look behind his left shoulder at Amanda, the first time he had looked at her since entering the courtroom.

'Yes,' he said.

Amanda's cheeks and ears suddenly flushed but she held his gaze, frowning slightly, apparently in both concentration and concern.

'Are you sure?'

'Yes.'

'Is it her? Are you sure it's the girl you saw?' Judge Massei insisted.

Quintavalle again turned to stare at Amanda. 'I'm sure now, yes.'

Later, when a TV interview with Quintavalle was shown on a giant screen, glimpses of Amanda's life before her arrest unexpectedly unfolded before the court – Amanda smiling and laughing in family photographs; a tipsy Amanda wagging her finger at the camera at a party with her student friends; Amanda looking hunted in the garden of the cottage on the day Meredith's body was discovered. Today's Amanda stared at the images of herself, looking as if she was about to cry.

When it was the turn of Raffaele's lawyer Maori, he tried to undermine Quintavalle by pressing him on why he hadn't called the police the moment he recognised Amanda in the newspaper. Why did he wait a whole year to come forward?

Quintavalle replied he'd only come forward because the journalist Fois had persuaded him to. He simply didn't think that what he'd seen was important. 'And besides, I wasn't all that keen to get involved, just as I'm not that keen today,' Quintavalle said.

But Maori wouldn't let go. 'But the question is why he presented himself a year after. So—'

Mignini interrupted him to jump to Quintavalle's defence. 'Objection, because the witness has to say the truth – when he testifies, or how he was found, is of no interest. What's important is what the witness says. The fact that he comes forward after some time is sadly because of reasons we all know about.'

Mignini continued: 'Witnesses should come forward immediately, but many of them say: "Well, what I say doesn't matter at all." They don't understand the importance of what they have to say.'

But Judge Massei overruled Mignini; the issue of how Quintavalle had come to testify would help to assess his reliability, the judge said.

Pressed once more, Quintavalle gave a curt answer. He had decided to testify when the journalist had told him he should. 'That's all there is to it,' he said.

As the weeks passed, with the prosecutors relentlessly working their way through dozens of witnesses, Amanda looked increasingly drawn in court. She no longer had a smile stamped on her face when she entered; she walked head bowed, with her shoulders hunched forwards, visibly shrinking from the touch of the guards who escorted her. But she still nodded and smiled at Judge Massei, who sometimes responded with a tight smile.

She was now finding it hard to keep her mind busy with her language studies as she used to. The long succession of witnesses unsettled her. Shortly after Quintavalle's testimony, she saw Ghirga in prison.

'So what does it mean? I don't have any hope?' she asked him
– 'it' meaning the array of witnesses at the trial.

'There's still hope, don't worry,' Ghirga said.

But he worried that it would be difficult to save her. He noticed
that Amanda never asked him outright whether she would be
convicted or not; nor did she ever ask him how long a prison
sentence could be. In court, when a witness said something that
worried her particularly, she would take hold of Ghirga's hand
and squeeze it, seeking comfort.

In front of prison guards, however, Amanda was a closed book.
One of them confided: 'Amanda's always smiling, always cheerful.
Every time I ask her how she is, she just says: "OK, fine." She's
never opened up. I've seen her cry, but only for little things like
the cellmate who made her clean all the time. She's never cried
over her fate. It's as if she doesn't seem to realise what's happened
to her.'

27 March 2009

It was cold in the courtroom and the elderly widow Nara Capezzali
kept her white anorak on as, her hair perfectly permed and
clutching the handbag which rested in her lap, she described in a
homely, slightly husky voice the scream she said she'd heard on
the night of Meredith's murder from her flat opposite the cottage.
The court sat as if spellbound by her words.

'I've got gooseflesh. I can almost . . . hear it again,' Capezzali
said, her hands quivering at the recollection of how she'd heard
what she described as a woman's scream after getting up to go to
the bathroom.

The judges and jury stared fixedly at her, stern-faced. Amanda sat
rock still, while Ghirga next to her shook his head from side to side.

'A scream,' Capezzali went on. She tried to make the noise
again, her voice rising: '*Aaaaaahhh . . .*' As she made the sound,
she let go of the strap of her handbag to raise her right hand and
make a long drawn-out sweeping gesture.

Mignini's questioning of Capezzali was however suddenly thrown off course when she mentioned that at about 11 a.m. the next day, she had gone to buy some bread and had read the newspaper placards on Piazza Grimana with news of Meredith's murder and exclaimed to a couple of friends: 'Oh God, I heard it, so it was this girl!'

Mignini struggled to put her back on the right track. She had always said in the past – to the journalist Fois, to Mignini himself and to other journalists who had interviewed her – that she'd heard the scream on the night of the murder. But the murder wasn't in the newspapers until the morning of 3 November, two days later. The prosecutor was convinced that the elderly widow was simply getting confused because of the stress of appearing in court.

'Are you sure you saw those newspaper placards that morning, or did you see them on a later occasion?' Mignini asked.

Raffaele's lawyer Bongiorno intervened, appealing to the judge in an attempt to have his question ruled out of order – she didn't want Mignini to give the witness a chance to correct herself: 'Your Honour, this is a typical question to try to—'

Judge Massei turned to Capezzali and attempted to clear things up himself: 'Excuse me, you say you saw the newspaper placards; what did you see as you walked past this newspaper kiosk?'

'I didn't see the newspaper placards, maybe it was the day after, because I go shopping every day, it's not as if I can remember . . .' Capezzali replied, now sounding thoroughly confused. Capezzali remained vague, and flustered, throughout the rest of her questioning, to Mignini's visible frustration.

After two hours of continuous questioning by Mignini and defence lawyers, she again had the court spellbound. Asking Capezzali about a TV interview she'd given, Amanda's lawyer Dalla Vedova asked whether her interviewer was a man or a woman. She replied first that it was a man, then that it might have been a woman. Apparently seeking to underline her confusion, Dalla Vedova screened the interview to show the journalist was a woman.

The interview, and Capezzali's reaction to it, chilled the court. On screen, she sobbed as she talked of 'a scream that was almost inhuman'. On the witness box, Capezzali herself sat with her eyes closed and her head down, looking on the verge of tears; moments later, she wiped tears from her eyes.

One woman juror also cried, dabbing her eyes and nose with a paper handkerchief. Another juror sat with his hands clasped in front of his forehead, as if what was happening was too distressing for him.

Mignini stood up to request that what he called Capezzali's 'silent crying' be entered into the court records. Judge Massei agreed to his demand.

Amanda, who had sat immobile as usual, turned to look at Ghirga; he shrugged.

When Judge Massei suspended the hearing for a break shortly afterwards, Ghirga stood up, looking sombre, while Amanda leant forward and stayed hunched over her desk, cheeks resting on her clenched fists, for several long seconds.

44

Suffering from a bad hernia, the tramp Antonio Curatolo was wheeled into the courtroom on an office chair by a clerk and an assistant of Mignini. They then lifted him, still in the chair, onto the witness box where he took his oath. He wore jeans and a blue denim jacket, a black and white hat, and a blue scarf tucked under his grey beard; his battered brown boots gaped open, laces undone.

Gently guided by Mignini, Curatolo testified in a strong, clear voice that on the evening of the murder, when he was sitting on a bench on Piazza Grimana reading a news magazine and smoking the odd cigarette, he'd noticed a boy and girl 'who looked like they were boyfriend and girlfriend' in a corner of the basketball court.

The pair talked animatedly to each other and every so often one of them would get up, walk over to a railing and look over towards the gate of the cottage. Curatolo had gone away just before midnight to spend the night in a nearby park. They'd disappeared shortly before that.

'How were these youngsters dressed?' Mignini asked.

'Their clothes were a bit dark,' Curatolo replied.

'Can you describe them to us – what did they look like?'

'They were a bit short. They looked nice, I thought.'

'Dark hair, light hair? Excuse me *Signor* Curatolo, can you see them in this courtroom, these youngsters?'

Curatolo turned stiffly to his left and took a long, slow look at Raffaele and then at Amanda. 'Yes,' he said.

Judge Massei: 'Can you point to them?'

Curatolo pointed with a bony finger. 'It's her and him. But I'd seen them before that evening too.'

Amanda, who was leaning forward over the desk in front of her, remained impassive. Raffaele swung his chair from side to side.

Curatolo added that the next day, in the early afternoon, he'd seen police and *carabinieri* officers at the cottage.

When Mignini sat down, Bongiorno started her questioning by making Curatolo repeat several times that he'd first seen the pair he believed were Amanda and Raffaele at 9.30 p.m.

'Listen to that, the tramp is giving Amanda and Raffaele a new alibi!' exclaimed a journalist in the public gallery.

Bongiorno's insistence on the timing disconcerted Mignini. Until then, he'd assumed on the basis of Curatolo's statement to him in February that the tramp had first seen the pair some two hours later. But in Curatolo's statement – which the prosecutor read out in court – there was no mention of when he'd first seen the couple.

Pressed by Mignini, Curatolo said he hadn't been watching the couple all the time. He'd read his magazine for a bit, then he'd smoked a cigarette and had a look round the square, and then read some more. In all, he'd seen the couple four or five times that evening.

Under questioning by Judge Massei, Curatolo said that 'sometimes it looked as if they were joking together, and sometimes it looked as if they were quarrelling.'

Looking a little thrown by Curatolo's testimony, Mignini called his next witness – Fabio Gioffredi, a lanky-haired university graduate in his mid-thirties.

Gioffredi described how two days before the murder on 30 October, he'd seen four youngsters walk out of the cottage at about 5 p.m. as he went to fetch his car, which was parked across the road. They were walking silently up the drive to the gate. At the time, Gioffredi recognised only Rudy – he was 99 per cent certain it was Rudy, because he'd already seen him before outside the university. A few days later, when he saw them on TV, he realised the three others were Meredith, Amanda and Raffaele.

Gioffredi was the only witness who said he'd seen the victim with all three accused of her murder. He recalled that Meredith was wearing jeans and army-type black boots with buckles, Raffaele a long dark jacket and Amanda a long, red '1960s-style' coat. He didn't see Rudy well enough to say how he was dressed because he was behind Raffaele. He was sure of the date because he'd bumped into someone else's car in the car park and had quarrelled with the driver. Like Curatolo before him, he too recognised Amanda and Raffaele in court.

After Gioffredi had been dismissed, Raffaele stood up. In his thin, reedy voice, he said Gioffredi couldn't have seen him with Rudy because he didn't know Rudy. Second, he'd never seen Amanda wear a long red coat. 'And third, that day I was elsewhere as my lawyers will demonstrate, with documents to prove it, later in this trial,' Raffaele said, thanking the court before sitting down again.

Both Mignini and his colleague Comodi had hesitated before putting the next witness down on their list – the Albanian farmhand Hekuran Kokomani. His testimony had been bluntly dismissed as 'irrelevant ravings' by Judge Micheli, who'd convicted Rudy and sent Amanda and Raffaele to trial. To make matters worse, the police had arrested Kokomani and accused him of drug-dealing in mid-February after finding eight grammes of cocaine in his flat; Kokomani had protested he was innocent and denied it was his.

But the prosecutors felt that he was a credible witness and decided to summon him. Armed guards took Kokomani's handcuffs off before he entered the courtroom but he walked in, head bowed, with a guard on either side of him. As with Amanda and Raffaele, the two guards then stood behind him while he gave evidence.

A thickset figure with a heavy butcher's face and a military-style haircut, dressed in a blue and white tracksuit, Kokomani looked nervous and gave his name in a whisper. Almost as soon as he started giving evidence, Judge Massei asked him to speak slowly and clearly. The judge was to make the same request again and again, to little effect.

Mignini kept insisting that Kokomani should speak in his native Albanian as he had a woman interpreter sitting next to him, but Kokomani kept answering in very poor Italian. His replies were often bewildering, prompting the usually unflappable Judge Massei to look lost for the first time since the trial had begun, his cheeks buried in the palms of his hands, and one juror to scratch his head in bafflement.

On the night before the murder or on the night of the murder itself – Kokomani wasn't sure which – he'd been driving past the cottage after dinner when he saw what looked like a black bag in the middle of the road; he braked but touched it with his bumper. He realised the 'bag' was in fact two youngsters when they stood up.

'These two kids here,' he added, indicating Amanda and Raffaele – the third witness to identify them in court that day.

As far as he could tell, the two had rowed with each other for a few seconds then Raffaele walked up to Kokomani, who was still sitting in his car, and punched him. Kokomani punched Raffaele back, sending his glasses flying.

Startling the guards standing behind him, Kokomani suddenly raised his hands above his head and mimed clutching a knife horizontally in both hands.

'The girl pulled out a knife with both hands and she said: "Come here and I'll show you!" ' Kokomani said, adding the knife was between twelve and sixteen inches long. Raffaele then said to Kokomani: 'Forget it, she's a girl; she can't do anything to you.'

After more requests from Judge Massei for him to speak up and to articulate, Kokomani ploughed on with his story: 'After the girl held the knife up, I threw a handful of olives in her face.'

Judge Massei, looking stunned: 'You threw a handful of olives?'

'Yes, at the girl.'

'And where were the olives?'

'I had them in a bucket in front of the seat.'

Kokomani's story – which often amazed his audience – was by no means finished. A black boy near the cottage whom Kokomani recognised as Rudy – Kokomani said he'd seen Rudy before at a bed and breakfast where he used to work as a waiter – had started shouting at him, and then demanded the loan of his car. Kokomani refused, and asked Rudy: 'What's that girl doing with a knife?'

'It's a party, we're cutting the cake,' Rudy replied.

At this point, Kokomani heard what sounded like a young woman in the cottage shouting for help or quarrelling – he didn't know in what language but it wasn't Italian – but Rudy told him it was just some music. Kokomani finally drove away and as he did so he saw that Raffaele was now holding a knife, which looked shorter than the one Amanda had.

When her turn came, Bongiorno lost no time in seeking to ridicule Kokomani. She zeroed in on his claim to have seen Amanda and Raffaele not only in November but also a couple of months earlier, in late August or early September. According to Kokomani, the couple was in a bar with a man in his sixties whose hair was 'a bit white and a bit red' and 'who said he was Amanda's uncle – maybe he was her lover, I didn't ask him for his ID papers!'

Bongiorno pointed out that Amanda and Raffaele had met only in late October, but Kokomani insisted he'd seen them together the previous summer.

When Bongiorno made Kokomani describe again how he'd thrown olives at Amanda, two jurors grinned broadly as he talked. Amanda turned to glance at Ghirga, who tapped his skull three times to mean the witness was mad.

In a smug tone of voice, Kokomani boasted about how the olives had struck home: 'I hit her spot on . . . In the face, she started to yell.'

Many in the courtroom burst out laughing, and several jurors smiled.

Kokomani proved the most bewildering witness the trial had seen so far, contradicting himself repeatedly. In his previous statements, he'd first estimated that he'd seen Amanda and Raffaele in the middle of the road at about 6.30 p.m., then that it had been 8.40 p.m. In court, he told Bongiorno it was about 9 or 9.30 p.m., before telling Judge Massei it was 8.30 or 9.30 p.m.

After Kokomani had testified that he'd noticed a gap in the middle of Amanda's front teeth when she shouted at him and brandished the knife, her lawyer Dalla Vedova asked him: 'Can you see Amanda today? Can you describe the space between the teeth?'

Kokomani muttered something incomprehensible.

'Perhaps if you look at her teeth . . .' Dalla Vedova suggested.

Amanda bared her teeth as Kokomani looked at her. 'Now she's got them stuck together,' he said, to more laughter in the courtroom.

Mignini put a brave face on a bad day. Kokomani, he insisted later, may have tried to 'overdo things' in court, and his refusal to use the interpreter was infuriating, but he'd seen Amanda, Raffaele and Rudy on the night before the murder. As for the tramp Curatolo, he'd seen Amanda and Raffaele on the night of the murder – which contradicted their alibi that they hadn't moved from Raffaele's flat that night.

45

The pathologist Luca Lalli, who had carried out the autopsy on Meredith, was the first expert witness to testify at the trial. Behind closed doors – Judge Massei ordered the public and the media to leave out of respect for Meredith – Lalli described his findings on the time and cause of death. He had found no unequivocal signs of sexual violence on Meredith's body, but he didn't rule out the possibility that she had been forced into having sex.

Judge Massei asked Lalli about Meredith's final moments: 'If there was during this period a very loud scream, a horrifying one – one of the witnesses said she heard it – when would you situate it? When she was struck in the neck?'

'I think it's unlikely the scream was at the moment of the most serious stab to the neck, because it would have been difficult to make the sound. It's possible the scream was at any time before that wound was inflicted. So theoretically that could be the moment when the girl was struck on the right side of the neck, where the wound wouldn't have made her incapable of screaming,' Lalli said.

'And if that's the case, the scream would have been one of pain or of fear? Or . . .'

'That's impossible, impossible to say . . .'

'An immediate reaction to pain?'

'Well, given the nature of pain, it takes a bit of time for a wound to produce pain so it's just as likely it was a scream of fear as of pain. We can't distinguish the moment in which the girl screams because she sees the weapon approaching, from the moment she realises the weapon has struck her and at that point screams out of fear and pain.'

Lalli's conclusions differed from those of his boss Professor Mauro Bacci, the head of Perugia's forensic medicine institute, who with two more colleagues had been asked by Mignini to study the results of the autopsy. For Bacci and his two colleagues, there was 'every probability' that the sex Meredith had shortly before her death 'could have had a violent connotation'. They pointed not only to the bruises in the genital area but also to bruises that indicated the killer or killers had tried to immobilise her.

The three experts found that the worst wound had provoked a haemorrhage and caused Meredith to inhale a great deal of blood. The kitchen knife seized at Raffaele's flat, and on which Meredith and Amanda's DNA had been found, was compatible with both the most serious wound and with one of the smaller ones, but then so were many other knives on the market. It was incompatible however with one of the two smaller wounds, because in order to enter the neck so deeply, its blade would have made a wider wound on her skin than the one Meredith suffered.

The experts gave a revised estimate for the time of death. Given that Meredith had eaten her dinner between 6 and 9 p.m. – and not at 9 p.m. as first thought when Lalli had estimated the time of death at 11 p.m. – and that she had left Amy and Robyn's home at 8.45 p.m., they said Meredith had died between 9.30 p.m. and midnight.

4 April 2009

A crowded courtroom watched in tense silence as, looking meek despite his athletic build, Rudy was escorted by guards to the witness box. He didn't look at either Amanda or Raffaele. Over the past few days, newspapers had furiously debated whether he would agree to give evidence and make a stunning revelation, or whether, as was his right, he would refuse to say anything. It took Rudy just a few seconds to end the suspense.

Judge Massei asked him whether he would answer questions or not.

Rudy glanced at his lawyers and then said simply: 'I exercise my right not to answer questions.'

The judge immediately dismissed him and Rudy walked out, again without a look at either Amanda or Raffaele.

The Kerchers' lawyer Maresca had been hoping for much more. 'Rudy's lost another opportunity to clarify his situation. He's going down the wrong road,' he commented afterwards.

18 April 2009

At the request of Raffaele's lawyers, the court abandoned the Hall of Frescoes for a couple of hours to visit the scene of the crime they were trying to reconstruct. Raffaele's defence team wanted to show the court that Meredith's killer – they hinted heavily this could only be Rudy – had indeed broken into the cottage through the window of her flatmate Filomena's bedroom.

The request surprised Maresca. 'I don't see the point of it. The Supreme Court has already said the thief would have had to be Spiderman to climb a dozen feet up a bare wall, and more importantly Judge Micheli acquitted Rudy of theft – so there was no break-in, only a fake one,' he said before the visit began.

Outside the cottage, the jury was divided in half – men in one group, women in the other – and the men went in first led by Judge Massei. The prosecutor Comodi tagged on to the men's group, along with the lawyer Bongiorno and the detective Napoleoni.

The floor was such a mess – it was strewn with clothes, papers, books and CDs – that they all had to pick their way through. The flat was filthy and the air inside smelt stale. It was almost completely dark in the flat – the only light came from the doorway – so Comodi borrowed a small electric torch from a police officer and opened a couple of windows to let in both light and air.

At first, no one spoke as they just stood in the sitting room and looked around. Comodi found the silence in the cottage deafening.

Bongiorno broke the silence to ask Judge Massei if a clerk who had a video camera could film the drawers where kitchen utensils were kept. He agreed, and Bongiorno tried to open what looked like the first drawer. She pulled and pulled but with no success, and finally gave up. Napoleoni had known all along the first drawer was a fake one – the handle was purely decorative – but she was damned if she was going to help Bongiorno.

Holding her torch up by her head, Comodi led the group down the corridor. The others followed her gingerly and stopped briefly to look inside Amanda's tiny room. Then Comodi went next door into Meredith's room. Using her torch, she walked across it avoiding the pool of blood on the floor and opened the window and shutters. The sunlight streamed in. The view over the rolling hills was at its spring best – a view Meredith had never seen.

The blood on the floor had caked completely dry. It was a dark colour. The splashes and streaks of blood on the walls had also darkened with time. The judges and jurors gazed for a long time at the photographs of Meredith and her friends still on the walls.

Looking around the room, a juror commented: 'But this isn't a small room like Amanda's. How many of us are in here now?'

Quick as a flash, Comodi replied: 'Seven.' She was secretly delighted by the question, as the defence had claimed Meredith's room was too small for three killers to attack her in it.

Bongiorno said nothing.

Another juror asked Comodi where the body had been found, and she gestured with her hands to indicate its position. As she spoke, the jurors looked from her to the bloody floor and she felt they fully realised the horror of what Meredith had been through.

But soon, that horror proved too much for Comodi herself. Just as on her first visit to the cottage the previous summer, she again felt as if she was going to suffocate. Excusing herself she walked out of the cottage, asking Mignini to replace her inside.

Later, the judges and jurors walked slowly round the cottage. One juror stared at the iron grating outside the door to the semi-basement flat, then up at the terrace above.

'*Presidente*,' he called out to the short Judge Massei, using his formal title, 'even you could manage to climb up here.'

The judges and jurors then went to examine the smooth wall under Filomena's window.

One woman juror remarked: 'If you ask me, anyone trying to climb that wall would have come to a sticky end.'

Comodi noted with satisfaction that this juror clearly didn't buy the claim that a burglar had broken in through Filomena's window. For Comodi, the defence had scored an own goal.

23 April 2009

Back in the Hall of Frescoes, as Comodi questioned Claudio Cantagalli from Perugia's forensic police, the judge allowed the public and the media to remain while a film of the crime scene was screened.

Amanda ignored the film at first, chewing gum and doodling on a piece of paper with her head down. Looking up suddenly, she flashed a big smile to Raffaele, making a gesture with her right hand over her stomach as if she was about to vomit, then laughed silently – a joke, according to one of his lawyers, about the stomach cramps Raffaele was suffering from.

Moments later, Amanda's face tensed as she stared at her bedroom on the screen. When the images switched to Meredith's room – the quilt, the foot sticking out from under it, the bra nearby – Amanda suddenly leant forward over her desk and put her left hand over her brow as if covering her eyes.

But from then on she would occasionally steal sideway glances from under her hand at the screen to her left. She looked away when the quilt covering Meredith, or traces of blood on the walls of Meredith's bedroom, appeared. Raffaele, in contrast, stared steadily at the screen throughout, chewing gum all the time.

Later, as the court reconvened after a lunch break, Raffaele and Amanda again smiled at each other. Raffaele held up a *Bacio* chocolate – the name also means 'kiss' in Italian – signalling that he wanted to give it to her. But guards stopped him.

'AMANDA AND RAFFAELE'S BANNED BACIO' a local paper headlined the next morning.

27 April 2009

Thin rain fell on what was once his daughter's home and leaden clouds hung low over the hills behind it as a bare-headed and grim-faced Curt waited outside the cottage, carrying a large blue suitcase and a big, empty shopping bag. A detective waved him in and he strode through the gate and up to Napoleoni who was sheltering under the porch.

Judge Massei had lifted the order sealing off the cottage and it was now time for Curt to retrieve some of Amanda's belongings before it was handed over to the owner, a wealthy elderly woman who lived in Rome and was preparing to rent it out again.

Guided by Napoleoni, Curt walked through the flat, which smelt unpleasantly dank with the rain, and turned into his daughter's room. Someone had opened the window. No one spoke as, watched by a couple of detectives, Curt pulled a handwritten list out of his pocket and picked out the items Amanda had asked him for – rock-climbing equipment and language-learning books. The only sounds were of the wind and the rain, and the swishing of car wheels on the wet road a few yards away.

Curt packed the suitcase and then the shopping bag, while an estate agent accompanied by a painter and a builder inspected the flat, estimating the cost of repairs and a new coat of paint.

The rain was still falling as an emotional Curt walked away from the cottage, carrying Amanda's belongings. 'The flat's a disaster, everything's been thrown around or broken,' he said as he walked to his car. 'It's a very sad situation in there. It's the house where a young lady lost her life. But being able to take Amanda's things out today, I kind of feel it's a step towards her coming home.'

Asked how his daughter was, Curt replied: 'She feels less free with every day that passes; she says it's as if she has less and less air to breathe.'

After Curt had left, a couple of police officers stuffed everything he had left behind into black rubbish bags, which they threw into a van parked in the garden. All that was left of Amanda's stay in the room was a small mess of spilt, dark tea leaves on her wooden desk.

Next door, Meredith's room was also stripped bare and her belongings placed in the boot of Napoleoni's car. Two workers sent by the city council quickly cleansed the room of the stains left by her murder. Moments later, the only trace of the killing was a damp grey smudge on the wall between the bed and the cupboard, where they had to rub particularly hard to get rid of the bloody streaks which Mignini thought were left by Meredith, trying to steady herself.

46

Comodi, who had agreed with Mignini that she would take on the forensic part of their case, sat peering at her laptop and muttering to herself as the court waited for her to start screening a film of the crime scene. Raffaele, sitting a couple of yards away to her right, offered to help and a stunned Comodi accepted.

The computer science graduate swiftly found out that Comodi's laptop couldn't play her DVD because it lacked the right program, so he slipped the DVD into a laptop on his desk, connected it to the giant screen in the court, and told her to go ahead.

The film Raffaele was helping to screen for the court included key evidence against him – it showed the forensic police finding Meredith's bra clasp on her bedroom floor, and on which DNA belonging to her as well as Raffaele and Rudy was later found.

Comodi couldn't have been more amazed by Raffaele's gesture. She wouldn't have been surprised if he'd just given her a mocking smile as if to say: 'I could help you, but I'm a defendant, so tough!' His kindness made her think he was at heart a good, well-brought-up boy. But at the same time it was another sign that, like Amanda, he hadn't understood anything about the trial or what was at stake for him. It was as if the pair were merely observers, watching the trial as if it was a film they had no part in.

Didn't they realise, Comodi wondered, that barely two weeks from now, the biologist Patrizia Stefanoni of the Rome forensic police would be presenting what she saw as even more damning evidence against them both?

18 May 2009

In the week leading up to Stefanoni's testimony, Comodi drove to Rome for long discussions with her and her colleagues. It was Stefanoni who'd found the DNA traces on the kitchen knife and on Meredith's bra clasp.

The two prosecutors had left the forensic witnesses until last on their list, as they felt this was the strongest part of their case. The forensic experts were the crucial witnesses; they were the ones who would give the court objective, irrefutable evidence – stronger than an eyewitness who could fail to make a convincing appearance in court, and be dismissed as unreliable.

The case against Amanda and Raffaele could stand or fall on whether the court not only understood the work done by the forensic experts, but also accepted it as scientifically above reproach. The defence lawyers would try to discredit all the results the teams had obtained, and the prosecutors were not going to leave anything to chance.

In the Rome offices of the forensic police, opposite the Cinecittà film studios, Comodi gathered the experts who had worked on the case, including those who had taken and analysed traces of blood and fingerprints. As they began to talk about the trial, Comodi realised they were nervous. They were confident they had done their jobs properly but they were worried about the grilling the defence lawyers would give them, and about being dragged under the media spotlight. To help them prepare for their ordeal, for almost an entire morning Comodi fired at them all the questions she thought the defence might put to them.

Why, she asked, was Meredith's bra clasp not taken from her bedroom until forty-six days after it was first spotted just after the murder? There was no doubt this was a serious mistake, and she expected Raffaele's defence lawyers to throw as much doubt as they could on Stefanoni's discovery of their client's DNA on the clasp. They would be sure to suggest that the clasp had been contaminated. They might go so far as to accuse the forensic police of manipulating the evidence.

'DNA doesn't have wings!' Stefanoni exclaimed. 'How can anyone say that we manipulated tests to throw the blame on Raffaele or Amanda? Do people really think we're monsters who want to crucify kids we've never met?' She didn't like the idea that her professionalism or her integrity could be called into question – her lab was internationally respected, and she'd been sent to join the investigation team struggling to identify victims of the 2004 Boxing Day tsunami in the Indian Ocean.

Of course, Stefanoni said, in an ideal world no one would have entered the cottage between her first search just after the murder and her second on 18 December. Police searches had disrupted the crime scene but that didn't mean the DNA of any of the accused had entered the cottage. The detectives them-selves, or even Mignini, would have been much more likely to leave fingerprints or their DNA behind, and this simply hadn't happened.

As part of their preparations for the next hearings, Comodi, together with Stefanoni, watched the films the forensic police had made at the crime scene. As the prosecutor watched the patholo-gist Lalli uncover the body, she was deeply moved by Meredith's gaze. Comodi had seen a dozen or so bodies in murder cases, but she had never seen eyes that expressive in a victim. For Comodi, Meredith's stare was one of surprise, as if she was thinking: 'No, it's not possible.'

Comodi was also struck by the beauty of Meredith's features; somehow, she looked more beautiful than in the photographs of the Halloween party.

'Thank God I wasn't on duty that night,' Comodi thought to herself.

22 May 2009

'THE LONGEST DAY FOR AMANDA AND RAFFAELE' was the headline of the local *Corriere dell'Umbria* newspaper on the day Stefanoni appeared before the court. Tall and slender with long dark hair, and dressed in an olive green trouser suit and a beige shirt with a frilly collar, she strode confidently into the courtroom, a computer bag slung over her shoulder.

At Comodi's prompting, Stefanoni launched into a long, precise explanation of the nature of DNA, its relevance to police investigations, and the rigid testing procedures adopted in her laboratory. She spoke in a self-assured tone of voice with a slight, warm Neapolitan accent, pointing to the charts she displayed on the screen using a red laser pen – as if she was giving a presentation at a science conference.

Her explanation was sometimes so technical it was difficult for the court to grasp. Comodi glanced at the jury. She saw that their attention was waning but it was vital to establish in the minds of the court that this was rigorous science, not guesswork.

Stefanoni then described, room by room, the 460 biological traces which included the bloodstains and traces of footprints, found not only in the cottage but also in Raffaele's and Rudy's flats.

Amanda and Raffaele sat as usual facing the two judges and jurors, their lawyers beside them and two prison guards in jaunty blue berets standing behind each of them. They looked so young and slight the guards seemed unnecessary. Raffaele wore a pink T-shirt and Amanda a plain mauve top, her hair scraped back in a ponytail secured with a blue bobble, a little-girl slide on each side of her head.

She sat pale and tight-lipped as Stefanoni talked, occasionally turning to see the screen, her face serious and intent as if she were back at university, listening to a complicated lecture. She looked away from the screen when it showed the quilt covering Meredith's body, and glanced only briefly at shots of the kitchen knife found in Raffaele's flat. Occasionally, she'd reach under the desk to squeeze Ghirga's hand.

When her turn came to question Stefanoni, Raffaele's lawyer Bongiorno focused on the trace of his DNA which the biologist had found on one of the hooks of the bra clasp, quizzing her relentlessly on the methods she and her team had used to collect evidence in the room. Who had entered it? Had anyone walked out and then gone back in again? How often had they changed their gloves and shoe covers?

'Is it correct to say, in general terms,' Bongiorno asked with mock humility, 'that if I'm wearing a glove which already has someone's DNA on it and I touch this microphone, I can transfer the DNA to it?'

'Only if this DNA is part of a fresh, watery trace, because if the DNA is in a substance which is completely dry, such as dried blood or saliva, I won't transfer the DNA when I touch something. The fact is, I got negative results from lots of samples, like the second time I scratched traces on the wall, which were clearly blood and had DNA in them. The traces had deteriorated, and I didn't get anything out of them,' Stefanoni replied.

Bongiorno then screened film of Stefanoni and her colleagues examining the flat, continually pausing it to challenge her about their work.

As images of Stefanoni taking hold of the bra clasp in Meredith's room a month and a half after the murder came up on the screen, Bongiorno gave a short running commentary: 'That's you. There, look at this point you take the . . . you see the hooks?'

'Yes, yes,' Stefanoni replied.

'Right now you're touching the strap.'

'Yes, and then I turn it round.'

'There, the hooks, the hooks, can you see? Can you see the hooks?' Bongiorno exclaimed excitedly, pointing at the screen.

Stefanoni was unruffled. 'One yes, the other one's hidden by my thumb.'

'Can you confirm to me the answer you gave me in pre-trial hearings that you didn't touch the hooks with your gloves?'

Stefanoni, herself pointing at the screen: 'Excuse me but you can't see that I . . . you can't see on these images [whether I did or not] . . .'

Bongiorno: 'All right, everyone will make up their own minds.'

The exchange caused tension in the courtroom with prosecutors and lawyers talking over each other. Judge Massei called for calm and intervened to clarify the issue: 'You say you didn't touch the hooks?'

'In those images I didn't, perhaps I did . . .' In any case, Stefanoni explained, she and her colleagues had just slipped on new gloves when they entered the room intending to look for the missing clasp.

Bongiorno sought to imply that Stefanoni had been less than professional in her discovery of Raffaele's DNA on the clasp: 'Just to clarify, when you did this test you already had Raffaele's profile?'

Stefanoni, as calm and professional as ever: 'Certainly . . .'

'So you already had Raffaele's profile from his saliva swab and you asked yourself: "Can Raffaele's profile fit in this chart I have here?" '

'No, you don't ask yourself the question first, that's not right.'

Bongiorno insisted: 'But you had it—'

'But it's not as if I knew it by heart! I don't even know my own by heart! It doesn't work like that.'

As Bongiorno continued to imply that Stefanoni had wrongly interrupted the results of the DNA test on the clasp, the biologist pointed out: 'But there's something you can't explain away – the Y chromosome, you can't ignore that.' She meant the Y chromosome found on the clasp could only be attributed to Raffaele or to a male relative.

'Let's forget about that for now,' a flustered Bongiorno observed before moving on.

Just as Bongiorno had focused on the bra clasp, Amanda's lawyer, Dalla Vedova, concentrated on the kitchen knife – her DNA had been found on the handle, and Meredith's on the blade. Dalla Vedova asked Stefanoni first about the way the knife had been sent to her from Perugia, in a cardboard box rather than in an evidence bag.

'Was the box sterilised according to you?' he asked.

'But we don't have sterilised exhibits . . .'

'But the evidence bag is.'

'No, not even the exhibits are sterile, God forbid! . . . For me sterile means something which doesn't have any microorganisms. We don't have anything which is sterile. Not even our gloves; they're in a box.'

While Dalla Vedova quizzed Stefanoni, Amanda wrote several pages of suggestions on what he should ask and passed them to him. He too sought to undermine Stefanoni's work, trying to cast doubt over the way she had concentrated and then amplified the sample on the handle in which Amanda's DNA was found. He also challenged her over her decision to apply a swab to the part of the handle where the hand butted against a small prominence that prevented it from slipping onto the blade.

Stefanoni explained: 'I have to analyse the exhibit in an objective way, so I analyse the exhibit within the context of a murder – and not as if it was being used for cooking.'

'Anyway, when someone cuts bread, how do you think they hold the knife? Don't they hold it the same way?'

'No, you don't hold it the same way.'

'Why?'

'Excuse me, but I don't stab a piece of bread, I—'

'I cut it,' Dalla Vedova completed the sentence for her.

The point where she'd taken the sample, Stefanoni added, 'indicates someone sticking a knife through something rather than someone cutting something.' She mimed a stabbing gesture with her clenched fist.

Several jurors looked taken aback at her gesture, and a few spectators in the courtroom gasped. Judge Massei again had to ask for calm as the prosecutors and lawyers argued among themselves.

After nine hours in court, Stefanoni dabbed at her eyes with a handkerchief – her contact lenses were giving her trouble. It was her first sign of strain; she had remained calm and professional throughout her testimony. Judge Massei suspended the hearing, and asked her to return the next day.

23 May 2009

Dalla Vedova pressed Stefanoni on why one of her colleagues, when working in the small bathroom used by Amanda and Meredith, had used a single swab to pick up trace marks of blood on the edge of the bidet and on the bottom near the plug. The sample contained mixed traces belonging to both Amanda and Meredith.

But Stefanoni doggedly insisted that her colleague had been right to use a single swab because the trace was a single one, as proven by the thin pink rivulet running from the edge of the bidet down towards the plug.

Later Mignini gave Stefanoni, who had analysed thousands of DNA traces in the course of her career, a chance to defend her professional record.

'For how many years have you been doing this job?' Mignini asked.

'Almost seven years.'

'Almost seven years. Have you dealt with cases similar to this one?'

'Yes. Yes, yes.'

'Do you remember whether you have always followed the same methods?'

'Yes.'

'In both taking samples and in assessing them?'

'Yes.'

'So, do you remember any cases of exhibits being contaminated?'

'No. We've never had any problems of the kind.'

Judge Massei also asked Stefanoni about the defence lawyers' charge that the bra clasp had somehow been contaminated with Raffaele's DNA.

'If the clasp had been contaminated with DNA from another source, what could that source be?' the judge asked.

'Look, no other trace of Raffaele's DNA alone was found in the flat. There's only one trace of his DNA and that's on a cigarette end, but it's mixed with Amanda's . . . So there's no reason to say that his DNA is present somewhere else and could have accidentally contaminated the clasp,' she replied.

When Stefanoni left the witness box after another six hours – in total, she'd been giving evidence for fifteen hours over two days – the two prosecutors were both jubilant. Mignini warmly shook her hand as she left the courtroom, while Comodi kissed her on both cheeks.

'You know who said: "You should never fight a battle you can't win"? Lenin,' Mignini said afterwards with a smile. 'If you're a defence lawyer and you're up against a witness like Stefanoni, the best thing would be not to ask any questions at all.'

47

For the first time since the trial started, Amanda looked downcast when she greeted the prison chaplain Father Saulo in jail.

'The worst thing is that I feel powerless. People are saying things which aren't true, and I feel there's nothing I can do about it,' she said.

But Amanda was soon her calm, smiling self again. Father Saulo marvelled at how self-possessed she was, and how unaffected she seemed by what was said against her in court. Sometimes he would mention something about the trial – such as experts testifying that the knife found at Raffaele's flat was compatible with Meredith's wounds.

'Is this positive or negative for you? It looks negative to me,' Father Saulo would ask her.

But whatever Father Saulo mentioned, Amanda always interpreted it as something positive.

The priest couldn't make up his mind whether she was an amazing actress, whether she was deceiving herself, or whether she was simply innocent.

On one visit to the prison, Father Saulo saw that Amanda had done a drawing of two human heads facing each other – both wearing blindfolds. Some women prisoners were putting on an adaptation of the parable of the Prodigal Son, and the drawing was part of the backdrop. The priest thought she'd done the drawing well – but he had no idea what it meant.

6 June 2009

Meredith's mother Arline, a small, fragile-looking figure dressed all in black, her face heavily lined, looked at neither Amanda nor Raffaele when she walked past them to take her turn on the witness box. Her former husband, John, and Meredith's sister, Stephanie, also wearing black for their first day at the trial, watched from a back row where they sat next to the detective Napoleoni, who proudly wore her police badge on a chain around her neck.

Arline answered questions from her lawyer Maresca in a low voice, with the help of an interpreter.

Arline talked of how Meredith had gone to live in the cottage: 'She found a flat on the student noticeboard at the university. She picked that place because of the view through the window and it's very close to the university. The Umbrian countryside, it's beautiful.

'There were two Italian girls and they seemed nice because they took her to the landlord and translated everything for her. There was also supposed to be an American coming in a month,' Arline went on.

Arline clearly found it hard to use Amanda's name. Describing the start of Meredith's relationship with Amanda, she said: 'I think the American girl arrived on 26 September, and Meredith invited her out for lunch and introduced her to friends and, um, Amanda said that she only wanted to socialise with Italians to help her with the language.'

Speaking in Italian, Maresca asked Arline how she had found out about the death of Meredith. The interpreter mistakenly translated the question as: 'How did you take the death of Meredith?'

The brutality of the question took Arline aback. She sat silently for a moment, sighed, then said as the interpreter held her hand: 'Her death was unbelievable, unreal, in many ways it still is. I'm still looking for her. It's not just the death but also the way it was done, the brutality of it, the violence, the great sadness it brought to everyone. And it's such a shock to send your daughter to school and she' – tears came to Arline's eyes – 'doesn't come back any more. We will never get over it.'

Maresca asked Arline if Meredith had been worried about anything in Perugia.

'Mainly the course she was doing. She never really said there was any trouble in particular but all my children try and shield me, they don't tell me everything because they don't want to worry me' – Arline chuckled – 'but if she'd come back home she would have told me. She wouldn't have wanted to worry me being so far from home.'

Later, Mignini asked Arline what Meredith had told her on 31 October, the day before she died, and on 1 November.

'The thirty-first when she rang she said she was going round to her girlfriends' house, they would do their make-up and dress up for Halloween so she was looking forward to that. Then on the first when she rang she said she was really tired because she'd stayed up so late. She said she was going to her friends' to watch a DVD. I think it was the English girls who were at Leeds; I don't remember if she mentioned them by name. She was going to come back early and have an early night.'

When it was Stephanie's turn to testify, Maresca asked her whether her sister had been physically strong.

'Yes, she did gym when she was little, she did karate, and once we did boxing in a gym together,' Stephanie replied.

Would Meredith have defended herself when attacked?

'Absolutely, 110 per cent. Mez had a very strong character and physically she was very strong. She was very passionate about things that were important to her – her family, her friends, coming to Italy and she fought for her place here.'

When Meredith's father John, the last of her relatives to testify, recalled how he had found out about Meredith's death from a newspaper colleague, Stephanie cried silently. Arline put her hand on her daughter's shoulder to comfort her.

*   *   *

Amanda's lawyers thought hard about whether they should summon her to testify at the trial. They decided she should give evidence, believing it would be a key part of her defence. Ghirga believed that Amanda needed to gain credibility in the eyes of the court. There was a limit to how much the lawyers could achieve on her behalf. Amanda speaking for herself would be the best way of increasing her credibility, he thought.

He was confident that Amanda would be up to it. He didn't mind whether she cried, or whether she suddenly put a stop to the questioning, as was her right. What mattered to him was what she said, and that she should come across as sincere and credible.

'Just say what you want to say, and be yourself,' Ghirga told her.

But in the run-up to her giving evidence, her lawyers prepared her carefully. They went over not only what she was going to say but how she was going to say it. They told her that she must look at the person asking the question, but that she should then look at the judges and jury when answering.

'Really, I hadn't noticed that!' a surprised Amanda exclaimed.

According to her stepfather, Chris, she was 'looking forward' to testifying. 'It freaks her out but she says this whole thing isn't so new anymore. She's got her story and she's going to tell it. She's not shy. If the prosecutors yell at her, she'll just clam up; we parents never had to do that with her. The prosecutors may want her to cry, but I don't think the judge will let them treat her badly. But Amanda may cry, she's pretty easy to get to tears,' he said.

The Kerchers' lawyer, Maresca, didn't expect it would come to that. 'Amanda may last an hour or she may last two days, it depends just on whether she manages to control her feelings or not. Her lawyers will jump in and stop everything if she looks as if she's about to break down,' he predicted.

48

12 June 2009

'AMANDA-DAY' read the newspaper placards on a hot, sunny morning as swifts swooped and shrieked over the satellite dishes of the TV vans on the square outside the law courts; her testimony attracted almost as many journalists as on the first day of the trial six months earlier.

Wearing a white blouse with short sleeves, cream trousers and her hair in the usual ponytail, Amanda started chewing her nails soon after entering the courtroom and taking her seat. Her face was wan, slightly shiny with sweat; there were deep black lines under her eyes and a big blister on her upper lip.

Before she was called to the witness box, her lawyers requested that TV cameras be allowed to film her testimony, a request that was accepted by Judge Massei. Comodi muttered in a low voice: 'I knew they'd put on a show!'

The swallows' cries could be heard through an open window as two guards escorted Amanda the few feet to the witness box. She walked slowly and stiffly, and licked her lips as she sat waiting, her back straight and her hands clasped in her lap. A woman guard stood with arms crossed behind her, and an interpreter sat next to her. Amanda, her mouth open, took two deep breaths.

'Amanda Knox,' she said in a loud, clear voice when Judge Massei asked her to say her name.

The lawyer Carlo Pacelli, representing the bar-owner Patrick Lumumba whom she'd accused of murdering Meredith before retracting her statement, was the first to question her. A kindly, old-fashioned figure, Pacelli greeted her politely: 'Good morning *Signorina* Amanda.'

Calm and self-assured, and at first speaking in English, she admitted to Pacelli that yes, she used to smoke marijuana 'every so often' with her friends. Asked about her relations with Patrick, she replied – in the present tense before correcting herself: 'I like Patrick very much, I liked him very much.' He had always treated her well and she wasn't scared of him.

Pacelli asked Amanda about the night of the murder. How long had she taken to reply to Patrick's text message telling her not to come to work that night?

'I think I replied as soon as I saw the message,' Amanda said.

Pacelli, quick as a flash: 'The fact is, you replied after about twenty-five minutes. Why did you wait such a long time?'

'I don't remember now.'

Asked why she'd deleted Patrick's message, Amanda said: 'I had limited space in my mobile, and when I received messages I didn't need to remember, I deleted them.'

Pacelli moved on to the night of 5 November 2007 and her statement to police that Patrick had killed Meredith. Why had she said she'd met Patrick at the basketball court on Piazza Grimana that evening before they went to the cottage?

Amanda embarked on a lengthy account of how the police had questioned her. She hadn't expected to be questioned that night – only Raffaele had been summoned – but detectives asked her who she thought could have killed Meredith and about what she'd done that evening. They'd asked to see the messages on her mobile phone. When she'd said she couldn't remember sending a reply to Patrick, they'd called her 'a stupid liar' and accused her of trying to protect someone.

'They put the mobile in front of me and they said: "Look, look at the messages. You were going to meet someone?" And when I denied it they went on calling me "stupid liar" and from then on I was so scared, they were treating me so badly and I didn't understand why.'

A police interpreter had then suggested that Amanda might be traumatised and couldn't remember the truth. 'This thing seemed ridiculous to me, because I remembered I was definitely at Raffaele's flat, I remember having done things at Raffaele's flat. I looked at emails and then we watched the film [*Amélie*], we talked and we had dinner, and I didn't leave the flat then,' Amanda said.

Detectives shouted at her and threatened to jail her for trying to protect someone. 'I started to imagine that perhaps I was traumatised as I'd been told. They went on saying I'd met someone and they went on putting so much emphasis on the message I'd received from Patrick and so I was almost convinced that I'd met him, but I was confused,' Amanda said.

The detectives Napoleoni and Ficarra, who sat in the back row of the courtroom listening closely, shook their heads repeatedly as she described the way she'd been treated.

Taking Amanda step-by-step through what she had told the detectives and Mignini about the murder, Pacelli said: '*Signorina* Amanda, you heard poor Meredith scream on the evening of 1 November.'

'No.' From then on, Amanda switched to the fluent, often colloquial Italian she'd learnt in prison.

'In your statement of 6 November 2007 at 5.45 a.m. you said that you heard Meredith scream. How did you know that Meredith screamed before she was killed. Who told you?'

'So, when I was with the police they asked me if I'd heard Meredith's screams. I said I hadn't and they said: "How's it possible that you didn't hear Meredith's screams if you were there?" I said: "Look, I don't know, maybe I had my hands over my ears," and they said, "OK, let's write it like that, that's OK." '

'On the sixth of November, the police didn't know that Meredith had screamed before she died.'

'I imagine they might have imagined it, God knows!'

'You said you were in the cottage when Meredith died, you were in the kitchen?'

'No.'

'Who said that to you, who suggested it to you?'

'It was suggested to me; they were following a line of reasoning. So they asked me if I was in Meredith's room when she was killed, I said no, they said to me: "But where were you?" I told them: "I don't know." They said: "Maybe you were in the kitchen," I said: "OK, fine." '

Pacelli turned to the note Amanda had written in English just after her arrest at midday on 6 November 2007, and which she'd given the detective Ficarra as 'a gift': 'When you wrote that memorandum, were you hit by the police?'

'No.'

'Were you badly treated?'

'No.'

'Did the police suggest its content?'

'No.'

'You wrote this memorandum freely?'

'Yes.'

'Of your own free will?'

'Yes.'

'Look, in this memorandum you say: "I confirm the statements made the previous night concerning the events which may have happened at my house with Patrick." You freely and spontaneously confirmed these circumstances, these statements.'

'Because I wasn't sure what was my imagination and what was reality, and so I wanted to say that I was confused and I couldn't know, but at the same time I knew I'd had to sign these statements, so I said: "OK, fine, I said these things, but I'm confused and I'm not sure." '

Amanda looked a little less tense when Ghirga's turn to question her came. He began by asking Judge Massei's permission, which was granted, to question his client using the familiar '*tu*' form of address – perhaps an attempt to give their exchanges a more informal, reassuring, tone for the court.

As Ghirga took her through the days leading up to the murder, and her relations with Meredith, Amanda looked and sounded self-assured. Her tone was even chatty at times – jarring with her surroundings – as when she played down her clash with Meredith over cleanliness: 'There's no doubt I wasn't the cleanest in the house, but for example the only times that Meredith had said something to me, the toilets here are a bit different from the ones in the United States and often you've got to use this kind of brush to clean the toilet after you've flushed it and often I didn't remember to do it, so once she told me [about that]. It was a bit embarrassing and then fine, cool!'

If Amanda's testimony was a stage performance as the prosecutors believed, her most polished turn was her account of the evening of the murder. Guided by Ghirga, she rarely faltered as she gave a lively description of how she and Raffaele had gone to his flat to watch the film *Amélie* – '*Bellissimo* [wonderful], my favourite film,' she said, adding: 'We thought: come on, let's watch this one.'

When Patrick sent her the text message saying she shouldn't come to work, she'd been delighted because she wanted to stay with Raffaele – 'I jumped up saying: "Hey, I don't need to work!" '

That evening they'd also read Harry Potter in German, which Raffaele was learning, and listened to a bit of music. They had dinner – 'fish and a salad' – at about 9.30 p.m. and afterwards, while Raffaele was washing the dishes, water had leaked from under the sink. Raffaele didn't have a rag to mop it up so Amanda said she'd bring one from the cottage the next morning. They'd then smoked a joint together and gone to sleep – 'We made love first,' Amanda clarified, unprompted.

With only the odd interruption by Ghirga, Amanda talked at length about her return to the cottage the following morning. She'd thought, 'That's strange!' when she saw the front door open – 'But I thought that if someone hadn't closed it properly then of course it would open, so perhaps someone went out quickly or went to the flat downstairs to fetch something or they went to take out the rubbish – *boh!*'

She again thought 'That's strange!' when she saw drops of blood in the sink – 'I had these piercings, I had so many of them and I like piercings . . . At first I thought they came from my ears but then when I scratched them I saw they were dry.'

And she yet again thought 'That's strange!' when she saw blood on the bathmat after having a shower – 'Maybe someone had a period and hadn't cleaned up, OK.'

But the strangest thing was seeing the excrement in the big bathroom used by Filomena and Laura – 'They were very clean but I thought, "Well, who knows?" Fine, I didn't know what to think but it was a bit strange so I took this mop and I went to Raffaele's flat.' She wanted to tell Raffaele about what she'd seen and she took the mop with her to help him clean up the previous evening's leak.

Ghirga then gave Amanda an opportunity to explain her reactions after the body was found. At the police station on the afternoon Meredith's body was discovered, she'd talked of it being in the cupboard, covered with a blanket – it was in fact lying on the floor – because, she said, that's what she'd heard from her flatmates and their friends just after they'd all been ordered out of the cottage.

A few days later, on the night she'd accused Patrick and again at the police station, she'd asked detectives: 'Shouldn't I have a lawyer now?' She only said it, she explained to the court, because of the films she'd seen on TV – but 'a detective told me that it would make things worse for me, because it would show I didn't want to collaborate with the police, so I said no.'

The judges and jurors looked surprised when Ghirga asked about the red mark on her neck which witnesses had seen just after her arrest and Amanda replied bluntly: 'It's a love bite.'

Like Ghirga, Dalla Vedova also talked to his client using the familiar '*tu*' form of address. He asked Amanda why she'd switched off her mobile on the evening of Meredith's murder.

'Because I didn't want to be called again to go to work, I didn't want to be bothered,' Amanda said. She added that she didn't usually turn her mobile off at night, because she used it as a watch.

Dalla Vedova asked Amanda whether she had cried after Meredith's body was found, as she sat in a car outside the cottage to keep warm.

'Yes, yes I cried but always while I was hugging Raffaele. First he gave me his jacket and then he cuddled me, because I was really trembling. I didn't know what to think. I was really in shock so he cuddled me, he kissed me, he told me not to worry and so I cried, practically inside this protection that he offered me.'

After Dalla Vedova had finished, Judge Massei asked Amanda whether she was tired.

'If it's not a nuisance, I am a bit tired,' Amanda answered politely.

Six hours after she had first started speaking, Judge Massei declared the day's hearing at an end. The next morning, Amanda would face a cross-examination by Mignini.

49

The swifts were again screaming in the sunshine as Mignini, dressed in jeans and a light beige jacket and looking flustered, walked into the courtroom. Apparently impatient to get started, he lost no time in taking his jacket off and slipping on his black prosecutor's robe with a gold tassel on each shoulder. 'Leave Amanda to me,' he'd told his colleague Comodi.

This, he hoped, would be his chance to prise what he was convinced was the truth out of Amanda. He still felt frustrated that she had put a stop to his interrogation in prison seven months earlier just when he felt sure she was about to crack. No doubt her lawyers would do all they could to protect her from any pressure the prosecutor tried to put on her this time, but he was confident that she was bound to make some mistakes at least.

Amanda, dressed in a white and patterned top and jeans, with a pink elastic band holding her neat ponytail in place, nodded several times at the court before sitting down at the witness box. She sat with her forearms resting on the desk in front of her, hands clasped, staring steadily at Mignini as he began by asking her what she had done on the day of Meredith's death.

Amanda's lawyers soon tried to block Mignini's cross-examination, interrupting him with objections to his questions as he pressed Amanda on why she had switched her mobile phone off after receiving Patrick's text message that evening. Visibly irritated by the lawyers' interventions, Mignini pushed on.

Amanda explained she was on Raffaele's bed in his flat at the time, and that she didn't want to risk Patrick calling her to tell her to go to work if customers turned up unexpectedly.

Mignini pointed out that when he interrogated her in prison, she'd said she switched it off both to save the battery, and to prevent Patrick calling her again.

Mignini then focused on her accusation that Patrick had raped and killed Meredith. Why had she stated the previous day: 'Patrick's name was suggested to me, I was beaten, I was put under pressure'? He asked her to tell in as much detail as possible what had happened at the police station on the night she made the accusation.

Amanda had hardly begun her reply when Mignini interrupted her with another question. Amanda snapped: 'Can I go on?'

Mignini apologised to her, but Dalla Vedova jumped in to reprimand Mignini, which prompted more tense exchanges between the prosecutors and defence lawyers, and an appeal for calm from Judge Massei.

Speaking rapidly and gesturing with her hands, Amanda repeated her accusations against the police, saying they'd threatened to jail her if she didn't tell the truth and had told her Raffaele had said she'd left his flat on the night of the murder. They told her she must try to remember something she had forgotten.

Amanda spread her hands over her cheeks as she went on: 'I was thinking: "What have I forgotten? What have I forgotten?" and they were going: "Come on, come on, come on. Do you remember? Do you remember? Do you remember?", boom, on my head' – she mimed being hit on the back of the neck – ' "Remember!" I went, "*Mamma mia!*" and then boom, "Do you remember?" Those were the cuffs on the head.'

Mignini told her curtly that she had failed to demonstrate that detectives had 'suggested' Patrick's name to her – a remark which prompted more protests from her lawyers, who pointed out that he wasn't allowed to comment on her replies.

As her lawyers quarrelled with Mignini – he grew so frustrated that he shouted, 'I will complete the cross-examination!' – Amanda looked on the verge of tears, bowed her head and stayed that way for a dozen seconds.

Ghirga leapt up from where he had been sitting, which was out of Amanda's field of vision, and hurried down the front row to his left, apparently wanting Amanda to catch sight of him. He asked for a five minute break.

But when Judge Massei asked whether Amanda wanted to stop testifying, she said she would go on.

Judge Massei gave Amanda another opportunity to explain herself. 'Did they say to you: "Say it's him"?' he asked.

'No,' Amanda replied.

'They said to you: "Remember, remember, remember." '

'They didn't say it was him, but they said to me: "Ah, but we know who it is, we know you were with [someone], that you met that person." '

'That's what the suggestion amounted to?'

'Yes.'

Mignini challenged her, saying what she had just said contrasted with what she'd told him when he interrogated her: at the time, she'd said, 'A moment before I said Patrick's name, someone was showing me the message I'd sent him.'

Amanda replied simply: 'I explained better today.'

'What happened next?' Mignini asked.

'First I started to cry. Then, when all these policemen were saying to me: "But you have to say why, how it happened," – they wanted all the details but I didn't know how to give them – I started to imagine a scene, images which maybe could have explained the situation. Patrick's face, Piazza Grimana, my house, a green thing which they said could be the sofa . . . It was always "I don't know", "maybe", imagining . . .' Amanda said, waving and flapping her hands as she talked.

Later, Mignini asked Amanda why she had cried when he and several detectives escorted her to the cottage to check on the knives in the kitchen, three days after the murder.

'It's true that I cried when looking for the knives because having to see if something was missing, it shocked me, because it was as if all the time I couldn't accept the fact that Meredith had been killed,' Amanda said.

As she spoke, Amanda raised her hands and put them over her ears. Mignini noticed the gesture – she had done the same gesture when he'd interrogated her, and he was sure it was an unconscious attempt to blot out Meredith's screams, which he was convinced she'd heard.

The prosecutor switched to the day Meredith's body was discovered: 'Raffaele tried to break down Meredith's door. Why did you say it was normal that the door was locked when Filomena arrived?'

'When the police arrived, they asked Filomena if the door was ever closed. She said: "Never." I said that "never" wasn't true, I thought it was strange that the door was closed but sometimes Meredith locked it. Normally it was open. I just wanted to explain it wasn't always open . . . I was worried she could be inside and had hurt herself, there were so many strange things in the house, the door closed with the window broken.'

Two hours into the cross-examination, Judge Massei asked Amanda whether she wanted a break and Amanda said yes. It was only a short respite, but Mignini paced around, looking irritated; he believed that Amanda was lying to herself, and of course her lawyers were out to stop him getting to the truth.

When the hearing restarted, Mignini asked Amanda: 'Did you try to break down Meredith's door to fetch your desk light?' The prosecutor suspected that Amanda had brought her light into Meredith's room soon after the murder; it was found there by police when the body was discovered.

'We didn't know the light was in there,' Amanda said in a disapproving tone.

Mignini ended his cross-examination.

The Kerchers' lawyer Maresca was the first to ask Amanda what Meredith's death had meant to her. 'You said yesterday that you had many friends, both in America and in Perugia. Did you consider Meredith Kercher a friend?' Maresca began.

'Yes.'

'And did you suffer for the loss of this friend?'

'Yes, to be precise I was more . . . I was very shocked, I couldn't imagine a thing like that.'

'Do you ever remember her in your everyday life? Do you ever think of this friend who lived in the same house as you?'

'Yes, I remember her, but in the end I knew her for a month and first of all I'm trying to go on with my life' – several journalists muttered in disapproval – 'so, yes, I remember her, I'm very sorry for what happened, sometimes it seems it doesn't seem real, but I really don't know what to think about it. Yes, I suffered.'

'So, yesterday you answered questions about some of your behaviour at the police station, the wheel, gymnastics, stretching and so on.'

'Yes.'

'Do you think this behaviour was suitable, given a tragedy of the kind?'

'I think everyone deals with a tragedy their own way and as I'm used to trying to feel normal in difficult situations, that's my way of feeling more secure. Because in the end I was very, very scared by this thing, very shocked. I didn't know how to deal with the situation and so for me it was surreal, I still had to accept the fact that it had happened. So my behaviour, yes, I know I'm a bit like that, carefree, but that's the way I am.'

'But in that moment were you scared or sad, or both?'

'I was so . . . I was very disoriented.'

Maresca asked Amanda about what she had told Meredith's friends about the way she had died. 'You told Meredith's friends at the police station that she had died slowly. Why on earth did you say this?'

'I heard that she'd had her throat cut, and from what I saw on *CSI*, these things are not quick or pleasant. So, when they said: "Let's hope that she died quickly," I said: "But what are you saying? She had her throat slit." But, dammit, not . . . *Bleargh* . . . This brutality, this death . . . *bleargh* . . . it really did shock me. That's the thing which struck me, the fact of having your throat slit, it seemed something really yucky and so I imagined it was a death that was slow and very, very scary, a really shocking death . . . really yucky, disgusting, really . . .' Amanda said, crossing her hands repeatedly in front of her chest.

The court looked surprised at her use of expressions like '*bleargh*' and 'yucky', and one woman juror held her head in her hands as she listened.

The last to question Amanda was Judge Massei. 'There are a few little questions which I'm afraid will be put to you in a disorganised way, because they occurred to us when we met during breaks [in the hearings],' he said.

'Certainly,' Amanda said.

The judge's words were deceptively reassuring – the 'little questions' he fired at Amanda were in fact so brief and incisive that the whole courtroom listened very closely; no lawyer daring to interrupt.

'Did Meredith ever go to Raffaele's house?'

'No.'

'She never went. Did you ever bring kitchen objects from Via della Pergola to Raffaele's house?'

'No.'

'When you turned your mobile off [on the evening of Meredith's death], did you tell Raffaele you were switching it off?'

Again and again, Amanda replied 'I can't remember' to Judge Massei's questions. She couldn't remember whether she had told Raffaele she was switching her mobile off. She couldn't remember whether she'd heard Raffaele's mobile or house phone ring afterwards. She couldn't remember whether she'd seen Raffaele use his mobile that evening.

She didn't know whether Raffaele had used his computer after they'd watched *Amélie* and had dinner. She couldn't remember whether she'd switched her mobile back on when she woke up the next morning. She couldn't remember when Raffaele had used his mobile for the first time that morning.

Judge Massei then asked Amanda about an aspect no one had ever raised with her before. 'What kind of heating was there in Via della Pergola?'

The question surprised Amanda. 'Heating?'

'Yes.'

'Not a lot, I remember that in my room it was often cold, so I had a carpet on the floor. Honestly I never switched on any kind of heating in my—'

'When you arrived at ten, you didn't switch on any kind of heating?'

'I never—'

'So the heating is turned off that morning?'

'I didn't look at any kind of heating.'

'Was the house warm when you walked in?'

'No, no, there was—'

'It was cold.'

'Yes, that's true.'

'The front door was wide open, it was cold.'

'Yes.'

'Was there heating in the bathroom?'

Again, Amanda repeated Judge Massei's question: 'In the bathroom?'

'Yes.'

'I never used heating in the bathroom, so . . .'

'So the bathroom was cold.'

'Yes, pretty much.'

'Raffaele's home was warm? What was the bathroom like, was it heated?'

'Yes.'

With his sharp, no-nonsense style, Judge Massei had planted in the minds of the jurors an idea which made Amanda's account of her return to the cottage yet more odd: if she was to be believed, she had chosen to take a shower in a cold flat rather than in Raffaele's heated bathroom.

Amanda appeared to lose some of her self-assurance as Judge Massei pressed on; she occasionally lowered her gaze and her face looked flushed.

He asked Amanda about the bloodstained light switch in the bathroom. 'Did you use the light switch in the bathroom? Did you press it once, or twice? Did you turn the light on in the bathroom?'

Again, Judge Massei surprised Amanda. 'Ah, the light?' she repeated.

'Yes.'

'I don't remember if I put the light on or not.'

'You don't remember,' Judge Massei noted aloud before going on. 'Excuse me, I also wanted to ask you, when you called [Filomena] Romanelli, it's the second of November, the first time, where were you?'

'OK, the first time . . .'

'Romanelli says that this phone call was at about 12.10 p.m.'

'OK, I think that the first time I called her I was at Raffaele's flat, I asked him what he wanted to do and he said I should call my flatmates. So I called her when I was in Raffaele's flat. But afterwards I think she called me again when we were walking to my house.'

'So you called Romanelli while you were at Raffaele's flat?'

'Yes.'

'That's what happened?'

'Yes.'

'You make your first phone call from Raffaele's flat.'

'Raffaele's, yes.'

'I point out to you that, at least according to Romanelli's testimony, the circumstances were different.'

'OK.'

Judge Massei read aloud Filomena's account of Amanda's call: 'She told me she'd had a shower, that she thought there was blood and that she was going to Raffaele's.'

'Ah, OK, so it was when I was walking to Raffaele's.'

'So you weren't at Raffaele's.'

When after five hours in the witness box, Judge Massei told Amanda her testimony was over, she smiled brightly in relief. She stood and, head bowed, was led back to prison.

'Amanda's lawyers managed to make Mignini furious so he wasn't as hard-hitting as he could have been,' an investigator commented afterwards. 'But Judge Massei was relentless and no one stopped him. Amanda did very well – her lawyers coached her very well, and I'm sure they told her not to cry whatever happened. But she hasn't cleared up any of the doubts in her story.'

If the questions put by Judge Massei on behalf of the court were any guide to their thinking on the case, the investigator wasn't the only person to have doubts about Amanda's story.

50

A week after Amanda took the witness box, it was her mother Edda's turn. Speaking through an interpreter, Edda was questioned gently by both of Amanda's lawyers.

Asked by Ghirga what Amanda had told her about Meredith and her two other flatmates, Edda replied in a soft, unemotional voice: 'She really liked all three of them.' Amanda had never talked about any problems with Meredith over the running of the flat; 'She said they got along great.'

Ghirga soon sat down again and his colleague Dalla Vedova quizzed Edda to paint a sketchy portrait of Amanda's life in Seattle. While Amanda doodled on a notepad, he asked Edda about her job as a schoolteacher and about Amanda's father, Curt – 'Amanda's father lives with his wife and two other daughters.'

'They live in Seattle?' Dalla Vedova asked.

'Yes, they live near us.'

'So Amanda sees her father regularly?

'Yes, he lives very near us,' Edda repeated.

Asked why Amanda had chosen Perugia for her studies abroad, Edda replied: 'She wanted to go to an Italian city that wasn't too touristy, because she wanted to learn about Italian people and their culture.' She'd worked hard to earn the money to pay for her trip.

Like Ghirga, Dalla Vedova also asked Edda about her daughter's relations with Meredith.

'She told me about the fun things she and Meredith did,' Edda said.

20 June 2009

Challenging the prosecution's reconstruction of Meredith's murder, Raffaele's lawyers called as a witness Francesco Introna, a professor of forensic medicine from the University of Bari, not far from Raffaele's hometown.

Introna, in his mid-fifties, told the court he'd become involved in the case at a late stage and had based his report on the results of the autopsy – which he hadn't attended – and had also consulted photographs and films of the crime scene.

Introna first challenged the prosecutors' estimate that Meredith had died between 11.10 p.m. and shortly after midnight. He maintained that she had died between 9.30 and 10.30 p.m. because, he argued, the stress of the attack she suffered had within that time range interrupted the emptying of her stomach following her dinner.

Introna's reconstruction of Meredith's last moments was also completely at odds with the prosecution's. The kitchen knife seized at Raffaele's flat simply couldn't be the murder weapon, he argued, brandishing a similar one together with a tape measure in court. Dissecting the size, depth and bruising around each of the three wounds as the images were projected on the giant screen – Judge Massei had previously ordered the public and the press out of the courtroom – he said it was impossible that such a knife, with a blade six-and-a-half inches long, could have caused any of them. Instead, a knife with a blade three to three-and-a-half inches long had been used.

When he screened images of the autopsy, commenting on them as he did so, a woman juror blanched and looked as if she was about to faint. Judge Massei interrupted the hearing to give her time to recover.

Introna went on to give his detailed interpretation of how Meredith had been attacked. Her bedroom was too small for three attackers to have killed her, he insisted – and there was only one murderer. With the court's permission, he asked two female lawyers to act out the scene, telling them how they should move as he described it.

The attacker, he began, had entered her room, holding a knife in his right hand, when Meredith was undressing – she was naked from the waist down – intending to sexually abuse her. Standing behind Meredith, he had grabbed her by the neck, clamped a hand over her mouth and nose to stop her screaming, and pressed the blade of a knife against her cheek to make her stop moving. Still threatening her with the knife, he sexually assaulted her. Meredith tried to break free and screamed. The killer cut her face and pushed her to the ground. She was on her hands and knees when the killer immobilised her with his legs and, raising the back of her bra with his left hand, cut it with the knife he was still holding in his right hand. He then stabbed her in the neck several times.

6 July 2009

Like the consultant Introna hired by Raffaele, the forensic pathologist Carlo Torre, called by Amanda's lawyers, also argued that the kitchen knife could not have caused Meredith's wounds and that Meredith had been killed by only one attacker.

Torre, a professor of forensic medicine at Turin University with more than thirty years' experience of studying high-profile cases – including murders by the terrorist Red Brigades in the 1970s – also agreed with Introna that a smaller knife with a blade just over three inches long had caused the wounds. The largest, fatal injury had been caused by the attacker stabbing Meredith a first time and then moving it back and forth in the wound.

But Torre's reconstruction differed from Introna's. Unlike his colleague, he believed the attacker had faced Meredith – not stood behind her – and that she had been lying on her back when she was stabbed, not crouching on her hands and knees.

14 September 2009

As the last witnesses and expert consultants gave evidence after a summer recess of almost two months – Amanda had put on

weight since the last hearing and looked more drawn, Raffaele
was as pale as ever – the two defence teams challenged the scientific evidence again and again. Adriano Tagliabracci, a professor
of forensic medicine from Ancona on the Adriatic Coast hired by
Raffaele, criticised Stefanoni's work as she sat between the two
prosecutors. She had failed to document her work properly, he
said, and had written 'too low' four times alongside an entry for
the samples taken from the kitchen knife.

'It could have been contamination in the laboratory. It could
have been anything. "Too low" means it shouldn't have been used
for analysis,' Tagliabracci said.

The results of the tests on the bra clasp were also too low to say
that Raffaele's DNA was on it, he continued. But he added that
the clasp could have been contaminated with Raffaele's DNA.

Stefanoni shook her head repeatedly as she listened to
Tagliabracci. She spoke quietly to Comodi, who interrupted him
several times and accused him of insulting the biologist.

19 September 2009

Two forensic police officers gingerly brought the kitchen knife
taken from Raffaele's flat into the courtroom. Wrapped in plastic
and lying in a white box, it was shown to the court and then to
expert witnesses – the experts put on latex gloves and masks to
cover their mouths and noses before approaching it.

The forensic pathologist Mariano Cingolani, one of three
experts who'd been appointed by a judge shortly after the
murder, doubted that it had caused the smallest of the wounds to
Meredith's neck.

'Many other knives are more compatible with that kind of
wound,' he said, arguing that the cut would have been bigger if
that knife had been used, given the wound's depth. But he added
there was no way of knowing for certain as both the position of
Meredith's neck at the time of the stabbing and the elasticity of
her tissues were unknown.

Amanda, her face expressionless, looked at the knife for a few seconds and then glanced at Raffaele.

25 September 2009

Professor Carlo Caltagirone, a Roman neurologist hired by Amanda, gave the court the only specialist analysis of her personality – albeit a very limited one. His brief had been to assess whether the stress she was under during police questioning – which her lawyers said lasted forty-one hours over the six days from the discovery of the body to the day of her arrest – could have affected her memory. He based his evidence on the 'two or three hours' he'd spent with her in prison, and on the texts she'd written just after her arrest.

'It's possible that someone's memory can be modified under stress. A situation combining pressure and prolonged tension can cause someone to remember something which never happened – a false memory,' Caltagirone told the court.

'Amanda is a person who is apparently serene and outgoing but in fact she bottles up stressful situations inside herself. Being questioned for a very long time in a foreign country, with someone telling her she may be guilty of something, and failing to grasp the gravity of her situation would have led to a lot of stress,' he said.

He described Amanda's 'cognitive condition' – the way she acquired knowledge through thought, experience and the senses – as 'very good . . . typical of a young woman.'

9 October 2009

After the last of the witnesses had testified, Amanda and Raffaele's lawyers made one final attack on the forensic evidence, demanding that the court appoint leading experts to carry out independent reviews.

Raffaele's lawyer Bongiorno argued that given scientific evidence had taken on such importance in the trial, these reviews were 'indispensible'; the 'future of a fine young man' was at stake.

Raffaele's team requested reviews on the DNA traces found on the bra clasp and on the kitchen knife; the time of Meredith's death; whether the knife was compatible with Meredith's wounds; whether the wounds were inflicted by one or several killers; and on whether the widow Nara Capezzali could have heard the scream she believed she had heard on the night of the murder – Bongiorno wanted experts to establish how many decibels were needed for the scream to be heard in her flat across the road from the cottage.

On Amanda's behalf, Ghirga also requested reviews on the DNA found on the kitchen knife as well as on the foot- and shoe prints found in Filomena's room, in the corridor of the flat and on the cushion under Meredith's body.

Neither the judges nor the jurors were impressed. After debating the requests for just under two hours, they rejected them all. Announcing the decision, Judge Massei said there was no need to acquire further evidence.

The ruling was a blow for Amanda and Raffaele. She raised her eyes to the ceiling then looked worriedly at her lawyers; Ghirga patted her on the back. Raffaele bowed his head and cried briefly.

Judge Massei consulted the prosecutors and lawyers, and announced that the final hearings would take place in six weeks' time with each party in turn making their closing arguments.

Amanda and Raffaele were taken back to their cells. There was little they could do now to influence the court; they resigned themselves to a long wait.

23 October 2009

Christ Mbette, a twenty-two-year-old nursing student from the Congo, became the first person to sleep in Meredith's room since her murder. The cottage's owner had redecorated the flat – Meredith's bedroom was given a fresh coat of paint and all the furniture replaced – and rented it out to Mbette and two female students from the Congo and Cameroon. The owner had yet to find someone to rent Amanda's room.

One TV show had wanted to broadcast a live programme from the flat, but the owner turned the request down and made her new tenants promise not to film or take any photographs inside it.

Mbette told a journalist: 'My friends are pulling my leg; they tell me to be careful and that sooner or later I'll see Meredith's ghost. My girlfriend has told me to pray to God and that I mustn't be scared. But I'm not afraid: even if I saw Meredith's ghost tonight, it wouldn't do me any harm, given the kind of person she was.'

31 October 2009

The eve of the second anniversary of Meredith's murder was also the deadline for prisoners at the Capanne jail to submit their entries in a writing competition organised by a local charity. Among them was a short story entitled 'My Love', by Marie Pace. The name was a pseudonym, and the author was in fact Amanda – Marie was her second Christian name, and '*pace*' means 'peace' in Italian.

A bizarre story, written in Italian, it takes the form of a letter written by a man to a girl 'with blonde hair'.

In the letter he asks the blonde girl: 'Do you remember that unexpectedly warm night in November?' That night, the man and the girl he is now writing to had been sitting on the porch of his house, while inside a party with booming house music was under way.

Some time later that evening the girl disappeared and the narrator tells her in his letter how he searched for her. 'I swam through the waves of warm bodies wet with sweat and drink ... You weren't in the kitchen.'

The letter continues: 'I saw you lying on the floor, you were no longer wearing either your jacket or your sweater. In that moment I didn't understand anything ... I realised you'd lost consciousness. When I came back they'd already taken you to hospital but I want you to know that I didn't mean to abandon you, but in that moment I didn't understand anything.'

The man expresses regret at failing the girl: 'If I'd had another chance I would have helped you and I would have been much closer to you. Your image is burnt into my eyes.'

The letter ends with the words: 'Forgive me.'

Amanda's entry won third prize, and £90.

18 November 2009

Rudy appeared before an appeal court in an attempt to have his thirty-year jail sentence overturned. Speaking quickly and earnestly – he used no notes and had clearly rehearsed before-hand – Rudy began by dashing any hopes that he was going to confess to the murder.

'For the last two years people have thought I'm hiding some-thing, but I can't talk about things I haven't seen and that didn't happen to me,' he said.

He repeated his story about meeting Meredith on the night before the murder and how she agreed to see him again at her home on the evening she was murdered: 'We started kissing each other until we realised we'd gone too far ... We stroked each other's intimate parts. She asked me if I had a condom and that's when I realised we'd gone too far as it was only the first time we'd been together.'

He again described how he had gone to the toilet and heard the doorbell. Moments later he heard Meredith quarrelling with Amanda about some missing money, and had rushed out of the bathroom after hearing a scream. But this time he failed to testify that the man armed with a knife whom he saw 'almost inside Meredith's room' could have been Raffaele, as he'd said previ-ously. He did repeat however that he'd seen Amanda's silhouette as she fled the cottage.

Rudy went on: 'I didn't know what to do but I had the clear-ness of mind to take the towels from the bathroom and try to stop the blood that was coming out of Meredith's neck. Meredith was dying and she tried to speak. I took her hand. I was in a state of shock. I felt as if I was going mad. There were so many unanswered questions in my head. And I got scared.'

He described running home and added: 'I'm not hiding anything, I'm not a liar. Even today, if I close my eyes and I think of those moments, everything goes red in front of my eyes.'

He sat down, only to get up again a few minutes later and turn to the Kerchers' lawyer Maresca. 'I want the Kercher family to know that I didn't kill or rape their little girl. I'm not the one who took her life away. The only thing on my conscience, from which no court can absolve me, is not doing all I could to save her life, although I don't even know if my actions would have saved her. That's the only thing I can apologise for. Thank you.'

As Rudy addressed him, Maresca stared back at him for a few moments then looked down at his papers.

After the hearing, Maresca was scathing in his dismissal of Rudy's latest account: 'He's lost yet another chance to explain what happened in that cottage.'

For Maresca, Rudy's apology was too little, too late: 'If Rudy was telling the truth, why didn't he run out into the street and stop a car or something to ask for help? He says he was scared? Can you imagine how scared Meredith was when she saw the knife about to stab her in the throat? I just can't feel any pity for him at all.'

51

Thick fog shrouded the valley below the law courts – only a few cypress-clad hilltops sticking out from it like islands in a grey sea – as Mignini, frowning slightly in concentration, paced up and down the Hall of Frescoes, waiting for the day's hearing to begin. Today was the day he was to make his closing argument – his last chance to persuade the court of his case.

'How do you feel this morning?' a journalist asked him.

'Fine, fine, I slept well. I just have a bit of a headache,' Mignini replied.

'Feeling nervous?'

The prosecutor smiled. 'No. My worry is that there isn't enough light in here. I'm long-sighted so I've brought a little electric torch with me in case I can't read my papers. I've got a lot to get through.'

Mignini had left nothing to chance, or improvisation. He had spent long afternoons in his office, his desk cluttered with the files of the investigation and transcripts of the trial, painstakingly typing up everything he intended to say in court.

Just before 10 a.m., Mignini cleared his throat huskily three times and started his summing-up. As he did so Amanda – as if the sound of his voice had given her a sudden chill – slipped on over her beige pullover a red hooded sweatshirt with a photograph of The Beatles on the back. She then sat still, staring at Mignini and occasionally taking some notes. Raffaele, in a bright fuchsia-coloured sweater, swung his chair from side to side.

Mignini read his text over half-moon glasses – he didn't need the torch he'd brought with him. He called Meredith by her nickname – 'Mez' – and spoke in a tone that was mostly slow and calm, even chatty at times.

Mignini began by demolishing the claim that Meredith had been killed by a lone burglar – in other words, Rudy. No burglar would have chosen Filomena's window to break into the cottage; it was too visible from the road, and besides it was too high to reach from the ground. Nothing was stolen, and the glass from the shattered window was found lying on top of the jumble of clothes on the floor of Filomena's room, meaning it had been broken after the clothes were thrown around. The truth was that Amanda and Raffaele had faked the burglary to ward off suspicion.

'The aim was to make it look as if an outsider had broken in and to divert suspicion from those who had the keys to the flat that night . . . The key to the mystery is in Filomena's room,' he said.

He poured scorn on Amanda's claim that she took a shower when she went back to the cottage despite finding the front door open and blood in the bathroom.

'Is this normal?' Mignini asked, raising his voice and waving the papers in his hands. 'Why would anyone do that?'

Drugs had undoubtedly had their part to play in the murder. Both Amanda and Raffaele had smoked hashish that evening. And, according to Amanda, Raffaele had once confided in her that he had in the past taken cocaine and acid. Cocaine, Mignini said, could cause aggressiveness – together with paranoia, in extreme cases – followed, in the 'down' phase, by depression. But acid or hallucinogenic drugs could cause, particularly in young and psychologically immature individuals, 'lasting and permanent psychoses'; Amanda had also said that Raffaele suffered from depression. And Rudy had also taken drugs in the past, including cocaine.

It was likely, Mignini argued, that Amanda had met Rudy shortly after 8 p.m. on her way home on the night of the murder;

she may have arranged to see him at the cottage later, and that he would bring drugs with him.

The tramp Curatolo – one of the many witnesses whose testimony Mignini related in detail even though, he charged, the defence had tried to 'demonise' them – had seen Amanda and Raffaele together in Piazza Grimana near the cottage for the first time between 9.30 and 10 p.m. The couple left the square between 11 and 11.30 p.m. and arrived at the cottage, with Rudy, soon afterwards.

The judges and jurors kept their eyes riveted on Mignini.

Shortly after a lunch break, the prosecutor gave the court a new reconstruction of how Meredith had died. He was careful to point out that nobody knew for certain how events spiralled into sexual abuse and murder. Nevertheless, the reconstruction was based on examination of Meredith's wounds and bruises, on forensic evidence such as Amanda and Meredith's DNA on the kitchen knife, and Raffaele and Rudy's DNA on Meredith's bra, and on studies such as the blood-splatter analysis on the cupboard in Meredith's room. Based also on the new testimony at the trial of witnesses who heard a scream on the night of the murder and expert consultants, it was much more detailed than the one he'd given another court at the preliminary hearings just over a year earlier.

When Amanda, Raffaele and Rudy entered the cottage, Mignini hypothesised, Meredith may have been stretched out on her bed, working on an essay she had to hand in soon. Meredith was probably annoyed to see that although it was so late, Amanda had brought home not only Raffaele but also Rudy, and told her so; she may also have reprimanded Amanda about some money that had gone missing.

Amanda, Raffaele and Rudy were 'under the influence of drugs and, probably, of alcohol too,' Mignini continued. Amanda had been nurturing hatred for Meredith for some time and this evening – the first on which the two were the only flatmates in the cottage – was for Amanda 'an opportunity to take revenge on this English girl who was too serious and too "quiet" for her liking . . . on that "simpering" girl.'

Rudy asked to use the bathroom, while Amanda, with Raffaele next to her, quarrelled ever more sharply in Meredith's room. Suddenly, as the three stood near the cupboard, Amanda reached out and banged Meredith's head against the wall, while Raffaele, standing on Amanda's left, pulled her hair in one hand and grabbed her right arm in the other.

As Mignini described Meredith's last moments, Amanda, who had until then been staring almost fixedly at him, bowed her head and started crying noiselessly, her cheeks flushed. It was the first time in the eleven-month trial that she cried in court.

The only movements she made were to quickly, furtively wipe her eyes and nose. Her lawyer Ghirga patted her briefly on the shoulder. The female guard standing behind her bent forward, apparently asking her if she needed anything.

Raffaele, emotionless, leafed slowly through the closing argument prepared by one of his lawyers. Amanda continued to cry.

Two of the jurors, shocked by the scene Mignini described, were staring at him, their hands covering their mouths. Oblivious to Amanda's tears, and looking only at the judges and the jurors, the prosecutor continued. Again and again, he said, Amanda banged Meredith's head against the wall near the window. Her fingers left bruises around Meredith's nose and under her chin.

Rudy returned from the bathroom and joined in the assault – 'there's a competition between him and Raffaele to please Amanda . . . Rudy does all he can to win Amanda's approval,' Mignini said.

Meredith fell to the floor in front of the cupboard, her head towards the window and her feet towards the bed. Amanda was on her right, Raffaele on her left, and Rudy facing her.

'By now it's an uncontrolled crescendo of violence and a sexual "game". The three tried to undress Mez, and slipped off

John Follain

her jeans . . . Amanda had pulled out the kitchen knife . . . Rudy sexually abused Mez with his fingers. She tried to defend herself, suffering wounds to her right hand,' Mignini said.

It was easy to imagine, Mignini continued, that Amanda was so angry with Meredith for criticising her uninhibited attitude to sex that she insulted her flatmate and perhaps shouted at her: 'You acted the goody-goody so much, now we're going to show you. Now you're going to be forced to have sex!'

With Meredith on her knees, facing the cupboard, Raffaele used his knife to cut off her bra. Like Amanda, Raffaele also used his knife to threaten and wound Meredith.

By now it had become clear to the attackers that Meredith would not yield to sexual violence; 'at that point, the "game" had to come to an end,' Mignini said. Amanda tried to strangle Meredith, and Raffaele stabbed her once in the neck, then a second time. Realising the violence was unstoppable and that the three were like 'frenzied furies', Meredith gave 'that terrible and desperate scream' heard by two neighbours, the elderly Capezzali and the schoolteacher Monacchia. Mignini raised his voice when he reminded the court that Capezzali had said she thought she was in 'a house of horrors'.

Mignini lifted his right hand as if holding the kitchen knife. It was after the scream, he said, that Amanda stabbed Meredith in the throat, inflicting the deepest – and fatal – wound.

Rudy went to the bathroom to fetch some towels to stop the blood; Amanda also went to the bathroom where she left traces of her blood mixed with Meredith's. Amanda and Raffaele then grabbed Meredith's mobile phones and fled. Mignini estimated the time of death at between 11.20 p.m. and midnight.

Sitting practically immobile with her head bowed, Amanda was still crying. The guard behind her bent forward to speak to her a second and third time but Amanda just shook her head.

Soon afterwards, Amanda whispered to Ghirga: 'It's not right, it's not true.'

She told Ghirga that she wanted to get up and tell the court that Meredith was her friend and that she'd never had anything to do with Rudy. But she then told him she didn't have the strength, and said she wanted to leave the courtroom and go back to jail.

Ghirga talked gently to her and squeezed her hand; he persuaded her to stay and Amanda soon stopped crying.

In the small hours of the night, Mignini continued, Amanda and Raffaele returned to the cottage. Amanda covered the body with the quilt. She and Raffaele cleaned up as best they could, mopping the floor to remove traces of blood, then they staged the fake burglary in Filomena's room.

Later, Raffaele told the police that nothing had been stolen. 'How could Raffaele have known with such certainty that nothing had been taken from Filomena's room, long before she found out and told the police, if it wasn't Raffaele and Amanda who staged the burglary?' Mignini asked.

There was a similar reason for Amanda saying shortly after the murder that Meredith's body was 'inside the cupboard'. Mignini explained: 'Only someone who was at the scene at the moment of the crime could have "placed" the victim inside the cupboard. "Inside the cupboard" mustn't be taken literally; it meant the victim was in front of the cupboard when she received the fatal blow.' When the body was discovered by the police, it had been shifted a few feet away, by the bed.

Amanda had accused the police of pressuring her into accusing Patrick of killing Meredith, but as her own testimony had made clear, they had never done anything of the kind; they had only asked her about a text message she had sent him. At no time had they 'suggested' his name to her.

'Amanda knowingly accused an innocent man ... Amanda didn't lift a finger to clear him while he languished in jail – neither her nor her mother, whom she'd confided in about the accusation being false. And as luck would have it, she'd accused a coloured man – as Rudy is,' Mignini said.

Mignini ended his closing argument after seven and a half hours.

As Judge Massei ordered a break, Amanda hugged one of her female lawyers, and rested her head on her breast for a moment. She then walked out of the courtroom, her cheeks flushed and her eyes red and swollen. That day, her family told the media that they had bought a ticket for Amanda's return home, confident that she would be acquitted.

'She knows she's innocent. We know she's innocent ... Hopefully we'll get to bring her back before Christmas,' her father Curt said.

52

The day after Mignini had described how the prosecution believed Meredith died, his colleague Comodi requested permission to screen an animated film reconstructing the murder and made with digital imaging. Amanda's lawyers protested that the film would be sensationalist and an unfair influence on the court but the judges and jurors gave her permission to go ahead.

The film was Comodi's idea. At first she simply wanted to demonstrate that there was plenty of space in Meredith's room for the victim and three killers – the defence had argued it was too small for more than one attacker. But when she realised the film's potential, she decided to show the entire reconstruction. 'It's one thing to hear a reconstruction, and it's another to actually see it,' she told Mignini. 'For lots of people, what they see on TV exists; what they don't see on TV doesn't exist.' She instructed the production company making the film to base it solely on the evidence, showing only what was in the case files.

With lights dimmed, a crowded courtroom watched in tense silence as the twenty-minute film showed figures resembling Amanda, Raffaele and Rudy entering the cottage, the assault that followed and the murder, with the scene shown from different angles. Graphic photographs of the wounds on Meredith's face and neck, and the bruises on her body appeared alongside the images. When the fatal stab wound was inflicted, the screen turned red.

Other scenes showed Amanda and Raffaele return to the
cottage, take their shoes off and, after fetching a lamp from
Amanda's room, stripping Meredith of some of her clothes, placing the quilt over her and then cleaning part of the flat with a mop.
The film ended with the staging of the burglary, and Amanda
and Raffaele standing outside the cottage while the recording of
his calls to the police were played to the courtroom. Amanda, her
chair turned away from the screen, never even glanced at the film;
Raffaele watched it all attentively.

Moments after the sound of Raffaele's voice had faded away,
and with many in the courtroom still shaken by the film, Mignini
rose and began his final request for the sentencing of the accused.
Amanda took a deep breath as he started to speak.

The prosecutor began with a devastating description of the
characters of Amanda and Raffaele. Amanda was a narcissist,
he said, who nurtured anger and was unusually aggressive. She
manipulated people, indulging in theatricals and in transgres-
sive behaviour. She had little empathy for others, suffered from
'emotional anaesthesia', and had a tendency to dominate relationships in order to satisfy her immediate needs. She was quick to
dislike those who didn't share her opinions, and had a deep disre-
gard for the dictates of authority.

As for Raffaele, he was remarkably emotionless and depend-
ent on others. 'He has never shown any regret, he's always been
impassive and ice-cold,' Mignini said.

But the prosecutor did have something positive to say about
Rudy: 'He at least showed a flicker of pity. He stayed on, he tried
to stop the blood from Mez's wounds and he didn't slander
anyone,' Mignini said.

As he spoke, Amanda scribbled on a sheet of paper which she
then showed her lawyers – 'Why does he say this about me?' she
wrote. 'He doesn't know me!' she added, and then: 'How can he
think I did this?'

Looking at each of the judges and jurors in turn, Mignini urged
them: 'At this moment, the most serious mistake you could make

would be to look only at the accused and forget what they are accused of and the victim of the crime. Instead you must remember her, now more than ever.'

The court had to pronounce itself, he said, on 'a murder committed together with sexual violence, carried out for futile motives, of a twenty-two-year-old girl who was due to go back to London in a few days' time for the birthday of her mother, to whom she was particularly close.'

'She would have gone home to hug her sister Stephanie, her father and her two brothers. Mez – that's how we call her now – will never go home again to hug her loved ones. She was killed in a horrifying way and now her relatives can only go to the cemetery, and stand quietly in front of her grave.

'Meredith Kercher has been literally eliminated for ever.'

With his love of history, Mignini couldn't resist quoting in Latin the politician and jurist Ulpian, of Ancient Rome: 'Justice is the constant and perpetual will to render to every man his due. To live honourably, to harm no one, to give to each his own.'

'You must give them what they deserve. A life sentence.' Because of the gravity of their crimes, the prosecutor said, Amanda should spend the first nine months of her sentence in solitary confinement during the day, and Raffaele the first two months.

Amanda, her loose hair falling untidily over her face, clasped and unclasped her hands. Two tears ran down her cheeks – 'tears of impotence' her lawyer Dalla Vedova called them later.

As he made his request, Mignini felt he was doing his duty. According to the penal code the maximum punishment for murder aggravated by a sexual attack was a life sentence. Amanda and Raffaele were also accused of other crimes – theft, carrying a knife, faking a burglary and, in Amanda's case, falsely accusing Patrick of murder – and he couldn't see any room for granting them a reduced sentence, particularly given their behaviour after the murder. Mignini also had to take into account the sentence imposed on Rudy; he had been condemned to thirty years in prison, but if his hadn't been a fast-track trial, it would have been life.

And yet Mignini also felt sadness, and compassion, at what awaited Amanda and Raffaele if the sentence he requested was passed by the court. He thought of his own teenage daughters, and of Amanda's parents and what a life sentence imposed on their girl would mean for them.

Soon afterwards, a friend told Mignini: 'I imagine the seven and a half hours of your closing argument were the worst hours of your life.'

Mignini replied: 'Actually, the worst was the minute in which I asked for the life sentences.'

Amanda had felt too overwhelmed the previous day to stand up and speak, but that afternoon she finally found enough strength to do so. She began confidently enough, but her voice soon quivered.

'I wanted first of all to say sorry because yesterday I wanted to say a couple of things, but I was very moved and I didn't manage it. Today I'm more level-headed. I wanted to say that Meredith was my friend and I didn't hate her,' Amanda said, fighting back tears.

'The fact that I could have killed her is absurd; the idea that I wanted to seek revenge on a person who was nice to me is absurd. I repeat that I didn't have any relations with Rudy ... *Mamma mia ...*' – the latter said almost in a scornful tone, as if the very idea of her having anything to do with Rudy was offensive.

She concluded: 'And everything that I've heard about myself in the past few days is pure fantasy, it has nothing to do with reality. I just wanted to say this. Thank you.'

27 November 2009

Mignini had accused Amanda of murder and demanded she be jailed for life, but his wasn't the most virulent attack against her at the trial. That was made by Patrick's lawyer Carlo Pacelli, who precisely nine months earlier had with old-fashioned courtesy addressed her as 'Signorina Amanda' when he questioned her.

Today, he lashed out at her, often raising his voice. Amanda was 'diabolic', 'perfidious and cunning'; she had a dual personality and was 'unclean on the outside because she was dirty on the inside'. The lawyer compared her to Judas for embracing Patrick one day and sending him to jail the next.

'Who is the real Amanda Knox?' Pacelli asked. 'Is she the angelic person we see here? Or is she really a diabolical she-devil, an explosive concentrate of sex, drugs and alcohol? She is both. But the latter is the Amanda we saw on 1 November, 2007.'

Amanda didn't even bother to glance at him. Once again, she resorted to writing a note and then showing it to her lawyers: 'In prison, you don't become a better person; you become worse if you don't have an inner light that guides you.' Away from the courtroom when guards escorted her to the bathroom during a break, she burst into tears.

Speaking after Pacelli, the Kerchers' lawyer Maresca spoke in a much more measured tone. He highlighted the Kercher family's support for the investigators, thanking the latter for their work.

'It's absolutely devastating to think that kids so young committed such a serious crime but the evidence that's been accumulated says just that,' Maresca said. He asked for damages of £22 million to be paid – 'a symbolic sum, because the life of a young girl has no price.' In Italy requests for such amounts were common, and a way of underscoring the seriousness of the crime.

Maresca ended with the words: 'To he who has caused suffering, suffering must be imposed . . . Mez cannot have her life back. For the others [Amanda and Raffaele], the only path is that of repentance, of faith.'

That evening, as Edda and Curt sat in Ghirga's office shortly after their arrival from Seattle for the last week of the trial, *carabinieri* officers served them with a notice that they were under investigation on suspicion of slandering the Homicide Squad – a crime with a potential prison sentence of up to three years.

The investigation had been launched at the request of Napoleoni and the entire Homicide Squad, who had filed a suit in September 2008. They accused Amanda's parents of slandering them in the interview they gave the author for *The Sunday Times Magazine* in saying that Amanda had been 'abused physically and verbally', hit on the back of the head by a police officer, and given no food or water for nine hours.

'The timing is very curious, with this coming five days before a high-profile case is going to come to a close, for an article written eighteen months ago,' Curt told a journalist. 'We just answered a reporter's questions about what Amanda had told us,' Edda added.

53

Of all the defence lawyers' final pleas, Bongiorno's was the most awaited. Raffaele's lawyer was the most heavyweight lawyer in the courtroom and she didn't disappoint with a sharp, well-researched summing-up delivered with only occasional glances at her notes.

She began by directly addressing the court and quoting Plato: 'I ask you to have the same frame of mind as the wise man, as the Socrates described by Plato; the one who, whatever he is considering at the time, says to himself: "I know that I don't know." '

What was beyond doubt, she argued, was that Raffaele and Rudy didn't know each other at the time of the murder. 'Rudy and Raffaele met each other in a courtroom during the preliminary hearings. The only link between them is the charge sheet,' she said.

She poured scorn on the witnesses who said they'd seen Amanda, Raffaele and Rudy together before the murder: 'One contradicted himself fifty-three times, the other remembers only things which are of use to the prosecution, but nothing which can prove his story.'

There was no motive for Raffaele killing Meredith. 'I'm waiting to find out why Raffaele, who was about to graduate and who was in love, should have taken part in the murder of Meredith whom he hardly knew. I want to know why he did it,' Bongiorno said.

She tipped coloured sticks of the Mikado game out onto the desk. 'The aim of the game is to pick up as many sticks as you can without moving the other ones. If Raffaele was in Via della Pergola on the night of the crime, he's a Mikado world champion.'

She went on: 'There are no prints belonging to Amanda or Raffaele in Meredith's room; only super-champions of this game could have managed that. People will say they cleaned up; but then they cleaned up only their traces, because that room is dripping with Rudy's prints. And because Alberto Intini, the head of the forensic police, says that "only a dragonfly in flight" can enter the room without leaving any traces, well then the two youngsters are innocent because they're not dragonflies, that's for sure.'

Bongiorno attacked Mignini's latest reconstruction of the murder: 'There used to be just one murder weapon, and now there are two. And in any case the big knife chosen by the prosecution, pulled out at random like a lottery number from a drawer where there were another hundred, is even for court-appointed experts compatible only with the will to threaten, not to kill. What shall we do? Change the charge sheet?'

For investigators, she said, finding the kitchen knife in Raffaele's flat served to give him a role in the murder; they saw him as just an appendix to Amanda, 'a drone'. But the kitchen knife wasn't the murder weapon.

'It's been excluded that the DNA found on the blade was blood. What's more, it's only at the end of the trial that we were told the genetic substance which was analysed was too low to be attributed to anyone,' she argued.

Nor was Meredith's bra clasp, on which the DNA of Raffaele, Rudy and Meredith was found, a valid piece of evidence. 'It was spotted by the police on 2 November 2007 close to Mez's body and was rediscovered forty-six days later under a rug which had at first been rolled up beside the desk . . . It's not genuine evidence. Either the prosecution explains to us how it came to be moved, or it should have the courage to throw it away.'

Bongiorno surprised many in court by making an impassioned defence of Amanda; she clearly believed that to save her client Raffaele, she also had to save his ex-girlfriend. Tackling Amanda's 'confession' that she was at the cottage at the time of the murder and heard Patrick kill her, Bongiorno said that on the night she made that statement to police, 'Amanda was denied her right to silence'; at the time, she added, Amanda spoke only a little Italian and she didn't know the country's laws.

Again staring straight at the judges and jurors, Bongiorno asked: 'Do you think it's so very strange that she became desperate, that she said things that weren't true, and that she didn't have the courage to correct what she had said afterwards? To understand that, you have to decipher Amanda.'

The prosecution, Bongiorno said, had described Amanda as 'a ripper' – as in 'Jack the Ripper'. She added: 'The truth is that Amanda is a fragile and weak girl and not a ripper. The ripper would have defended herself, she wouldn't have let herself be duped by the police' – a reference to the night on which she made her 'confession'.

The clue to Amanda's nature was in the memorandum she wrote five days after the murder in which she said her friends thought she was like Amélie – the faux-naïve heroine of the film she and Raffaele said they watched on the night of the murder – *because I'm a bit of a weirdo, in that I like random little things, like birds singing, and these little things make me happy.*

Amanda was 'the Amélie of Seattle' for Bongiorno. 'She looks at the world with the eyes of a little girl, like Amélie: a naïve, slightly extravagant, spontaneous young girl who is 60% imagination and 40% reality,' Bongiorno said.

Amanda and Raffaele were not murderers but adolescents who had been discovering love. 'The two would have committed such a savage murder after having watched such a romantic comedy? Does that seem logical?' Bongiorno asked.

Bongiorno appealed to the court one last time: 'I began by quoting Plato and urging you to doubt. When you deliberate, don't be afraid of having doubts, of verifying, of contradicting each other. The role that you are performing is something I've never wanted to have because I don't feel capable. Only you and God have the power to sit in judgement.'

1 December 2009

With the court due to start deliberating their verdict in three days'
time, Amanda took up pen and paper yet again. A note she left
behind on her desk after a hearing was headed: '*What I want to
say at the end.*'

She wrote that she planned to thank the court and added: '*I'm
afraid of losing myself because I'm afraid of being convicted for something I'm not, which I didn't do.*'

In court, Amanda adopted a more sombre look. Gone were the
Beatles T-shirt and sweatshirt; her hair gathered in a neat plait that
started on the crown of her head, she dressed elegantly in a black
polo-neck sweater and cream trousers.

2 December 2009

A stickler for routine, Amanda's lawyer Ghirga started his day as
usual on a high metal stool outside the Caffè Turreno before strid-
ing down to the law courts. But today, the day he was to make his
closing argument on Amanda's behalf, he brought his daughter
Giulia into the courtroom with him and sat her down just a few
feet from Amanda and himself, near the big steel cage; Ghirga
wanted his daughter, who was almost the same age as Amanda, to
be close to him as he spoke.

'Good luck!' a friend greeted Ghirga as he arranged a dozen
piles of handwritten notes and case files all over his desk.

'It's out of my hands,' Ghirga, his white hair immaculately
combed, shot back – as if he had already resigned himself to a
guilty sentence.

Ghirga's plea clearly came from the heart; he sounded sincere,
impassioned, often patting Amanda's shoulder when he mentioned
her. Her arms folded, she sat staring fixedly up at him as he talked,
her lips sealed tight. Taking the court through the investigation,
the former sweeper for the Juventus team first tackled Napoleoni
and her female colleagues of the Homicide Squad head-on.

The squad, Ghirga said, had seen Amanda 'snogging' – 'What a horrible word!' he added – with Raffaele in the garden of the cottage, and had immediately started tapping her phone. 'This is a clash between women, between Amanda and the women of the Flying Squad, which she has had to put up with from the very beginning,' Ghirga said, making sweeping gestures with his hands and nearly shouting. 'The vibrator, the condoms, the Vaseline pushed the investigation towards a sex crime. That's how the image of a man-eater was born – the student who brought boys home.'

A couple of journalists in the courtroom wondered why Ghirga had zeroed in on the women investigators – 'Is he being sexist? Is he implying Napoleoni and the others suspected her out of female bitchiness?' one journalist whispered. Whatever the reason, Ghirga had apparently chosen to ignore the fact that most of Napoleoni's colleagues in the Homicide Squad were in fact men – the head of the Flying Squad was a man and so was the lead prosecutor who had more authority over the investigation than any of these women.

Amanda was no man-eater, Ghirga continued: 'She only brought one man home, on the night she went to the Red Zone [night club] with Mez. Amanda, who hadn't met Raffaele yet, brought a Roman boy to her room. Meredith was in her room with [her neighbour] Giacomo.'

Now turning himself into a referee, Ghirga sanctioned the prosecutor Mignini for failing to give Amanda a lawyer on the night she made her 'confession' and 'leaving her defenceless for hours'. Ghirga raised his voice to a shout: 'What Amanda suffered that night was a red-card foul. This is a very serious omission which we can't tolerate.'

Ghirga's attack left Mignini visibly fuming, but the prosecutor said nothing.

The only reason Amanda had made that 'confession', Ghirga went on, was that she had 'freaked out completely after four days of stress ... There was no deliberate intention, no will' to trap

Patrick, and so she should be acquitted of the charge of slander. She had simply started to say what the police wanted to hear.

Ghirga again hit out at Mignini, denouncing his new reconstruction of how Meredith died. 'Everything's changed in the prosecution's case – the position of the victim, the weapons, the time of death. The sexual motive has fallen through, so here's hatred; but the text messages between Amanda and Mez prove their friendship,' Ghirga said.

Going further than any other lawyer or expert consultant at the trial, Ghirga then ruled out the kitchen knife as the murder weapon, stating categorically: 'There was an involuntary DNA contamination in the laboratory.' But he gave no evidence for this.

As he ended his plea, Ghirga urged the judges and jurors: 'I ask you – or rather Amanda's parents, two desperate parents,' – Ghirga turned to point at Edda and Curt – 'ask you to acquit her.'

Ghirga again touched Amanda lightly on the shoulder. 'Amanda asks you for her life. Give Amanda her life back,' he said.

The strain of the past two years, and his own emotional commitment to Amanda – of whom he'd confided 'I'd love to have her as my own daughter' – suddenly proved too much for Ghirga as he found himself choking back tears. He stopped, blinked several times and took a sip of water.

'I'm a little moved. What you've seen isn't an act, I want to do my utmost to persuade you,' Ghirga said.

He thanked the court, then affectionately pinched Amanda's cheek before sitting down.

Over lunch with Napoleoni and the Kerchers' lawyer Maresca afterwards, Mignini fretted about whether any of Ghirga's arguments had persuaded the court.

'Ghirga threw a lot of mud, and mud sticks,' Mignini worried.

Back at the Caffè Turreno later that day, Ghirga confided: 'I bumped into a couple of the jurors on my way out of court. One said "Bravo" to me, and another said I'd moved him.'

'Does that mean they'll acquit?' a journalist asked.

'Nope,' Ghirga replied.

With a keen sense of timing, Rudy suddenly branded Amanda and Raffaele 'murderers' – the first time he had ever done so. In a letter to his lawyer, he raged against what they and their lawyers had said about him at the pair's trial.

'Two murderers, Raffaele Sollecito and Amanda Knox, are deservedly on trial for the murder of a splendid girl,' Rudy wrote. 'Instead of admitting their guilt, but above all the horror they committed, Sollecito and Knox do nothing but slander people, spreading falsehoods and hoping to get off scot-free . . . Enough is enough.'

3 December 2009

The night before the court was due to withdraw to decide their verdict, Amanda woke up at 3 a.m. and, tormented by anxiety, spent the rest of the night wide awake.

That afternoon, in a trembling voice, she addressed the court for the last time, speaking in her fluent Italian. Dressed in a bright, lime-green coat, she stood with her cheeks flushed, her arms rigid, the tips of her fingers occasionally stabbing the top of her desk.

'Many times over the past few days, people have asked me: "How do you manage to stay so calm?" But I'm not calm. A few days ago I wrote on a piece of paper that I was afraid of being called what I'm not and I'm scared of having the mask of a murderer forced on to my skin.

'As far as the decisions to keep me in jail these past two years are concerned, I can say that I feel disappointed, sad, frustrated. Many tell me that if they'd been in my situation they'd have already torn their hair out or smashed their cell but I don't do these things, I don't get depressed because I take deep breaths and I try to find positive things to think about.

'I have to thank the prosecution because quite honestly they're trying to do their job even if they don't understand, even if they don't succeed in understanding. They're trying to ensure justice after an act which took someone away from this world, and so I thank them for what they're doing.

'But the most important thing is that I thank you because it's up to you now. And so, thank you. So . . . that's it.'

After Amanda finished speaking, Judge Massei decreed a break but she didn't have the strength to move; she staggered slightly and grabbed Ghirga's arm to steady herself.

'Some water please,' she said, then added: 'I'm fine, it's nothing.'

54

On a drizzly morning at 10.35 a.m., Judge Massei led his colleague Judge Cristiani and the six jurors out of the courtroom after the last lawyers had spoken. Both judges, in black robes and white ruffled neckbands, and the six jurors, wearing tricolour sashes, walked a few yards into a small, sparsely furnished room where they would now begin their deliberations.

A pale, drawn-looking Amanda, her hair freshly plaited, and again wearing her bright green coat, turned to glance at her family – Edda and Curt and their spouses, as well as her sister Deanna – as two guards approached to escort her out. Head bowed, she breathed in and out slowly and deeply as she was led away. Raffaele, in a black polo-neck sweater and brown trousers, looked straight ahead of him as he followed her. Both would await the verdict in their prison cells.

The junior prosecutor Comodi watched Amanda and Raffaele leave and suddenly thought to herself: 'They're going to be convicted, I'm sure of it.' She then thought: 'How absurd, how terrible for two such young kids to have so many years in jail ahead of them.'

As the courtroom was cleared, journalists tried to guess how long it would take for a verdict to be reached. According to one judicial source, Judge Massei had let it be known that he expected a decision by the early hours of the next morning. A rumour said his clerk hadn't booked a hotel for judges and jurors for the night, so the verdict would come some time during the night at the latest.

The prosecutors, Mignini and Comodi, spent part of the day at their offices across town from the law courts, trying to make a start on the huge backlog of work on other cases that had accumulated during the trial.

Staring out at the rain, a calm, even genial, Mignini told a visitor: 'I like the rain. It's clean.'

Down the corridor, the usually vivacious Comodi was more downcast. 'This is the worst day. There's nothing we can do any more, and it's now that I feel things the hardest. I feel so sorry for Raffaele; I really pity him for getting involved in all this. But I don't feel sorry for Amanda,' she said.

The rain had stopped by the time the two prosecutors left for lunch, to be replaced by fog which crept up from the valley below Perugia to blanket the main Corso Vannucci so thickly that the cathedral was visible only from some fifty yards.

The Kerchers' lawyer, Maresca, spent much of the afternoon walking around in a futile attempt to stop thinking about the long wait. He bought a couple of Christmas presents for his young daughter.

Shortly after 5 p.m., the Kercher family arrived at their hotel outside the city centre, sharing a taxi. Meredith's parents John and Arline, her sister Stephanie and her brothers John and Lyle said nothing as they walked through a crowd of jostling TV crews and photographers. Arline had a stunned expression on her face and Stephanie put a protective arm around her mother's shoulder as she guided her to the lift up to their rooms.

Soon afterwards, they met their lawyers Maresca and Perna in the lobby of the hotel. Over strong coffees, Maresca told the family he thought the court would find Amanda and Raffaele guilty, but he added: 'In theory, they could also be acquitted.'

Arline looked taken aback. 'But if there's all that DNA of theirs in the house!' she protested.

'Yes, there's their DNA, but the experts named by the defence have been challenging how it got there,' Maresca said.

'When will the verdict be?' the Kerchers asked.

Probably that night, Maresca said, but it could come as late as two o'clock in the morning. The Kerchers looked surprised, but resigned themselves to wait.

At his church, not far from the prosecutors' offices, the prison chaplain Father Saulo busied himself preparing for early evening Mass. As ever, he had stayed away from the law courts.

'It seems impossible to me that the Amanda I've known these past two years could have done it,' Father Saulo told a visitor. 'As for the Amanda of before . . . well, I don't know.'

But that evening, Father Saulo prayed for her acquittal.

At 8 p.m., the judges and jurors took a break from their deliberations to have dinner. As they couldn't leave the room where they had now been closeted for eleven and a half hours, a nearby restaurant delivered the meal: a first course of pasta, followed by a main dish of meat and vegetables, and a dessert.

Anxious to keep their minds sharp, they shared a single bottle of red wine between them.

A two-minute walk away, the prosecutors, Mignini and Comodi, were having dinner with the Kerchers' lawyers, Maresca and Perna, at the *Ristorante del Sole*. All four of them were tense – they kept their mobile phones by their plates, waiting for the call from Judge Massei's clerk which would tell them when the verdict was to be announced – but did their best not to show it. For moral support, Mignini brought along his wife Cristina, who was three months' pregnant with their fourth child.

As they picked at their food – pasta followed by *tagliata*, thinly-sliced cuts of almost raw beef – the prosecutors and lawyers dissected the trial from beginning to end. They had plenty of time to do so now.

The call came at 9.35 p.m., on Comodi's mobile.

'They're coming out at midnight,' the clerk told Comodi – there was no need to say who 'they' were.

Comodi thanked her, and gave her the names of her companions to save her making pointless calls.

No one felt like eating any more. Wanting fresh air, Mignini and Comodi went for a walk down the Corso Vannucci. Comodi was struck by how surreal it all was – here she was, strolling along in the Friday night crowd just as if she was enjoying an evening out like them but she was waiting for the verdict in a murder trial. And Christmas lights were twinkling high over her head; she had always hated Christmas decorations and at that moment she hated them more than ever.

More than two hours to wait, Comodi thought.

Maresca headed to his hotel to change – it was a ritual of his to change into casual clothes after the court withdrew, and then change back into a suit and tie for the verdict. He texted an American journalist who was dining with colleagues at a wine bar opposite the cathedral and told her the verdict would come at midnight.

His message electrified the party. Their meal forgotten, the journalists first called their newsrooms, then rushed to pay the bill and join the queue that was building up quickly outside the law courts. By 10.30 p.m., a crowd of more than a hundred journalists and locals thronged the square waiting for the doors of the law courts to open.

Shortly before midnight, the key protagonists of the eleven-month trial were back in the courtroom. Without exception, the prosecutors and the lawyers wore mournful expressions and waited in silence, or talked briefly in hushed voices, as if they were at a wake. Mignini sat quietly, sucking at an unlit pipe. Comodi sat next to him, not moving. Amanda's lawyer Ghirga stood facing the public and press gallery, looking grim, his hands thrust in his pockets.

On one side of the courtroom, by the steel cage, Edda and Curt stood waiting silently with their spouses. A woman lawyer stroked the cheek of Amanda's sister Deanna.

At the opposite end of the courtroom, the Kerchers sat just as quietly. They were all dressed in black.

Guards led Amanda in for the last time. Still wearing her green coat, she ignored the Kerchers as she was led past them, and gave just a curt, unsmiling nod to her own family before sitting down with her head bowed. Ghirga patted her on the back. Two guards stood behind her, an extra three guards standing a few feet away.

Raffaele greeted his lawyer Bongiorno with a tight smile and a kiss on both cheeks.

5 December 2009

At four minutes past midnight, a bell rang for a couple of seconds. More than thirteen hours after they had left it, the judges and jurors filed back into the courtroom. All looked strained; several of the jurors looked exhausted.

Amanda stood up and glanced at Judge Massei, nodding her head slightly in greeting as she had always done when the court entered. She swallowed and looked as if she was making an effort to breathe deeply. Ghirga gripped her right arm.

'In the name of the Italian people . . .' The court remained standing as Judge Massei, the crucifix hanging on the wall just behind his head, began to read. He looked only at the paper he held in his hands, reading quickly in a low monotone.

'In the trial against Knox, Amanda Marie, and Sollecito, Raffaele, given articles 533 and 535 . . .'

Amanda realised immediately that she had been convicted. Ghirga had warned her that if the judge began by quoting these two articles, then that meant a guilty verdict. Amanda's head dropped forward and her chest heaved as she started to sob. Ghirga clasped her right arm even more tightly.

Judge Massei, his voice so quiet he could barely be heard: '. . . Declares Knox, Amanda Marie, and Sollecito, Raffaele, guilty of the crimes they stood accused of under sub-heading A . . .'

Two rows behind Amanda, her father Curt and his second wife Cassandra turned away from her for a moment as Cassandra asked an American journalist a few feet behind her: 'Guilty?'

'Yes,' the journalist replied.

The blood drained from Raffaele's face but he stood immobile, staring straight at the judge. His stepmother Mara, standing a few feet behind him, cried out in dismay then collapsed onto a chair.

The Kerchers' lawyer Maresca glanced towards Meredith's parents next to him and made a little punching gesture into the air with his left fist to tell them the pair had been found guilty. He then turned to give a little nod to Stephanie and her two brothers standing behind him.

Judge Massei ploughed on. '. . . condemns Knox to the sentence of twenty-six years in prison . . .'

Amanda's shoulders shook as she sobbed more heavily. Two rows behind her, Curt shook his head slowly from side to side, his face and body otherwise rigid. Edda looked shattered but dry-eyed. Deanna sobbed like her sister, and one of Ghirga's secretaries stroked her arm.

'. . . and Raffaele Sollecito to the sentence of twenty-five years in prison . . .'

Raffaele made no movement, still staring straight at the judge, but his stepmother began to wail, occasionally drowning out the judge's quiet voice.

Arline Kercher and her daughter Stephanie stared at Amanda and tears filled their own eyes.

Without pausing to glance at the scene before him, Judge Massei continued to read. The court found Amanda and Raffaele guilty of complicity in murder, illegally carrying a knife, sexual assault, simulation of a crime – and in Amanda's case, slander. Only once did he say the word 'acquitted' – Amanda and Raffaele were cleared of stealing £270 from Meredith and her credit cards, but they were convicted of stealing her two mobile phones.

The court granted Amanda and Raffaele a reduced sentence for their youth and their clean records, and ordered them to pay £900,000 in compensation to each of Meredith's parents, and £720,000 to each of her siblings. Amanda, also convicted of slandering Patrick, must pay him £9,000 in damages. Both must also pay legal costs.

Mignini felt first a wave of serenity at the fact that the court had backed him. He had done his job properly, and justice had been rendered to Meredith. But his satisfaction was tinged by sorrow both for Meredith, and for Amanda and Raffaele – they were all so young, he thought.

Mignini then caught sight of the crucifix behind Judge Massei and he drew comfort from it. In his suffering, he thought, Christ represented us all – prosecutors, defence lawyers, the accused and the victim – and was also a bearer of hope.

His colleague Comodi sometimes felt a wave of exultation when a verdict went her way. But not this time. 'Good, this is right,' she thought to herself. But she felt no happiness.

Standing not far from the prosecutors, the detective Napoleoni thought how terrible this case was. For her, the most terrible thing about it was that there was no motive for Meredith's death. 'The only motive was the emptiness inside these kids, their lack of humanity. Meredith died for nothing, and she was killed by people who should have been her friends,' she reflected.

If there was one thing the case had taught her, it was that a young woman could die 'for no reason at all'.

When Judge Massei finished reading and turned to leave, followed by his colleague and the jurors, a still-weeping Amanda turned towards Ghirga and buried her face in his shoulder. Deanna wept uncontrollably, gasping for air.

Ghirga, still clasping Amanda tightly by the arm, then escorted her out of the courtroom, Amanda leaning heavily on him as if to stop herself slumping to the floor. It wasn't Ghirga's job to escort her, but no one stopped him and a woman guard held her other arm.

Amanda sobbed so heavily she didn't see those she passed on her way out – the prosecutors Mignini and Comodi, Napoleoni and her police colleagues, and finally the Kerchers. Raffaele followed, walking stiffly, a dazed expression on his face. Arline stared at both Amanda and Raffaele as they passed only a few feet away.

Moments later, as Amanda was escorted to the prison van, she gave a desperate scream which could be heard in the courtroom: 'No, no, no!' she shouted.

'Will you fight on?' a journalist asked Curt.

'Hell, yes,' he replied.

Comodi was in a hurry to leave. 'Giuliano, let's go,' she said to Mignini.

As she said goodbye to Arline, Meredith's mother kissed her on both cheeks.

'Thank you very much,' Arline said.

Comodi just smiled; she couldn't manage to say anything.

'What we've done is very little,' Comodi thought. As a mother of two girls herself, she realised that Arline felt comforted by the fact that those who had killed her daughter had been found and punished. 'At least Arline can tick that box, but for the rest of her life she'll be mourning a missing daughter,' she thought.

Meredith's father John embraced Mignini, then turned to Napoleoni; he hugged her, cupped her cheeks in his hands and then hugged her again.

'Got to go,' he told Napoleoni with a smile. 'See you some time.'

★   ★   ★

Stephanie wiped the tears from her eyes and shook Napoleoni's hand. 'Thank you, for Meredith,' Stephanie said to her.

Napoleoni stared at Stephanie and was stunned by what she saw. She had always been struck by how much Stephanie looked like her younger sister but today, with Stephanie having grown her hair longer, Napoleoni thought: 'She's just like Meredith now.'

She felt as if it was Meredith who was standing in front of her.

Soon afterwards, when Stephanie was asked what the last two years had been like for her family, she hesitated and then replied: 'It just feels as if our lives have been on hold. It won't ever be the same without Mez so . . .' – she left the sentence unfinished, then added: 'She is still a very big part of our lives. She's still very much with us.'

Meredith's friends Sophie, Amy and Robyn had arranged to be connected to each other via the Skype network when the verdict came. Sophie was in a hostel in Ecuador, on holiday; Amy and Robyn were both back in England.

Sophie's first reaction to the verdict was relief that Amanda and Raffaele had been found guilty. But a twenty-six-year sentence, she quickly realised, meant Amanda would be in her early forties, at the most, when she walked free. Sophie had wanted Amanda jailed for life, but she would still have a life ahead of her.

But Sophie hoped that after the verdict, Amanda and Raffaele would start to realise that they weren't going to get away with what they'd done. Perhaps one of them, or Rudy, would confess.

55

Two weeks after Amanda and Raffaele were convicted, an appeal court reduced Rudy's sentence from thirty years to sixteen. The court had singled out his youth, his clean record, his difficult childhood, his decision to return to Italy to give himself up after fleeing to Germany, and his apology to the Kerchers, even if this was only for failing to save her.

But Rudy was anything but grateful for the verdict. 'I'm not pleased because I'm innocent,' he told journalists as he was led out of the courtroom. The Kerchers had their own reasons for being unhappy with the verdict and their lawyer Maresca fumed against the 'drastic reduction' in Rudy's sentence.

The decision baffled Amanda. 'I don't understand why they reduced his sentence. He's never told the truth. He keeps accusing me even though he knows I've got nothing to do with Meredith's death,' Amanda protested when her mother Edda visited her, bringing a cashmere sweater as a Christmas present.

Edda tried to explain the court's reasoning. Her daughter listened attentively, then burst out: 'Rudy's got nothing to do with me. I saw him twice, briefly. I hope that one day he'll say the truth at last and stop dragging me into this horrible thing. I've never pointed a finger at him, I've never accused him.'

As the two said goodbye – Edda had to go home to Seattle and wouldn't be back in Perugia until the spring – Amanda told her mother not to worry about her. 'I'll be strong. Both of us must be strong,' she said. 'I've been told that appeal trials work in Italy – it's rare that an innocent is left in jail.' Then she added: 'I'm so scared.'

Amanda showed Edda a big yellow envelope she kept in her cell. She'd written on the envelope: 'Positive letters, to read when I'm home.'

Amanda explained: 'Lots of people believe me. I receive hundreds of letters. People write to me from all over Italy, from the States, from Canada, from Ireland. Even from South Africa. Boys and girls, and parents who have children who are the same age as me. They tell me to be confident.'

Only two letters, from the UK, sneered at her. 'Enjoy jail,' one of them said.

Amanda handed the envelope to her mother. 'I've put in here the letters from people who believe in my innocence. I'd like to reply to all of them but there are too many. Take them home with you. I'll read them when I'm free.'

22 February 2010

A case that had dogged Mignini like no other came to a climax in a courtroom in Florence. This time he was not the prosecutor but the accused, charged with serious misconduct in his investigation of a suspicious death linked to the 'Monster of Florence', a serial killer who murdered couples in the 1960s and 1970s. The Florence prosecutor Luca Turco had portrayed Mignini as 'driven by a crusader's fervor' in his work, for whom 'everything that was critical of the investigation was an attack against it'.

Flanked by his lawyers, Mignini stood to hear the verdict. He was sure that the court would acquit him of all charges. His pregnant wife Cristina and one of their three daughters stood nearby, as did the Kerchers' lawyer Maresca who had come to show support.

Mignini was stunned when the judge gave him a suspended prison sentence of one year and four months for abuse of office,

ruling that he had illegally tapped the phones of three police officers and three journalists reporting on the 'Monster'. Michele
Giuttari, the former head of Florence's Flying Squad, was given
a suspended sentence of one year and six months for the same
crime. Both Mignini and Giuttari were banned from holding
public office, but this too was suspended. The death they'd inves-
tigated was that of a Perugia doctor, Francesco Narducci, in 1985;
they believed it was a murder linked to the 'Monster'.

The court acquitted Mignini of the more serious charge of
aiding and abetting Giuttari. They also acquitted him of abuse of
office in his conduct of another investigation into a taped conversation between Giuttari and a Florence prosecutor, in which the
latter accused his superiors of blocking the investigation into the
'Monster'. Giuttari was also acquitted of other charges.

Mignini couldn't understand why he had been found guilty
of ordering illegal phone taps. No prosecutor had the power to
tap phones without first obtaining permission from a judge. And
yet no accusation was made against the judge who'd given him
permission.

'My conscience is clear, I did nothing wrong,' Mignini told
journalists just after the verdict, announcing that he would appeal.
He was the victim of a Florentine power struggle, he said. The trial
should never have been held in Florence, because other Florence
prosecutors were involved in the case.

Asked whether the ruling might throw any shadows on his
handling of the Kercher investigation, Mignini replied: 'Judges
and jurors have ruled on the Meredith case. Today's verdict,
instead, involves only me.'

But from Philadelphia a new lawyer appointed by Amanda's
family, Theodore Simon, immediately seized on Mignini's conviction. In America, he said, a prosecutor would never have been
allowed to continue working on a case while facing an indictment
himself; the Italian system meant that the fairness of the trial and
the integrity of the verdict could be called into question.

4 March 2010

Three months after sentencing Amanda and Raffaele, Judges Massei and Cristiani released their review of the evidence – a massive, 427-page report in which they painstakingly dissected all the key elements presented in court before offering their own reconstruction of Meredith's last moments.

The review focused at length on contradictions and inconsistencies in Amanda's accounts. Amanda had variously said that on the night of the murder she and Raffaele had dinner at about 9.30, 10.30 or 11 p.m. But when Raffaele's father called at 8.42 p.m., Raffaele told him that he was with Amanda and that 'while he was washing the dishes he had realised there was a leak' in the kitchen – so the couple had dinner much earlier than Amanda claimed. She had lied to create an alibi for the couple.

Amanda also claimed that she slept through the night and awoke in Raffaele's arms at 10–10.30 a.m. on 2 November. But she never made any mention of the fact that Raffaele's computer was turned on at 5.32 a.m. to play music for a half hour, nor that he switched on his mobile phone at 6 a.m., nor that he spoke to his father at 9.30 a.m.

That morning, Amanda said, she took a shower and washed her hair at her cottage. This was hard to believe, as she had already done so at Raffaele's flat the previous evening. Moreover, the judges couldn't understand why Amanda should have gone to the cottage for a shower, given that the couple planned to leave that morning for a day trip to the medieval town of Gubbio.

The first call Amanda made on 2 November was to her flatmate Filomena, according to Amanda's testimony. But in fact her first call was to Meredith's English mobile phone, at 12.07 p.m. The judges held that she made the call because she wanted to check that no one had found Meredith's two phones, before calling Filomena to tell her about the 'burglary' at the cottage. If Amanda really had wanted to find out where Meredith was, as she claimed, why then didn't she also call her Italian phone? The truth was that Amanda and Raffaele knew perfectly well that Meredith couldn't answer.

In the email she sent to her family and friends in Seattle on 4 November, Amanda said she had panicked after Meredith failed to answer her when she banged on her door and shouted her flatmate's name. Raffaele had then tried to knock the door down but failed, and that was when they had decided to call the police.

Amanda said Meredith's door was normally closed, and yet Raffaele tried to force it open. His attempt was only a 'timid' one, the judges said – he had stopped trying after only one kick. And when the police arrived at the cottage, there was no sign of the panic Amanda mentioned. Amanda and Raffaele drew the police's attention not to the closed bedroom door but to the broken window and the mess in Filomena's room, the open front door, and the bloodstains in the bathroom. It was Filomena who alerted the police to Meredith's closed door, the judges pointed out.

The review defended the work of the police detectives, the forensic police and their DNA analysis, and the two prosecutors, who had painted 'a comprehensive and coherent picture, with no omissions and no inconsistencies.' And yet the judges dismissed as worthless the testimony of the farmhand Kokomani – who said he saw Amanda, Raffaele and Rudy together – as well as that of the graduate Gioffredi – who said he saw all three with Meredith.

The judges struck a cautious tone in reconstructing the murder, describing their scenario not as set in stone but as the most likely based on the evidence they had examined. Their reconstruction was as follows:

On the night of 1 November, Amanda and Raffaele finished their dinner at his flat at about 8.40 p.m., and walked to Piazza Grimana, the square opposite the University for Foreigners. The tramp Curatolo saw them there between 9.30–10 p.m. and about 11 p.m. Rudy saw the couple there too, and started talking to Amanda who introduced him to Raffaele. At about 11 p.m., the three walked to the cottage; Amanda let them in.

For the judges, it was impossible to establish why Rudy had gone to the cottage. Perhaps he wanted to stay the night there, or spend some time with Amanda and Raffaele and use the bathroom, or say hello to his friends in the semi-basement flat. Whatever the reason, it was likely that he had found out there was no one in the downstairs flat, and told Amanda and Raffaele.

The trio must have realised immediately that Meredith was home. Meredith, who almost always left her door open, was still dressed and awake in her room, reading the history book her friend Robyn had lent her earlier that day.

Shortly after arriving at the cottage, Rudy went to the bathroom while Amanda and Raffaele went to her bedroom 'to be together, and to be intimate' – Amanda testified she and Raffaele had sex that evening, but at his flat, after smoking hashish.

On leaving the bathroom, Rudy let himself be carried away by what he saw as a situation 'heavy with sexual stimulus' which went to his head – 'two young lovers in their room and Meredith alone in the room next door.' He approached Meredith's room and walked in, wanting to have sex with her.

All Meredith wanted that evening was to be left in peace to study and go to bed early. She had a new boyfriend, she had no interest in Rudy and she rejected his advances. Amanda and Raffaele heard her repulsing him. They intervened – not to defend Meredith, but to help Rudy assault her.

Why did Amanda and Raffaele turn against Meredith? For the judges, the couple was probably drugged on hashish, and their motive was 'erotic sexual violence'. Forcing Meredith to yield to Rudy was 'a special thrill, which had to be tried out'.

The wounds which Meredith suffered, the DNA traces and the bare bloody footprints in the flat were proof of Amanda and Raffaele's participation. Given Meredith's character and physical strength – she had taken karate lessons – no lone attacker could have undressed her, sexually abused her, inflicted so many wounds and murdered her.

At some point during the assault, Amanda went to her bedroom to fetch the kitchen knife, its blade six-and-a-half inches long. Raffaele, they surmised, had probably persuaded her to keep it in the big handbag she always carried around with her, so that she could defend herself if attacked in the street at night.

At first, the judges continued, Amanda may have used the kitchen knife simply to threaten Meredith. But as Rudy and Raffaele struggled to undress a fiercely resistant Meredith, Raffaele took out another, smaller knife with a blade one-and-a-half inches long which he always carried on him. He cut the bra strap on her back. Immediately afterwards, as Rudy sexually assaulted Meredith with his fingers, Raffaele stabbed her in the neck with the same knife, inflicting a wound one-and-a-half inches deep – that knife was never found.

Meredith's 'scream of pain and terror' – the scream heard by the widow Capezzali – prompted one of her attackers to clamp a hand over her mouth to silence her, while Amanda stabbed her in the throat with the kitchen knife, this time inflicting a wound three inches deep. Meredith tried to jerk her head away but as she struggled she was pushed back onto the knife. Embedded in her flesh it now cut through her epiglottis (the flap of cartilage behind the root of her tongue), in effect stabbing her yet again.

When Meredith died, which the judges estimated was shortly after 11.30 p.m., Rudy rushed out of the cottage. The widow Capezzali heard him climb the iron stairs leading up from the car park opposite the cottage.

Amanda and Raffaele stayed behind. They cleaned themselves up in the bathroom, leaving several traces of Amanda and Meredith's blood, as well as one of Raffaele's bare foot stained with Meredith's blood.

Amanda and Raffaele then looked out through her bedroom windows and through those in Filomena's room to make sure no one had heard Meredith's scream and was coming to investigate. As she did so, Amanda left bare footprints stained with her own blood together with that of Meredith in both rooms. The couple decided to break Filomena's window to stage a burglary, which they did with a stone Raffaele brought in from the garden.

The couple walked back into Meredith's room. Careful not to step in the pools of blood on the floor, they took her two mobile phones and covered her virtually naked body. Neither of them noticed when a small piece of glass from Filomena's broken window fell on the floor. They left, locking the bedroom door behind them. The widow Capezzali heard them running down the cottage drive making a 'scurrying' sound, as she remembered it, on the stones and dry leaves in the drive.

Early the following morning, Amanda and Raffaele returned to the cottage and wiped away some but not all of their traces. They probably thought that the small bloodstains in the bathroom were insignificant. The judges found that Raffaele had, as he claimed, called the *carabinieri* before the postal police arrived at the cottage.

At the end of their report, the judges explained why the court had granted Amanda and Raffaele a reduced sentence. Until the murder they had been good students, their only 'unseemly' act that of taking drugs. Both Amanda and Raffaele were very young, inexperienced and immature, and this had been aggravated by the fact that they were far from home, their families and long-time friends.

A series of 'casual contingencies' lay behind the murder: Amanda and Raffaele suddenly finding themselves at a loose end that evening; the couple bumping into Rudy; the three of them present in the cottage at a time when Meredith was the only other person there. The murder had not been planned, nor was there 'any animosity or spite' towards the victim – a view which differed from the prosecution's.

There was one final reason for granting Amanda and Raffaele a reduced sentence. Covering the body with the quilt indicated not only pity for Meredith, but also 'a rejection of [the crime] that had been committed and therefore a kind of repentance.'

The same feelings also prompted Amanda and Raffaele to keep their distance from Meredith's bedroom when the door was kicked down and her body discovered – 'they didn't want to see Meredith's body, and the blood that had been spilt,' the judges wrote.

56

Amanda looked almost angelic as she recited the Lord's Prayer. '... *And forgive us our trespasses, as we forgive those who trespass against us, and lead us not into temptation, but deliver us from evil,*' she intoned in a strong, steady voice, her blue eyes bright, her small hands turned palms upwards by her chest.

Attending an Easter Mass in the chapel of the women's section at the Capanne prison, Amanda wore the red sweatshirt with a picture of The Beatles on the back that she had often worn to court, with black leggings and grey and white trainers. A small brown pouch was slung across her shoulder and chest. She had cut her dark brown hair short, pageboy style, which made her look younger and somehow more frail than at her trial. She was more smartly turned out than the other prisoners, who were in baggy tracksuits – the pouch looked coquettish and her hair formed a neat curl in front of each ear. She sported silver nail varnish.

An Italian magazine had quoted Amanda as saying her new haircut was '80% for practical reasons, because I can dry it quickly and it feels cooler. And 20% to express a kind of rebellion, to show how this situation is devastating me.' (Her parents said the magazine had spoken only to her mother Edda.)

Earlier that afternoon Amanda was the first prisoner the author, who had been granted permission to visit the prison, came across. Shadowed by a guard, she was pushing a trolley with a couple of box files on it. She smiled politely at another guard who made room for her and disappeared into an office.

'Amanda's working,' Rita Rapponi, chief supervisor at the women's wing, explained. 'She goes round the cells to ask prisoners what they want to buy and then she takes the orders and their money books down to the guardroom.' Orders included coffee, cigarettes, newspapers, magazines and strawberries. It was also Amanda's job to distribute the purchases.

How was Amanda? 'She's pretty well,' Rapponi replied. 'Amanda's confident that the future will bring freedom for her. She doesn't break down in tears. It's nothing like her night of tears after the verdict when we had to comfort her.'

During the service, Amanda sat bolt upright and chanted along with the others and laughed with them when Father Saulo, helped by two Franciscan friars, cracked jokes. When the priest, after the Lord's Prayer, invited the congregation to exchange a sign of peace, Amanda shook hands with the women next to her and kissed them on the cheek.

The service ended with the women chanting in unison, over and over again, 'Let our suffering be your joy' – a chant they had adopted as their own. Then they applauded and got up to return to their cells. Amanda rushed up to Father Saulo and the two friars and hugged each of them in turn. She chatted with them, then started walking back down the aisle.

Father Saulo called out: 'Amanda! Do you know John?' She stopped and smiled as Father Saulo introduced the author. Her handshake was firm, her eyes still bright, her cheeks flushed after the chanting in contrast with the pallor of the rest of her face.

Asked how she was, Amanda replied with a smile: 'Fine.' She then asked abruptly, her eyes now wary: 'Who are you?'

Told about this book, she replied with another broad smile – 'Oh great!'

As Amanda was banned from granting interviews under prison rules, the author asked whether he could write to her; Amanda said yes. She was then led away back to her cell. The author sent her a letter shortly afterwards, but this went unanswered.

For the supervisor Rapponi, Father Saulo and the nuns and friars who visited Amanda and the other inmates almost daily had helped 'to make her less tense, less emotional. Now she's got her feet firmly on the ground.'

Amanda had built a rapport with Father Saulo, but she kept both the guards and the other prisoners at a distance; the only exception was her American cellmate. 'It's understandable. Amanda is a foreigner so she gets close to someone who speaks her own language. She gets on well with the other prisoners, she's never quarrelled with anyone, but she doesn't have a deep relationship with anyone else. She's very reserved,' Rapponi said.

Despite this reserve, most of Amanda's fellow prisoners not only liked her, they believed she had committed no crime. 'She's a great girl, she's never been a problem. She behaves so well. Most of us think she's innocent,' one prisoner said. 'She respects other people and she's never sad,' another echoed.

Amanda never talked to either the guards or the other prisoners about Meredith's murder. Prisoners didn't talk about the reason that, rightly or wrongly, got them into jail. 'Most of us don't talk about their crimes. The worse the crimes are, the less people admit they're guilty,' one of them said.

Bernardina di Mario, the prison governor, also had only praise for her most infamous prisoner. 'Her behaviour is excellent. She's calm, she's serving her time with serenity. She works, she studies, she isn't a nuisance,' di Mario said. 'It wasn't the case during the trial, but these days she's always smiling. The blow of the verdict has become softened.'

In the 130-square-foot cell she shared with her fellow American – a woman in her early fifties held on drugs charges – Amanda spent much of her time reading through the thick judges' review which her lawyers had brought her.

If the review made Amanda's spirits flag, she betrayed no sign of it. To the contrary, she appeared optimistic, telling the supervisor, Rapponi: 'I'll be out soon.'

1 November 2010

On the third anniversary of Meredith's death, her family brought flowers to her grave in Mitcham Road Cemetery, near Croydon. 'I miss you,' read a message from her father John. The family also left dozens of messages from her friends, who wrote to her about their boyfriends, or their new jobs, as if she were still alive.

'Like us, they hope – really, they do – that Meredith might somehow know what they have written,' John explained later in an article he wrote for the *Daily Mail*. 'None of us, you see, wants to forget her for even one second. So she is here, among us, everywhere.' At her home in Surrey, Meredith's bedroom was left just as it was when she'd left it, with make-up lying next to a pile of books on a table.

'Sometimes, even now, I find it hard to believe she is not still with us. Her passing is easier to bear if I pretend she has just gone away for a while; that some day soon she will ring me – her voice bubbling with laughter and enthusiasm – to tell me about her latest adventure,' John wrote.

22 November 2010

Two days before the start of Amanda and Raffaele's appeal trial, John watched a breakfast-time interview with her parents Edda and Curt on the ITV1 programme *Daybreak*. 'Once again, I felt the pain and the anger and the raw grief resurface,' he wrote in the same article.

Amanda had been convicted of killing his daughter, and yet she had been accorded the status of a minor celebrity. 'Sometimes it seems that there is no escape from her or her jaunty nickname, "Foxy Knoxy" (doubly hurtful, for the way it trivialises the awfulness of her offence),' John protested.

For the first time, he expressed anger at Amanda's parents: 'Curt Knox and his ex-wife Edda Mellas have never expressed their condolences to our family for our grievous loss. There has been no letter of sympathy; no word of regret. Instead, I have watched them repeatedly reiterate the mantra of their daughter's innocence.'

He acknowledged that, to many, Amanda seemed an unlikely killer. 'Yet to my family she is, unequivocally, culpable.'

John had no illusions about what awaited his family. The appeal would drag on for months which would make it ever harder for the Kerchers 'to grieve for Meredith in peace'. And if Amanda was found guilty on appeal, she might then take her case to Italy's Supreme Court.

'Put simply, our ordeal could go on for years.'

57

24 November 2010

The Amanda who walked into the Hall of Frescoes at the start of the appeal trial had little in common with the Amanda who had smiled, chatted and laughed with her lawyers and guards during her first days in the same courtroom almost two years earlier. Now twenty-four years old, she looked pale, and thinner. Heavy dark circles were etched under her sad eyes.

Returning to the same courtroom unnerved her. 'I'm scared. Why are you bringing me here? This is where I was convicted in December,' she protested as she was led in. She managed to smile faintly at Raffaele, greeting him in a low voice: '*Ciao*, how are you?' Raffaele, in contrast, was his usual smiling self, yet at the same time there was a lost expression on his face.

The prosecutor Comodi was struck by the change she saw in Amanda. 'It's as if the light inside her has gone out,' she thought. Comodi herself felt depressed as she waited for the new trial to begin. Amanda and Raffaele had already been convicted; the same lawyers, she knew, would wage their new battle chiefly by repeating old arguments; and they were all back in the same courtroom.

In coming months, Comodi and her colleague Mignini would take turns in sitting by the chief prosecutor in the appeal court, Giancarlo Costagliola. Costagliola had a long career behind him – in the late 1970s, he had sent police to a Milan hotel to block illegal negotiations on the transfers of soccer stars, and over the next ten years he had sent what amounted to a small army of Mafiosi to prison in his native Naples.

The two judges now presiding over the fate of Amanda and Raffaele had both been picked from the civil courts, and not the penal ones as several of the judges there had already been involved in the case.

For the past five years, the senior judge Claudio Pratillo Hellmann – a tall, imposing figure in his late sixties with silver hair and black bushy eyebrows – had dealt mainly with labour and welfare cases. But he was no stranger to penal offences as he had previously headed the law courts in the town of Spoleto. Although he too came from the civil section, the secondary judge Massimo Zanetti had more recent experience of penal cases, having dealt with several in recent years. He was to dismay prosecutors by stating, in his outline of the case to the court: 'The only certain and undisputed fact is the death of Meredith Kercher.' Six jurors – five of whom were women – would also decide whether Amanda and Raffaele's conviction should be upheld, or quashed.

Because Raffaele's lead lawyer, Bongiorno, was absent – she was heavily pregnant with a son due in January – Judge Pratillo Hellmann kept the first hearing short, ruling that photographers and TV crews would be allowed to record only Amanda and Raffaele entering and leaving the courtroom.

When the hearing was over, Amanda's lawyer Ghirga confided: 'Amanda is tense and worn out. She's worried and demoralised. Let's hope she regains her peace of mind.'

11 December 2010

Looking frailer than ever, Amanda stood up in court and took off her heavy black coat. Dressed in jeans and a grey sweater, her head bowed, she began to read in Italian from her handwritten notes.

She began with a lengthy apology. She'd always found it difficult to express herself, even with her friends, she said. 'I am the
weakest in this courtroom as far as expressing myself goes,' she
said, her voice tense.

Taking a deep breath, she addressed Meredith's family – none
of whom were present – for the first time in more than three
years. 'To Meredith's family and her loved ones, I want to say
I'm very sorry she isn't here any more. I cannot know what you
feel but I have little sisters too, and the idea of their suffering and
of losing them for ever terrorizes me,' Amanda said, beginning
to sob.

'What you are suffering and what Meredith suffered is incomprehensible, unacceptable . . .' – Amanda paused for more than ten
seconds as she sniffed repeatedly, the only sounds in the hushed
courtroom. 'I'm sorry that all this has happened to you, that you will
never have her next to you where she belongs. It isn't fair and it can
never be. But you are not alone when you remember her because I
am thinking of you too. I too remember Meredith,' she said.

Sitting some distance away behind Amanda to her left, the Kerchers'
lawyer Maresca found it unbearable listening to her words about
the family. He didn't like what she was saying, he didn't like the tone
in which she said it, and he didn't like the fact that she was addressing the Kerchers only after Meredith's father had pointed out that
Amanda's parents had never offered their condolences.

He got up and walked out of the courtroom.

Amanda didn't notice Maresca leave, and went on to apologise to
Patrick, the owner of the bar where she used to work, whom she'd
initially accused of killing Meredith – this was another first, as she
had never apologised to him before.

Describing how afraid she'd felt after Meredith's death, she
praised Raffaele, whose eyes were fixed on her, as 'a source of
reassurance, comfort and love'. Three years on, the truth about
her and Raffaele had still not been recognised. 'I am innocent.

Raffaele is innocent.' Amanda's voice was now steady, and she articulated each syllable. 'We did not kill Meredith.'

Amanda appealed directly to the judges and jurors: 'I ask you to recognise that an enormous mistake was made, and that no justice is rendered to Meredith or her loved ones by taking our lives away from us.' She said how the prosecution had depicted her as 'a dangerous, diabolical, jealous, uncaring and violent girl . . . but I have never been that girl. Never.'

'How could I be capable of using such violence as Meredith suffered? How could I hurt a friend of mine' – Amanda's voice rose – 'with such violence as if this was more important and more natural than all I have been taught, my values, my dreams and my whole life?

'All this is not possible. I am not that girl.'

Amanda's eyes were still wet as she sat down after speaking for a quarter of an hour – the longest and most emotional statement she had made in any of the court hearings.

But for at least one investigator watching her in court, Amanda's protestations were insincere. 'Amanda is very wily, and she's certainly not the first convict who claims she's innocent – the great majority of convicts in any prison will tell you they're innocent. My guess is that Amanda has convinced herself that she is,' he said.

'It's possible that she is feeling awful about Meredith's death, and that's why she's almost apologised to the Kerchers, for the first time. What strikes me is her extraordinary self-centredness; what she said was all "me, me, me",' he added.

For their part, the judges and jurors had sat attentively through Amanda's statement, their eyes fixed on her. Their faces betrayed no emotion.

16 December 2010

Three weeks after the start of Amanda and Raffaele's appeal trial in Perugia, the Supreme Court in Rome – Italy's highest court

– sealed Rudy's fate. Five judges upheld his sixteen-year prison sentence.

The judges refused to be drawn on whether Amanda and Raffaele were also guilty of Meredith's murder; their responsibility, they wrote, was to judge Rudy only. However, they made no secret of their belief that Rudy had not been alone in murdering Meredith, describing as 'convincing' the findings of the lower courts that she had been killed by 'several people'.

Meredith had died for 'futile motives' – a desire to have sex with her, which she had resisted. The judges denounced 'the brutal and dictatorial violence of a multiple, collective conduct which reveals in its sad protagonists the orgiastic will to give vent to the most criminal impulses.' This, the judges added, 'caused a deep sense of dismay, revulsion and contempt in every individual of average morality.'

The judges highlighted the DNA and handprint evidence found against Rudy, dismissed his claim of a flirtation with Meredith, and quoted a remark Rudy had made on 19 November 2007, nearly three weeks after the murder. Messaging his friend Giacomo Benedetti on the Skype network, Rudy had typed: '*I got scared they'd put the blame only on me.*'

The ruling was the first definitive condemnation in the Kercher case as, in Italy, the presumption of innocence held until all appeals – the last, to the Supreme Court – had been exhausted.

In Perugia, a senior investigator hailed the verdict as 'a milestone' for Amanda and Raffaele. 'It will put them in a tighter spot,' he said.

18 December 2010

Amanda sat as if praying with her eyes closed, her elbows on the desk and her hands clasped in front of her face as Judge Pratillo Hellmann read out the appeal court's decision on requests which had been made by the defence teams for a new review of DNA evidence and for new witnesses to be called.

The court, the judge announced, had decided to grant demands for a fresh review of DNA traces on Raffaele's kitchen knife and on Meredith's bra clasp. The forensic police had found traces of Amanda's DNA on the knife handle, and traces of Meredith's on the blade. On Meredith's bra clasp they had found traces of Raffaele's DNA as well as Meredith's own.

The judge explained that the court had approved the requests in line with the principle that an accused person could only be convicted if their guilt was 'beyond any reasonable doubt' and because the assessment of highly technical DNA analysis was 'objectively difficult'. He appointed two experts to analyse the DNA traces found by the forensic police. If that was not possible due to the destruction of samples during testing, they would establish the reliability of the police findings and investigate 'possible contamination'.

The court also granted a request to summon Antonio Curatolo, the tramp who had testified that he saw Amanda and Raffaele near the cottage on the night of the murder, as well as several new witnesses whom the defence hoped would refute his testimony.

Amanda burst into fresh tears at the news – but this time, she was smiling through her tears. A couple of rows behind her, her mother Edda clapped silently and started sobbing too; she had felt sick during the wait for the court's decision, but her nausea vanished immediately, she said later. Tears also came to Raffaele's eyes; he turned to smile at his family. Before Amanda was led out of court, Edda went up to her. Edda told her she loved her, and urged her to hang on. Amanda just beamed at her.

For Amanda and Raffaele, it was the first courtroom victory in months. Amanda's lawyer Ghirga called it 'a victory in the search for truth'. Raffaele's lawyer Bongiorno proclaimed it 'a turning point'. His other lawyer Maori went even further. 'At last, after three years, the trial is just beginning,' he said.

Although the prosecutors publicly welcomed the new review as a chance to demonstrate yet again the validity of the DNA tests, in private they were less confident. The last thing the court needed, one investigator said, was a repeat of the case of Luigi Chiatti, the so-called 'Monster of Foligno' – whom Raffaele had admired in a blog before Meredith's murder. Chiatti had first received two life sentences for killing two boys. But in the appeal trial, an expert new to the case had pronounced him unsound of mind, with the result that his sentence was reduced to thirty years.

'What if the experts don't agree among themselves?' the investigator worried. 'That would just confuse the court. And what if you get an arrogant expert who claims to know everything and slams the tests by the forensic police? The court is supposed to reach a verdict independently, based on all the evidence, but there's a danger an expert could influence it too much.'

For one lawyer convinced of Amanda and Raffaele's guilt, the new review was ominous. 'Allowing a review is pointless, and it's without doubt a very dangerous thing to have done,' he said.

After the hearing, when Amanda was led back into the women's wing of the Capanne prison, several fellow inmates clapped and cheered.

58

Almost precisely two years after the tramp Antonio Curatolo had been wheeled into the Hall of Frescoes to testify that he had seen Amanda and Raffaele in Piazza Grimana on the evening of the murder, the prosecution called him again as a witness. This time the white-haired Curatolo slowly hobbled in using a crutch. A prison guard – acting more as a helper than a guard – escorted him to the raised platform in front of the judge and jury and held a chair steady as he lowered himself into it.

Curatolo wore a navy-blue tracksuit and sneakers – a prisoner's uniform. His life as a tramp had ended abruptly a month earlier, when he began his one-and-a-half-year jail sentence for drugs charges.

Mignini immediately asked him when he had seen Amanda and Raffaele.

'I think it was on Halloween, because there were lots of kids around,' Curatolo replied.

Mignini caught his breath; his colleague Comodi was so shocked that she jumped up and walked out to have a cigarette. Amanda and Raffaele stared intently at Curatolo. The court which convicted them had established that Curatolo saw the couple on the evening of the murder – 1 November – but now he was stating it was the previous evening instead.

Mignini pressed on. 'What happened the following day?' he asked.

'In the afternoon, at about one or two p.m., the *carabinieri* came to ask questions . . . At a certain point I saw the "extra-terrestrials" – that's how I call the men dressed in white overalls – with their equipment, they were outside and inside the cottage,' Curatolo replied.

His latest remark indicated that he had indeed seen the couple on the evening of the murder, as the forensic police – clad in white – had arrived at the cottage on the afternoon of 2 November.

'Do you know when Halloween is?' Mignini asked.

'On 1 or 2 November,' Curatolo replied – an error which made his testimony even more confused.

But he remembered it had not been raining on the evening he saw the couple – in fact, it had rained on Halloween, but not on the night of the murder.

Mignini made one last attempt to save Curatolo's testimony. 'You're sure that the day after you see these young people [Amanda and Raffaele], there were police and men in white overalls in the cottage?'

'Yes, as sure as I'm sitting here,' Curatolo replied.

Mignini said he'd finished – he had questioned a witness who had been labelled as key to the prosecution for only ten minutes.

Raffaele's lawyer Bongiorno seized on the opportunity Curatolo had given her. She asked him whether on the evening he said he saw Amanda and Raffaele he had also seen people in fancy dress.

'Yes, there were kids in fancy dress,' Curatolo said. He added that he'd also seen buses taking people to nightclubs on Perugia's outskirts.

At the previous hearing, the defence lawyers had tried to wreck Curatolo's credibility by summoning staff from several nightclubs located outside Perugia together with the operators of the shuttle bus services; the new witnesses testified that there were no buses to their nightclubs that night, but they couldn't rule out the possibility that other nightclubs had had some, or that other buses could have been hired for a private party. Municipal buses were known to have been in service that night.

Curatolo looked taken aback when the secondary judge Massimo Zanetti started his questioning by asking where the former tramp used to relieve himself.

'In the thickets, by the side of the road,' Curatolo said.

'So you'd move away [from the square]?' Judge Zanetti asked in a terse, stern tone.

'Yes, I'd move away. But I was always close to it.'

'Why did you choose to be a tramp?'

'Because I'm an anarchist by nature. Then I read the Bible and I became Christian-anarchist.'

'And so?' Judge Zanetti demanded curtly.

'And so I chose to lead the life of Christ . . .'

'Did you take drugs?'

'I have always used drugs.'

'Now?'

'No.'

'In 2007?'

'I took heroin. And heroin isn't a hallucinogen.'

After the hearing, Amanda's stepfather Chris Mellas exulted: 'It couldn't have gone better. Curatolo confirmed it was Halloween and there were the buses for the nightclubs,' he said. Asked about Amanda, he replied: 'Amanda's eating more, and she feels a bit better about how the trial is going.'

But a senior investigator insisted Curatolo had seen Amanda and Raffaele on the evening of the murder. 'The linchpin is that Amanda was working at the bar Le Chic on Halloween, so Curatolo couldn't have seen her on Piazza Grimana. He's confused about when Halloween is. He says it wasn't raining on the evening he saw Amanda and Raffaele, and that he saw the forensic police the day after. You know, you can be imprecise but still be reliable. The precise witness, who says he remembers everything to the second, is usually the least reliable.'

The questions Judge Zanetti had put to Curatolo, and his harsh tone of voice, had struck the investigator. 'Why was he asking Curatolo about relieving himself and about drugs? Does he want to show that Curatolo wasn't always at the square, and that he was high on heroin that night?'

'The appeal court should stick to discussing the earlier court's review of the evidence, but here people want to redo the whole trial. It's not looking good . . .'

17 June 2011

On a warm afternoon, Amanda's lawyer Ghirga sat sipping mineral water on a tall metal stool outside the hillside Caffè Turreno, watching locals and students strolling past. New witnesses would be heard in court the next day, but Ghirga, sporting sunglasses and a mauve Lacoste polo shirt, could afford to relax – he had had plenty of time to prepare.

Almost three months had passed since Curatolo's second appearance. The deadline for the DNA experts to submit their review had come and gone as they had demanded more time. The slowness of the trial was nothing extraordinary for Ghirga, who had spent most of his life in Italian courts; it irked him however that Amanda had to wait what he saw as an outrageously long time behind bars for a verdict.

'So, will the court acquit Amanda and Raffaele?' a journalist asked Ghirga.

Ghirga looked mildly surprised by the question. 'Everyone asks me that, but I don't know. How could I? What I do know is that the jurors who acquit them will have to be heroes to do so, simply because Amanda and Raffaele will have been in jail for almost four years. There'll be consequences, including demands for damages . . .' Ghirga left the sentence hanging.

'You feel the court is pro-Amanda?' the journalist insisted.

'I can't say!' Ghirga exclaimed. 'The facts are that the court agreed to a new DNA review – no lawyer could have asked for more than that. Plus, we're showing the court that the prosecution's evidence, taken one element at a time, doesn't stand up.'

'And how's Amanda? What is she expecting?'

'Amanda is more hopeful than she was, but she says: "It's not going to be like the first trial is it, everybody nice and friendly and then they screw us?" She's more angry than she used to be,' Ghirga replied.

But he gave the impression of being more optimistic than he wanted to let on.

The prosecutor Comodi, in contrast, was increasingly unhappy with the way the trial was going. She felt the defence – and only the defence – had been playing a series of cards one after another, with the prosecution scrambling to catch up. For her, the prosecution wasn't getting through to the court as it had in the first trial. She worried the court might acquit Amanda and Raffaele – all it would take was for the defence to plant enough doubt in the minds of the judges and jurors about some of the evidence.

She herself had no such doubts, and sometimes felt so frustrated she wanted to give up on it all.

59

'What a charming cast of characters!' a prosecutor joked as he went through the list of five convicts that Amanda and Raffaele's lawyers had summoned as witnesses for the day. They included a child-murderer and a mafia collaborator, and all of them claimed they had evidence showing the pair were innocent of Meredith's murder.

Amanda needed the support of these fellow convicts, but the elegant way she dressed for the day appeared to signal that she had nothing in common with such underworld company – a long flowered skirt, smart black flats, a sleeveless navy-blue top and pearl-drop earrings.

Gone was the prisoner's 'uniform' of jeans, sweatshirts and sneakers she had worn so often at the previous trial. Gone also was the Amanda who used to gesticulate, grin broadly and even laugh as she chatted and joked with guards in court during the first trial; now she only talked briefly with one guard, gave him just a couple of tight smiles and kept her hands still.

The first witness on the stand was one of Italy's most notorious killers – Mario Alessi, a Sicilian bricklayer who five years earlier had kidnapped eighteen-month-old Tommaso Onofri for ransom, only to murder him by hitting him in the temple with a shovel because he was crying. Alessi was serving a life sentence, and had also been convicted of sexual assault in a separate case.

A tall fifty-year-old who clenched his powerful hands as he walked in to court, Alessi looked unwell and had to be led out again moments after having his handcuffs removed, complaining of feeling faint. A clerk called an ambulance, but he was soon pronounced fit to testify and brought back to court; he had suffered a sudden drop in blood pressure.

Bongiorno, Raffaele's lawyer, led Alessi through what he had told her when she visited him in the Viterbo prison after he had written to her. Alessi had befriended Rudy in prison, and if the Sicilian was to be believed, Rudy had changed his story yet again.

Alessi spoke in a steady, unemotional tone, but he often chewed his upper lip in a nervous twitch. He testified that in November 2009 – nine days before Rudy's appeal trial was due – Rudy had taken him by the arm in the prison courtyard and said: 'We've got to get away from the others because we've got important things to talk about.'

Out of earshot of other prisoners, Rudy told Alessi: 'As you know, my trial's coming up in a few days. I'm very worried.'

'Cheer up, you've got to face it,' Alessi told his friend.

'That's not the point; the point is whether to tell the truth or not,' Rudy said.

'Isn't the truth what we've all heard?' asked Alessi, who'd been following the case on the TV news.

'No, the truth is completely different, and only two of us know it,' Rudy said.

Alessi also told how, over the next two hours in the prison courtyard and as they talked to each other from their cells, a tearful Rudy explained how he had first seen Meredith while out drinking with a friend identified only as 'The Drunkard' in a nightclub. Later, with another friend identified only as 'Fatty', Rudy had followed Meredith to find out where she lived.

A few days later, Rudy and 'The Drunkard' went to Meredith's house. A surprised Meredith let them in, and the three of them sat down. 'I asked Meredith if she'd like to have a threesome,' Rudy recalled. Meredith got up and told the two men to leave. Rudy went to the bathroom, and spent some fifteen to twenty minutes there.

As he told his story in court, Alessi said in a cold, detached tone of voice: 'Rudy came out and found a different scene.'

Alessi paused to take a long drink of water, then went on in the same unfeeling tone as before: 'Meredith was on her back on the floor, Rudy's friend was holding her down. Rudy got astride Meredith and masturbated himself, then he and his friend switched positions. Rudy held her with one leg pushing down on her back while his friend forced her to have anal intercourse. Then suddenly this knife appeared, almost out of nowhere, the friend pointed it close to the neck of the girl, and the girl injured herself as she gesticulated.'

Rudy then looked for something to pack Meredith's wound, but his friend snapped at him: 'Now what are you doing? We've got to finish off this slut, otherwise we'll rot in jail.' With the knife – 'a small knife, with an ivory handle' – the friend continued to attack Meredith, and killed her.

Later that evening, Rudy met 'The Drunkard' in a nightclub. The friend gave Rudy some money and told him: 'Get out of Italy!'

Alessi ended his account by saying that he had quarrelled with Rudy afterwards, because Rudy had failed to keep a promise to tell the truth at his appeal trial. 'I couldn't tell the truth,' Rudy had told him afterwards, 'because if I had, the sentence wouldn't have been thirty years, it would have been more.'

Alessi claimed he had challenged Rudy: 'You've got a nerve, how can you say these things when you told me these two kids are innocent?' The two had come to blows and had to be separated by a cellmate. From then on, they stopped talking to each other.

Bongiorno had one last question for Alessi: 'So Rudy's role was to help Meredith?'

'Yes,' Alessi replied.

This was apparently too much for Judge Pratillo Hellmann, who pointed out: 'Well, the judicial truth is different ...' – a reference to Rudy's murder conviction, which the Supreme Court had upheld.

Maresca, the Kerchers' lawyer and father of an eleven-year-old girl, held up an A4-size copy of a photograph of Alessi's victim, the toddler Tommaso. It showed Tommaso's chubby face; the boy had curly hair and big wondering eyes.

Maresca held the photograph steady for a moment; Alessi only glanced at it, but the judges and jurors stared – as did Amanda and Raffaele.

Maresca made no effort to keep the contempt out of his voice. 'You recognise this child?' he asked.

'No,' Alessi said.

'That's fine, *we* recognise him,' Maresca shot back.

Pressed by Maresca, who was given a helping hand by Judge Pratillo Hellmann, Alessi said that he had broken off his friendship with Rudy because he thought the latter was 'a despicable person' who had left two innocent people – Amanda and Raffaele – in prison. Alessi had fallen headlong into a trap. Maresca promptly flicked through the rulings which had led to Alessi's life sentence, which accused him of lying again and again, and of trying to frame an innocent person.

'We believe this *Signore* [gentleman]' – Maresca spat the word out, he didn't even deign to name Alessi – 'is lying, and the "despicable person" is someone else.'

After Tommaso had been seized from his home, Alessi had pretended he knew nothing about his fate, telling a TV interviewer: 'All children are angels who come down from the sky. Children must be left in peace. They need to be with their parents who brought them into the world.' And, appealing to the camera: 'Let him go now; free Tommaso.'

When Alessi gave that interview, he had already killed the boy.

That day, the court was given a variety of gangland witnesses to believe in – or not. Marco Castelluccio, a short and burly robber and police informer, hid behind a light blue screen and was flanked by two bodyguards, one with a gun in its holster slung across his chest. He testified that he had once heard Rudy say that Amanda and Raffaele were innocent.

But Luciano Aviello, a member of the Naples mafia who had turned state's witness, claimed that not only Amanda and Raffaele, but also Rudy, were innocent of Meredith's murder. Aviello, a boyish forty-two-year-old, said the killers were in fact his brother Antonio – who had long disappeared – and an Albanian named only as Florio who had been commissioned to steal a valuable painting but had burgled the wrong house. The pair had been spotted by 'a woman in a dressing gown' whom they stabbed to death.

Maresca pointed out that Aviello had been convicted of slander no fewer than nine times, and his credibility was later decimated by police officers and fellow prisoners; his account, they said, was a tissue of lies.

After the hearing, an exasperated Comodi burst out: 'Ok, so now we've heard the jailbirds. Can we get back to the case now?' She was convinced that the experts' DNA review, due by the end of the month, would decide the outcome of the trial.

But before then, and at the prosecution's request, the court was to summon Rudy to hear what he had to say about the story he had supposedly told the child-killer Alessi. It would be only the second time since Meredith's death that Rudy would come face-to-face with Amanda and Raffaele. The first time – more than two years earlier at Amanda and Raffaele's first trial – Rudy had refused to answer any questions whatsoever.

The prospect of Rudy testifying in front of Amanda and Raffaele prompted many observers to wonder – yet again – whether he would now say more about how Meredith died. Surely Rudy knew more, much more than he had revealed so far about the part Amanda and Raffaele had played in the murder, they speculated. The prospect was so tantalising that the *Corriere dell'Umbria* newspaper promised its readers 'the mother of all hearings'.

27 June 2011

'The mother of all hearings' began with Rudy walking into court wearing a white T-shirt with 'ARMANI' in big capital letters across the chest. He had a slight slouch, as if to show the day's proceedings didn't matter all that much to him; he didn't look at either Amanda or Raffaele as he waited for the guards to unlock his handcuffs.

Behind the judge and jurors, the sun's strong rays struck the bars outside the windows, their shadows projecting a stark grid-like pattern on the glass panes. The Hall of Frescoes felt more like a dungeon than ever.

Amanda wasted no time in trying to tell the court just what she thought of anything Rudy might have to say. Guards were still fiddling with Rudy's handcuffs when her lawyer Dalla Vedova asked for permission for her to address the court. But Judge Pratillo Hellmann was in no hurry to hear her. Given that Rudy was waiting to testify, hearing Amanda now was 'inopportune', the judge said curtly.

The lead prosecutor, Costagliola, asked only a handful of questions of Rudy – just enough to have him deny ever telling his fellow prisoner Alessi anything at all about Meredith's death. The two had only 'chit-chatted', Rudy said.

When Mignini's turn came, he played a card he had been keeping close to his chest. He held up a copy of a letter which Rudy had sent his lawyers in May of the previous year after Alessi's account first emerged; it had been leaked by a private TV network. A clerk carried the copy over to Rudy, who curtly confirmed he had written it.

Mignini went on to read the letter out. A virulent rant against Alessi, the letter denounced 'blasphemous insinuations' and slammed the child-killer as 'a foul being with a stinking conscience', 'an ogre who had no pity on a little boy'. Mignini read the letter through to the end; what mattered was the final sentence in which Rudy wrote of 'the horrible murder of a splendid and wonderful girl by Raffaele Sollecito and Amanda Knox.'

Amanda and Raffaele just sat and stared as Mignini took his time in sitting down again. For the first time in court, Rudy had unreservedly accused the two of killing Meredith.

Dalla Vedova tried to make Rudy tell the court exactly what part Amanda and Raffaele, according to him, had played in the murder. But Rudy refused to say more.

'You confirm this part [of the letter] about Amanda and Raffaele?' Dalla Vedova insisted.

'I decided to write it after hearing absurd things and feeling like a puppet being manipulated by other people. It's not up to me to decide who killed Meredith. I've always said who was in the house that damned night,' Rudy said.

As he sat listening, Mignini turned to beam broadly at the Kerchers' lawyers behind him – the defence questions were back-firing on Amanda and Raffaele.

'Rudy involving Amanda and Raffaele is news. Why did he never say this before?' Dalla Vedova persisted.

Visibly irritated, and with a slight sweat shining on his fore-head, Rudy shot back: 'It's not as if there is my truth, and the truth of Tom, Dick and Harry. What there is is the truth of what I lived through that night, full stop.'

Moments after Rudy was led out, Amanda tried to demolish what the court had just heard. 'I just wanted to say simply that the only time Rudy, Raffaele and me have been together in the same place is in court. I'm shocked and anguished' – her voice broke and tears came to her eyes – 'by his testimony. He knows we weren't there then,' Amanda said.

The Kerchers' lawyer Maresca was jubilant after the hearing. 'The defence did us a huge favour. They should never have kept going at Rudy about his statement that Amanda and Raffaele are the killers,' he said.

If Amanda's mother Edda was feeling in any way discouraged, she didn't show it. She played down Rudy's attack, saying he'd been vague. 'It's unfortunate that Rudy didn't take the chance to redeem himself . . . Amanda just wanted to say to him: "You know the truth, you know I wasn't there, speak up, tell the truth." ' Edda said.

How did she feel the appeal trial was going?

'I think the appeal is going great, very well. I think that when the DNA [review] comes out, it will be even better,' she replied firmly.

60

For once, the TV crews allowed into the Hall of Frescoes for the start of each hearing focused not on Amanda but on two academics busying themselves with a laptop and piles of files as they sat side by side at a desk in front of the judges and jurors.

Carla Vecchiotti and Stefano Conti – specialists in forensic medicine from the University La Sapienza in Rome – had finally completed their independent review of the DNA evidence on the kitchen knife and on Meredith's bra clasp. Today, they would brief the court on their findings.

Their review was a blow for the prosecution. They accused the forensic police of violating international guidelines on the collection of evidence at the crime scene. The attribution of the DNA trace on the knife blade to Meredith was 'unreliable' because Patrizia Stefanoni, the lead biologist, had failed to follow international standards on testing such a small sample which could have been the result of contamination, they said. But they confirmed that Amanda's DNA was on the handle.

The experts also confirmed that one of the traces on the bra clasp was indeed Raffaele's, but again cautioned that it too could be the result of contamination – especially since the clasp was retrieved from the floor of Meredith's bedroom forty-six days after the murder.

When Amanda, who had had her twenty-fourth birthday the previous month, first heard news of the review she was watching

TV in prison. She laughed and cried with joy; fellow prisoners came up to her and hugged her. 'For the first time, someone believes me,' she told her lawyer, Ghirga.

For the first time in months she looked almost buoyant as she sat in court waiting for the experts to testify, smiling frequently as she chatted with her lawyers.

With the courtroom plunged in semi-darkness as images of the knife and the bra clasp were projected on a large screen, the moustachioed Conti, a rotund, balding figure, quoted guidelines on crime scene management from a host of police and forensic manuals – chiefly from American states such as New Jersey, North Carolina and Wisconsin.

Screening extracts from videos made by Stefanoni's forensic team while it was gathering samples at the cottage, Conti then listed more than fifty alleged failings – several of which drew gasps from the public gallery. The team failed to put on new gloves after bagging each sample; it used plastic bags for samples instead of paper bags which prevent condensation; the officer who picked up Meredith's bra clasp passed it to a colleague before placing it back on the floor, and then bagging it; there was a smudge on the fingertip of one of the gloves which touched the clasp, so the glove was dirty; an officer wore no gloves when he picked up Meredith's bra; an officer shook Meredith's knickers over the floor before bagging them . . .

Dressed in a light summer dress and sitting with the prosecutors a few feet away, Stefanoni scribbled furiously, or did quick searches on her laptop, as Conti worked his way down his list.

The prosecutor Comodi sprung to Stefanoni's defence, interrupting Conti repeatedly and suggesting that he was going beyond his brief.

But Comodi was herself interrupted by a roar of 'Silence!' from the usually unflappable Judge Pratillo Hellmann, which made many in court jump in their seats. Comodi apologised and promised to let the expert finish without any more interruptions.

Conti's list went on and on. One person dressed in jeans and a sweater entered Meredith's room and touched the body; another touched the edges of one of her throat wounds; Stefanoni's gloves were smudged with blood and split over her left index when she picked up a sample; the officer filming the police video walked in and out of Meredith's room without changing his shoe covers; an officer was recorded saying: 'It's absurd, I've complained about how incredibly disorganised this is'; at Raffaele's flat, officers took empty shopping bags from his kitchen to bag the objects they seized . . .

Conti's colleague Vecchiotti, a stern-looking figure with straight black hair speaking in a clear, clipped tone, followed up with another broadside, this time on Stefanoni's laboratory work. Stefanoni, she alleged, had failed to specify the size of the DNA sample she found on the blade of the kitchen knife; that sample was too small – technically, it had a 'low copy number' – and the risk of contamination was too high for it to produce a convincing result. This meant Stefanoni had been wrong to attribute it to Meredith.

'Contamination is always possible,' Vecchiotti kept repeating.

She criticised only mildly Stefanoni's analysis of the DNA traces on Meredith's bra clasp, agreeing that Raffaele's Y chromosome was on the clasp; there were also traces of Meredith and several, unidentified males.

But again, Vecchiotti cautioned: 'This piece of evidence [the bra clasp] was recovered forty-six days after it was first found in a context which strongly suggests contamination.'

After the hearing, Amanda's mother smiled broadly with relief. 'I'm not celebrating until she walks out, but it's definitely looking better. A lot of this stuff was brought up in the first trial but it wasn't accepted then. Now it's got more importance because it comes from court-appointed experts,' Edda said.

But Maresca, the Kerchers' lawyer, turned against the two experts, saying their attacks were 'inquisitorial'. He added: 'The Kercher family is very worried about what's happening. The forensic police did a serious job, but what's being alleged is that we've just been playing around until now.'

A tense Comodi rolled her eyes upwards when a journalist asked her whether the prosecution's case could collapse because of the experts' testimony. 'Are you joking? Are you joking? Don't make me get mad!' she exclaimed.

Comodi refused to predict the verdict. 'No one can get inside the heads of the judges and jurors. And frankly I don't want to,' she said.

Over a decaffeinated coffee in the late afternoon sunshine at a bar opposite the cathedral, Amanda's lawyer Ghirga looked exhausted, stunned and quietly delighted by that day's hearing. He usually slept well before a hearing, but that morning he had been up at 5.30 a.m., too nervous to sleep any more. The only thing that had surprised him today, he said, was the image of the smudge on the glove which touched the bra clasp.

'The rest was in the video of the forensic police, but why were we accused of lese-majesty [high treason] when our experts said the same things?' Ghirga asked rhetorically as he waved a couple of pigeons off the next table.

Did he think Amanda might be acquitted on the basis of the experts' review? 'I can't even begin to imagine that happening. I don't know what I would do, whether I'd laugh or cry,' he said. 'One thing's certain: if Amanda's acquitted, she won't hang around. She'll swim to America if she has to.'

30 July 2011

Five days after their first testimony, it was now the turn of the two experts, Vecchiotti and Conti, to be 'in the dock' as they braced themselves for questioning by Comodi. As the prosecutor entered the courtroom, looking strained at the start of what would no doubt be a marathon session, she joked: 'I've stuffed myself with camomile.'

Before the prosecutor began, the two experts were taken to task by Piero Angeloni, the head of the national forensic police.

In a letter read out by Judge Pratillo Hellmann, Angeloni accused the two experts of attacking 'the professionalism and dignity' of his staff. The latter, he wrote, worked on no fewer than 25,000 crime scenes a year, were highly trained, had the latest technology at their disposal, and were regularly monitored and approved by the European Network of Forensic Science Institutes (ENFSI). Never before, Angeloni concluded, had his staff come under criticism such as the two experts had levelled at them.

Clad in her black robe, and briskly fanning herself with a fan of white lace in the hot courtroom, Comodi got to her feet and started by asking the two experts about their qualifications – a clear attempt to undermine their credibility.

Sounding slightly piqued, Conti described himself as a forensic medicine specialist and listed a string of credentials from work for the civil aviation authority to mass disasters, medical computer science and microphotography. Vecchiotti fired off a longer list. She too was a forensic medicine specialist and taught forensic haematology at a school for police superintendents. She had worked on many high-profile Italian murder cases, and carried out more than seventy studies on forensic genetics.

Comodi tried to probe the two experts about their experience but the judge stopped her. 'Keep to the review,' he told her.

Comodi complied by challenging the experts' methods, making Vecchiotti acknowledge that she had not asked to visit the laboratory of the forensic police, nor had she asked what cleaning routine they followed in order to reduce the risk of contamination.

'How could you talk about the staff failing to clean their work surface if you didn't check their procedures?' Comodi asked.

'I based myself on the files of the case,' Vecchiotti replied.

'Does a surgeon write about putting on his green mask and his cap before an operation?' Comodi exclaimed, theatrically miming the gestures she described.

'I don't know the procedure in operating theatres,' Vecchiotti replied.

Judge Pratillo Hellmann intervened to ask about the DNA trace attributed to Meredith on the knife blade. 'I would like to be enlightened,' the judge said graciously. 'Is there a trace which can be attributed to Meredith?'

'It was never established how much DNA there was. We don't know anything, we don't know if Meredith's DNA was there . . . There's a complete profile but it isn't reliable,' Vecchiotti replied. The profile wasn't reliable because the test should have been repeated two or three times, she said.

To chuckles in court, Vecchiotti kept calling Comodi '*avvocato*' (lawyer). Comodi kept correcting her, and exclaimed after yet another '*avvocato*': 'Please concentrate. Does my face look like that of a lawyer or of a prosecutor?'

Sitting next to Comodi, the lead prosecutor Costagliola tugged at her robe, whispering to her to keep calm.

The more questions Comodi asked, the more sombre Amanda became. She sat quietly for much of the hearing, head bowed forwards, shoulders hunched.

Again and again, Comodi pressed Vecchiotti on her statement that both the trace attributed to Meredith on the knife and Raffaele's on the bra clasp could be the result of contamination.

Vecchiotti said she had no idea that Stefanoni had carried out so-called 'negative tests' intended to exclude the possibility of contamination. The tests had been filed with an earlier judge, and Judge Pratillo Hellmann later admitted them as evidence at the trial.

Nor did Vecchiotti know that Stefanoni had analysed the traces on the knife in her laboratory six days after last handling Meredith's DNA.

'Are six days enough to guarantee that a test tube doesn't come into contact with another test tube?' Comodi asked.

'They're sufficient if that's the way things went,' Vecchiotti replied stubbornly.

'You can't cast doubt on everything the forensic police writes!' Comodi fired back.

In a similar exchange, Comodi got Vecchiotti to agree that laboratory contamination of Meredith's bra clasp had also been avoided, as Stefanoni tested Raffaele's sample twelve days after last handling his DNA.

Turning to the other expert, Conti, Comodi then tried to show contamination away from the laboratory was also extremely unlikely, if not impossible. She questioned Conti about the search of Raffaele's flat, and he quoted the veteran police officer Armando Finzi's testimony that he had used just one pair of gloves during the entire time.

Comodi pointed out that the police had seized only a couple of newspapers in the flat before Finzi took the knife from a kitchen drawer, and that Meredith had never been in the flat.

'There was no DNA of Meredith's on the newspapers. Is it reasonable to say there was no DNA of Meredith's on the handle of the kitchen drawer?' Comodi asked.

Conti conceded it was.

'You agree Amanda's DNA was on the knife handle?'

'Certainly,' Conti replied.

Comodi drove her point home. 'So only the blade was contaminated by Finzi, not the handle?'

Comodi also challenged Conti on his assertion that dirty gloves were used to handle Meredith's bra clasp.

'Is it possible those gloves were dirty with Raffaele's DNA?' Comodi asked.

'Everything's possible,' Conti replied.

An exasperated Comodi burst out: 'And that Martians . . .'

Raffaele's lawyer Bongiorno jumped up to object, but the prosecutor turned to the judge and protested: 'An expert's answer can't be that everything is possible.'

Judge Pratillo Hellmann chided Comodi with a joke: 'Let's keep to the review, otherwise these two [experts] will end up accused of something themselves!'

★   ★   ★

Comodi moved on, and challenged Conti over his numerous criticisms of the handling of the crime scene at the cottage.

The person dressed in jeans and sweater who touched Meredith's body and one of her wounds was the forensic pathologist, she informed him. The officer who was recorded complaining about the lack of organisation was not in Meredith's flat but in the downstairs flat below, which had a separate entrance.

'We agree that the semi-basement flat is not the crime scene?' Comodi asked.

'I can ask you a rhetorical question: if it isn't, what reason did the police have for going there?' Conti retorted – a comment which drew him cries of derision from police detectives attending the hearing.

During a break from the hearing Stefanoni, who was the experts' main target, voiced her frustration at their allegations. 'If there was contamination, how come our forensic team's DNA was found only on some bloody handkerchiefs outside the cottage, when we took a total of 460 samples in all, including at the cottage and at Raffaele's flat? I didn't leave my DNA anywhere!' she exclaimed indignantly.

'At the cottage we took 136 samples, and only two of them had Raffaele's DNA on them – one was on the bra clasp in Meredith's bedroom, and the other was on a cigarette end in the kitchen which also had Amanda's on it. So how could contamination have happened?' Stefanoni protested.

Towards the end of her questioning, Comodi asked Vecchiotti about the alleged contamination of the bra clasp: 'Is it possible for [Raffaele's] DNA to end up only on the clasp?'

'Possible,' Vecchiotti said.

Comodi insisted: 'Probable?'

'Probable,' Vecchiotti retorted.

At 4.30 p.m., after five and a half hours, Comodi fired her last shot at Vecchiotti.

'Has it ever happened that you were appointed by a judge, and the judge failed to follow your findings? I can give you the ruling of the Cosenza court . . .' Comodi said.

Her words were drowned out by furious defence lawyers; the judge ruled her out of order. Comodi had no more questions.

Shortly afterwards, Amanda was frowning as she was led out of the courtroom.

61

After a long summer break, the prosecutors launched a new tactic as the appeal trial reached the last stretch during which all sides would make their closing arguments. They were convinced that the court had focused too much on only a few issues – the DNA review especially – and now they wanted to give as thorough an account as possible of their whole case.

Mignini began his summing-up at the beginning – the afternoon that he had first walked into the cottage and seen Meredith's body: 'I still remember the staring eyes of this girl, they will never leave me.' Mignini ranged widely – covering the break-in which he argued had been staged, the comments Meredith's friends Sophie and Robyn had made about tensions between Meredith and Amanda, Amanda's own behaviour at the police station, and the wounds Meredith suffered.

Amanda sat with her elbows resting on the desk, her hands clasped in front of her mouth as she stared ahead of her, keeping her gaze away from Mignini.

He accused defence lawyers of slandering the forensic police, comparing the tactic to that used by Joseph Goebbels: '*Slander, slander, something will always stick*. It's what the Nazis' propaganda minister used to say in the 1930s,' Mignini said.

He urged the court not to judge on appearances. 'They've been called "good-looking kids" but everyone has a dark side and it would be superficial to think that just because someone looks innocent they are not capable of killing,' he said.

He said that it was just when she felt she might be found guilty that Amanda had slandered the bar-owner Patrick. She had accused him not because the police had hit her in the neck, but because the police had told her that Raffaele was saying she wasn't in his flat with him on the evening of the murder. 'It wasn't the police who suggested Patrick's name, it was Amanda who suggested it,' Mignini said, turning to point at Patrick sitting a few feet behind him.

'The slander is inextricably tied to the murder.' Mignini raised his voice: 'There is no justification for it whatsoever! There is no justification for it whatsoever!' The police had simply wanted to find out the truth.

Reaching the end of his summing-up after more than four hours, Mignini stressed the Supreme Court ruling on Rudy that several killers had murdered Meredith. 'And in this courtroom, Rudy accused his accomplices,' Mignini said, gesturing towards Amanda and Raffaele. 'You can't make a black boy pay for everyone.'

Mignini ended on a personal note. He had been shocked to read in an Italian newspaper that an American TV network had paid for a flight ticket home for Amanda, and for an interview with her – a report flatly denied by her family. 'I have never seen anything like this in a 32-year career. It's an offence not only to the prosecutors and the police but to this very court,' Mignini said.

'And above all, it's the last outrage to the girl from Coulsdon who ceased to live that night.'

24 September 2011

The junior prosecutor Comodi started mildly, asking the jurors to tell the judge if they felt the need for a break that day. But within seconds she was decimating the DNA review with a barrage of accusations against the two experts. 'They betrayed your trust, with false facts. Their whole manner was aggressive when they should have been impartial,' Comodi charged.

The experts were 'absolutely inadequate'. She could have easily demonstrated this but the judge had stopped her questioning them about their experience. 'If they'd been asked how many technical searches they had done, the answer would have been zero – zero,' she said, holding up her right hand to make a '0' with her thumb and index finger.

The court's task was not to give a mark for the forensic police's work, it was to assess the validity of their findings. 'Because that's what you'd have to say, that the specialists, (the biologist) Stefanoni . . ., all of them have lied,' she said. She claimed that contamination of the bra clasp was out of the question. 'The only movements of objects were around the room itself, or when they were taken out of it,' Comodi said. Nor was contamination of what she insisted was indeed Meredith's DNA on the knife remotely possible.

As for the lack of traces in Meredith's room, it wasn't automatic that a killer would leave such traces. Stefanoni had been convinced that she would find DNA traces of a killer in the streaks of blood on the walls. 'But there were none, so it's not that easy for DNA to remain, unfortunately,' Comodi said.

She went on to ridicule the defence argument that the testing with the chemical Luminol, which had highlighted bare footprints in Amanda's bedroom, the bathroom and the corridor attributed to Amanda and Raffaele, had reacted not to blood but to other substances it could detect. 'It's unthinkable that Amanda and Raffaele could have soaked their feet in a bucket of bleach, or fruit juice, or rust because only this could have produced the strong glow (of the Luminol reaction),' Comodi said. 'If the floor had been covered in bleach, the foot would have removed that substance and left nothing on the floor.'

Under Italian law, the accused had the right to lie, she said. 'But if an accused person gives a false alibi, that has to be considered an element against him.' Raffaele said he had been at his computer for much of the night, but the only human interaction on it had been at 9.36 p.m. that night.

'Amanda and Raffaele killed for nothing. What is there that is more futile than killing for nothing?' Comodi asked.

The court had to believe Amanda and Raffaele were guilty 'beyond every reasonable doubt' to convict them. That did not mean, she said, that the court could acquit them simply because they believed in an alternative explanation for the murder. 'An alternative theory . . . cannot be based on the presumption that anything's possible – that DNA flies,' she said.

At the close of the day's hearing, the lead prosecutor Costagliola made the prosecution's final request. He demanded life sentences for Amanda and Raffaele – asking that Amanda be held in isolation for six months, and Raffaele for two months.

Amanda sat with her eyes closed, hands clasped in front of her mouth, immobile save for taking long breaths through slightly-parted lips.

Outside the law courts, Amanda's father Curt was asked how she had taken the demand for a life sentence. 'She was prepared for that ... She's holding up, she'll be strong, she'll be ready,' he said. 'I still have great hopes.'

26 September 2011

'A diabolical she-devil, an explosive concentrate of sex, drugs and alcohol' – in late 2009, Patrick Lumumba's lawyer Carlo Pacelli had made headlines with his portrait of Amanda. Today, almost two years on, Pacelli didn't disappoint journalists when he made his summing-up. 'Who is Amanda?' Pacelli asked. 'Fascinating, intelligent, cunning and astute. She always seems fragile, with her face like a naïve doll.'

But he claimed that Amanda was 'muddy outside, a she-devil

inside'. She had lied in accusing Patrick of the murder to ward suspicion off herself. She was 'a sorceress of deceit'.

Patrick himself had no doubt that Amanda was guilty of Meredith's murder. Seated in a bar opposite the cathedral during a lunchtime break, he described himself as living proof of her guilt. 'I went to prison unjustly. I was called an assassin. Who said that? Amanda. I'm the proof that she is involved in the murder,' the soft-spoken Patrick said, pressing his open hands to his chest.

Now studying Media and Advertising after having to close his bar, he said he didn't know whether Amanda had dealt the fatal blow. But he was convinced of her guilt because of her behaviour after her arrest. 'First, she was held like me in isolation and in that situation, you really want to get out. We knew that to get out, you have to talk to a judge. But when [she appeared before] the judge, Amanda didn't reply to questions, she preferred to stay silent,' Patrick said.

'Why didn't she say that she had nothing to do with it, that I had nothing to do with it?' he asked. 'Second, she told her mother in prison later that she was sorry, that she knew I was innocent. But she never told anyone else, she kept this secret. So I think that all this time she hoped that they would find me guilty.'

For Patrick, Amanda was 'the world's best actress'. He explained: 'Look at how she cried when she told the cops I was guilty, and I saw her cry twice before a judge but she never said I was innocent.' The apology which Amanda had made to him at the appeal trial ten months earlier was just 'crocodile tears'.

'I don't hate Amanda, I never hated her,' he said. 'I've forgiven her but that doesn't mean justice mustn't be done.'

That afternoon, the Kerchers' lawyer Maresca told the court that all Meredith's family wanted was a 'fair' sentence – he asked the court to confirm the earlier sentence of 26 and 25 years in prison for Amanda and Raffaele respectively.

A big photograph of a beaming Meredith flashed up on the

screen in court. 'That's the girl, that's the splendid girl,' Maresca said, as judges and jurors turned to look. He urged the court not to let itself be influenced by the virulence of what he called 'the Knox and Sollecito clans' and denounced the media campaigns lobbying for their release. The Kerchers, in contrast, had rarely spoken publicly over the past four years. 'They awaited rulings in silence,' he said.

Meredith 'had her throat cut like in mafia murders ... She met her attackers in her house, not outside. She wanted to rest, she met her death in her room, close to the bed, where you feel most safe,' Maresca said. 'It's obvious that that night, those three were in that house. Beyond the bra clasp and the knife the court's been talking about for nine months, there's much, much more.'

Now six photographs of Meredith's body flashed onto the screen. One showed her lying virtually naked from head to toe on the floor of her bedroom. Others were close-ups of her head and of the wounds to her throat. The eyes of one woman juror became moist as she struggled to look. Amanda, head bowed, never looked at the screen; Raffaele glanced at the photographs occasionally.

'I want to tell you we are not in a TV film. I show you these photographs to make you understand the suffering of this girl as she died . . . She had no wounds caused by defending herself, which means she was held down by several people. Remember that when people talk about a single attacker,' Maresca said.

The photographs vanished from the screen and Maresca paused at length as he shuffled his papers to allow his words – and the photographs – to sink in. Judges and jurors, riveted, all stared at him.

Maresca ended with one last picture of Meredith – this time, of her alive and laughing. He asked the court to confirm the guilty verdict of the earlier trial, and quoted Isaac Newton: '*Truth is ever to be found in simplicity, and not in the multiplicity and confusion of things.*'

62

'Well, today we're opening a new front!' Amanda's lawyer Ghirga exclaimed with a broad grin as he walked through the law court's arched doorway. After three days of demands for a guilty verdict, it was now the defence's turn to launch its last offensive.

Giulia Bongiorno, the first to speak and as sharp and forceful as ever, may have been Raffaele's star lawyer but she lost no time in stressing that she would be pleading for Amanda too. This was an 'Amanda-centred' trial, with Raffaele in the dock as a supposedly idiotic, colourless extra. 'I think it's the first case in history in which an individual is held to account as merely the boyfriend,' Bongiorno said.

As for Amanda, she had been depicted as a character in *Venus in Furs*, a 19th century erotic novel by the Austrian writer Leopold von Sacher-Masoch in which the hero aspires to be treated like a slave by his lover. Waving a copy of the book in the air, she said Amanda had been portrayed as a *femme fatale*, ordering Raffaele about. Jumping to modern times, Bongiorno said Amanda had also been portrayed like the cartoon character Jessica Rabbit from the film *Who Framed Roger Rabbit?*: 'A woman who devours men, but who at the same time is faithful and in love. As Jessica says: "I'm not bad. I'm just drawn that way".'

Amanda's accusation of Patrick, Bongiorno claimed, was no attempt to throw the police off the track because in making that statement she had placed herself at the crime scene. 'If she'd been a real cunning "Venus in Furs", she would never have done that,' she said. There was nothing perverse about Amanda – the game she most enjoyed playing with Raffaele was making faces at each other before going to sleep. The two had indeed embraced each other at the police station after the murder 'but this was tenderness, not sex obsession'.

As Amanda wrote in her diary, they also liked to rub noses together, which she called '*unca wunca*'. This, Bongiorno said, had nothing to do with 'bunga bunga', the erotic after-dinner parties allegedly enjoyed by the prime minister Silvio Berlusconi – the joke prompted smiles from jurors and laughter from lawyers and journalists.

Turning serious again, Bongiorno acidly reprimanded Mignini – for not giving Amanda a lawyer when she made her 'false confession', and for failing to question Raffaele at the first trial. She then took to task the detectives of the Homicide Squad who, she said, had insulted Raffaele's relatives in the notes they scribbled on intercepts of their phone conversations. They had called them 'vipers' and 'bitches'. Bongiorno raised her voice: 'You don't call a suspect's relatives "cretins". This is unacceptable!'

But her heaviest attack was on the way the crime scene itself had been handled. She screened a series of photographs to show how police had made a mess of Meredith's bedroom before her bra clasp was finally recovered forty-six days after her death. The sequence appeared to unsettle the prosecutor Comodi, who had a coughing fit and had to leave the courtroom briefly. Bongiorno ploughed on regardless. 'The bra clasp is an exhibit which you must declare un-u-sa-ble,' she emphasised.

The DNA trace attributed to Raffaele on the clasp had failed to yield the genetic profile of only individual. It was a mixed trace, and experts said that such traces should be disregarded. The biologist Stefanoni 'for the first and last time in her life, made a mistake.'

Bongiorno then sought to use Rudy's traces to support her

argument. His presence at the crime scene was 'a proof worth thousands of proofs' because it demonstrated how anyone present in Meredith's bedroom would have left traces there. 'Why does that room speak only of Rudy?' she asked.

Bongiorno ended with one last attack on the prosecution: 'I heard that Amanda and Raffaele killed for nothing. To me that's a fitting epilogue to a trial in which Raffaele is "Mr Nobody", who killed for nothing. This whole trial is based on a DNA trace which has been demonstrated to be a mistake.'

Bongiorno turned to Amanda and gave her a copy of *Venus in Furs*, the erotic novel she had mentioned. Amanda thanked her with a smile.

29 September 2011

Ghirga began with a fatherly gesture – he turned to Amanda, 'this young friend, whose age means she's just between my daughter and my son'. Someone, he said, his tone suddenly turning angry, whose image had been 'massacred' in the media. He had met her 400 times in prison, and he was convinced of her innocence.

Throughout his closing argument, Ghirga alternated comical quips with loud, theatrical outbursts in which he lashed out at investigators. Stefanoni, the biologist, and Finzi, the officer who seized the kitchen knife, were 'too skilled and too lucky'. Stefanoni should have gone no further after writing in her notes that the DNA sample on the blade was 'too low' – Ghirga held up his silver pen to inches in front of his face and pretended to write the words in the air.

Indignantly, Ghirga rubbished the tramp Curatolo, who the prosecution claimed had seen Amanda and Raffaele near the cottage on the night of the murder. 'He came in here like Al Capone in a wheelchair,' Ghirga joked, making Amanda laugh. 'Curatolo sees them at 8.30 p.m. the first time, then he says he sees them at 11.20 p.m., then he says between 9.30 p.m. and 11.30 p.m.,' he said – which had prompted the prosecution to delay the time of death. The grocer Quintavalle, who claimed to have seen Amanda in his supermarket early on the morning after the murder – contradicting her alibi that she was at Raffaele's flat at the time – should also be ignored.

Ghirga blamed the police for Amanda's accusation of Patrick as the murderer. 'They've got into my head,' he quoted Amanda as saying of the detectives. It had been a terrible week for the police, he said: they had obtained nothing from intercepts, it was 3 a.m. and then they saw the text message 'and out came Patrick'. But Ghirga claimed that Amanda had immediately afterwards said her accusation was false, that it wasn't true that she had stuck to it. Nor, he said, was it conceivable that Amanda and Raffaele – 'these two artists of crime' – had cleaned up to remove their traces, leaving only Rudy's as the prosecution claimed.

Just as he had done at the end of the earlier trial, Ghirga turned to point at Amanda's family sitting behind him. 'Please consider the Knox clan, two extended families which have been united. Don't see them as creators of a plot from across the Atlantic. They are parents who deserve absolute respect,' he said.

He then turned once more to Amanda. 'Amanda isn't terrified. Her heart is full of hope. She hopes to go back home. I wish her that and ...' – Ghirga paused – 'I feel I'm going to cry, that happened last time too,' he said. But checking his emotion he added: 'She has so much courage, Amanda.'

2 October 2011

On the eve of the verdict, a Sunday, Mignini was in a tense and reflective mood after attending Mass at the cathedral as, a short walk downhill, TV crews jostled for position in the square outside the law courts – more than 400 journalists, mainly from the Italian, American and British media had been accredited for the final ruling.

Mignini tried to read the court's mind; he couldn't help looking back again and again over the past four years. He had only one regret: 'If I could do it all again, the only thing I would do differently would be to let the pathologist examine the body earlier than I did, to get a more precise idea of the time of death. But the biologist Stefanoni told me not to "to avoid any risk of contamination" – those were her words,' Mignini confided over an *aperitivo* in exceptionally warm sunshine.

He was clearly bracing himself for an acquittal. He had spent hours watching the body-language of the judges and the jurors – observing when they took copious notes on what the prosecution or the defence was saying, when they unconsciously nodded in agreement, or smiled at jokes by the one or the other. He felt the DNA review had very probably persuaded the court – assuming it needed persuading in the first place – to cast doubt over his entire case.

Mignini had looked into the chances of America ever extraditing Amanda to Italy if she was acquitted, and then found guilty when the case went to the Supreme Court for a second appeal. Officials told him that yes, there was an extradition treaty between the two countries, but no, America would never send Amanda back.

Meredith's three closest friends from Perugia – Sophie, Amy and Robyn – spent a long weekend together at Sophie's home near London as they waited; they had taken time off work to make sure they could be together when the verdict was broadcast live on the Monday.

They had spent much of Saturday talking about the case, and that night Sophie had felt very scared when she went upstairs, alone, to close the windows. She hadn't felt that frightened for a couple of years and knew it was because they had talked about the details of the murder.

Sophie believed Amanda and Raffaele were guilty and was confident they would be convicted; she couldn't even imagine an acquittal. Robyn kept telling her to prepare herself for a possible acquittal, but Sophie just couldn't.

3 October 2011

Monday, the day of the verdict. In jeans and a mauve shirt, Raffaele fidgeted nervously with the microphone for long moments before addressing the court for the last time. Then, reading from prepared notes in a low, feeble voice: 'I have never, *ever*, hurt anyone.' The prosecution had defined him 'as a boyfriend of Amanda who killed for nothing . . . and it's asked for a life sentence for this "Mr Nobody".' In the meantime, he was spending every day in prison 'where the end of every day is already a death.'

The judges and jurors listened to him with rapt attention, several of the jurors leaning forward as they concentrated on his words. Raffaele insisted he did not know Rudy Guede. Looking at the court, he said: 'I know you better than I know Guede. I've seen you many times, Guede I just saw in court a few times, and *basta* (enough).'

On the evening of Meredith's death, he had been living 'a beautiful, I could say idyllic, moment.' He was about to graduate and had met Amanda a little earlier – 'a beautiful, sunny, lively and sweet girl with whom I was due to spend the weekend'. They had only one desire – 'to spend the evening with endearments and cuddles, nothing more.'

Raffaele paused. 'I don't have much to say . . . but I would like to leave you a little gift,' He fiddled with a bracelet on his left wrist. 'On this bracelet, it's written: *Free Amanda and Raffaele* ... I think that now it's time to take it off,' he said. The bracelet, he said, expressed his desire for justice, for freedom – 'and that there be for Amanda and me new hopes, a new future.'

Raffaele took off the bracelet, and held it out to the court. His lawyer Bongiorno told him to put it down on the desk in front of him, and he sat down.

Amanda, wearing a light green blouse and black trousers, struggled to begin as she took pauses repeatedly and tried to take deep breaths. 'It's been said many times that I'm someone different from what I am . . .' – she paused to breathe again – 'fear . . .'

'It's alright, you can sit down,' Judge Pratillo Hellmann interrupted, kindly.

'Anywhere, I'm a bit . . .' She stopped, and said to herself out loud: 'OK.' She remained standing. 'I am the same person I was four years ago. The only difference is what I have suffered in four years, I've lost a friend in the most brutal, unexplainable way possible,' she said in her fluent Italian.

Four years ago she had never suffered, she didn't know 'what tragedy was.' She went on, the court hanging on her every word: 'I didn't know how to tackle it . . . So how did I feel when it was discovered that Meredith had been killed?' she asked rhetorically.

'I couldn't believe it. How was it possible that someone I was spending my life with, whose room was next to mine, had been killed . . . and if I had been there that evening, I would have been dead, like her.'

Amanda kept raising and lowering her hands, clasping and unclasping them as she spoke. She had helped the police out of a sense of duty, for the sake of justice. 'I was betrayed. I wasn't just squeezed and stressed, I was manipulated,' she said. 'I didn't kill, I didn't rape, I didn't steal, I wasn't there.'

She spoke again of Meredith: 'I shared my life with Meredith, we had a friendship, she was always nice to me. Meredith was killed and I have always wanted justice for her. I'm not fleeing the truth, I *insist* on the truth, I *insist* after four desperate years on my innocence, on our innocence because it is *true*.'

'I want to go home. I want to go back to my life. I don't want to be punished and deprived of my life for something I didn't do, because I'm innocent ...' Amanda paused again, and struggled to breathe deeply. 'I have much respect for this court and so I thank you. I ask for justice,' she finished.

A good actress, Sophie thought, as she watched Amanda live on TV from her home with Amy and Robyn. Amanda had chosen all the right things to say and had rehearsed her lines well.

Sophie was struck by Amanda echoing the words she had said

in front of Meredith's friends at the police station almost four years earlier: 'It could have been me in her place.'

Judge Pratillo Hellmann cautioned the courtroom: 'This is not a soccer game so there is no space for rival groups of fans. Let's remember a beautiful girl died in a horrible way so when we read the verdict, please, let us have respect and silence.'

At 10.45 a.m., he led the court out of the Hall of Frescoes. They would be returning shortly once it had been cleared, to consider the verdict there. Guards led Amanda and Raffaele back to prison to await the verdict. It was their 1,450th day behind bars.

63

Shortly after the court withdrew, Meredith's mother Arline, her sister Stephanie and her brother Lyle flew into Perugia. They had got up at 3.30 a.m. that morning to catch their flight. Officers of the Homicide Squad met them at the airport and escorted them to a hotel opposite the prosecutors' offices, where they met their lawyers Maresca and Perna.

At lunchtime, Maresca and Perna left the Kerchers with David Broomfield, the British consul in Florence. The two lawyers then set off for the centre of Perugia to meet the prosecutors at the *Ristorante del Sole,* where they had dined together as they awaited the verdict at the end of the first trial. They hoped that returning to the same restaurant might bring them luck, but none of them were in high spirits.

At a packed news conference at their hotel that afternoon, the Kerchers refused to be drawn on what verdict they wanted. Asked whether they felt abandoned by the media's neglect of Meredith, Stephanie – her resemblance with her late sister struck many journalists – replied: 'It's nearly four years now . . . Mez has been almost forgotten in all this, there isn't much about what happened in the beginning. It's really hard . . . We're here to remember Meredith, and the city she loves.'

Could they forgive Meredith's killers? 'Forgiveness doesn't come into it without a final ending,' Stephanie said. 'You have to remember the brutality of what happened that night, what Meredith went through that night, the fear and the terror and not knowing why.'

At 8.45 p.m., Amanda's family and friends filed into the court-room, Amanda's mother Edda holding her daughter Deanna by the hand.

Half an hour later, Arline walked in slowly, a woman officer of the Homicide Squad guiding her with an arm around her shoulders. Arline, Stephanie and Lyle sat down in the back row and waited. As soon as Mignini saw them he went up to kiss Arline and Stephanie on the cheeks, and to shake hands with Lyle.

At 9.35 p.m., Amanda and Raffaele were led in. Amanda kept her black coat on over her shoulders although the courtroom was warm – partly because of the lights set up by a handful of TV crews which the judge had agreed could film his reading of the verdict. Amanda talked to her lawyers, every so often taking slow, deep breaths. Her face showed intense strain. She glanced at the door through which the judges and jurors would come, then looked away.

At 9.46 p.m., the bell rang, the clerk called out 'The Court!' and everyone stood. After eleven hours of deliberations, the judges and jurors walked to their places. Judge Pratillo Hellmann adjusted the collar of his robe, put on his glasses and began to read.

'In the name of the Italian people,' the court found Amanda guilty of slandering Patrick and sentenced her to three years and eleven days in prison – a sentence which it said had already been served as Amanda had spent almost four years in jail.

Amanda stood almost motionless, the only sign of movement the deep breaths she was concentrating on taking.

The court, the judge went on, acquitted both Amanda and Raffaele of all the remaining charges, including murder, sexual assault and staging a break-in – it ruled that there had been no such staging.

Amanda became convulsed by sobs, but managed to hug each of her lawyers tightly. From behind her came a couple of whoops, muffled cries and a brief burst of applause. Edda and Deanna stood next to each other, in tears and looking bewildered, before Deanna managed to get past a couple of prison guards to hug her sister.

A few feet away, Raffaele remained impassive save for a timid smile. His lawyer Bongiorno spun round and gave him a bear hug, slapping his back loudly. The court filed out again and six guards rushed Amanda away as, bent forward, she sobbed heavily; she was due to be released at the prison within a couple of hours.

The Kerchers sat down and looked straight ahead of them, their eyes averted from the outbursts of joy to their right. Stephanie began to cry, and Lyle put his arm around her. Arline sat still, chewing her lower lip.

Seeing her lawyer Maresca looking crestfallen, Arline asked him: 'Are you alright?' Maresca was amazed that she should be concerned about him at such a moment. 'Yes, yes,' he replied, 'and you?'

'Yes, ok,' Arline replied.

Mignini went up to the Kerchers and shook hands with each of them in turn. 'I'm sorry,' he told them.

Sophie, Amy and Robyn were sitting side-by-side on a sofa, holding hands as they watched TV, when the verdict came.

Robyn burst into tears and Sophie hugged her. Sophie and Amy felt numb. Sophie felt what she was seeing on the screen wasn't really happening, and both she and Amy were angry with themselves for not feeling anything. Then Sophie started crying, but that was because she saw Robyn was so upset.

Sophie turned the TV off; she didn't want to see Amanda leave court. The three friends just sat there for a long moment, the only sound that of Robyn crying, before Sophie turned the TV on again.

Late that night they wrote a card for the Kerchers, wishing them well.

Outside the law courts, a crowd some 4,000 strong had gathered to await the verdict and almost filled the cobbled square, some of them perched on lamp posts for a better view. When the lawyers for Amanda and Raffaele emerged, they were greeted by whistles and chants of '*Assassini, assassini* (murderers, murderers)!' and '*Vergogna, vergona* (shame, shame)!' Raffaele's lawyer Bongiorno had to be escorted by police officers as she made her way to TV reporters waiting to interview her. Perugians had long been over-whelmingly convinced of Amanda and Raffaele's guilt, and were stunned by the reversal.

A beaming Ghirga ignored the protests. 'Perhaps I don't fully realise it yet but I think I've won the most important trial of my life,' he said.

Within moments of the verdict, prosecutors said they would be appealing against the verdict to the Supreme Court in Rome; they wanted it overturned in the hope that a re-trial would be ordered. For a bitter Comodi, the court had partly decided the outcome before the trial even began – the secondary judge Zanetti, she recalled, had said at the start that the only certainty about the case was Meredith's death. The Kerchers' lawyer Maresca said the family would support the prosecution in that appeal.

Late that night, Amanda was driven out of the Capanne prison in a black Mercedes with tinted windows, headed for a hotel on the coast south of Rome, close to Fiumicino airport.

4 October 2011

On the morning after the verdict, Sophie was driving to the school where she worked as a teacher when it all hit her. She hadn't even been thinking about the verdict when she started crying 'out of nowhere' and had to pull over and stop the car.

She made it to the school but told her colleagues she didn't feel up to working that day. She needed to be on her own.

Sophie was tempted to just sit at home and do nothing, as she had in the first months after her friend's murder. But she decided she would go back to work the next day and keep going. 'They've already destroyed Meredith's life, I won't allow them to destroy mine – it's not what Meredith would have wanted,' she told herself.

That morning, as Amanda flew to London from which she would board another flight to Seattle, Arline, Stephanie and Lyle Kercher sat close to each other at the end of a long table in a bare, basement, conference room at their hotel. In an interview with the author, they were smiling and friendly despite the strain of the last few days. But their words highlighted their sense of bewilderment.

For Lyle, the acquittal felt 'like being back to square one'. He explained: 'It almost raises more questions than there are answers now because the initial decision was that it' – he didn't use any more specific term for the murder – 'wasn't done by one person but by more than that. Two have been released, one remains in jail, so we're now left questioning who are these other people or (this other) person?'

Did the family have doubts about any of the evidence presented by the prosecution? 'It's hard to say at the moment whether the DNA was contaminated,' Lyle said. 'We don't know if the jury looked at it and said actually there isn't enough DNA evidence to grant a conviction or even if it's incorrect. Perhaps the DNA matches with more than one person and therefore it's hard to say it's definitive.'

Did they still believe that Amanda and Raffaele were guilty, as John, Meredith's father, had written in a recent newspaper article? 'In a way we have to believe what the police say because they are the ones compiling the evidence,' Arline said. 'We haven't a clue. I think that's what he was saying. It's the police, it's their job.'

'It's difficult for anybody to make a valid opinion on any case, not just this one, unless you're a trained expert,' Lyle echoed. 'There are forensics, detectives, psychological profilers and so on who are trained to do this and read the information and draw the hypotheses from that, which of course no lay person really is. So if that's the conclusion they come to then we're happy to stand by that.'

'We have to accept, don't we, just like now we have to accept this,' Arline said.

'And that's why it's so disappointing, because we don't know,' Stephanie said.

Asked about predictions in the world media that Amanda stood to earn millions of dollars from book and film deals back in America, Lyle expressed disquiet. 'I think any right-minded person would find it difficult to gain profit from such an incident. I'm sure Amanda and Raffaele, like us and anybody else really, want to get back to a normal kind of life which if it was me would mean maintain as low a profile as possible rather than feed media attention.'

'Of course, that's a decision that's out of our hands and it really boils down to any individual's integrity and preferences,' he added.

What was their strongest memory of Meredith?, the author asked. 'Her smile, definitely her smile,' Stephanie replied. 'Her laugh and her smile just make you laugh as well and we giggle for hours,' she added with a short laugh – and speaking in the present tense.

'I think it's as Stephanie says, her wicked sense of humour I think I shared with her. I always remember her for that, she's always been full of life and very funny,' Lyle said.

'Yes, a lovely, lively person,' Arline nodded with a warm smile. 'A whirlwind going through the house at times because she was late. She was always on the run.'

5 October 2011

Unexpectedly fuelling the Kerchers' sense of bewilderment, Judge Pratillo Hellmann told Italian radio in an interview just two days after the verdict that Amanda and Raffaele may be guilty of Meredith's murder – even though his court had acquitted them.

The judge said he was certain that Rudy knew what had happened that night, but hadn't said so. 'Maybe Amanda Knox and Raffaele Sollecito also know what happened that night, because our acquittal verdict stems from the truth which was established in the trial. But the real truth can be different,' he said. 'They may be responsible, but there isn't the evidence.'

He added: 'So, perhaps they too know what happened that night, but that's not our conclusion.'

22 November 2011

Mignini lost Amanda and Raffaele's appeal trial, but six weeks later he won an appeal of his own. In February 2010, a judge had given the prosecutor a suspended prison sentence of one year and four months for abuse of office. The judge said he had broken the law in tapping the phones of three police officers and three journalists who were working on a suspicious death linked to the serial killer known as the 'Monster of Florence'.

But now a Florence appeal court overthrew the guilty verdict, ruling that the judge who convicted Mignini was disqualified from hearing the case because a local prosecutor was also involved. At the same time, the court also quashed a suspended prison sentence doled out to Michele Giuttari, the former head of Florence's Flying Squad.

It ordered the case files be sent to prosecutors in Turin in northern Italy. But legal sources said the investigation would be eventually dropped as it was expected to exceed the limit set on the length of time a case could drag through the courts.

15 December 2011

In a 143-page review of the evidence, Judges Pratillo Hellmann and Zanetti gave their reasons for granting Amanda and Raffaele their freedom.

Amanda had indeed slandered Patrick during police questioning but, the judges maintained, she did so under 'considerable psychological pressure'. At the time she was a young foreign girl who had difficulty speaking and understanding Italian well, and she didn't have a lawyer. An interpreter urged her to try to remember what had happened on the night of Meredith's death, telling her that she might well feel confused after the trauma she had suffered. The questioning 'of obsessive duration' by day and at night had been 'a real torment' for Amanda and, exhausted, she had accused Patrick in the hope of ending it – 'she gave detectives what they wanted to hear: a name, a murderer.' What she said about Patrick was more like 'a macabre dream' than a description of what actually happened.

The judges refused to take into account Rudy's accusation that Amanda and Raffaele had murdered Meredith since he had not been summoned before the appeal court to testify about the night she died. Instead, Rudy had been summoned to testify about the accounts of his fellow prisoners, who claimed he had described her murder to them. The judges dismissed the testimony of these fellow prisoners as unreliable. In any case, the judges said, his accusation against Amanda and Raffaele wasn't an account of events that had taken place but 'only a personal conviction'.

Nor did the judges give any importance to Curatolo's testimony. He was a tramp, a former heroin addict who dealt in drugs, and most importantly he was unsure whether he saw Amanda and Raffaele on the night of the murder or on the previous night. In the judges' opinion, Curatolo had probably seen them on the night before the murder – on 31 October.

Similarly, the grocer Quintavalle was 'not very reliable'. As he himself admitted, he had initially had doubts over whether the young woman he saw in his shop early on the morning after the murder was Amanda. As a result, he did not tell Mignini about the episode until a year later.

Repeatedly challenging the findings of Judge Massei's court, the judges estimated that Meredith died not at about 11.30 p.m. but rather no later than 10.13 p.m. They based this on an account Rudy gave a friend – he said Meredith died between 9 and 9.30 p.m. – and phone traffic on her mobile phone. If the tramp Curatolo was to be believed – and the judges repeated that he shouldn't be – then his testimony alone would be enough to clear Amanda and Raffaele because he placed them in Piazza Grimana at that time, the judges wrote.

The Massei court had established that the kitchen knife found in Raffaele's flat had been used to kill Meredith. But according to the appeal judges, it was not a murder weapon. Quoting defence consultants, they argued that a smaller knife had caused the most serious of the wounds on Meredith's neck. The judges branded as 'really bizarre' the Massei court's suggestion that Amanda might have taken to carrying the kitchen knife in her handbag in order to protect herself. She had been going out alone at night for years and was unlikely, they reasoned, to start carrying a knife simply because Raffaele, whom she had not known for long, urged her to do so.

Even more improbable was the idea that Amanda and Raffaele would put such a murder weapon back in the kitchen drawer. 'Is it really likely,' the judges asked, 'that two normal, even "good" young people, who were certainly shocked by what had happened . . . after taking part in such a barbaric murder, would have not only conceived the cold and diabolical idea of keeping the knife, instead of getting rid of it, even putting it back with the rest of the cutlery, but also the callousness and the gall to go on using that cutlery, and perhaps the knife, to prepare meals in the days after the crime?'

The judges then examined what they called 'the cornerstone' of the Massei court's reconstruction – the DNA evidence. Clearly mindful of the prosecution's attacks on the competence of the forensic experts they had appointed to review DNA evidence on the kitchen knife, and on Meredith's bra clasp, the judges warmly praised Professors Vecchiotti and Conti. The two came from one of Italy's most prestigious universities – La Sapienza in Rome – they were both experts in the field of forensic genetics and 'they both deserve the full confidence of the court as professionals and as individuals.'

The judges quoted the two experts at length, approving their findings without reservation. They agreed that the forensic police had failed to follow guidelines set by the international scientific community in its work on both the knife and the bra clasp. There was no trace of Meredith's DNA on the knife blade. No blood was found on the knife, and the presence of starch on the blade showed that it hadn't been cleaned.

As for the bra clasp, the judges doubted that the DNA profile attributed to Raffaele was indeed his, because a different interpretation might be possible given that the traces of several different individuals had been found on it. They concluded that Raffaele's trace was 'probably' the result of contamination before the sample – which they recalled had been mislaid for forty-six days in the cottage – was finally retrieved by the forensic police.

Again quoting defence consultants in order to challenge the Massei court's verdict, the judges suggested that the bloody right footprint found on the bathmat in the cottage's small bathroom wasn't Raffaele's, but perhaps Rudy's. The Massei court had also mistakenly argued that the footprints found in the corridor, in Amanda's bedroom and in Filomena's bedroom – and previously attributed to Amanda and Raffaele – were shown to be tainted with blood when highlighted with the chemical Luminol. It was more likely that the Luminol had reacted to bleach, or to traces of fruit juice or vegetable soup, the judges argued.

What's more, there was no reason to think there had been a 'staged burglary' at the cottage. The intruder – the judges pointed a finger at Rudy – may have used a nail in the wall under Filomena's window to climb up to it, and a defence consultant had shown it was possible to throw a stone through the window from a short distance.

The Massei court had argued that bits of glass found on top of jumbles of clothes in Filomena's room were evidence of a staged burglary. But the appeal court judges quoted Filomena herself, as well as other witnesses, as saying that the bits of glass were both on top of and underneath the clothes. The judges argued that an intruder's 'obviously frenetic rummaging' through her belongings could have caused bits of glass to end up on top of the piles of clothes. As for Raffaele telling the police that nothing had been stolen, the judges explained this was not because he had helped stage a burglary but because Amanda hadn't noticed anything important missing when she first checked the flat.

In rare agreement with the prosecutors, the judges acknowledged that Amanda and Raffaele had failed to prove their alibi – that they spent the night at his flat. But they also ruled that prosecutors had failed to disprove the alibi. The fact that there had been no human activity on Raffaele's laptop between 9.10 p.m. and 5.32 a.m. didn't rule out the couple's presence that night. Besides, none of his other computers had been examined as their hard disks had been destroyed after police seized them. Nor did the fact that their mobile phones were either inactive or switched off during the night mean they had left the flat.

There was nothing unusual in Amanda leaving Raffaele's flat in the morning to go and have a shower at home, despite having had one the previous evening after the couple had sex. Raffaele's shower wasn't working properly, and her underwear and clothes were at the cottage.

On the subject of Amanda and Raffaele's embraces, and Amanda's cartwheel and yoga exercises at the police station, the judges explained that this was due to their 'need to find a bit of normality in a tragic situation'. There was also a simple explanation as to why Amanda had bought some underwear a couple of days later – she needed it as police had sealed off the cottage. 'That she bought a thong . . . really cannot be seen as a mark of an insensitive spirit or obscene inclinations, because it's a fashionable item of clothing which is very popular with both young and not-so-young women,' the judges wrote. Nothing in Amanda and Raffaele's behaviour after the murder could be seen as an indication of their guilt.

In their final conclusions, the judges criticised the Massei court yet again. The words 'probable' and 'improbable' featured no fewer than thirty-nine times in the earlier court's review of the evidence, the judges pointed out, adding that 'its reconstruction of events was always based on probability.' The motive advanced by the Massei court – 'sexual erotic violence' to force Meredith to yield to Rudy – was itself 'not at all probable'.

The judges added: 'the sudden decision of two good, well-meaning young people to do evil for evil's sake, and for no other reason, is all the more incomprehensible because it aims to help Rudy Guede – with whom they had no relationship and whose character and social background is different from theirs – to commit a crime.'

The judges refused to explain why and how Meredith died. 'It isn't up to this court to state what really happened, nor whether one or more people carried out the crime, nor whether other investigative scenarios were neglected or not. What this court notes is only the lack of proof of the guilt of the accused,' they wrote.

Acknowledgements

I owe a special debt of gratitude to the following:

In Perugia: prosecutors Giuliano Mignini and Manuela Comodi, and detectives Giacinto Profazio and Monica Napoleoni; warmest thanks to Arline, Stephanie and Lyle Kercher for granting me an interview and to Lyle for his help with sources; the Kercher family's lawyers Francesco Maresca and Serena Perna; Amanda Knox's lawyers Carlo Dalla Vedova and Luciano Ghirga; her stepfather Chris Mellas; Raffaele Sollecito's lawyers Giulia Bongiorno, Luca Maori and Marco Brusco, and Raffaele himself for corresponding with me; Rudy Guede's lawyers Valter Biscotti and Nicodemo Gentile; Rudy's father Roger; Diya 'Patrick' Lumumba and his lawyers Carlo Pacelli and Giuseppe Sereni; Letizia Magnini, lawyer for the cottage's owner; Mauro Bacci, Luca Lalli and Giulia Ceccarelli at the University of Perugia's forensic medicine institute; Pasquale 'Pisco' Alessi; and Fabrizio Fornari, criminologist. Many thanks to those who allowed me to enter the cottage at Via della Pergola in April 2009 shortly after police removed the seals.

At the Capanne prison, which I visited in March 2009 and April 2010: governors Bernardina di Mario, Antonio Fullone and Giaccobbe Pantaleone; Fulvio Brillo, head of Perugian prison guards; Father Saulo Scarabattoli, chaplain; and the prisoners Vanessa Davis, Cinzia Gonnella, Anna Kalu and Carmela Pascucci who agreed to be interviewed.

In Rome: Assunta Borzachiello, at the DAP prison administration service; Alberto Intini and Patrizia Stefanoni at the forensic police; Maurizio Masciopinto and Filippo Bartolozzi at the interior ministry's press office; Vincenzo Mastronardi, criminologist; and Massimo Montebove of the SAP police trade union.

In Seattle, which I travelled to in December 2007 and in May 2008: Edda Mellas, Curt Knox and their daughter Deanna for giving me a lengthy interview; David Marriott; Kent Hickey, president of the Seattle Preparatory School; Mike James, president of the Seattle–Perugia Sister City Association; Levi Pulkkinen, the *Seattle Post-Intelligencer*; Christina Siderius, the *Seattle Times*.

Heartfelt thanks to my journalist colleagues, especially Ann Wise, *ABC*; Claudio Sebastiani, ANSA news agency; Marta Falconi and Alessandra Rizzo, AP news agency; Elio Clero Bertoldi, *Corriere dell'Umbria*; Fiorenza Sarzanini, *Corriere della Sera*, Francesca Bene, Giuseppe Castellini, Antioco Fois and Luca Fiorucci, *Giornale dell'Umbria*; Peter Gomez, *Il Fatto Quotidiano*; Italo Carmignani, *Il Messaggero*; Erika Pontini, *La Nazione*; Meo Ponte, *La Repubblica*; Barbie Nadeau, *Newsweek;* Mario Spezi, *La Nazione*, Andrea Vogt, the *Seattle Post-Intelligencer*; John Witherow, editor of *The Sunday Times*, Sean Ryan, my foreign editor who sent me repeatedly to Perugia and gave me time to research and write the book, Robin Morgan and Cathy Galvin, who commissioned two cover stories for *The Sunday Times Magazine*, and Kate Mansey, now at the newspaper, who described in detail her interview with Raffaele. Thanks also to novelist Douglas Preston and Charlie Gauvain, at Eye Film and Television.

I'm very grateful, again, to my wonderfully supportive agent Clare Alexander, and to Rupert Lancaster, my publisher who championed it all from the beginning, as well as the rest of the team at Hodder & Stoughton, especially Jason Bartholomew, Meryl Evans, Tara Gladden, Ben Gutcher, Kerry Hood, Alice Howe, Laura Macaulay, Kate Miles, Maddie Mogford and Justine Taylor. Warm thanks to Giovanna Punzo and Antonio Cristofari for their hospitality, to my parents for their encouragement, and especially to my mother for her work on early drafts.

And lastly, thanks to my wife Rita and my son Sébastien for their patience and much more.

Picture Acknowledgements

Giancarlo Belfiore: 2 below left and right. Nick Cornish: 1 above, 2 above left, 3 below, 4, 5, 6, 7 below, 8 below. Roberto Settonce, courtesy *Giornale dell'Umbria*: 2 center right, 3 above. Perugia Police Department: 2 above right. Sophie Purton: 1 below. 8 above: © Tiziana Fabi/AP/Press Association Images.

Every reasonable effort has been made to contact the copyright holders, but if there are any errors or omissions, Hodder & Stoughton will be pleased to insert the appropriate acknowledgement in any subsequent printing of this publication.